UNEQUAL TIME

UNEQUAL TIME

Gender, Class, and
Family in Employment
Schedules

Dan Clawson and
Naomi Gerstel

Russell Sage Foundation
New York

The Russell Sage Foundation

The Russell Sage Foundation, one of the oldest of America's general purpose foundations, was established in 1907 by Mrs. Margaret Olivia Sage for "the improvement of social and living conditions in the United States." The Foundation seeks to fulfill this mandate by fostering the development and dissemination of knowledge about the country's political, social, and economic problems. While the Foundation endeavors to assure the accuracy and objectivity of each book it publishes, the conclusions and interpretations in Russell Sage Foundation publications are those of the authors and not of the Foundation, its Trustees, or its staff. Publication by Russell Sage, therefore, does not imply Foundation endorsement.

Library of Congress Cataloging-in-Publication Data

Clawson, Dan.
  Unequal time : gender, class, and family in employment schedules / Dan Clawson and Naomi Gerstel.
    pages cm
  Includes bibliographical references and index.
  ISBN 978-0-87154-014-0 (pbk. : alk. paper) — ISBN 978-1-61044-843-7 (ebook)
  1. Medical personnel—United States—Social conditions—Case studies.
2. Medical personnel—Time management—United States—Case studies.
3. Hours of labor—United States.   4. Time management surveys—United
States,   5. Manpower planning—United States.   6. Work environment—United
States.   I. Gerstel, Naomi.   II. Russell Sage Foundation. III. Title.
  RA410.7.C52 2014
  658.4'093088610—dc23   2014006874

Text design by Suzanne Nichols.

RUSSELL SAGE FOUNDATION
112 East 64th Street, New York, New York 10065
10 9 8 7 6 5 4 3 2 1

Contents

List of Tables and Figures

For additional material please go to https://www.russellsage.org/
publications/unequal-time

About the Authors

DAN CLAWSON is professor of sociology at the University of Massachusetts Amherst.

NAOMI GERSTEL is Distinguished University Professor in the sociology department at the University of Massachusetts Amherst.

Preface and Acknowledgments

THIS PROJECT BEGAN longer ago than we care to think. It began when we first thought about where our interests intersected and whether collaboration would be fruitful. Naomi's work, with numerous collaborators, had shown that families, when confronted by what might appear to be the same problem, responded in varying ways, depending on class, gender, and race. She had a special interest in addressing the time it took to complete not only a first shift (spent in a job) and a second shift (spent in marriage, housework, and child care) but also a third shift (spent caring for extended kin) and looking at the ways in which these were related—especially how time spent in the "greedy institutions" of jobs and marriages could detract from the time spent on other matters. In related but separate work, Naomi focused on the Family and Medical Leave Act, showing that, despite what the law said, it reinforced inequality of race, class, and gender and also that employers were ignoring the law, or obeying only a portion of it.

Dan had recently completed a study of the labor movement in which he argued that most of the time labor is in retreat, but in occasional (relatively brief) periods it makes dramatic gains. During those periods of upsurge, the labor movement takes up new issues, reaches out to underrepresented demographic groups, and adopts new forms of organization and new tactics. Thinking about the issues that might drive an upsurge, he thought the most likely seemed to be how workers and their families handled the time demands of jobs. For many people the problem is overwork. Those whose lives require them to be constantly available for work would like to take back the forty-hour workweek, not to mention the fading concept of evenings off and weekends free. Meanwhile, other people—almost one in seven in 2014, according to the Bureau of Labor Statistics U6 unemployment rate—want to work but can't get any job, or they can't get enough hours in their job to pay the bills. A movement to challenge these twin realities, Dan concluded, might draw widespread support and trigger new alliances and new tactics.

Our interests clearly intersected, and the more we worked on the project the truer that became, to the point that we can no longer tell which of us wrote what—we very much doubt that even one page remains in the book that was written by one of us, and only one. The order of authorship is alphabetical; we contributed equally and would list our names with equal prominence were there a way to do so.

We worked with many others. The project was shaped by so many people that we couldn't hope to acknowledge them all. That's especially the case for those whose written work and conference presentations have influenced us, even when—perhaps especially when—that work is not specifically cited here, or the citations give only a hint of the work's impact on our thinking.

We collected, coded, and analyzed more data than for any project either of us had done before. Our interviews were (mostly) transcribed by Karen Mason and Martha Stone; anytime we needed to get an interview transcribed by someone else we learned just how good they both were. They not only got what was said accurately (not always an easy task) but captured nuances of language. Several librarians helped us track down sources or brought us materials we had not known existed. We are especially indebted to Steve McGinty at the University of Massachusetts Amherst and to Clare Gabriel and Katie Winograd at the Russell Sage Foundation. We also thank Galo Falchettore for research services at the Russell Sage Foundation during our visiting scholar year.

Our warm thanks go to both the graduate and undergraduate students who helped create the data needed for this project. Undergraduates did so primarily by entering data, especially concerning the schedules people actually worked as opposed to those they were officially scheduled to work. These students included Dylan Barnett, Daniel Goldberg, Ming Li, Valerie Lucas, Julia Medhzitova, Denise Miller, Julia Popkin, Matt Rosenbaum, and Stephanie St. Paul. Julia also helped code union contracts. Zoe Crowley analyzed coded interviews and helped call attention to the most compelling examples.

In coding interviews and union contracts, graduate students Laura Heston, Melissa Hodges, Marianne Joyce, and Mary Koppes worked hard to maintain inter-coder reliability; besides making worthwhile points, they also proposed changes to our coding that often shaped our thinking. Three other students conducted some of the early interviews with survey respondents: Dana Huyser deBernardo, Jason Rodriguez, and Rachel Rybaczuk. Dana was also a key person who helped to create, administer, and analyze the survey.

Three graduate students did significantly more. Carla Russell Shows did all of the ethnographic observation at our fire station and almost all of the observations at our private-sector EMT company; she also conducted interviews with EMTs and others. Jackie Stein observed union negotiations, coded contracts, and took primary responsibility for analysis of the union contracts. She also worked on (and made usable) the survey data with which we began this project. Jill Crocker was with the project longer than anyone but us and did the widest range of tasks: conducting numerous interviews, observing at the Berkman nursing home and the surgical practice doctors' office, coding both interviews and contracts, supervising data entry (and creating the system to do so) for the schedule data, managing and analyzing all the schedule data, and generally being actively involved in every phase of the project except the actual writing of the book. We could not have done the research without her. All three students—Carla, Jackie, and Jill—met with us often and published papers on aspects of the project. Jill wrote a dissertation using the data to address forms of resistance.

A large project requires funding, and many different sources gave generously. We gratefully acknowledge research support provided by the National Science Foundation (SES-0549817; SES-0959712), the Alfred Sloan Foundation, the Russell Sage Foundation, the National Association of Emergency Medical Technicians, the Center for Research on Families at the University of Massachusetts Amherst, and the Political Economy Research Institute. Several people at these organizations went above and beyond the call of duty in offering us feedback and suggestions: Sally Powers, Beth Rubin, Kathleen Christiansen, Jerry Epstein, and Eric Wanner. When we were first writing the proposal as faculty scholars in the Center for Research on Families, both Sally Powers and David Arnold helped us formulate the research design. Linda Rahm consulted with us and advised us. Joan Roche made enormous contributions, from helping us gain access to organizations to going through the arduous IRB process at hospitals and discussing the project as it developed.

When we had a complete draft of the manuscript, we circulated it to a number of people who gave us a range of penetrating comments and suggestions, many (but by no means all) of which were incorporated into the book before you. Reading a manuscript is a huge undertaking. More people than we had any right to expect each took many hours to suggest ways to make this a better book. Those who read the manuscript and provided helpful comments, sometimes many pages of them, include Laura Clawson, Mary Ann Clawson, Stephanie Coontz, Francine Deutsch, Lisa Dodson, Kathleen Gerson, Suzanne Gordon, Lisa Harvey, Rosanna Hertz, James Jasper, Arne Kalleberg, Stephanie Luce, Margaret Nelson, Rhacel Parrenas, Maureen Perry-Jenkins, Susan Rosen, Sarah Rosenfield, Natasha Sarkisian, Donald Tomaskovic-Devey, Joan Williams, and Robert Zussman. Fran Deutsch was endlessly willing to talk with us about the project and read multiple versions of the manuscript, even in the midst of medical treatments. Amy Armenia, Robby Aronowitz, Michelle Budig, Paul DiMaggio, Nancy Folbre, Julia Henly, Arlie Hochschild, Steven Lopez, Ruth Milkman, Michael Schwartz, Judith Stephan Norris, and anonymous reviewers at the *American Journal of Sociology, Gender & Society,* and *Social Problems* gave us useful comments on proposals, chapters, ideas, and articles using the same data. We presented work from this project at various meetings, classes, workshops, and seminars and received useful feedback from those who attended, including not only many of those listed earlier but also Michael Ash, Annette Bernhardt, Bruce Link, Julie Pinkham, Richard Sanders, Eve Weinbaum, and Viviana Zelizer.

We thank as well Susan Lambert and a second (anonymous) reviewer for the Russell Sage Foundation, who read the revised manuscript and provided long, detailed, and insightful comments. Susan suggested the term "web of time" for what we had been calling a "network of time"; we liked that formulation much better, and it has helped our own thinking. Suzanne Nichols was an excellent editor, supporting us always, nudging us when needed, summarizing reviewer comments, and providing her independent suggestions. Cynthia Buck provided outstanding copyediting; the book reads much better as a result. Jean Blackburn's careful oversight (and her fast turnaround time) were much appreciated.

Naomi Gerstel: I owe a special debt to Robert Zussman, who read everything we wrote—from multiple proposals to many drafts of the interview schedule to many versions of every chapter. His advice about the larger issues that the book should and could address, along with his precise and evocative turns of phrase, were immensely useful—even if the truth was sometimes painful. And his companionship and conversation meant I was never bored. My daughter, Katie Zussman Gerstel, brought me much joy even as the book pulled me away. As a key part of my web of time, she not only responded with generosity to how much time the book took but discussed chapters with wit and insight. Robert and I sometimes wonder if aliens invaded her body because over the course of writing this book we witnessed her turn from an occasionally (but only occasionally) cranky teen into a young woman who sometimes seems like a saint. Eva Gerstel, my sociologist mother, listened to a number of chapters. Her commentary, enthusiasm, and love—now and in the past—helped in ways impossible to recount.

Dan Clawson: My thinking is continuously shaped by conversations with two sociologists, Mary Ann and Laura Clawson. It's often difficult to know what is my own and what I've adapted from one or another of them; that's true for the ideas I've contributed to this project, and perhaps even more so for some of the bad formulations I proposed and was persuaded to abandon. Many people want to leave work behind, to create a separation between work and the rest of life. Given what most people's work is like, that makes sense. But I'd like to see a world where work is joyful and creative, a space of freedom and self-fulfillment. One of the ways I'm luckiest is that work often provides such a space for me. I have family members who share these interests; we often find it stimulating to talk about politics and our work, learn from each other, and find this a source of support and bonding.

Finally, we wish to thank our many helpful and thoughtful respondents, whom we cannot name because of our need to maintain confidentiality. They were witty and insightful. We appreciate the time and wisdom they shared with us, especially given their often difficult and unpredictable schedules.

PART I | Introduction

Chapter 1 | Unpredictability and Unequal Control in a Web of Time

BECAUSE LIFE IS ROUTINELY UNPREDICTABLE, our control over time becomes a crucial resource for keeping a job and having a family—but control over time, much like income, is contested and powerfully shaped by gender and class inequalities. Those inequalities reverberate through a "web of time" in which our daily schedules are connected to the schedules of others, especially our employers, our coworkers, and our family members.

Take one example of a reverberating event that is both inevitable and unexpected: your child gets sick. All seemed well at bedtime, but at 5:00 AM your child is feverish and throwing up. It's an important day at work, so what is to be done? Consider the responses of the people we interviewed for this book: a male surgeon (earning $360,000 a year), a woman nurse (earning $70,000), a male firefighter who is an emergency medical technician (EMT) ($47,000), and a woman certified nursing assistant (CNA) ($16,000). Although a child's sickness could happen to any of them, the control they had, the ways they responded, and the people they can rely on were very different, with class and gender organizing those differences.

The surgeon, who performed elective surgeries, had access to the operating room (OR) only one day a week, and he had operations scheduled on a day when his child got sick. Although married to another surgeon, his wife worked only half-time, so there was a two-out-of-five chance she would be home for the day and could care for their sick kid. If it happend on a day when they both worked, the nanny would have taken care of their child; after all, that was why they had a nanny. In fact, the problem they worried about was not so much a sick child as a sick nanny. As the surgeon told us:

That's the biggest problem of all, because if the nanny calls on Wednesday, calls Wednesday morning, God forbid, and says (*in a hoarse voice*) "I'm sick, I can't come in." . . . Now, we both operate on Wednesdays—you know, what do you do on those days? And that's really hard, and we have some of our neighbors who have kids who sometimes we can call and say, "Can you do . . . ?" But if our kid is sick *and* the nanny's sick, we don't want to pawn our sick kid off on somebody else, so sometimes we have to call and cancel the day in the OR to accommodate that. So the kids really throw a monkey wrench into the whole schedule.

Later in the interview, he explained that he himself had never canceled a day in the operating room, but his wife had.

The child of the firefighter EMT, who was a paramedic, got sick in early December, a particularly bad time: from hunting season to the end of the year, his coworkers took their remaining sick days, so it was hard to keep the station staffed. Normally, the captain tries to get someone else to come in. If he can't find anyone, the captain mandates that an already on-duty EMT stay for another five-hour half-shift. The EMT didn't want to be the reason someone else was mandated, but he was confident that if the person mandated faced a serious problem taking the extra shift, then another coworker would volunteer to take the five hours. Sometimes the firefighter's wife would stay home if their child was sick, but as likely as not, he would. The EMT explained that if a child gets sick, "of course that's a reason to stay home." Under the union contract, staying home with a sick child was a legitimate use of sick days, and he didn't worry about being penalized.

The nurse's child got sick on a school vacation day, which meant that the unit was already short-staffed. If she called out and the hospital couldn't find a replacement, the nurses on the floor would be stressed and might be less willing to swap the next time she needed help. But for the nurse, the first point was that a sick child was her responsibility, even though she earned more than her husband. Asking her husband to stay home didn't occur to her. She explained that nurses don't want to call out and the managers at the hospital "really, really look down upon you calling in an hour before"; nonetheless, when nurses do call out, "nobody ever questions it." She felt awful about leaving her coworkers jammed up, but like her coworkers and even her manager, she just assumed that a mother has no choice but to stay home with her sick child and that it is the hospital that needs to be flexible.

The nursing assistant's problem was that in the span of six weeks she had already had to call out for a sick child twice. Although she had sick days left, if she called out four times over a ninety-day period, she would be fired. Calling out that day would be number three: if she called out again over the next seven weeks, for any reason at all, she would be fired. The nursing assistant was a single mother with three kids, one of whom was periodically hospitalized for asthma. She had spent time in a homeless shelter before becoming a nursing assistant, she earned $1,100 a month plus earnings from whatever extra shifts she could pick up—almost double what she got on welfare—and she was determined to keep the job. Normally, on weekdays her kids went to government-subsidized day care or school. "So for day care on the weekdays, I pretty much don't have a problem, but if one of them is sick or let's say he had a high fever the night before, day care won't take them in, so I also have their dad and my aunt." She also relied on her grandmother. This support system was important—but her vulnerability to being fired for excessive absences indicates the limits of even a pretty solid support system.

In this book, we look at these four occupations in the medical-health sector—doctors, nurses, emergency medical technicians, and nursing assistants—and examine how those in these occupations seek to control their work hours and schedules, which are routinely subject to interruption by unpredictable events. We chose to study medical occupations and organizations for a reason: in these settings, someone has to be on duty 24 hours a day, seven days a week, 365 days a year—no exceptions. A hospital or a nursing home can't leave a patient unattended, not even for an hour. People in the medical-health jobs we focus on seek to control their schedules differently as they confront and create distinctive institutional realities on the job and at home and act on distinctive ideas about how they should organize time. These differences, however, are far from random. Quite the reverse: they are rooted in systems of inequality. People in these different occupations have unequal control not only over their own time but over that of those around them—on the job and at home.

Although little research has examined inequality in schedule predictability and control, plenty has been written about the total number of hours that Americans work and the time divide in those hours. First, research suggests, there are "sharply graded educational differences": the more-educated work more hours, and the less-educated are unable to get enough hours. "Long workweeks," note Jerry Jacobs and Kathleen Gerson, are "most common among professionals and managers."[1] And that literature suggests that there is a gender divide as well: at 2,000 hours a year, men work substantially more paid hours than women, who work 1,729 hours. Assuming that people take two weeks off annually, on average men are working forty hours a week and women are working thirty-five.[2]

We designed our research with this time divide in mind. So the four occupations form a classic two-by-two table of class and gender. Doctors and nurses are relatively advantaged and are professionals, and EMTs and CNAs are working-class. This class difference is one source of inequality. Gender is a second source of inequality: members of two of the occupations—nurses and nursing assistants—are overwhelmingly (more than 90 percent) women; members of the other two—doctors and emergency medical technicians—are predominantly (70 percent) men.[3]

In this book, we make three broad and largely novel arguments:

1. *Normal unpredictability:* The book identifies and analyzes the pervasiveness of routine disruptions. We argue that it is those events that are sure to happen sometime but not expected today that routinely throw schedules into chaos and create havoc in people's jobs and families. Such chaos happens now more often than in earlier decades.

2. *Control over unpredictability:* We argue that employers, organizations, employees, and their families all struggle to control basic schedules as well as the unpredictability that disrupts them. That control is negotiated, contested, and shaped by unequal relations at home and at work. These issues of control are tied to the *joint* operation (or intersection) of class and gender. Their operation indicates the socially patterned character of control over time.

3. *The web of time:* Although many see a schedule as an individual affair, we argue here that a schedule is also collective—it is based on relations within occupations and organizations as well as across them, within families, and among them. These relations together make up a "web of time" in which changes in one person's schedule cascade to create changes in the schedule of another person at the workplace and outside of it. The subsequent meshing of schedules leads to cooperation and accommodation, struggle and conflict—between employees and supervisors, among coworkers, between regular workers and per diems, among different organizations, between spouses, parents, and children, and with other kin. The character and power of relations in that web vary by gender and class.

NORMAL UNPREDICTABILITY

Normal unpredictability—events that are predictable in the aggregate but unpredictable in their particular timing—throws schedules into chaos. The problem is that such disruptions are common—even pervasive—in health care as elsewhere.

Scholars often write about hours and schedules in a couple of ways: the first assumes a standard work week schedule of Monday to Friday, nine to five. The second, growing in prominence, recognizes the pervasiveness of nonstandard hours—outside of the "normal" nine-to-five frame. Both of these assume a fixed schedule—that people work at predictable hours on regular days scheduled in advance. We develop a third frame—one that assumes normal unpredictability. This perspective takes us into a dimension that is less often discussed but is central to understanding the problems that both people and organizations face in managing and negotiating work schedules.

Other researchers have emphasized schedule unpredictability in low-wage jobs, but we have found that unpredictability is also pervasive in relatively stable jobs, whether low-wage or well-paid.[4] While others focus on employer actions that create schedule instability, we examine jobs with stable schedules whose unpredictability is often caused by employee actions—within an employer framework of lean staffing. The unexpected is, paradoxically, both routine and normal. We may not know when we (or our kids, or our partners, or our parents) will get sick, whether it will happen today, tomorrow, or not for a couple of months. We do not know when our coworkers will quit or stay home. We do not know when we will receive an unexpected bill that can be paid off only with overtime pay or when we will feel pressure to leave our job early or stay late. But we know that these things happen. We had access to records for one nursing home employer showing when people actually worked as opposed to when they had been scheduled to work. We found that for every two shifts employees worked according to the planned schedule there was one shift that went not according to schedule. Sometimes a schedule was changed by management and sometimes it changed because an employee couldn't make it into work. Unpredictability in this sense is entirely routine.

Anyone whose car has broken down, whose kid's school has called a snow day, or whose manager has made a request to stay several hours past the scheduled work day knows the challenge posed by these situations. These kinds of events become tests of our ability to manage our jobs and our lives: can we handle these disruptions with such ease that we barely notice them, like hiccups, or do they become a major stress, threatening our job and family, our health and happiness?

CONTROL OVER UNPREDICTABILITY

Employers want control over workers' time. Life for employers would be much simpler if they could be sure that workers would always show up as scheduled, that if asked to work extra hours workers would always put the job over their families without complaint, that workers would quietly and cheerfully go home (without pay) whenever demand slackened, and that workers would never quit a job no matter what demands it made. Life for workers would be simpler and happier if they had control over their time—if they could work whenever they needed money and had an inclination to work, but could take off whenever they faced other demands or simply lacked enthusiasm for work. In practice these scenarios are pure fantasy for both employers and workers, but each group seeks to move toward these ends.

Some important research has examined control over time. Because it uses survey data, that research tends to treat control as an outcome instead of an ongoing set of interactions. We take a different approach, showing the ways employers and employees, coworkers and family members, continually negotiate and contest control over work hours and schedules.[5]

Some of the struggle for control over work hours and schedules is individually contested, some of it comes from social movements and organizations (like unions), some of it centers on legal regulations that resulted from past (perhaps long forgotten) protests, some of it stems from a changing local organizational culture and structure, and some comes from family members. These conflicts are resolved in several ways. Some solutions are win-win: ways are devised of enabling employees to deal with the unpredictable without inconveniencing the employer (and possibly even saving the employer money). Some impose minor costs on employers but enable them to retain valued employees. Other resolutions to these struggles are (largely) victories for employers that require employees to find some way to meet their employer's demands. And a few resolutions to conflicts over control of time are unequivocal victories for workers; many such victories for workers were won in past struggles and have become embodied in custom or law as rights.

Flexibility, a term we hear with growing frequency, is part of this continuing struggle over control. The term "flexibility" is typically used to imply something good—that a person or organization has the necessary leeway and resilience to deal with unexpected problems. Our terms "unpredictability," "disruption," and "churning" are different from this more widely discussed concept of "flexibility," but tied to it. "Unpredictability" implies an event that disrupts our routine and must be dealt with. One way to do so is to have a flexible job; another is to have a flexible family willing (and able) to adjust to our job demands. (Most discussions of flexibility at least implicitly assume that flexibility is rooted only in "family-friendly" jobs and that families and their divisions of labor are inflexible.)

Much of the recent academic literature and much of the political debate focus on flexibility for employees, but this often turns out to mean flexibility only for professionals and managers. Moreover, many employers have taken over the term and now use it to mean that workers should be flexible in the face of employer schedule demands.[6] One union official told us that flexibility is a "new management buzzword" and that "flexibility is the new word for control by management." Another put it more forcefully: "For management, flexibility means the ability to do anything they want with their workforce without any obligation for the workforce to have their rights acknowledged." The increasing deployment of the rhetoric of flexibility indicates a trend to unpredictability—while masking a struggle to control it.

Gender-Class Intersections

The solutions to unpredictable events vary by class and gender and indicate the collective character of control. Researchers have emphasized the ways in which gender or class shape hours and schedules. By contrast, we argue here that what matters is not just gender or class, but the ways in which gender and class intersect and the complications, even paradoxes, that result from those intersections.

Gender-class intersections affect not only the rules managers create and the ways they apply those rules but also the goals that workers seek. Male doctors, for example, work long hours and simultaneously complain, often bitterly, about those hours. Though they grumble, they also largely control those hours, or at least collaborate with their peers to determine them. Pamela Stone has uncovered what she terms a "rhetoric of choice" among women executives, but we find the opposite among male doctors: a widely shared "rhetoric of constraint."[7] To put it simply, male doctors make a lot of money that they come to believe they need; they also earn respect and honor from their peers when they work long hours because "the ones who work the most are looked up to." Thus, the advantages sought by these doctors lead them to say that their schedules require that their wives (and hired caregivers) respond to demands at home. A paradoxical and disquieting pattern develops: most male doctors choose to be absent from home for long hours, but bemoan the fact that they must do so.

Nurses also have significant control over their work schedules, albeit considerably less than doctors. The widespread and extensive demand for nurses gives them leverage in choosing not to work (for pay) unless doing so creates a schedule that fits with their family needs. Organizations respond to nurses' use of this leverage by, in effect, restructuring the workplace (in small or large ways) to accommodate nurses' family responsibilities. We asked a nurse administrator what would happen if a nurse came to her and said: "I can't do this schedule anymore." She said she would answer: "Well, let's figure out what you *can* do, and we'll look at the master schedule, and I'll change the master if I can, to better accommodate you." If a nurse needs to miss a day to stay home with a sick child, she typically does so with little resistance from her supervisor or director (who may very well share the nurse's view that it is a woman's job to take care of her family).[8] If nurses have children or elderly parents with recurring health problems, they know about and make use of the Family and Medical Leave Act, which permits them, with few questions or repercussions, to take a day off to provide care, even if their director is convinced that they are abusing the law. A nursing director reported that she supervised a dozen employees who were taking FMLA leaves, that she believed probably six of them were abusing the FMLA, but that if nurses call up to say, "I'm not coming in tonight, I'm taking an FMLA day," then "there's not a thing I can say about it, it's already approved. It doesn't matter what the staffing is on the unit."

Here we see very clearly something that most commentary misses: balance doesn't just happen. Balancing work and family often depends on employee leverage and resistance, which are rooted in the power of the group, not just individual insistence. Nurses, at least in hospitals, challenge and replace the rigid gendered-male schedule practices with flexible organizational practices that are, in many ways, gendered-female.[9] That is, nurses feminize organizations: both cultural schemas and organizational practices are reshaped to offer schedules that provide relatively well-paid employment that simultaneously makes possible devotion to family.

This organization of time looks very different from how time is organized not only for male doctors but also for women nursing assistants. At one nursing home, CNAs faced a highly punitive sick leave policy under which they could be fired even if they still had sick time available and even if they were taking an epileptic or asthmatic child to the hospital, a circumstance covered by the FMLA. Almost none of the nursing assistants knew of the Family and Medical Leave Act or the rights it offered them; indeed, the nursing home's records showed that over a six-month period only a single missed day was recorded as an FMLA day. As a result of such policies, nursing assistants often go to work even when they are sick—with unfortunate consequences for the frail and elderly patients they care for—and sometimes leave their children home alone, with a healthy ten-year-old watching a sick eight-year-old. Nursing assistants repeatedly complained about the policy (to us), but they had little leverage or control. As one single mother noted: "Everyone thinks it's crazy, or that it doesn't make sense, but what are you going to do? You're not going to be able to really change it. They do what they want, basically. I've been here four years, and I know that. They change the rules when they want to change them and stuff, so, you just gotta sit back and deal with it."

The intersection of gender and class creates a paradox. Given the oppressive conditions they face on the job, it would make perfect sense for low-paid nursing assistants to use whatever schedule control they have to escape work. To the contrary, many of the nursing assistants we spoke with (more than in any of the other occupations) said that they used their job as a strategy to escape home. One reported, "I feel better when I'm at work. I feel, you know how some people, they drown theirself in the bottle because sometimes they'd be so miserable and unhappy? That's me. To me at work is . . . it's like a big old ice cream cone." Finding this pattern led us to draw on but recast Arlie Hochschild's broad argument about the time bind that turns work into an escape from home.[10] Yes, sometimes work is more appealing than family. Paradoxically, in our study it was the low-wage women in particular who said that work was a kind of haven. They found it so because they developed strong relationships on the job with coworkers and residents but also because they faced stress at home— stress created in part by the conditions they faced at work. They sought longer hours because they needed the money from jobs that were difficult, even exploitative, but they also sought additional hours to escape their stressed and stressful families.

In concert, these cases reveal the intersection, or joint operation, of gender and class, but in ways rarely articulated. When class advantage gives people more control over their schedules, they often use that control in conventionally gendered ways. Male doctors use their control to devote themselves to long hours at their jobs; female nurses use their control to devote themselves to their families. Class disadvantage, on the other hand, restricts people's ability to behave in gendered ways. Nursing assistants may sometimes wish to be available to care for their families, but the need to earn enough to live on often requires them to make their job a priority; EMTs are led to make child care more of a priority than it might otherwise be. That is, class advantage reinforces gender expectations, while class disadvantage helps deconstruct gender.

Is Unpredictability Inevitable or Socially Created?

Some unpredictable events are acts of God or nature that happen to everyone: the snowstorm that drops an unexpected two feet, for instance, or your father's heart attack.[11] But today social trends—changes in the economy and in the family—are expanding and exacerbating the unpredictable events and problems with which we must contend.

Much of the chaos caused by unpredictability is created by an economic system in which employers increasingly squeeze workers and run on razor-thin staffing margins.[12] Much of what turns unpredictable events into mini-crises is created by staffing so lean that any absence creates a problem. The chaos is also driven by the growing number of organizations that hire irregular or contingent workers, like per diems and temps, to fill some of the holes left not only by disruptions in workers' lives but also by unexpected changes in demand for employer services. In effect, employers have outsourced some of the unpredictability to these irregular workers whose very livelihood depends on unpredictability, both in their own schedules and in the schedules of regular workers. While this practice may solve some of the problems for the short-staffed organization and help out regular staff, it leaves many problems unresolved, especially when the regular workers have specialized skills, knowledge of local routines, or personalized relations with clients. These increasingly common organizational practices—understaffing and the hiring of irregular workers—all too often create stress, conflicts, and divisions.

Workers are often aware of the difference between a natural necessity and an employer exerting control by squeezing workers. For example, at one for-profit ambulance company known among EMTs as "The Evil Empire," the company routinely held over workers, requiring them to stay an hour or more past the end of their scheduled shift (with no advance notice). When we made the (employer) case to one EMT that sometimes holding workers past the end of their shift cannot be helped, we got a sharp response:

INTERVIEWER: What about holdovers? I'll make the following argument to you and you make the response: "Well, holdovers, there's nothing we can do about them; they're just determined by what's out there and there's no choice about it. You may not like being held over, but how else could we do it, because these people need to be taken care of."

RESPONDENT: Which ones? Which ones? The ones that call 911 or the ones that have been sitting in a bed for three hours up at St. Mary's[13] [hospital] because you couldn't schedule properly? If you're going to hold me over to go do a transfer out of the hospital, or to send every other truck up to the floor to do a transfer, and now you have no coverage for the city and you're making me stay an hour and a half past my shift? That's not fair—you're taking advantage of me. If a call comes in because every other truck is on a 911 and you need me to go do a 911, I won't say one word—I'll go do it.

New technologies further increase the sway of unpredictability. Some of that, as Leslie Perlow points out, is a result of the all-too-present emails and cell phones.[14] But it is also the case that managers increasingly rely on technology that helps them wield control and create scheduling policies that intensify instability. The *New York Times* recently reported that "workers' schedules have become far less predictable and stable" because

> powerful scheduling software, developed by companies like Dayforce and Kronos over the last decade, has been widely adopted by retail and restaurant chains. The Kronos program . . . breaks down schedules into 15-minute increments. So if the lunchtime rush at a particular shop slows down at 1:45, the software may suggest cutting 15 minutes from the shift of an employee normally scheduled from 9 a.m. to 2 p.m.[15]

In concert with the increasing disruptions wrought by economic changes, broad trends in the family have made normal unpredictability even more common. In *The Time Divide,* Jacobs and Gerson suggest that as many wives and mothers entered the labor force in the past generation there was a substantial increase in the working time not of individuals but of families.[16] This increase in hours produced more opportunities as well as more unpredictable schedules and strategies to control them. Today, with more and more women in the labor force as part of dual-earner couples, husbands are less able to "outsource" unpredictability to stay-at-home wives. In addition, the high rates of divorce and the increase in the number of babies born outside of marriage have led to many more people being single parents, especially single mothers. Solo parenting increases the number and impact of unpredictable events with which the parent must cope. Moreover, the rise in intergenerational households increases unpredictability (though the extended kin in these households may also serve as a resource to control or resolve that unpredictability).

Overall, these related trends in both the economy and the family create stress about "crazy schedules." Normal unpredictability, then, has increased. How should we interpret this? As individual malaise or systemic failure? In the lead article of the *New York Times* "Sunday Review" section, Tim Kreider argued recently that "the 'crazy busy' existence so many of us complain about is almost entirely self-imposed."[17] We disagree. While many of us may live in a bubble where we see neither how our lives are part of broader patterns nor how our situation compares to the situations of others, unpredictable events stem not primarily from personal issues created by life's vagaries but instead are produced by broad and unequal institutional factors in the market and in families. Moreover, for the members of our four occupations as well as for others, these normal disruptions are simultaneously influenced by class and gender differences.

Suppose one of our respondents experienced a fender-bender in a parking lot, and as a result, his or her car could not be driven without a $1,000 repair. A male doctor earning $200,000 a year would have to use the family's other car, get dropped off by his wife, or rent a car. The car accident would be a nuisance and a hassle, but ultimately it would not be that big a problem and it would not cause him to miss even a day of work. For a $20,000-a-year nursing assistant whose income as a single mother supports her family, this accident would be a disaster that might cost her the job. Unable to afford repairs and lacking insurance, she needs a car to get to her job and has no good options by which to deal with the situation.

These contrasting experiences lie at the heart of this book, much of which deals not only with the challenges of setting basic schedules, important as that is, but also with the ways in which disrupted schedules are fixed.

THE WEB OF TIME

Most research on time, whether it relies on time diaries or surveys, looks at disparate individuals. This literature does not (and cannot) take account of the ways in which the allocation and expenditure of time is collective—within and between occupations, within and between organizations, and within and between families. Together these relations compose a web of time in which the allocation, experience, and control of time is a collective project. Because people are linked, changes in one person's schedule often create changes in the schedule of another person, both in the workplace and outside of it. Sometimes relations in the web create problems by increasing unpredictability; sometimes they provide solutions. The web leads to both, since it depends on cooperation and accommodation. But it also creates struggles for control and other conflicts in and between occupations and organizations.

Consider one example. An emergency room night nurse realizes that she is going to have to stay late, maybe because a coworker hasn't shown up, or maybe because a critically ill patient arrived just before the end of her shift. If this nurse were married to a doctor—a fairly frequent pairing—it would be highly unlikely that her husband would pick up the slack at home. (In fact, a nurse married to a doctor might choose not to work in the highly skilled but highly unpredictable world of an ER.) This nurse, however, is married to a firefighter, and as we will show, some firefighters take significant responsibility for their children. She calls her husband to let him know she will be late getting home and he will have to see the kids off to school. As a result, he will be late for his day shift at the fire station. He calls the station, talks to the outgoing crew, and one of them volunteers to cover for him until he can come in. This arrangement is made informally; no record is kept of it. In the web of time, a firefighter stays past the end of his shift because his coworker's wife had an unexpected patient. An unpredictable event at one point in the web reverberates throughout the web.

In *Patterns of Time in Hospital Life*, Eviatar Zerubavel stresses that "the structural components of the sociotemporal order are collectivities."[18] Zerubavel studied a single organization, but the web operates to shape schedules beyond a single organization. Looking at relations among workers within as well as across occupations and organizations reveals how such decisions cascade, altering choices and institutional requirements for other workers at a range of sites and then affecting what happens in those families and jobs as well. For example, when some workers decide to stay late out of a concern for their clients or their coworkers on the next shift, other staff are sometimes required to stay as well. That initial decision to stay late cascades to affect both regular and irregular workers, since the use of per diem workers, who are supposedly at the bottom of the pecking order, allows institutions to fill shifts but also to cancel the shifts that full-time regular workers depend on. Overall, this web then has a number of components or substructures: it consists of those grouped in single occupations (nurses, for example), those in linked occupations (like doctors and nurses), and those relations that operate across units within a single organization (such as the ER and the medical floor). This web also operates across organizations as workers shape one another's schedules (as when a doctor at night tells a patient to go to an ER, or an ambulance moves a patient to a nursing home). So, too, families are increasingly an important component of this web operating across occupations and organizations. When a worker unexpectedly must add hours to the end of his or her day, a spouse must rush home, a child must take care of another child, or a grandmother must keep the kids as her adult daughter takes the double shift she needs to support her family. The web relieves even as it intensifies the chaos of unpredictability.

The Coworker Solution

Coworkers are a key part of this web of time, although they are often all but invisible in the research that examines work hours and schedules. When the work-family literature addresses the problem of a worker needing an exception to the normally required schedule, the emphasis is primarily on managers and supervisors, who may make special arrangements for valued workers.[19] A change in a worker's basic schedule almost certainly requires a manager's approval, but for the unpredictable events that can cost people their jobs—or at a minimum make the difference between high and low stress—we find that managers usually are not the key. Instead, one of the most important ways in which workers gain some control over their lives is through coworkers, who provide the solution whether the problem is seeing their child's school play or getting vacation time off when they want or need it.

If a worker's nine-year-old tells her that he has a big part in the school play, to be performed at 2:00 PM two days from now, the manager will tell her that this is not enough notice and she can't change her schedule. She could call out sick, but if a manager shows up at the same school event, she might face sanctions (as reported by one of the respondents in our study). But if a coworker exchanges days off with her and agrees to work that day for her, the problem is solved: she will make it to the play and will not face workplace repercussions. Management can solve the easy problems that come with plenty of advance notice. Coworkers, however, often solve the tough problems, the unpredictable events that need a solution right away. Employers gain from coworkers' reliance on each other, since they are the ones, rather than managers, who are filling the schedule hole. But this pattern also makes workers feel that management is rigid and uncaring, while coworkers are the people they can count on in a pinch.

Families as a Source of Compliance and Resistance

Family members shape one another's schedules by making it more or less possible to add or cut hours of work. The role of families in schedule flexibility has two sides. On one side, it is often said that families, and especially children, become a reason for workers to keep their heads down and go along with employer demands, even unjust and unreasonable ones, since they need to keep their jobs in order to provide for their families. In fact, this is often the case, as corroborated by workers themselves. For example, an experienced nursing assistant told a new aide to control her "attitude," and another reminded her, "When you have to feed your kids, you have to behave differently just to keep the job."

The other side to this story is implicit in the literature on work and family but often is less foregrounded: families are a key source of resistance. Families, and especially children, are central to the web of time; children are the single most important reason why workers refuse an offered schedule, why they demand another schedule, or why they fail to meet the official schedule. The scheduler at a nursing home noted that "the majority of the call-outs are babysitting issues." Nurses, nursing assistants, and EMTs do not necessarily think of staying home with a sick kid as "resistance" to their employer's demands, but that choice is a clear statement of what is more important to them, and it is often accompanied by a firm assertion that, if push comes to shove, they are willing to risk—or lose—their job for their kids. For example, the nursing assistant discussed in our opening vignettes had a child with serious asthma, such that attacks sometimes required hospitalization. When that happened, "I mean, if they were to call me at work, I'm sorry, I don't care if my supervisor says no—if it's for my kids, I'm leaving." Sometimes there is no emergency but kids still come first—for example, on special occasions. As one EMT explained: "I missed Sidney's second birthday, and it killed me to not be there, and I vowed from that point on I would never miss another birthday, whether it meant calling out sick, or it was vacations, getting docked a day's pay." Going to a child's birthday party, attending the school play, or taking one's child to the hospital all require adjustments from employers and family members in a cascading web of time.

To be sure, family matters to both advantaged and disadvantaged workers, but who is considered family by these two groups? One way to understand the differing meanings of family is to look at who is and is not included in a respondent's typical web of time. All four occupations shared the dilemma of trying to deal with the unpredictable needs of children (who create unpredictable events far more often than spouses or other relatives), but "family" meant something different for those in advantaged and disadvantaged occupations. For the two professional occupations, doctors and nurses, family usually meant a spouse and children. For the two working-class occupations, EMTs and nursing assistants, family usually included extended family as well—grandmothers, siblings, cousins, and aunts or uncles. In our opening vignette, for example, the surgeon turned first to his wife for assistance, then to the nanny, and finally to neighbors; he made no mention of extended family. The nursing assistant's aunt and grandmother, on the other hand, were key parts of the solution to her problem. The content and impact of this web, then, is shaped by gender and class.

This book develops these broad arguments—about normal unpredictability, control over unpredictability, and the web of time—using a variety of data. Our focus is on the four occupations and eight organizations we studied in the medical sector, but we believe that the processes we identify and analyze apply far more generally. Since developing our analysis, we constantly remark in our own lives on the normal unpredictability of faculty life, the web of time for construction workers renovating our houses, the struggles to control schedules at hotels, coffee shops, and restaurants, and a thousand other instances. We believe that although there are important variations from one occupation or organization to the next, our theoretical points apply in some fashion across a range of occupations and organizations. The next chapter briefly discusses our methods, and the following one provides background on the four occupations and eight organizations we studied.

Chapter 2 | Concepts and Methods

THIS CHAPTER SETS OUT our research design, briefly presents our data and methods, and then discusses key concepts and decisions. It is the most academic, nuts-and-bolts part of the book. Other readers may want more detail, which is available on the book's website at:

https://www.russellsage.org/publications/unequal-time.

RESEARCH DESIGN

We began this study with a broad aim: to develop a research design that would allow us to understand inequalities in hours and schedules and the social processes that produce them. Initially we considered many occupations, but after substantial discussion, we decided to examine four linked health care occupations, for reasons both substantive and methodological.

Studying linked occupations and the particular organizations in which they are situated would allow us, we thought, to examine the ways in which work hours and schedules are collective experiences, the products of interactions and power relations both on the job and at home. The design would allow us to examine the influence of the local in several ways: it would show the impact on workers not only of broad structural influences but also of their particular occupations with their unique coworker connections and negotiations or struggles with managers; we would be able to see particular organizational (and unit) practices and policies; and the design would facilitate an examination of the different kinds of relational cultures in particular families and the power operating inside those cultures. Examination of these areas could provide, we thought, the "thick description" necessary for understanding interactions, institutions, and contexts that produce temporal inequality and control over it.

Most studies of work hours use surveys to examine a heterogeneous collection of individuals scattered across a range of occupations. Some studies examine organizations or occupations but focus on a single occupation, a single workplace, or a single employer. But such a design encompasses, for our purposes, a population that is either too broad and scattered or too narrow and focused. In contrast, our decision to study intermeshing occupations and organizations in a single sector of the economy allowed us to analyze the contexts shaping hours and schedules. At the same time, looking at these linked occupations and organizations enabled us to identify, conceptualize, and analyze a web of time operating within and among the occupations and organizations. This design allowed us to analyze the connections between occupations and organizations in that web—how those within a single occupation and those within different occupations and across organizations shape one another's schedules. For example, not only do two ER doctors in the same unit affect one another's shifts, but if one ER doctor decides to stay late, the ER nurse may have to stay late as well. Or a patient discharged from the ER early may be sent to a nursing home, where a CNA does an additional shift to provide that patient with hospital-level care; in turn, the CNA's sister may have to look after her kids. This multifaceted web was a key component of our research design and became one of the central foci of our study.

We chose health care as a strategic research site because the temporal issues that are present in many industries appear with particular clarity in this location. Not only do many parts of the medical system rely on diverse shifts in organizations that operate 24/7, but as part of the growing service sector rather than the diminishing manufacturing sector, health care is in some sense the prototypical industry of our time. Health care accounted for 17.5 percent of total gross domestic product (GDP) in 2010[1] and 24 percent of government transfers in 2009.[2] Medical occupations also share a similar economic environment: they operate in an industry where rapidly increasing costs coexist with strong pressures to hold down costs.[3] Finally, a crucial methodological advantage is that, at least in the Northeast, where we conducted the research, employees in all of these occupations must register with the state, and that made it possible to draw the random sample that we used in the initial survey.

Our study is unusual in both scope and complexity: we take on four occupations and eight organizations, and do so using multiple methods. Although we focus on health care, many of the processes we analyze operate in other sectors of the economy. Because prior research has established gender and class as key determinants of work hours, we chose four linked

Table 2.1   Four Health Care Occupations, by Class and Gender

Gender	Class	
	Professional occupation	Working-class occupation
Male-dominated	Physicians Percentage women: 32 percent Mean income = $187,000	EMTs Percentage women: 22 percent Mean income = $54,000
Female-dominated	Nurses Percentage women: 93 percent Mean income = $55,000	Nursing assistants Percentage women: 93 percent Mean income = $21,000

Source: Authors, 2005, Survey of Hours and Schedules. See the website for the equivalent national data.

health care occupations that vary by class and gender: doctors, nurses, EMTs, and nursing assistants. The research design creates sociology's classic two-by-two table, gender by class (see table 2.1).

Note that the working-class male occupation (EMT) earns almost as much as the female-dominated profession (nursing) and significantly more than the female-dominated working-class occupation (nursing assistant). The data for the occupations in our study closely approximate the national data, except for the EMT incomes.[4] According to national data, EMTs earn a median income of $33,000—significantly below the median income of the EMTs who answered our survey. Later we discuss the reasons for this income difference in more detail, but here we note that the most important reason for it is the high proportion (62 percent) of our EMTs who worked second jobs—higher than in any other group in our study.

Also fundamental to our research design was that we studied these four occupations at eight organizational sites, described in greater detail later in the chapter.

DATA: MULTIPLE METHODS

We collected five types of data in two counties in the Northeastern United States whose demographics approximated those of the national population.[5] First, at the end of 2004 we mailed a survey to a random sample of two hundred people in each occupation. As mentioned earlier, the state registration requirement gave us a crucial methodological advantage by making it possible to draw a random sample. To obtain the survey samples, we tracked down lists based on state registries of all those legally certified to work in the four occupations; these came from a different agency for each occupation and ranged from 120,000 nurses to 19,000 EMTs. The overall response rate was 64.5 percent, with a rate greater than 50 percent for every occupation.[6] When relying on this part of the data, we refer to the survey as our source.

Second, from 2006 to 2008 we completed 208 intensive face-to-face interviews. One-quarter of the interviews were with individuals who managed schedules in the four occupations: administrators, schedulers, human resource personnel, union representatives, and temporary agency officials.[7] Three-quarters of the interviews were with direct-care providers distributed across the four occupations; about one-quarter of these were survey respondents who indicated a willingness to be interviewed, and the rest were respondents chosen at our observation sites.[8] At the sites, we selected respondents to ensure variation by occupation, gender, and shift. Occasionally, we selected someone because he or she seemed particularly observant. Approximately 80 percent of those whom we approached agreed to participate and then did the interviews; a few agreed and then did not show up for the interview (this happened most frequently among the CNAs); and a small number of those whom we approached turned us down. Respondents selected where the interview would take place; many chose their home, some chose their job site, and a few chose a restaurant or other public locale. Interviews averaged well over an hour each. We transcribed more than four thousand pages of interview material, developed a coding scheme and codebook covering themes, coded all interviews using NVivo 8, and held weekly meetings to address questions and inconsistencies in coding.[9] When using these data, we refer to "interviews" to distinguish them from those points where we rely on the survey.

Third, we observed from the summer of 2007 to the summer of 2009, for a total of 615 hours, at the four kinds of organizations. We observed eight different organizations, including:

1. *Two hospitals* (out of eight in the two-county area[10]): One hospital was a large urban teaching hospital and the other was a community hospital; both were nonprofit. Within each hospital, we observed both an emergency floor, where the workload was relatively unpredictable, and a medical surgical floor, where the workload was relatively predictable.[11]

2. *Two nursing homes* (out of thirty-four in the area): One nursing home was a high-end stand-alone nonprofit and the other was a less-upscale, midrange chain facility.

3. *Two doctors' offices:* We chose a family practitioner and a specialist surgical practice.

4. *Two EMS centers:* Our two sites were a public fire station and a private for-profit company. Both in the area we studied and nationally, much of the EMT service is provided by firefighters.

We observed on the day, evening, and night shifts, attending staff meetings, shadowing (really following) staff, and listening to conversations on and about different shifts, as well as just hanging around the offices, floors, and break rooms. These observations allowed us to watch (and sometimes ask questions about) relationships and interactions at the moment they occurred. The web of relations, and the chain of command embedded in it, becomes especially visible during the many periods of waiting—whether it is patients waiting in a "waiting room," nurses waiting for a doctor, or EMTs or CNAs waiting for a nurse. In group gatherings, such as those that routinely occur in locker and break rooms, we would sometimes ask a question about a shift or a schedule, and this very often led to a free-ranging discussion (and sometimes disagreement) among staff in the room. In the hospitals, we wore white coats initially but soon stopped when we realized that this clothing set us apart or led people to assume that we were medical staff whom they could ask for assistance with medical procedures. After a while, people either seemed to stop noticing we were hanging around or did very much notice us, wanting to give us a tip or make a point about something that they found of particular interest. Given the hectic pace of many of these medical settings (which we describe in some detail in the next chapter), our presence did little to interrupt the pressing flow of demands and events.

Fourth, while observing, we sometimes fortuitously located additional types of data that became useful parts of our analysis, such as official work schedules handed out in advance and the day-by-day schedules actually worked at one nursing home and two hospitals. At the different sites, we collected additional material that organizations developed, such as descriptions of workplace regulations—for example, the handbooks that hospitals gave to new employees and the material HR personnel posted to explain policies.

Fifth, and finally, in 2010 and 2011 we collected and coded 132 union contracts, observed at 24 union negotiating sessions, and conducted an additional 26 interviews with workers and union staff involved in union negotiations. For each of these events, our focus was on issues of hours and schedules.

The people we interviewed and observed were passionate, witty, and insightful, constantly challenging our preconceptions. It is their words, their stories, and their insights that make this book possible.

KEY CONCEPTS: GENDER, CLASS, AND RACE

Gender

The classic way of studying the effect of gender is to compare men and women in the same occupation, whether it be finance, the law, medicine, or construction. But women in male-dominated occupations are anomalous, as are men in female-dominated occupations. Such studies can generate important insights (which we draw on), but it is at least as important to analyze the situations of men and women working in occupations in which their gender group predominates; a high proportion of the working population is employed in such workplaces.[12] The overall gender composition of the occupation matters because it shapes the structure of organizational policies as well as the cultural schemas of both employers and employees (both on the job and at home).[13]

Our research design allowed us to examine gender as a relational characteristic that shapes *organizational* and *occupational* policies and practices rather than simply to analyze gender as a characteristic of individuals. For example, where nurses predominate in the workforce, as in hospitals, attracting and retaining quality staff requires that both the culture of the organization and the official staffing practices adapt to nurse demands—many of which emanate from their position at home. Moreover, the range of options is shaped not just by individual traits or what an individual asks for or wants (although those matter) but also by group processes, such as previous negotiations and struggles, and group realities, such as difficulty finding staff. And the culture and structure of nursing are tied to the other three occupations, whether the two dominated by men (doctors and EMTs) or the other one dominated by women (nursing assistants), just as they shape the gendered familial relations to which these workplaces are linked.

But gender composition by itself is not enough; inequalities are complex. Nursing assistants are also overwhelmingly women, but nursing homes have not reshaped their scheduling practices to meet the needs and preferences of these employees; instead, they insist that nursing assistants conform to a version of what Mary Blair-Loy calls a "work devotion" approach, with severe penalties for failing to do so.[14] That is, organizational practices and schemas depend not only on gender but also on class; the rules in an organization numerically dominated by nurses (as hospitals are) differ from those in an organization numerically dominated by nursing assistants (as nursing homes are). Our research design made it possible to explore such interactions and show that gender interacts with class in undocumented ways.

We compared gendered occupations rather than using the more common technique of comparing men and women within single occupations. The fact that the women's occupations are not the equivalent of the men's is a strength, not a limit, of our study. In the United States, women with a bachelor's degree earn $2,000 a year less than men with an associate's degree.[15] Given these patterns, it is not surprising that women professionals (nurses) earn only slightly more than working-class men (EMTs). And in our study, the EMTs had to work overtime and second jobs—an extra eighteen hours a week—to (almost) match the nurses' incomes. Doctors are the most highly paid, on average, of any profession. Although nurses' incomes do not match doctors' incomes, nursing is very close to being the most highly paid women's health profession, coming in fractionally behind occupational therapists. But as the Census Bureau reports,[16] the United States has only 67,050 occupational therapists, while there are 2,415,590 nurses. In effect, then, we studied the highest-paid health care profession dominated by women and contrasted it to the highest-paid health care profession dominated by men. The same asymmetry is found in the two working-class occupations: our working-class men were paid more than our working-class women and were subject to less punitive policies. In other words, this study's occupations correspond in key ways to the U.S. distribution, where gender privilege affects income and job conditions. Furthermore, again reflecting the reality of employment patterns, the occupations in which men predominate have a higher proportion of women than those in which women predominate, because women have entered male occupations more than men have entered women's.[17]

For the two occupations that were overwhelmingly dominated by women, gender comparisons within occupation were not feasible. There were too few men. In contrast, there were more women in the two male-dominated occupations (again corresponding to national data): 28 percent of the doctors and 30 percent of the EMTs we interviewed were women. The women EMTs, however, were very similar to the men on issues of hours and schedules, whereas the male and female doctors were more different. That difference may be a consequence of the fact that doctors have more control, and hence more choices, about hours and schedules. Men and women often use such choice to take sharply differing approaches—especially insofar as they organize hours and schedules around family responsibilities. Thus, given the numbers, similarities, and choices, doctors were the only occupation in which we could systematically compare women and men (see the chapters on families, chapters 8 and 9).

Class

Class is messy. We do not have a language or agreed way of recognizing class divides, but instead a welter of competing and alternative approaches, some of which obscure as much as they illuminate. The first alternative approach, and by far the most common in the media and popular discourse, is to use the categories lower-class, middle-class, and upper-class—frequently with assorted transitional categories (especially upper-middle-class and lower-middle-class)—and to assign one of these categories to individuals (or individual families). When surveys offer people a choice among these three categories, typically almost 90 percent of the population say that they are middle-class; that is, a majority of those below the poverty line say they are middle-class, as do a majority of the top 10 percent of the income distribution.[18] If we are all middle-class, then class does not really exist as a distinguishing or motivating characteristic and can be ignored. Politicians and newsmakers can present a person or family with wealth, power, and privilege as middle-class, then imply that those characteristics extend to everyone else. Put somewhat differently, there are many gradations in society but, in this view, we are all basically the same—some people simply have a little more and others a little less.[19] Because this framework is so common in popular discourse, all of us—including scholars who know better—end up using these terms, even though the statement that someone is "middle-class" conveys almost no information.

A second formulation, one that is far more analytic and insightful, comes to us from Max Weber and his many academic descendants; our own usage sometimes draws on Weber's conception. Weber saw class in terms of inequality of opportunity and the market. This view leads, among other things, to studies of consumption and to the creation and enforcement of distinctions like access to educational credentials. Pierre Bourdieu also took this basic approach, though with important differences.[20] How does a group establish boundaries—to create both internal coherence and a sense of group identity—and provide markers that maintain those boundaries and enable the group to exclude outsiders? In this formulation, class is not just an individual location; it also depends on social hoarding and social closure. In other words, the advantages of some come at the expense, disadvantage, or exclusion of others.[21]

In much of the analysis here, we take a third approach, one rooted in a tradition that extends and reinterprets Marx. In this approach, class is not only about relationships but also about relationships of power and domination. The key, as Mike Zweig writes, is that "class is about the power some people have over the lives of others, and the powerlessness most people experience as a result. . . . Classes are groups of people connected to one another, and made different from one another, by the ways they interact when producing goods and services."[22] This approach is not simply about the market advantage of one group over another, or the status distinctions between them. It addresses the domination entailed in their relationship: "This is a stronger form of relational interdependency than in a relation of simple exclusion," notes Erik Olin Wright, "for here there is an ongoing relationship between the *activities* of the advantaged and disadvantaged persons not just a relationship between their *conditions*."[23]

E. P. Thompson, who examined the changing work schedules brought about by the rise of industry, argued that class is not simply a result of a person's location within a social structure, but rather a result of common experiences and ways of understanding: "Class happens when some [people], as a result of common experiences (inherited or shared), feel and articulate the identity of their interests as between themselves, and as against other [people], whose interests are different from (and usually opposed to) theirs."[24] Thompson emphasized that as such, class is a historical phenomenon. What is key to this book—and our research design—is our understanding and analysis of class (like gender) as relational. This book shows that the process by which people share common experiences and see themselves as having the same interests as others in a similar situation (occupation)—interests that are different from and opposed to those of others (in a different occupation)—is not limited to a change that takes place over historical time. It also takes place in individual lives. Over the course of a year at work, for instance, a nursing assistant becomes much more conscious of the need to maintain solidarity with other nursing assistants and aware that their interests differ from those of nurses or "the big bosses." Class (along with gender) was a part of our research design from the beginning, but it is also a finding: we hope the material we present here helps readers become more conscious of some of the many ways in which class, combined with gender and race, shapes our lives and is thus a meaningful concept in the United States today.

We chose to study four occupations linked in one broad system—medical care—because that allowed us to examine the ways in which class, like gender, both entails relationships and depends on them: the character and content of each of these occupations—and their hours and schedules—interact in organizational fields. They are shaped by power relations within and among them. We begin by differentiating between professional and working-class occupations, but that distinction is a hypothesis, not an a priori absolute. Although we focus on class as a relation of power at work (which shapes and is shaped by relations of power at home), other indicators of class also distinguish these occupations. There are education differences in addition to the income differences presented in table 2.1: physicians must have a college degree plus at least four additional years of education, nurses must receive at least two years of nursing-specific education (and many have college degrees), but only three weeks of training are required to qualify as a nursing assistant or a basic-level EMT. (Paramedic training requires a year or two.) Moreover, there are large differences in the market positions of our occupations. Nursing aides' unemployment rate stood at about 9 percent over the last ten years, higher than that of any of our other groups. To be sure, EMTs had relatively low unemployment (with rates at about 3 percent over the last decade), but their rate was higher than nurses' (whose unemployment rate ranged from 1 to 2 percent over the last ten years) and doctors' (who faced almost no unemployment).[25] Furthermore, our survey shows that the following percentages for each occupation were paid on an hourly basis (that is, with their hours externally monitored by their organization): 98.7 percent of nursing assistants, 80.6 percent of EMTs, 67.4 percent of nurses, and only 2.0 percent of physicians. Doctors, nurses, and EMTs are primarily supervised and controlled by other members of the same occupation, but when occupational lines are crossed, not only do nurses answer to doctors (which has been much written about), but nurses also exercise power over EMTs and (especially) nursing assistants.

As feminist scholars have emphasized, class is based not only in the workplace but also in family relations and circumstances; those class relations, in turn, shape gender dynamics. Part of this dynamic depends on marital status (49 percent of the CNAs were married, as were 61 percent of the EMTs, 73 percent of the nurses, and 78 percent of the doctors), which is consequential not only for income but also for many benefits, such as health insurance; these benefits shape work hours and schedules.[26] If married, spouses' occupations also affect, of course, the family's class position. The biggest range of spouse occupations was among nurses, and the smallest was among physicians (essentially all spouses of doctors were trained as professionals, though many were not employed) and nursing assistants (essentially all were partnered with working-class people). The nurse married to a firefighter lives a significantly different life than the nurse married to an emergency room doctor; our sample included both. These differences shape relations at home, especially the division of household labor, which, as we emphasize later, is based not only on gender and on class but on the intersection of gender with class. Finally, class shapes the form that families take—whether people primarily rely on the nuclear family or are likely to turn to extended kin for support. We found much more involvement with kin among the two working-class occupations, and less among the professionals, especially the physicians. These differences affected where they lived, the vacations they took, and their sense of themselves and their relationship to the larger world, including their relationship to their job hours and schedules.

The Language of Class   In the United States today, ordinary people's understandings of class are typically not framed in the language of either social scientists or political partisans. Contrast this to gender. In 1963 Betty Friedan began *The Feminine Mystique* by discussing "the problem that has no name." At the time women thought that they as individuals were experiencing a set of personal problems, and they did not see those problems as stemming from the larger social system. A decade later the women's movement had transformed that understanding. By then women could see the connection between making coffee for the boss and staying home with the kids, between being denied admission to law school and getting whistled at on the street, between being invisible and being patronized, and they had come to understand these connections through the general framework of sexism—or at a minimum, gender discrimination.

Similarly, in today's world workers lack a language and set of categories with which to articulate issues of class, even as in some ways they are very clear about class differences and constantly refer to them.[27] Thus, consider the words of a nursing assistant complaining about a newly imposed sick leave policy that inflicted additional penalties on staff: "Like the DON [Director of Nursing], you know, the administrative. All the head people, they call out a day, do they get wrote up?" Or consider a discussion among three veteran nursing assistants who were schooling new hires about the known but still mysterious "they" (mostly, but not only, referring to nurses):

(handwritten margin note: defining difference)

AIDE 1: They watch everything.

AIDE 2: When you punch in, when you punch out.

AIDE 3: And not just when you punch in, but what you're doing when you punch in. Do you stand out here gabbing or get to work? They watch everything.

Or consider the other side of that relationship. As one feisty nurse manager said in a meeting of nurses on a hospital medical floor when they were talking about the relations and the division of labor between CNAs and nurses: "Our job as nurses is to delegate. It is the CNA's job to receive.

We can't go overboard, but this is the way it has to be. It is not about power and control. They need to understand how hard nurses work and don't have time." She then went on to emphasize that the nurses needed to recognize their superior position: "You are the overseers of CNAs. . . . Are you clear on your expectations? I am not suggesting we use bull whips. . . ." She stopped here in midsentence. Note her insistence that this relationship between nurses and CNAs was not "about power and control." She simultaneously insisted upon and obscured the class relations between nurses and CNAs.

Such interactions are by no means confined to nurses and nursing assistants. In doctors-only meetings to collectively plan their schedules, no one raises his or her voice to another doctor and there is a careful etiquette about how to frame schedule requests. When doctors are on the hospital floor, however, they often berate nurses for making them wait or for being called when they think they should not have been. A nurse sharing such an experience with another nurse sarcastically said, "I'm only a nurse." Or consider what was said to a firefighter who wanted to use a new piece of technology as soon as it arrived. His coworkers insisted that he wait until their jobs were protected, saying to him, "You don't know how these people operate. They're gonna jam this down our throats, and it's gonna end up backfiring on us." Workers refer to "the head people," "they/them," or "these people," and managers refer to "they/them" or "delegation." Workers say "we" and "us," referring to their coworkers, not their bosses and managers. Even as none of these are clear statements of class, all of these are clear statements of class. Their language shows a clear recognition of difference in how they are treated, how they are connected, and who has control, compared to some other imperfectly defined (but more or less powerful) alternative group. That class is experienced and expressed here in particular organizational and occupational contexts provides us with yet another rationale for studying such connected or linked contexts.

If class is about relationships and control, then it makes very good sense to see nurses as professionals and EMTs as working-class. Every day nurses routinely direct and control the activities of nursing assistants and other personnel. EMTs are among the personnel over whom nurses have power. In hospital emergency rooms EMTs work hard (often unsuccessfully) to get the attention of nurses, and nurses tell them what to do and sometimes treat them as second-class citizens. One EMT who was also a nurse but often worked as an EMT had this to say about hospital emergency rooms:

> One of the things I hate is having to identify myself to another nurse as a nurse. All of a sudden it lends validity to what I'm telling you. Oh, you're a

nurse! Okay, so the report you gave me as a paramedic is absolute BS, but now you're a nurse, oh, it's legitimate now. Like *now* I have credibility. There have been times where I have pulled that card, it's like a trump card. Listen, you need to listen to what I'm saying. I know you're busy and I know that this appears to be nothing, and I know you think that I am just a cowboy, starting lines and giving medications because I can, but here's why I'm doing this: (*whispers*) I'm also a nurse! Don't tell anybody, but this is why I did this! And oh, okay, all of a sudden it's like I know the secret handshake and everything is cool with these people.

This EMT/nurse was referring not only to the status distinctions between nurses and EMTs but also the power differences between them and their relations of control or domination. While nurses control EMTs, EMTs do not direct or control members of any other occupation.[28] Moreover, as we shall see, on some key dimensions of time, especially control over their own official basic schedules, EMTs resemble nursing assistants far more than they resemble nurses.

Race

In numerous disciplines today, many understand and promote an analysis of intersectionality and include in that analysis not only class and gender but also race.[29] It is difficult to disentangle class and race. Social class is not randomly distributed but instead is still deeply tied to race, a fact that becomes very clear among the workers in our study: three of our four occupations were overwhelmingly white. Only a small proportion of EMTs (5 percent), physicians (11 percent), and nurses (12 percent) we interviewed were nonwhite, while a majority of CNAs (58 percent) we interviewed were nonwhite.[30] These differences, which characterize not only the region we observed but the nation as a whole, make it extremely difficult to separate race from class in much of the analysis in this book. Moreover, because there were few black or Latino doctors, nurses, or EMTs in our sample, if we had discussed the situation of the few we did interview we would have been likely to uniquely identify them and compromise informant confidentiality. Nursing assistants, on the other hand, were about evenly divided between whites and people of color in our sample—with the people of color predominantly black (both African American and West Indian) or Latino (overwhelmingly Puerto Rican)—and we do, in some contexts, examine racial dynamics among the CNAs.

What our research emphasizes is not only the high correlation between race and class but also the fact that stratification and inequality occur and are sustained at the occupational and organizational levels. Nurses predominate in hospitals, while nursing assistants predominate (at least numerically) in nursing homes. At one of the two nursing homes we observed, 87 percent of the nursing assistants were people of color; at the other, only about 20 percent were. Both nursing homes provided stable jobs and good benefits, but the nursing home with a largely black and Latina workforce imposed harsh and punitive rules and management regarded workers as constantly trying to evade their responsibilities. The nursing home with predominantly white nursing assistants took a different approach. On the one hand, our findings reveal some of the ways in which local organizations are a key site for the production and maintenance of inequality, as some scholars insist but rarely study.[31]

On the other hand, these organizational differences further complicate efforts to assess the independent contributions of race. Other research documents the interaction of organization and racial composition: for example, Susan Lambert and Elaine Waxman find the same type of racial stratification in retail when comparing the composition of workforces in elite department stores and big-box retailers.[32]

In our study, we cannot look at racial patterns within or across occupations, although we can—and do occasionally—hypothesize that differences among occupations and organizations are likely to be tied not only to class and gender but also to racial dynamics.

Chapter 3 | The Context: Occupations and Organizations

MUCH RESEARCH ON TIME decontextualizes and disconnects individual workers from one another. These studies have yielded important insights, and we sometimes rely on them. But for our purposes, even these studies are limited: they cannot and do not provide a systemic view of the web of time, that is, of the ways time is a collective experience. These studies almost never embed workers in both shared occupations *and* organizations. Unless research embeds occupations in organizations, it is difficult to see the ways that time is layered, negotiated, contested, and shaped by unequal relations.

This chapter provides a detailed discussion of the four occupations and eight organizations we studied. For expository reasons, this chapter is divided in two—the first half covers the occupational context, and the second half the organizational context—though we argue that it is difficult to fully separate the two.

OCCUPATIONS: CHARACTERISTICS, TASKS, INTENSITY, AND RELATIONS

In discussing each occupation, we focus on four aspects: the basic demography of the group, the allocation of tasks (a division sometimes legally mandated, sometimes dictated by management, and sometimes worked out among coworkers), the intensity of work routines, and the attendant hierarchies and social relations. Here we devote relatively little attention to the unpredictability of hours and the degree of control over work and scheduling in each occupation, as this is a central concern of the rest of the book. Looking across occupations, we see that even though the tasks, intensity, and social relations at work are quite distinct, at least analytically, from the hours of work, they also clearly shape the experience of those hours.

Emergency Medical Technicians

EMTs have three levels of certification—basic (81 percent of all EMTs), intermediate (3 percent), and paramedic (16 percent). Although more than 80 percent of EMTs are certified at the basic level, only 46 percent of *employed* EMTs are at the basic level.[1] Our survey and interviews reflect data for employed EMTs. There is a major pay difference between basic EMTs and paramedics, with paramedics earning almost twice what basic EMTs earn.[2] Both in our area and nationally, much of the EMT service is provided by town and city firefighters.[3]

The typical emergency medical system (EMS) worker—both in our study and nationwide—is a young white male, and the job entails, at least part of the time, the expression of a kind of heroic masculinity.[4] The nature of the calls is similar, whether they work for a fire department or in the private sector; EMTs in our study talked about the attraction of the work and its pull on them:

> Am I going to get lucky tonight?. . . It's all about trauma codes, so the shootings, the stabbings, the bad car accidents—I want to be there for that. So that's the trade-off: I'll have these people treat me like crap, whether it's the patient or the family or the nursing staff or whoever. But the trade-off is, I might get a trauma code. I might get a shooting tonight, so it's worth it for that one call, that one good call. And I have to be honest, that one good call— and I'm not talking about the *nature* of the call, but the call where you see yourself making a difference—it is so worth it. And that I think is what has you come back.

Consider two calls that involved response by the same team of paramedics, each for a reported heart attack. In one, a forty-year-old white woman called self-reporting that she was having a heart attack. Taking a history on scene revealed that she had frequent anxiety attacks, that she was on medication for them, and that she had failed to take her medication that day; other signs indicated normal heart functioning combined with rapid breathing (forty-five times per minute, compared to a normal rate of ten to twelve), an indicator of an anxiety attack. The woman was taken to the hospital, but transported by basic-level EMTs rather than by paramedics.

In the other case, by good luck the paramedic team arrived at the scene just two minutes after a call for a man having a massive heart attack. They found the man to be clinically dead: no pulse, no breathing. Within about sixty seconds, the paramedics, working together as a team, used an "electronic gizmo" with pads applied to the man's chest to get a quick reading and analyze his condition. During the next several intense minutes, the medics used the "gizmo" to shoot two hundred joules of electricity through the patient's chest; they did CPR on him; they canulated the antecubital vein on his left arm; they installed a tube on that which had something approximating injection ports; and they used the tube to give the man a standard one-milligram dose of epinephrine, hanging a bag of IV fluids to flush that into circulation. They also intubated the patient—that is, they inserted a breathing tube, gave him oxygen, and administered amiodorone. The odds are not good for patients who, like this one, have a STEMI (ST segment elevation myocardial infarction) heart attack, but this patient survived and walked out of the hospital two weeks later. Medics resent being called "just" ambulance drivers; as one said, "I always say to my patients: I'm bringing the emergency room to you."

Medics may work at a fevered pitch for many minutes, then not have another call for a couple of hours. Much of the job consists of sitting around and waiting, then being ready to go all-out when called. That seems to be especially true for EMTs who are firefighters.

The EMTs who work for fire stations have the lightest schedules of any of the workers we studied. Although firefighter EMTs work more than forty hours a week at their main job—on ten-, fourteen-, or twenty-four-hour shifts, typically with two days and two nights on as well as with regular weekend duty—the *average* level of intensity while at work is lower than for our other occupations. At times firefighters must work at a "speed and efficiency can save a life" pace, but most of the time the work pace is quite relaxed.

To some extent that pace is inevitable: both fire calls and ambulance runs in fact seem to require that the organization maintain substantial excess capacity. The work must respond to need as it arises—the unscheduled, unplanned, and largely unpredictable emergency call to respond to an event, whether a fire or a heart attack, that has occurred at a variable and unpredictable distance from where the workers are stationed (unlike, say, a hospital, where staff are on-site). The unavoidable fact that other people's unpredictable life events are built into the organization of EMTs' jobs makes the pace of work unpredictable and uneven. As one firefighter paramedic explained to us: "You can go from nobody moving for hours to there's not one piece of apparatus left in the city, in less than five minutes. Everyone's called out and you're going." It might be more "efficient" to have fewer staff staying busy a larger percentage of the time, but if that involved an occasional one-hour (or even five-minute) delay, then houses would burn to the ground and heart attacks would kill people who could have been saved.

Although some amount of waiting and downtime are thus closely tied to the requirements of the position, a typical day for Ben, a firefighter, provides a striking contrast with our other occupations. The day shift begins at 8:00 AM with a shift change briefing and roll call:

> And then after that takes place, coffee is usually the main subject, so then during coffee, from, say, till about 8:30, quarter of nine, we discuss what we know is going to be coming up during the day or which equipment's got to go out for service and which equipment needs fuel, needs cleaning, washing, that sort of thing. And then probably between 8:30 and quarter of nine, we actually get going and start the day, accomplishing the things that we know that need to be done.

The morning work of these firefighter EMTs, while they wait for a call, is not an expression of heroic masculinity—quite the reverse. There is typically little to do other than cleaning the fire equipment and the station. The ambulance needs to be carefully checked and restocked, so that all supplies will be available, within their effective dates, and in exactly the right place. Several paramedics noted that having everything in place in exactly the right way can save precious seconds in an emergency; as one said, "I'm a neat freak, in the back of an ambulance especially, so I like things my way, so that when I go to grab it I know that it's there."

For Ben and his coworkers, the morning is actually the *most* strenuous part of the daily routine:

> So then, getting on towards like 11:00, 11:30 or so, we start fighting about lunch, what we're going to do, and then we have a lunch break [typically from 12:00 to 1:00]. But in the afternoon, it depends if it's a weekend or a weekday. During weekdays they usually have some . . . we have a drill instructor type of thing, and usually from, say, 1:00, 1:30, something like that, he may have some sort of program going for us—training, movies, films, what-have-you—that usually kind of absorbs some of the afternoon time.

This weekday training activity (not held on weekends) lasts until perhaps 3:00 or 3:30. Around 4:30, "usually the cadre—the chief, the deputy, and the training instructor—all those people go home"; for the rest of the shift, EMTs are "on our own." They relax and start to talk about dinner:

> So then we fight a little bit about what we're going to have for supper, so then we go out and do what we're going to do for . . . not go out but, you

know, get food or Chinese take-out or a pizza or actually cook, which we do also. And at that point in time, say 6:30 or something, we'll clean up whatever we've done, and most of the guys will just kind of relax and watch some TV. . . . Usually most of the guys go to bed somewhere between 10:00 and 11:00. We try and sleep if we can, and get up the next morning, say 7:00, and make some coffee and meet the crew coming in. It pretty much chews up the day.

This routine is interrupted, of course, by fire or ambulance calls. Most calls do not turn out to be significant emergencies, but that cannot be known in advance. One EMT estimated that the response to a typical call lasted an hour.

Although the amount of work actually accomplished is modest, appearances are important: "Chief doesn't expect to see you doing anything after 4:00 in the afternoon, and he doesn't expect to see you doing anything between noon and 1:00. But other than that, if he sees you hanging around, he wants you to be busy." A paramedic at another station summed it up when we asked if he worked a forty-eight-hour week: "I'm *at* work forty-eight hours a week. . . . Out of the forty-eight, I may actually work ten hours, eight hours of actually doing work. The rest of the time it may just be . . . at night, like I said, from 3:00 PM till, unless we have a class, 8:00 the next morning, it's free time—you can do whatever you want, you've just got to be in the building."

Whatever their work site, the days of the EMTs seem much less intense than those of any other group we examined. They rarely interact with members of the other occupations except in hospital emergency rooms (where they often wait for nurses). The average EMT workday contrasts starkly with that of the other working-class occupation—nursing assistants. Intermittent crisis management is not the main task in this occupation, which is dominated by women; instead, nursing assistants give almost constant hands-on care and often interact with the others, especially nurses, who direct them.

Nursing Assistants

Certified nursing assistants (CNAs) work an average of thirty-five hours a week, with an interquartile range of thirty-two to forty-six hours—significantly less than the weekly hours for the two male-dominated occupations. Compared with the other occupations, they also have less education (three-quarters have only a high school degree or less) and lower family incomes (under $30,000 a year for 63 percent of their households). Nationally, a majority (57 percent) have received public assistance at some point.[5]

The work shifts of nursing assistants are typically filled with far more intense activity than those of EMTs, especially on the day and evening shifts. Most CNAs work in nursing homes, where they are the hands-on caregivers for patients (often called "residents"). Although the relationships with residents in nursing homes are often closer than those to patients in hospitals, many of the tasks nursing assistants perform are similar, whether they work in a hospital or a nursing home.

The number of residents assigned to each CNA varies from one nursing home to another, from one shift to another, and from one unit to another. Long-term nursing home residents fall into two main groups: those with Alzheimer's, who may be physically capable, and those with serious physical incapacities, who may be mentally sharp. Both sets of residents require extensive care, often toileting, washing, diapering, dressing, and feeding, as well as care for minor needs, from taking a sweater off (or putting it on) to adjusting a seat or blanket.

We were not allowed to follow the nursing assistants into the residents' rooms. Steven Lopez, a sociologist at Ohio State University who became certified as a nursing assistant, has convincingly shown that it is impossible to obey all the rules and still complete all of the tasks associated with getting the residents up, washed, and dressed by breakfast time.[6] Aides *had* to take shortcuts that compromise residents' health, such as washing their hands much less often than specified in the rules and washing residents less thoroughly than specified. On top of resident care, CNAs must chart food eaten, excretion, and assorted other parameters not only to track patient health but also to qualify for reimbursement because, as Timothy Diamond writes, from management's point of view, "if it's not charted, it didn't happen."[7]

Management insists on the impossible: that all rules be followed *and* that all resident care be completed on time. Management can do so by staying willfully ignorant of the need to take shortcuts. Thus, when a problem develops, management insists that the issue is human error—an aide's failure to follow prescribed procedures—rather than insufficient staffing or a rigid division of labor. This way management can blame the CNAs rather than themselves.

There are tasks to be done throughout the day, and residents are constantly ringing bells to have nursing assistants do things for them. Ringing bells are often a source of stress and conflict among nursing assistants—which resident is ringing, who will answer, how fast should the response be, how fast *can* it be—and between nursing assistants and their nurse supervisors.

Not only are the nursing assistants constantly attending to the physical demands and needs of the patients and residents, but they also do much emotion work. They are often the staff with whom the nursing home residents have the closest relationship. We observed residents insisting that only a particular CNA was acceptable as someone to take them to the toilet or adjust their bed. We saw nursing assistants crying about residents, and some came in on their days off to check on them.[8] Although facing high death rates among those they cared for, these nursing assistants did not develop the "detached concern"—a kind of emotional distance—that Harold Leif and Renée Fox deemed important for doctors, who see so much death and dying.[9] Nor did CNAs think they should develop such detachment. Sometimes they would say, "We're just ass-wipers, that's all we are," but at the same time it was a job they could and did feel good about—taking care of other human beings who mattered to them.

As these women attended to residents' physical and emotional demands they were supervised by professionals—the nurses, with whom they were in constant contact and who typically were other women.

Nurses

Nurses' work hours are the same as nursing assistants' on average (though significantly less than the hours worked by EMTs or doctors)—about thirty-five hours a week, with an interquartile range of thirty-one to forty-two hours. Like CNAs (but not EMTs), nurses' days tend to be filled with intense activity, but their assigned duties are very different from those of nursing assistants (and are often mandated to be different by both the law and management). As hospitals and nursing homes have shifted routine tasks—like taking vital signs and drawing blood—to nursing assistants, nurses have come to have less intimate contact with patients.[10]

Most of the nurses in our study are RNs (registered nurses), although it does include some LPNs (licensed practical nurses), who have less education and earn less money than RNs, as well as a few nurse-practitioners and midwives, who typically have more specialized education and higher earnings than other RNs.[11] About half of RNs have a BA degree. While almost half of CNAs are women of color, 95 percent of RNs reporting race identify as white.[12] Organizationally, a majority (56.2 percent) of the nation's 2.9 million registered nurses work in hospitals; only about one in sixteen (6.3 percent) work in nursing homes, and the remainder work in other settings.

Hospital nurses are constantly on the go. We moved quickly as we followed one hospital charge nurse, who commented: "The hospital did some observation and drew diagrams of following nurses. It looked like a ball of spaghetti, because they go back and forth, around and around."[13] We shadowed an emergency room charge nurse for an hour and were exhausted simply following her around.[14] Going from one task to another every minute or two, this nurse moved quickly as she constantly balanced multiple and conflicting priorities.

Although charge nurses (especially those in ERs) have some of the most demanding nursing jobs, the pace has increased for almost all nursing jobs. The average length of a hospital stay in the United States has decreased substantially and is now the lowest in the industrialized world.[15] In the past a patient staying in the hospital for a week would have required intense care for the first two days, a middling level of attention and care for two or three days, and only occasional assistance in the last two days. Now the web of time has shifted: a patient with the same condition that used to require a one-week hospitalization is now in the hospital for only two days (or less)—those two days being the period when the patient needs a great deal of attention and care. As hospitals discharge patients "quicker and sicker," a nurse may still be caring for six patients, just as she did ten or twenty years ago, but the six patients are all in the first two days of post-op and therefore require much more care, making the nursing job more demanding and tiring.

The emergency department charge nurse whom we shadowed interacted with a wide range of staff, including not only other nurses but also nursing assistants, EMTs, and orderlies (whom she directed), a couple of doctors (who directed her), a patient advocate, and patients and patients' families (to whom she tended). Her subordination to doctors was clear. Although another nurse complained to her of a particular decision a doctor had made, hoping she would intervene, the charge nurse instead supported the doctor and quickly moved on.

In nursing homes, nurses primarily dispense medications and are much less directly involved than CNAs in the routines of residents' daily lives. Many residents are taking a number of different medications, and by law only a nurse may dispense medications. Although nursing home nurses primarily interact with one another, they also supervise nursing assistants, deal with the concerns of residents' families, are called in by nursing assistants to look at any resident with a potential medical complication or care issue (such as a rash or a bruise), and complete even more paperwork than nursing assistants. Nurses may assist with the routine care of residents, but if asked to do so (for example, to take a resident to the toilet), they are more likely to assign a nursing assistant to the task than do it themselves. Whether spending time on paperwork or patient care, nurses often complain about the pace and content of their days. A hospital nurse who used to be a nursing assistant lamented that now, as a nurse, she had no time to spend with patients and her time was spent instead on the paperwork required by the state and insurance companies.

Doctors

Wherever they work, doctors' days are filled with activity from the moment they arrive on the job until the moment they leave. (And typically their work activity continues after they leave for home, where they answer emails, read journals for recertification, and do still more paperwork.) Physicians often arrive early for their long days, and across the settings we observed—from private practices to hospital emergency rooms—numerous doctors told us that they rarely took a lunch break. Instead, while they sat at their computers going over paperwork or reviewing charts when they had a couple of minutes between patients, they would snack, paying little attention to what they ate—and often enough after discussing the importance of a good diet with the last patient they had seen.

Although the doctors more than any other group we studied had autonomy and control over their own routine and that of others, that autonomy has eroded in the last generation. In 1983 fewer than 25 percent of physicians were employees; by 1996 a majority of young physicians were employees.[16] But even doctors who work as employees signal their relative power by not signing in. At one hospital, a doctor explained why doctors, who were supposed to swipe in, did not: "Because it makes us seem like players on a team so other people in other groups, like the nurses, don't feel like they have to swipe in and the doctors don't." Then he continued: "But the doctors don't do it and payroll knows this, and they don't use the swiping system for the doctors." Few individuals tell doctors what to do, and doctors tell lots of other people what to do. Among the occupations we studied, doctors were the ultimate decision-makers, and that control paid off quite literally: although their income depended on where they worked and their specialty, doctors in our study earned a lot of money—more than three times the average of any other group we studied. To put it quite starkly, one doctor earns on average what nine nursing assistants earn. In our survey, more than 80 percent of those doctors were white; whites and Asians combined were 94 percent of all doctors.

Doctors are not, and do not feel, completely autonomous. Some primary care and hospital physicians allude to the control of other doctors, especially specialists, but most doctors, whether in hospitals, private practice, or group practice, emphasize the control exerted by impersonal, external, and distant factors rather than more personal and immediate sources of control such as other doctors. They complain that their "hectic" schedules are primarily caused by insurance company paperwork, medical malpractice fears, and state regulations, which combine to add substantial hours beyond the time they spend seeing patients, lengthen the workday needed to maintain the incomes they seek to attain, and limit the time they can spend with any given patient.

When they are employed by hospitals, doctors now primarily work either in emergency departments or as hospitalists—a relatively new kind of physician who is hired by a hospital and works only for the hospital. We shadowed a doctor in the same emergency department where we shadowed a charge nurse, and like that nurse, this hospital doctor moved quickly, rarely sitting, rarely stopping.[17] Even when he talked to another staff member, they just kept walking. But this ED doctor's daily routine was in some sense far narrower than that of the nurse. He had a more limited number of tasks—getting medical histories, using the material filled out for him by other personnel (like nurses), making medical decisions, and signing off on those decisions (which only doctors can legally do). This doctor's network on the floor was smaller: he got information from a nurse and talked briefly to his daughter and wife (whom he told to handle the home situation), but the rest of his time he was interacting with patients or other doctors. And perhaps most importantly, his movements (like his departure) were under his own control rather than controlled by others around him, and in fact he shaped the pace and activities of those others. Our shadowing notes ended about 8:00 PM, when the doctor said good-bye, telling us he had to leave. The notes report: "He had told me this was going to be his last night on the ED for three weeks. As he leaves, I say, 'So are you going on vacation?' He said, 'No, I've just rearranged my schedule to do some research and then Passover's coming.'" As this quote implies, this doctor had chosen to rearrange his schedule, and he had chosen to go home for the holiday. Even if rearranging his schedule had required some coordination, at least with other doctors, his remark indicates his use and level of control.

The second kind of doctor working in hospitals these days, the hospitalist, works in a specialty that has proliferated rapidly over the last couple of decades—from no more than 1,000 in 1995 to approximately 30,000 in 2011.[18] They have taken over hospital care from private physicians, and the growth in their numbers has dramatic consequences for the hours and schedules of other doctors in the medical system. Hospitalists move from one patient on one floor to another patient on another floor, often three or four flights away, carrying a list of patients and room numbers on stapled pages that are ragged by the end of the day.[19] They go to each patient's room, often for only a minute or two. After seeing a patient, the hospitalist spends several minutes documenting on the chart what he or she has seen. Moving between patients, sometimes hospitalists run up the stairs because they find the elevators too slow. Following one hospitalist, we observed a number of occasions when he would arrive at a patient's room only to discover that the patient had been taken away for a test. One time, after taking a phone call from a specialist, he hung up and said:

> Hospitalists always use the phrase "it's a slippery slope" to describe their relationship with specialists, like cardiologists. They say when they sign up that they will give you a specific number of patients. We always ask them how many patients. But then it grows and grows. We can't do that. It is too much for us to keep up with given the number of hospitalists we have. Primary care can limit patients; we have more trouble.

Perhaps this remark speaks to the declining autonomy of physicians as they increasingly seek and gain employment from large institutions, such as hospitals. But it also speaks to the ways in which doctors form a web of time—shaping one another's practices as they go about their days. Regardless of where they work, however, doctors have intense days, filled with constant activity, an unpredictable number of patients, a limited range of personnel with whom they interact, and little sociable downtime. They work hard. Nevertheless, even if their control is waning, they have more control of their own days than do those in the other three occupations.

THE SETTING: ORGANIZATIONAL CONTEXT

Occupations exist and interact within organizations. In this section, we focus on the eight organizations we observed: two hospitals, two nursing homes, two doctors' offices, and two EMT centers. These organizations vary across four basic dimensions: who works there, what kind of work they do, who has control, and the character of the organizational control strategy.

First, there is wide variation in the range of the direct-care employees who work and interact in each of these organizations. Fire stations and emergency medical services employ only one of our groups, the EMTs.[20] Nursing homes mostly employ nursing assistants, but a significant number of nurses and an occasional doctor are also on staff. Doctors' offices employ not only doctors but some nurses and nursing assistants. Hospitals employ the largest range of direct-care occupations, including their own staff nurses and smaller but significant numbers of nursing assistants and doctors; even EMTs do some of their work on hospital floors. Hospitals provide a particularly useful lens through which to see how the four occupations—doctors and nurses, nursing assistants and even EMTs—form a deeply intertwined web of time and shape each other's schedules as they go about the business of their day. The workers in these occupations—connected but also divided by relations of class and gender—sometimes support and coordinate with one another, but sometimes engage in struggles with each other.

Second, organizations shape tasks and routines. A nurse in a hospital has different tasks from the tasks of a nurse in a nursing home, and a different set of relations. Even within the hospital, there is a significant difference between the emergency department and the medical floor.

Third, the character of the hierarchy differs from one organization to the next, although some elements are common across settings. Doctors have the most autonomy and control wherever we look, while nursing assistants have the least. Nurses have power over nursing assistants in both hospitals and nursing homes and occasionally exert power over EMTs. Analysis of inter- and intra-organizational relationships makes clear that what varies is not simply the content and unpredictability of the day but the control over that content.

Fourth, even within the same type of organization, even dealing with the same occupation, organizations adopt different control strategies.

Hospitals

To protect the confidentiality of the research sites, we do not provide exact numbers, but one of our two hospitals, which we call Outercity, is more than four times as large as the other, which we call Countryside. Outercity is a level I trauma center and a teaching hospital with well over 500 staffed beds, 200 medical residents, and over 750 nurses; in total, it employs more than 5,000 people and is one of the largest hospitals in its state. Its expenses are around $750 million annually, with about $290 million of that spent on payroll. Outercity logs more than 175,000 patient-days per year and almost 800,000 outpatient visits per year.[21]

Our other hospital, Countryside, is a community hospital with about 150 beds, about 200 nurses, and slightly over 1,000 total personnel. These figures make it an average-size hospital for the state, where many are smaller, but Countryside is dwarfed by Outercity. Countryside's expenses are around $140 million per year, with almost $70 million of that going to payroll. It logs somewhat under 30,000 patient-days per year and has slightly over 200,000 outpatient visits per year.

Outercity is nonunion, thriving, expanding, and taking over other area hospitals. Countryside is struggling financially and laid off staff in 2010, for the third year in a row; this action was very publicly opposed by its unionized nurses, who took out an ad in the local paper denouncing the decision. After our observations ended, the hospital agreed to merge with another hospital—much to the chagrin of many staff.

Of course, each hospital has many floors providing different kinds of services; in each hospital we observed both in an emergency department (ED) and on a medical floor.[22] We chose these two floors because they provide stark contrasts: the ED is more fluid, unpredictable, and even chaotic, while the medical floor is more predictable and controlled. Personnel in emergency rooms have the least control over the flow of patients and tasks; in contrast, those on medical floors have more control over these flows.

In the web of time, the EDs of both hospitals served as a gateway for patients—to hospital rooms, physicians' practices, other hospitals, nursing homes, or the patients' homes.[23] The two EDs were quite different in other respects, however, even though the medical floors of these two hospitals looked fairly similar. One physician's description of the Outercity ED as "controlled chaos" was accurate. The waiting rooms and the ERs they served were all windowless, with glaring fluorescent lights. A doctor explained that the rooms were windowless "because people work at night and don't want to know what time it is." The main waiting room was loud: adults and adolescents talking, children running around, babies crying, loudspeaker announcements, TVs on. (Note that the widely recognized term "waiting room" underscores the web of time, in both hospitals and doctors' offices: those seeking assistance and in need of services assume that they must wait on those with expertise and authority, who will not themselves waste time—and money—by waiting.)

At Outercity, entry to the ED itself was controlled by security guards. This entry often had a few psychiatric patients, sometimes tied down, sometimes screaming. Then came a long hallway that was frequently packed with people, some of them on stretchers, being attended to by staff. It was hard to move around the hallway and the emergency room, and it was hard to hear. Some patients were not waiting for rooms but for funeral arrangements. One morning around 10:30 AM a nurse pointed to a dead person and told us that he had died at 6:30 AM. He was still surrounded by hugging and crying relatives as the nurse dealt with the funeral home.

After being assigned to a space, the living patients—some moaning, some bleeding, some sleeping, some with family, some alone—still waited in the hallways for a "room," which was really just an area cordoned off from the adjacent "room" with curtains. Then they waited in the room for a nurse or a nursing assistant, and then they waited for a doctor. An elderly patient who was worried that he had suffered a heart attack asked a nurse, "When am I going to get a bed?" She replied: "It's going to be a long time—there aren't any beds in the hospital. People have been waiting since yesterday; maybe tomorrow you'll get a bed."

Inside the main ED, different types of staff mingled, waited, and moved about, forming a web of time and a chain of command. Personnel with the most status and power usually waited for the shortest amount of time, while those with little status or power often waited for longer periods of time. EMTs often came to the waiting room with patients or waited at the triage desk, where we heard one, after waiting patiently for the triage nurse, mutter, "She just wouldn't talk to me." He later explained: "I just needed five seconds of her time." Nurses moved quickly from patient to patient, often calling for assistance, whether from male orderlies, who did the heavy lifting, or female nursing assistants, who turned patients, put in catheters, or took patients to the bathroom. Translators were often called in over loudspeakers, and occasionally calls went out for patient advocates or ministers.

EMTs, nursing assistants, nurses, and patients all waited for the doctors. About twenty-five doctors (some of whom were residents) worked for this urban ED; they tended to gather at one corner, reviewing patient data on a computer reserved for them and sometimes eating (because they often didn't think they had time to take a break for a meal). Sometimes they went to the separate trauma room, where they made immediate decisions, occasionally to stitch or perform a procedure. But in most cases, after reading the chart, the doctor went to see the patient in an ED "room" and decided to send the patient home, to a hospital room they knew would (eventually) open up, to the ED transition room (the separate eight-bed waiting room for ED patients who were admitted to the hospital but for whom floor beds were not yet available), or to another hospital. (Faxes would come in from other area hospitals saying, "We have bed availability.")

The Outercity waiting room got more and more crowded as the day passed. As one nurse depicted this waiting room, "It's usually slow till about 2:00, and then all hell breaks loose. The whole world changes, it gets crazy, it turns into a circus."[24] In our field notes we noted that, on what a nurse described as a quiet day, she "did not stop moving." Another nurse said of the ED transition room that it was even more hectic than the main ER, commenting, "Imagine you sat down to work [in an office job] and the phone kept ringing and you kept trying to do some work and someone calls every five minutes."

There is little social talk among hospital personnel. They do not have time. But there is work talk at the end of the day: each shift ends with incoming and outgoing nurses, and then separately incoming and outgoing doctors, who gather at the whiteboard to exchange information about each patient still on the board. From our field notes: "Observing in the hospital provides a very different meaning to what a shift is. When you see the frenetic character of an emergency room, you understand all the more how 12 hours is an extraordinarily intense, long period of time to work."

In contrast, at Countryside, the smaller hospital, life in the ED felt less chaotic. And while there were clearly power differences among the staff— doctors exerted control over nurses and nurses supervised nursing assistants—the differences seemed less dramatic than at Outercity. While hardly a relaxing unit most of the time, Countryside was less stressful than Outercity.

Cots rarely filled the hallway. On a day when they did, our notes said: "Though a very busy day for Countryside, this would seem like a quiet day at Outercity." That day a nurse said, with a great deal of concern, "Did you hear what is going on? There are no beds in the hospital. This is so bad." What seemed routine at Outercity seemed like a crisis at Countryside.

At Countryside, as at Outercity, staff would wait for one of the ER doctors to appear and make a decision about each patient; sometimes both nurse and patient got impatient, saying it felt like a long wait. At one point, a doctor, standing in front of the whiteboard, asked the secretary where a patient was; the secretary looked up at the whiteboard to find this information and told him. A nurse manager walking by commented: "Want to hear our little secret? The doctors are like little children. They can't find a thing. Never can. Nurses aren't like that." This was not an unusual exchange. "Doctors and nurses exchange barbs nearly every day," Robert Zussman notes, "blunting them only slightly with a frequently bantering tone."[25] This particular comment from the nurse manager suggests, first, that nurses have more knowledge about the routines of the ED than doctors do, but second, that doctors have more power and status, which nurses may occasionally resist but which they also acknowledge and even protect. What the nurse did not say, but we saw, was that asking others for such information rather than getting it oneself was another indication of status and control in this little community. The doctors did not have to go looking for information; their time, seen by them and also by other staff as too valuable, was carefully protected.

Despite these differences between their emergency departments, the medical floors at the two hospitals were more similar, although they obviously differed in size. Both were less hectic than the ED, even if both had lots of clocks around because, as one of the nurses said, "in the hospital, time is everything."

On both the Outercity and Countryside medical floors, there were approximately three times as many nurses as nursing assistants.[26] At both hospitals, nurses and nursing assistants sometimes argued about who should do what—especially when bells rang or lights outside the rooms started blinking, which commonly meant that a patient was calling for help with toileting. But on both medical floors, the CNAs and nurses did not spend much time interacting with doctors. Instead, doctors at both hospitals came in occasionally and moved quickly through the halls, sometimes talking to other doctors (and much less often to nurses or nursing assistants) or sitting at computers, usually alone. The night shift on both medical floors, with many patients asleep and all visitors, case managers, occupational therapists, doctors, nutritionists, and administrators gone, was much more relaxed, informal, and friendly, and less hectic than the other shifts.

There were rarely stretchers lining the hallways of either of these two medical floors. On both floors, the staff, nurses as well as nursing assistants, had some time to hang around—again, especially on the night shift, but also on the other shifts. On all shifts, medical floor staff moved more slowly than the ED staff. Nursing assistants as well as nurses sometimes briefly stopped and chatted or shared a laugh with each other—about their kids, vacation plans, a coworker, their health, or a course they were taking. Some sat and shared baked goods one of them had brought in. Most took their allotted fifteen-minute breaks. Occasionally a staff member would take a nap in the break room (especially on the night shift).[27] Fairly often, a nurse or nursing assistant would make a personal call—mostly to kids, sometimes to other family or friends.

We should not overstate. It was still hectic compared to EMT work sites. But the actions (or inactions) of staff on a hospital medical floor were striking not only because they were different from EMT sites but because they were different from the hospital EDs.

Clearly, then, the pace of work and the relations among staff depend in part on what kind of hospital they work in, and on what floor. But different hospitals do not seem as different as hospitals and nursing homes, in part because of who works in each. In hospitals there are more nurses, while in nursing homes there are more nursing assistants. Although hospitals pay more and might have more routine schedules, a number of nursing assistants (and even some nurses) prefer the work activities in nursing homes because they get to know the residents and even become close to some of them.

Nursing Homes

The basic work tasks were similar at the two nursing homes, but there were also significant differences between them in management style and approaches to workers, especially nursing assistants. One was a high-end, stand-alone, nonprofit, two-hundred-bed facility that we call Berkman. A substantial fraction of Berkman residents had private rooms, and their families were encouraged to visit and participate in their care. The facility was arguably the most highly respected in the region. The nursing home residents (who were called "residents," not "patients") were overwhelmingly white (95 percent) and predominantly affluent. Some, especially in the Alzheimer's units, were able to do most tasks for themselves; others needed to have almost everything done for them. Some residents, especially on the non-Alzheimer's floors, were friendly and socially engaging; other residents, especially in the Alzheimer's units, could be abusive and were capable of unpredictable actions that caused problems (at all hours of the day and night). Nationally, all nursing assistants working in nursing homes are at significant risk of injury: in a typical year, 17.3 percent receive back injuries, and another 15.6 percent suffer other strains or pulled muscles. But it is in Alzheimer's units that workers are most likely to be bitten (11.4 percent), to receive black eyes or other bruising (16.1 percent), or to be scratched or cut (44.4 percent).[28]

Berkman operated at 95 percent bed occupancy; the number of residents, and thus the number of staff needed, was highly stable. The low-wage direct-care workers were overwhelmingly women, primarily women of color (12.5 percent were white), while almost all the nurses were white (only 9 percent were black or Latina).

Most full-time employees worked their regular hours on one unit and to the extent possible were routinely assigned to the same residents. (For long-time employees this assignment was a given; for newer employees it was not inevitable.) Staff turnover was low by the standards of low-wage work. Staff and residents got to know each other well, and bonds of real affection developed. Although Berkman was a top-end facility, pay was comparatively low, even by the standards of other nursing assistant positions, which are always low-paid. The management at Berkman believed that because it provided some of the most appealing nursing home jobs to be found in its geographic vicinity, workers would accept lower wages. Starting pay was only $9.37 an hour, and went up slowly. As one longtime nursing assistant said to us, "I'm there going on eighteen years, and I'm making $12.33. If I'm there for the next ten years, I will never get to $15. Never."[29]

The other nursing home was smaller. Lucas Estates, a 120-bed rehabilitation and skilled nursing facility, was part of a larger group that included a couple of hospitals and more than a dozen nursing homes. Lucas was a clean, quiet, and pleasant facility, set outside of town. It was not nearly so upscale as Berkman; most of the patients (and they were called that, not "residents") shared rooms and were from more modest backgrounds. As at Berkman, essentially all the patients at Lucas were white. A key difference between Berkman and Lucas was that about 80 percent of Lucas nursing assistants were white, as were almost all Lucas nurses.

The difference in the racial composition of the nursing assistant workforce corresponded to a striking difference in management approach. The Berkman approach was punitive. The underlying philosophy, more or less openly articulated by the director of nursing, was that nursing assistants would do pretty much anything they could get away with. Nursing assistants, management believed, *could* do well if they truly wanted to, but were constantly struggling to find ways to cut corners and work the system to their advantage. The way to control such employees was through the imposition and enforcement of rules. A properly designed rule, with a carefully measured sanction that progressively increased with subsequent violations, would lead nursing assistants to do the right thing. Management occasionally tried to appeal to the better nature and professionalism of its workers, but such appeals were fairly minimal and unconvincing. Even for rewards, the emphasis was on giveaways of various coupons (for reduced-price movie tickets, for example); workers expressed contempt for some of these measures despite their economic need. The workers responded to many of these rules with anger, frustration, and a sense that nothing could change management's minds; they felt that managers did whatever they wanted and that, although nursing assistants could be angry and grumble, logic and appeals would not work with management. Berkman workers protected each other against management, but there were also some significant tensions among them: some workers bullied others, and there were racial tensions, with some Latina workers feeling that West Indians acted dominant, got away with murder, and exercised unjust power over other workers.

The Lucas approach was strikingly different. When arranging to do fieldwork at the site, we met with the administrator. She spent most of the meeting lecturing us on the hard lives that Lucas's nursing assistants led—earning low pay and having to meet the many demands put on them—and stressed that she did not want them harmed in any way by the fieldwork and wanted to be sure that we showed proper sympathy for them. Although Lucas had a milder form of the same attendance policy in place at Berkman, Lucas tried hard not to invoke it, and the sanctions policy was supplemented by a practice of awarding certificates to employees with perfect attendance and to the employee of the month and posting full-sized copies of those certificates in the break room. (We observed other employees looking over the certificates.) If a Lucas worker had an attendance problem, the administrator wanted to talk to her and find a way to work with her to solve it. At Berkman, administrators rarely performed any resident-care task, and if a resident asked to be toileted, the nurse would ask a nursing assistant to do so, sometimes ignoring the resident's request until an aide could be found. At Lucas, nurses and supervisors helped with serving meals, and just about every day the overall administrator of the nursing home made time to help serve residents lunch and would also toilet a resident if the need arose.

At Lucas, nursing assistants and nurses didn't necessarily love management, but comparatively speaking, they harbored little anger against managers and had a high level of respect for them. Lucas workers didn't all love each other, but there was a more effective culture of workers talking to each other—not about how to resist management, but about the need to pull their fair share of the load or to improve the way they carried out tasks. Lucas workers also seemed to cooperate better in doing each other's tasks and helping each other out.

To be sure, CNAs were at the bottom of the hierarchy and were paid less than half of what the nurses earned at both nursing homes (a structure of inequality that characterizes nursing homes all over the United States). But this comparison also illustrates the ways in which local organizational differences—here correlated with racial variation—are key to the allocation and experience of inequality.

Doctors' Offices

Today about half of practicing doctors work in hospitals, while the others work in office-based practices of varying sizes.[30] In addition to observing doctors on the medical floors and in the emergency rooms of the two hospitals, we also observed doctors in two private practice settings: one a very small primary care physician office, called CFP, and the other a group surgical practice called OHS.

Although doctors' offices are calmer and less bureaucratic than hospitals, they are hardly quiet and relaxed places. In the small private practice, CFP, there were two doctors, a nurse-practitioner, and about seven other staff members, all but one of whom were women, including an RN, a couple of nursing assistants, an accountant, a couple of receptionists, and a scheduler. Almost all were white. Although we do not have data on what the other staff earned, the (woman) doctor who was the head of the practice earned about $160,000 per year.

With classical music quietly playing in the background (to cover up any noise coming from patient rooms), CFP had a friendly atmosphere—staff chatted and laughed between patients and after hours, offered sympathy in response to stories about their children, gave one another little massages, or took a couple of minutes to play with the office dog (the head doctor's dog).

But the doctors were in control, and the staff worked hard to smooth the way for them. At one point, one of the doctors could not figure out where a particular patient was located and went back to the front office saying, with clear frustration, "Where is Jimmy? Can someone help me find a patient?" A receptionist pointed out the patient, and the doctor said, still a little irritated, "I am taking the patient to the blue room." A nursing assistant rushed out of a patient room and said, "I have already put someone in the blue room," and quickly made adjustments so that the doctor lost no more time. The receptionist shook her head, muttering, "Such a busy place."

The office closed for an hour every day for lunch. About once a week, lunch was provided by a drug company rep, who would try to launch into a standard spiel. But the doctor would interrupt: "I hate being asked questions, and I don't have time. Just tell me what you want to tell me. I have three minutes to eat." With little choice, the reps would say okay and then quickly present the favorable data about a drug they were selling. After a brief period, the doctor would end the discussion saying: "I gotta run. Give me the sample. Want my signature, okay." She would sign for the food, put on her coat, and leave to go see patients at another site. Total time this doctor typically took for lunch: less than ten minutes. Most other staff took the full hour, some sitting at lunch chatting, others going for a brief walk.

Like the other organizations where doctors work, CFP was usually a busy place controlled by doctors. But at this office, the doctor was neither a distant and resented presence nor a "child" to be mocked. To the contrary, the staff in this office often expressed considerable attachment to the head doctor.

The second doctors' office, OHS, was a surgical office with seven doctors and offices in three nearby cities; typically there were two or three doctors seeing patients at the main office, supported by a considerable office staff, a couple of medical assistants, a physician's assistant, and a couple of tech people. Core doctors in the practice were board-certified fellows of the American College of Surgeons; they had high incomes, about three times that of the primary care physician we observed. All of the doctors were white; six of the seven were men, and the only woman doctor had chosen to work part-time.

Patients were scheduled for fifteen-minute slots, but the office double- and triple-booked each slot (indicating the priority of the doctor's time not only over his or her staff but over the patients). The doctors chose to do it this way, they said, both because a significant number of patients canceled (in advance, at the last minute, or as no-shows) and because the doctors wanted to be constantly busy. Even in what should have been the most controlled and well-staffed of environments, unpredictability was pervasive.

The tech people had their own appointments with patients, but their appointments were secondary to what the doctors wanted. The techs were constantly adapting. For different reasons, the same was true of doctors: when a doctor in the office asked us to explain the study (which we usually explained in terms of work hours and schedules), his immediate, somewhat aggressive, response was to say, in a frustrated voice, "Oh, you mean how I had to cancel my entire morning because I couldn't get here from surgery? I was supposed to be in at 10:00 and couldn't get in until after 11:30. That's an example for you." In the web of time, doctors assume that they will be in control and that others will shape their routines to keep the doctors working and supported. Doctors get frustrated when time is beyond their control, whether because a surgery takes longer than scheduled or because other workers fail to anticipate the doctor's needs so as to enable him to use his time efficiently.

Doctors become frustrated on days when there are many patient no-shows, or when patients forget to bring films and have to go get them and come back, or, above all, when medical assistants do not have patients waiting in the exam rooms when the doctors are ready to see them. One afternoon when only one medical assistant was on duty to get patients to rooms, within five minutes two doctors expressed unhappiness, one saying, "I need a patient in a room please," and the other, "Let's keep the rooms filled, huh?" This is a frequent source of tension between doctors and support staff, and although doctors often use humor ("Okay, let's get our next contestant"), the edge is clear to everyone. Doctors cannot work until the patients are seated in the rooms, and doctors assume that someone else will take care of that.

Although doctors are dependent on support staff, at OHS there was no question who was in control: the doctors, especially the doctor who explained how he managed his schedule by saying, "I own the place. Everyone here works for me. Everyone." When this doctor came looking for a medical assistant, he joked that as part of the ongoing technology upgrade he was going to add the technology to put an electric collar on her; she was not amused.

The lead doctor explained: "We eat on the run. We do everything on the run. Once we're here, we're working." Although it was true that the doctors' pace—and his especially—was notably faster than that of the other staff in the office, he also set priorities: family came first, he reported, but time for exercise was also sacrosanct. Similarly, one morning he announced, "Today I am leaving at four o'clock. So if anything comes in from one o'clock on, it waits until tomorrow." When a key member of the office staff began to raise a concern, the doctor followed up with: "Well, that's how it's going to have to be."

Emergency Medical Systems: Fire Departments and Ambulance Services

We observed EMTs in two sites as well: a fire department and a private ambulance service. The fire department in the town of Longford (population somewhat over 20,000) had a chief, five captains (one for each of the four crews, plus a fire prevention safety officer), and about twenty-five privates, roughly six per crew, with an annual budget somewhat under $2 million. All firefighters had to have at least EMT-basic training, and all new firefighters hired in Longford had to be paramedics; at the time of our study, about half of the crew members were paramedics. (The captains, who had been there longer, were all basic-level EMTs.)

Fire departments nationally have been moving to take over EMT service, in part to maintain employment as the number of fires, and fire fatalities, has been cut in half in the past generation.[31] For the Longford Fire Department, ambulance calls were twice as common as fire calls (and even rarer were legitimate fire calls, that is, for serious fires). There were about five ambulance calls per day, with considerable variation: in the low week there were only sixteen ambulance calls, and in the high week there were forty-nine. Because fire calls were half as common as ambulance calls, paramedic firefighters worked harder than other firefighters.

The building was designed for significant downtime. Upstairs were living quarters (beds and toilets) and offices, a conference room, a kitchen (with stove, microwave, refrigerator, coffee maker, dishes and silverware, cabinets where some firefighters kept personal food, and a long table for meals), and a room with recliners, TV, DVD/VCR, and exercise equipment. They used these often.

Our second EMT observation site, Medic-Route, was a private company that provided a range of EMT services; one important service was acting as an intercept service for the fire department of a local town that had only basic-level EMTs. (With intercept service, when a 911 call requires a paramedic—for example, a suspected heart attack, or trouble breathing—the fire department responds, but paramedics from a private company, like Medic-Route, respond as well.) Medic-Route also provided backup for a private ambulance company, EHS, that was the primary provider for two low-income cities in the vicinity, covering their calls if all EHS ambulances were occupied.

Basic-level EMTs do 90 percent transports (say, from a nursing home to a doctor's office and back), and medics do 90 percent 911 calls. Medic-

Route was a relatively small local company, owned by a former para-medic; workers preferred it to EHS, a large national chain that they often referred to as "the Evil Empire" and characterized as owned by "suits" who "don't know what it's like to be a medic."

EMTs' preference for Medic-Route did not, however, mean that the work conditions were good—they were not. Medic-Route, housed in a run-down former factory, had lockers, some mismatched couches and chairs, a TV (from about the 1960s, but no cable or satellite service), rest-rooms, a microwave, fridge, soda machine, and table, and some old gym equipment. In the summer, the air conditioning worked only some of the time. There were stains on the ceiling and a bucket to catch leaks. But un-like firefighters, Medic-Route workers could leave the building to run er-rands, as long as they were constantly available to take calls. As one ex-plained: "We have a lot of downtime because one of the hallmarks of EMS is that you do calls when there are calls, but when there are no calls, there's nothing to do. We are free to travel in the cities that we're in, so if we want to run errands, that's fine, they have no problems with that." A typical twenty-four-hour shift for this paramedic, he reported, involved perhaps eight calls, each taking roughly an hour for response; the mix of calls in-cluded one cardiac arrest, a few other legitimate medical calls, and a few calls that did not require paramedic response. The routine level of activity was very different from a nursing home job, let alone a hospital emer-gency department.

CONCLUSION

This chapter's discussion of occupations and organizations provides background to contextualize the book's analyses of hours and schedules. Before observing the routines of our four occupations, we might have imagined that long workdays are the most demanding. Not so. We might have expected those with the most control to be the most likely to take lunch breaks. Not so. Gertrude Stein might say that a nurse is a nurse is a nurse, but we saw that the daily routines of a nurse in a hospital emer-gency department are different from those of a nurse in a nursing home Alzheimer's unit, and that they differ as well in pay, skill set, and work pace (even if they are more similar to each other than to the nursing as-sistants at either of these sites). We even saw that two nursing homes can take approaches to their workforces that are different enough (one far more punitive than the other) to shape their hours and schedules.

Examining workers in different, but linked, occupations and organiza-tions helps us understand the processes that shape time on the job. Look-ing across occupations reveals both "temporal coordination" and "temporal struggle," and a chain of command shapes the hours and schedules of those linked. Nurses supervise CNAs, and even though some tasks have in recent years been transferred from nurses to CNAs as a way to reduce hospital costs, the law mandates that only nurses can perform certain tasks.[32] The most tense, conflicted, and emotional interoccupational relations were those between nurses and nursing assistants. The nurse manager who commented that nurses are "overseers" of nursing assistants (see chapter 2) was indicating that nurses have a right to expect nursing assistants to comply with their requests and to organize their time at work around the nurses' demands. While some nursing assistants were enthusiastic about particular nurses, others were far less sanguine about the division of labor and time. Aides told us that nurses "always say I don't have time. To me, and personally, I think you do have time, you just have to make the time." Others, expressing their anger at this division, agreed: "Nurses, they're lazy, they don't help," and, "Sometimes the nurses just sit there behind the nurses' station, eating ice cream or something, and 'Oh, the bells are goin' off!' Okay! Try answerin' one occasionally!" and, "Why do I have to, you know, finish what I'm doing and go down when they're sitting, chatting about cooking recipes? To me, I find that unfair. You know, you're the peon."

The web of time and chain of command extend to EMTs. Especially in emergency departments, as EMTs hand patients off to nurses and occasionally interact with nurses, both solidarity and tension come into play. Solidarity with other medical workers comes from the sense of shared goals and also shared schedules: "I notice, relationship-wise, people who are in nursing or EMS or police work I do better with, because they understand that type of schedule, versus someone who works on Monday through Friday 9–5. . . . People in this type of work environment tend to stick together." But there is also a fair amount of tension between EMTs and nurses. As one EMT suggested, sometimes the "nurses treat us like crap." A number reminded us of how the nurses made them wait—and not always in the most gracious of ways. The EMTs were surprisingly understanding about this, often seeing the problem as structural, not personal. In the Outercity emergency room, one EMT observed,

> those people are overwhelmed. There is not enough bed space, not enough nursing staff, so every single shift you go in there knowing I'm going to get the tar beat out of me tonight. I am going to have so many patients and not be able to give them care, and I'm already maxed to the limit, and here comes another ambulance. You want to scream. . . . So you [the EMTs] get static from the nurses, because they can't unload on their patients, [but] I can yell at you—what are you gonna do to me? You're just an ambulance driver!

In turn, nurses, as we saw in this chapter, are subject to the control of doctors. By legal mandate, doctors exert power over patient care and hence over nurses. Certain procedures are legally limited to doctors—whether signing off on medical treatments, making end-of-life-decisions, or sending patients home. In both private practice and hospitals, most nurses accept that in the web of time they wait for doctors. As Zussman writes:

> Nursing has achieved a measure, albeit limited, of collective self-direction. Yet it is hospital administrators, many of whom are physicians, very few of whom are nurses, who set the broad parameters of nursing, who determine what is nursing's proper place. . . . Moreover, it is individual physicians— who are officially part of an entirely different hierarchy from nurses—who order the bulk of the therapies and procedures. . . . In this sense, nursing is, at least organizationally, a subordinate occupation.[33]

We saw doctors on the floor berate nurses for making them wait. To be sure, doctors occasionally develop a sense of solidarity with nurses. An emergency room doctor told us:

> When I got into the emergency room, it was a unique group of people. It's the camaraderie down there with the nurses, there's no, you know, blasting orders—we're a team. Everybody's a team. . . . If we're yelling at a nurse, things aren't going to get done. We all work together, and that's what I love about it. It's different than a lot of the services. You go to the operating room, you see somebody screaming at the surgery tech or the nurse, it's just not the way we work.

A nurse supervisor concurred, saying that in her unit the doctors "work very collaboratively with nursing" and noting that, although a couple of doctors took the view, "Do this because I'm the doctor," in the emergency room "that's never going to fly, not in this arena." As both made clear, relations between doctors and nurses (like relations between nurses and nursing assistants, or between nurses and EMTs) vary across settings.

These variations point to both a strength of the study and a limitation. Much research on work hours (and on the sociology of work more generally) looks at workers disconnected from other workers and from the organizations that employ them. Our research compares and connects these occupations, but there are limits to the comparisons. To what extent do the differences we observe arise from the selection effects of who is hired to work (or chooses to work) in one unit rather than another, and to what extent are these differences a treatment effect, with the organizational setting itself exerting the influence? For example, maybe nursing homes lead nurses to behave differently than they do in hospitals; maybe the nurses who choose to work in nursing homes are different sorts of people. These issues become most noteworthy when we face a striking difference of one sort or another. The Berkman nursing home had much stricter policies than the Lucas Estates nursing home; Berkman's nursing assistants were 87 percent people of color, while Lucas's were only 20 percent people of color. What was the relationship between the control strategy and the racial composition of the workforce? Having observed only two nursing homes, we can do no more than speculate about this; we certainly cannot offer definitive proof.

We aimed for a representative sample of the members of each of our occupations, and the characteristics of both our survey (drawn from a random sample) and our interview respondents (some drawn from the survey, most from our observation sites) closely track national survey data on these occupations. For our organizations and observations, on the other hand, we employed a strategy of maximizing contrasts: we not only looked at people in a range of different settings but intentionally contrasted a large teaching hospital with a smaller community hospital; an upscale, stand-alone nursing home with a middle-of-the-pack chain nursing home; a primary care practice and a surgical physician practice; and a fire station and a for-profit private EMS service.

Chapter 4 | Setting the Official Schedule

WHEN THEY ARE HIRED, regular staff members are typically given an official basic schedule that specifies in advance a number of work hours and a shift—day, evening, and / or night; weekday or weekend—that both they and their employer come to expect. These official schedules are disrupted much of the time, but in this chapter we begin by examining the framework within which those disruptions occur. After introducing the official schedule, we argue that its development is shaped by four processes, all of which create inequalities.

First, across the four occupations, management sets staffing ratios that provide the frame within which official schedules take shape; this control often becomes invisible as the distribution of shifts and schedules seems to take on a life of its own.

Second, class matters. Eviatar Zerubavel highlighted the importance of egalitarian principles and fairness "as a fundamental rule of scheduling" *within* occupational groups.[1] We show, however, that principles of scheduling are also unequally distributed *across* groups. For the two professional occupations, employers make efforts (for doctors a lot, for nurses somewhat less) to adapt schedules to what employees want and to give them some degree of control over when they work. These two advantaged occupations have also developed structural staffing alternatives that provide personnel to fill the designated slots that regular staff resist or reject. These alternatives become components of a web of time and offer the advantaged some control over their schedules. For the two working-class occupations, employers generally impose a rigid official schedule and expect employees to conform to it. For these occupations, we see fewer alternative staffing systems to fill in schedule holes.

Third, gender matters. In large part gender inequality in official schedules is organized around family and becomes a key part of the web of time—in very different ways for women and men. To a significant extent occupations gendered male make paid work a priority (men in these occupations tend to believe breadwinning remains their primary family responsibility) and often are officially organized so that workers will structure the rest of their lives, including their families, around the job schedule. In contrast, occupations gendered female *sometimes* recognize that even official basic schedules may have to accommodate family work.

Fourth, class and gender *jointly* shape official basic schedules and the priority of work and family. In professions dominated by men, employees often use their control to expand their work time; in professions dominated by women, employees often use their control to convince employers to adapt even their official work schedules to their lives outside of work, especially their domestic responsibilities. That is, workers themselves use class advantage in the service of "doing gender."[2] In contrast, the two working-class occupations—especially female nursing assistants and to some extent EMTs—have little ability to shape or control their basic work schedule. For both EMTs and nursing assistants, being in a disadvantaged class position makes it more difficult to enact traditional or conventional gender models than it is for the professionals. All too often this intersection has been overlooked in studies of time, which sometimes document the separate effects of gender and class but rarely their joint operation.

FRAMING THE SCHEDULE: MANAGERIAL PREROGATIVE

Who and what shapes the basic official schedule, and how many staff members are needed to fill it? Especially for health care organizations, the overriding scheduling challenge is developing a plan to provide continuous coverage twenty-four hours a day, seven days a week, 365 days a year.

We might expect that the number of staff members needed to provide safe, around-the-clock care would be set by empirical research and guided by legal mandate—just as it is for, say, some day care providers or flight attendants. By and large, however, this is not the case in health care. Instead, management personnel decide what staff ratios they think are necessary and then shape their basic official schedules around these organizational decisions. Their constructions of staff ratios do not derive from any set of best practices based in research or from legal regulations that set staffing ratios, except insofar as there is a legally enforced "duty of care." De facto staffing patterns result instead from managerial prerogative based largely on what managers assert are budget constraints (especially federal and insurance company reimbursement rates), the staffing necessary to meet what they see as safety and quality concerns, and the norms they develop in conversation with other managers in their organization and at other institutions. Both employers and employees in hospitals and nursing homes typically then take these staffing patterns as given and talk about the need to fill holes in the established schedule frame.

Though it was sometimes difficult to get managers to specify (even perhaps to themselves) the factors that shaped their staffing and scheduling decisions, we uncovered indicators of this control in all four occupations. For nurses, there was struggle over control of the staffing ratios. As Suzanne Gordon and her colleagues point out in their book *Safety in Numbers*, California is the only state "with legally mandated nurse-to-patient staffing ratios on all the units in their hospitals."[3] When the Massachusetts Nurses Association promoted a staffing ratio bill, the Massachusetts Hospital Association (MHA) called it "a prescription for disaster," and the *Boston Globe* opined that "staffing decisions are best left to the administrators [of hospitals], not state government."[4] We attended legislative hearings in Massachusetts that addressed the Patient Safety Act—a proposed act designed to address such staff ratios. Both sides—employees and employers—used the mantra of patient safety at these hearings to promote their interests. On one side, a coalition of Massachusetts nurses came out in favor of the act, stressing the problems of inadequate staffing for both patients and staff (and their families); they brought in nurses from California to explain why favorable legally mandated ratios saved lives. On the other side, the hospitals came out in full force against legally mandating staffing ratios. With its representatives sitting in the audience wearing lab coats with stickers on them saying No STAFFING RATIOS, the MHA said that "staffing decisions should always be based on the best interest of the patient, not a number," and argued that "no two patients, nurses, or hospitals are alike. They can't—and shouldn't—be treated as such."[5] The MHA reps insisted on the importance of local knowledge, that is, their own knowledge. Nurse staffing decisions were therefore best left unregulated, they argued, and should be decided by managers and executives, who know their own hospitals. In some sense, the MHA won: the act has been languishing in a state senate committee for a number of years.

By and large, nurse staffing remains unregulated, and so staffing decisions lie primarily with employers, who often tweak official schedules in response to shifting budgetary concerns (based in part on the competitive rates for wages and salaries), fluctuations in the patient census and acuity, and staff members' skill levels and scheduling demands (which employers cannot ignore primarily because of the market power of nurses). Describing her "historically based" staffing budget, one manager of several hospital floors said that unexpected staffing changes (people getting sick, others just leaving) made it necessary to constantly rework their staffing formulas. "In challenging times," she said,

staff have to work short . . . above the budget. So it ends up being a real challenge financially as well as for morale. If you approached any nurse right now, they'd say staff is short, they're working short, and they're right. And we patch them as best we can and try to fix the holes as best we can, but it's now beginning to impact patient satisfaction. . . . You then have to pull somebody from another floor. It's seeing the big picture and seeing what the house looks like. . . . This institution, just like the American Nurses Association, has a statement about mandatory overtime—that you don't want to see it abused, but you never want to remove it.

When probed, many managers insisted that their staffing formulas were close to intuitive or based on a kind of savvy they had come by as managers—the ones with an overview of the system and knowledge of the needs of the organization, its different floors, the patients, and the varied staff. One longtime administrator explained how she determined staffing ratios and schedules on her unit:

If—if you have a hundred patients, and you have one nurse, business smarts would say, well, who's going to—at what number is the patient going to start to leave? At what number is the patient unsafe? At what number does the staff person say, "This is ridiculous. I'm leaving here." So we look at all of those things, you know? And I'm very fortunate. I have a director that allows me to think this way. I am not business-smart. I'm not an MBA, you know, number cruncher. I just know from experience, and yes, from my knowledge, of what really works.

A comparison of our two hospitals further illustrates the use of managerial prerogative. As we saw in chapter 3, it became the expected routine in one emergency room for patients to wait around for a room for hours and hours; in the other, any such waiting was viewed by management as a crisis that required extra efforts to get additional nurses to come in. The difference in these two responses to the same scenario underscores the power of local management to decide on the "necessary" staff ratio and schedule.[6]

For the other professional group, physicians, there are even fewer regulations concerning adequate staffing ratios. Numerous journal articles and physician websites debate the question of adequate staffing. One article that discusses physician staffing in hospitals says that "'the sweet spot' of patient census remains elusive."[7] When we asked doctors in private practices and hospitals how they decided on the number of staff members they needed and how they determined their official basic schedules, they hemmed and hawed and talked about "rules of thumb," "magic numbers," and "informal discussions" with doctors in their own practices and in other practices. These "magic numbers" take on a life of their own. To be sure, physicians told us that staffing is determined in part by external agencies—including insurance companies, whose reimbursement rates limit the amount of time that doctors can spend with patients. But as one private practice physician remarked:

> Doctors say it [scheduling] is the fault of the insurance company, but that is code for a whole realm of other causes. They think it is too complicated to explain, so they just say it's the "fault of insurance company." "Insurance company" is code for the fact that the docs want to maintain their salaries for themselves and their families but also for their department and their institutions who need to attract staff.

Whether they blame insurance companies or the state, these relatively autonomous professionals often feel pressure because their managers (who typically are also doctors) "decide" on some acceptable income level (of course a level far higher than that of any of our other occupational groups), which sets a standard of staffing, which in turn dictates their basic schedules, which, in a paradoxical twist, they then often come to feel are "crazy."

Similarly, there are few staffing ratio standards for EMTs. Some locales seek to regulate staffing ratios for EMTs, but these regulations tend to vary from city to city and as such they come and go. Some towns and cities have recently saved local money by eradicating these ordinances—granting, for example, to the fire commissioner the authority to decide how many firefighters will work on any given shift. To be sure, there are suggested institutional guidelines from the Occupational Safety and Health Administration (OSHA) and the National Fire Protection Association. But in many other states there is no legal mandate; in Massachusetts, for example, the Superior Court recently overturned an arbitration award that established minimum staffing levels for city fire departments.[8] For the most part, EMT staffing remains a management prerogative based on budget allocations and local wage scales, which in turn shape the rigid basic schedules offered to EMTs.

Finally, similarly rigid schedules are offered to CNAs. For the nursing homes where most nursing assistants work, the U.S. Department of Health and Human Services (HHS) estimates that the threshold for adequate staffing is 2.9 CNA-hours per resident day, but the average is actually 2.3

hours. Even where there are established state minimums, enforcement is weak; moreover, a number of states have modified or eliminated expected ratios.[9] As we saw in the previous chapter, CNAs often cannot finish all the tasks they are assigned, but management insists that they do just that. These managers short-staff and then, if difficulties arise, insist that the problem is the nursing assistants' failure to finish the assigned tasks rather than the inadequate staffing allocation of the official basic schedules. In fact, there are external constraints rooted in public policy funding streams that seem to act primarily to *reduce* staffing. Medicaid and Medicare approve only a limited number of staff for reimbursement. An owner of a small nursing home explained how she came up with the number of necessary staff and the official basic schedules of the nursing assistants she hired:

> So I have to base my schedules and my times and my shifts around the needs of my patients. Um, for me, the most important things, number one, was our budget and trying to stay within the budget restraints that the government gives us. 'Cause most of our, um, payments come from Medicare or Medicaid, so it's a fixed budget. Um, we can't charge more to make up the difference for a raise or something like that. We are a fixed-income entity.

Steven Lopez recounts a very similar process in the nursing home he studied: "Resource limitations imposed by Medicaid and Medicare reimbursement rates mean that even nonprofit facilities desiring to maximize staffing cannot afford to hire enough staff to live up to basic care standards."[10]

Across the occupations, management told us that they had very little wiggle room. As we saw, this meant that management hired the number of workers they decided they needed. Management set the official schedules, which they then insisted on for these workers. (To be more precise, they insisted on these ratios and schedules except when they decided to change or negotiate them.) Each of the four occupations confronted this managerial frame—some with more power and ability to negotiate than others.

CLASS AND GENDER VARIATION IN OFFICIAL SCHEDULES

Examining the official schedules of physicians and nurses, Eviatar Zerubavel brought into theoretical focus the social conditions, cognitions, and moral premises that shape those schedules.[11] He emphasized the coordination that such schedules required and the organizational continuity they promoted *within* each group: "The structural components of the so-ciotemporal order are collectivities. . . . The persons who are in charge of designing them, that is the regulators of the social temporal order, must deal with such issues as vacation requests, night duty arrangements, or holiday or weekend coverage on a group basis."[12] It is precisely these collective patterns and issues enacted by medical occupations that we focus on here. But we go further, stressing both the similarity *within* groups and the inequality *across* groups.

Physicians' Official Basic Schedules

In response to our survey question, "How many hours did you work last week?" doctors reported an average of forty-five hours a week, with an interquartile range of forty to fifty-eight hours.[13] This was probably an underestimate. When probed about their work hours in intensive inter-views, doctors' estimates went up as they remembered to include staying late or going home to answer work emails, "doing paperwork" (a part of their job they complained about bitterly), or reading journal articles at night—perhaps forgotten in answering surveys because these activities are not counted as reimbursable and billable patient care.[14] But physicians also stood out because they had more control over their schedules than any of the other occupations.

Like other professionals, doctors are "elite workers" who "appear to have gained control over when they work at the expense of how long they work."[15] Such control is typically exerted through a group process rather than as a set of atomized individual choices. One way in which physicians' schedules are set is through a group meeting, attended by physicians only, where they do not decide staffing ratios but do establish who will fill the holes they assume must be filled. These meetings usually focus on filling holes in the schedule caused by events such as vacations, holi-days, and staff turnover. As a hospital doctor explained, "We sit down once a month and finish the schedule for all the holes that there are." An-other doctor at the same hospital explained, "We actually sit at a table and we go through the month. Every shift has to be covered somehow. It's very give-and-take."

The cultural style is to make mildly formed requests, as one doctor ex-plained: "I'll say, 'Here's my week I would like to be off. If I can be off here, that would be nice.'. . . You can never say 100 percent because it has to be covered." Sometimes the pressure gets a little sharper; doctors working in groups face a kind of peer pressure that they sometimes experience as "the tyranny of teamwork."[16]

INTERVIEWER: And what determines who will and who won't?

RESPONDENT: Umm . . . arm-twisting.

INTERVIEWER: How do you arm-twist?

RESPONDENT: I say . . . well, like, for example, "Gee, you're not working one shift this week. Do you think you can possibly do this shift?" In front of everybody else. Peer pressure.

An example from our fieldwork illustrates the group scheduling process and the power (and limits) of peer pressure among these autonomous professionals. Before the start of one hospital scheduling meeting in an emergency department (a part of the hospital where we might expect to find the least flexibility), some doctors were talking among themselves. Asked if they were talking about the schedule, one replied, "We're always talking about the schedule." Walking into the meeting at 7:30 AM, the head of the department said: "Oh, you are here for the worst scheduling meeting of the year" (because it included Thanksgiving, Christmas, and New Year's). Throughout the meeting, stress was evident, but what made it evident were the pauses and the silence. No one raised a voice; no one even sounded particularly angry (and these were people who did sometimes sound angry when they were talking to nonphysician staff). No one was explicitly told what to do, and no one had—or assumed—the authority to tell others what to do. (Even though there were differences in rank among those present: one doctor was head of the ED, while some were partners and others were not.) Instead, they used peer pressure. Although there were occasional long silences, with people avoiding eye contact and staring at the schedules in front of them that "dictated" what holes had to be filled, it took little time for the doctors sitting around the table to volunteer for those openings. One doctor, arriving a few minutes late, commented that he had been thinking of not coming but decided that was too dangerous; others laughed. During the meeting, one young doctor kept jumping up from the table to call his wife—to report the pressure on him to come in on one holiday or another. After a while the other doctors started to look irritated and began to tease him. The ED director gently reminded this younger doctor that he and his wife wanted a new kitchen and, with a smile, indicated that it was the young doctor's obligation to provide the domestic trappings they desired. The young doctor agreed to work Christmas Day. Like him, most of these doctors were responsive to the pressure of their colleagues—though of course some were more responsive than others, whether because of personality or position in a status hierarchy.

Although group decision-making was the most common approach and prevailed in pretty much all of our small groups of physicians, in larger and more bureaucratic units one doctor would make up the schedule for the group as a whole but filled designated scheduling holes off of their requests. One physician contrasted his large hospital to a smaller one:

> In smaller places, like Edison, the way they do the schedules, the guys just sit around and say, "This is what I need off." So our schedule as a whole has been the total opposite. Rick's given us a year's schedule, saying, "Here's your schedule; change what you need." And in some ways that takes some pressure off Rick.

It is important to take the pressure off the physician who prepares the initial schedule because "whoever does your schedule . . . there's always going to be a glitch that somebody's going to think something's happened just to them for some spiteful reason, because people are very protective of their time off." Therefore, "whoever does your schedule, you have to make sure you have a lot of faith in them." On their staff, Rick was considered "the most fair person; he's the most honorable, trustworthy person on our staff."

After the person regarded as the fairest and most trustworthy makes up the initial schedule, everyone gets a chance to identify problems and work with others to make changes in their assignments. The ability to do so is crucial:

> What works for us is knowing that you have something that you can work with and you have some control over changing. I think if we got a schedule and we couldn't change it, that would be very hard. . . . I think there's really this feeling of empowerment that it's us and we're not waiting till the whim of the scheduler to design our fate.

Nurses' Official Basic Schedules

In response to our survey question, "How many hours did you work last week?" nurses reported an average of thirty-five hours, with an interquartile range of thirty-one to forty-two hours, almost ten hours less than physicians. And unlike the physicians, when questioned further, they did not bring up additional work hours. For nurses, there was little blurring of boundaries: when they left the workplace, their paid work day came to an end.

With the exception of two midwives we interviewed (working in different locations), no nurses engaged in the group processes that physicians used to determine their schedules. Nonetheless, nurses, like doctors, had a great variety of official schedules. In part because of their favorable market situation—nurses' unemployment rate is very low, ranging from 1 to 2 percent over the last ten years—hospitals offered nurses official basic schedules that encompassed a wide range of hours and shifts. They offered shifts of varying lengths—six, eight, ten, or, increasingly, twelve hours for three days a week. One scheduler reported that she had twelve different shifts. Another listed the options: "I have 7:00 to 3:00, 7:00 to 5:00, 9:00 to 9:00, 11:00 to 9:00, 11:00 to 11:00, 3:00 to 11:00, 5:00 to 3:00, 7P to 7A, 7A to 7P, 9P to 7A, and 11:00 to 7:00." As one scheduler noted, this "is a scheduling nightmare."

Employers felt that they had little choice but to offer nurses these options. A nurse scheduler simply said, "People would come and interview and say, 'This is what I need to work.' And we'd say, 'Okay. Yup.'" An emergency room nurse scheduler remarked, "If I had someone turn up tomorrow and say, 'I want to work 3:00 to 1:30, four days a week,' and I didn't have the position available, I could probably get it for them." A nurse administrator in one hospital explained the range of shifts they offered by citing market competition: she told us that nurses will say, "Why should I come to Outercity when I can go to Haven (another local hospital) and get the shift I want?" Another hospital nurse administrator explained that nurses "know how marketable they are. So they do come with some challenges." She continued:

> I don't want them to leave, and that would be one of the reasons why people would leave—the schedule no longer works for their life. That's the main reason why people sometimes leave. . . . (*And if they come and say to you, "I can't do this anymore," what do you say?*) Well, let's figure out what you *can* do, and we'll look at the master schedule and I'll change the master if I can, to better accommodate them.

Much of the nurses' control came through individual negotiation—although the power to negotiate was rooted in their group's advantaged market position.

Twelve-hour shifts are a hot issue in hospitals. Of the two hospitals we studied, one relied primarily on twelve-hour shifts, and the other primarily on eight-hour shifts (even if they routinely changed these to meet nurses' demands). At both hospitals, neither administrators nor nurses agreed among themselves about which was preferable. An administrator at the hospital with eight-hour shifts complained, "I know that I'm losing nurses out there in the real world because they want twelve hours. They want to work more hours in a day to be off more days." Similarly, nurses often wanted to schedule themselves to work multiple days in a row, which one administrator saw as unsafe: "People want that in their schedule. It doesn't matter if they're unsafe or sleeping or falling asleep at the job, because they want those days off together." In our first interview with one scheduler, she reported that although the hospital had considered twelve-hour shifts, as a unionized hospital the nurses and their unions would have had to agree to make the change, and the older nurses in this aging workforce did not want to work so long at one stretch. Not long thereafter, however, the hospital did introduce twelve-hour shifts as an additional option.

Twelve-hour shifts are one hot issue in hospitals; another is what used to be called self-scheduling. An administrator's two-sentence statement showed the limitations of the term: "We have self-scheduling here." Then she added, "I have the final review of the schedule before it's posted on the unit." Administrators have changed the language and now call it "participatory scheduling." Another elaborated: "In my previous life we said 'self-scheduling,' and they [the nurses] felt like what they put down was what they were going to get, so we had to change that. . . . By changing that terminology to say that 'you're participating in it' gave them a new mind-set."

Self-scheduling is related to the issue of when the schedule should be posted: should the schedule be made up and handed out in four- to six-week blocks or fixed for the duration of employment? Administrators often preferred fixed schedules because, from the managerial perspective, moving to a fixed schedule required less effort and saved them considerable time. Some nurses agreed, preferring the fixed schedule so they could make plans for a date months in the future. But many others did not. Some even saw a six-week block as too long because it could not allow for unexpected interruptions:

> A good thing and a bad thing is we do our time six weeks in advance. So it's good because you can plan your life. I can get my babysitters and things like that. Unfortunately, things come up in six weeks that you didn't know about—doctors' appointments, random things that you weren't expecting to come up. Then you're kind of scrambling to fill that or switch your schedule or whatever.

Given the unpredictability in their lives, nurses sometimes pushed managers to compromise. Acknowledging that nurses' strong position meant that they might leave, one manager believed that the fixed-schedule approach was "not a staff satisfier" and remarked: "So that's what [the administrator] has to weigh."

Organizations as well as occupation shape nurses' official basic schedules. Hospitals offer nurses a wide range of options, but nursing homes require nurses to abide by the same rigid options that govern CNAs. The difference was captured by the words of a nurse at the Berkman nursing home:

INTERVIEWER: How much choice do you think you have over the hours that you work?

RESPONDENT: None! (*laughs*)

INTERVIEWER: What sort of circumstances do you think would maybe allow you to modify your schedule in that way? Can you imagine any?

RESPONDENT: Yeah—hospitals! (*laughs*)

But note that far more nurses work in hospitals than nursing homes; the staff in nursing homes consists primarily of nursing assistants. Because nursing homes employ a smaller number of nurses, these employers have less leeway. But perhaps it is also *because* nurses, who are more advantaged, tend to work in hospitals that these organizations decide to offer more flexible schedules.

Personnel Systems to Address Unpredictability for Nurses: Temp Workers and Flex Teams   If a regularly scheduled worker decides not to come to work, hospitals and nursing homes sometimes replace them by using external temp (or "pool" or "registry") agencies; these act as "private contractors . . . to carry out work within any number of facilities."[17] Although the agencies might be willing to provide any kind of employee, in practice temp agencies were never used for EMTs, rarely used for doctors (though there were a few doctors who sometimes moonlighted for agencies), only occasionally used for CNAs, and most often used for nurses. In 2001, 56 percent of hospitals used temporary nurses, and nearly six percent of hospital staff nurses were supplemental temporary hires.[18] Temp workers and the organizations that hire them become an important part of the web of time primarily for nurses. Why this class and gender distribution? It is harder to maintain adequate staffing for the professionals who have more power to stay away. This creates a demand. And women seek out intermittent work that can be scheduled around family demands.[19] This creates a supply.

To be sure, employers tend to view these temp agencies as a strategy of last resort. One director of a pool agency said exactly what managers and schedulers also reported. Commenting that "nursing homes for the most part hate agencies," he continued:

There's no—I don't want to say this the wrong way since I'm in the business and all—but there's no positive benefit to using an agency over using your own nurse. You would rather be fully staffed at all times. Every nursing home and hospital's goal is to not use us. Our goal is do a good job for them when they have to. So we don't have to sell them on using an agency; they have to use an agency because they don't have the nurses.

He then suggested that organizations use temp agencies because of inadequate organizational staffing and routine unpredictability in the lives of employees:

> The reason you're going to call us is because either you don't employ enough nurses to cover that ratio that you need, or because you employ that number but somebody's sick, somebody's on maternity leave, somebody can't come in for whatever reason. Most of our nursing homes that use us, use us on a daily basis, which means they're understaffed.

For the workers they hire, the flexibility provided by these agencies provides both some schedule control and some schedule instability. If all goes well, a nurse working through a temp agency has an ideal arrangement: she earns higher pay per hour and can decide when to work, and under what conditions. As the owner of a temp agency said, "When you work for an agency you in essence have an agent who represents you. . . . It's sort of a nice thing for them to be self-employed without being self-employed."

Temp agencies sell that flexibility. The website of one such national agency, Nursefinders, places at the top of its website the phrase "Find Flexibility, Find a Job." Another national agency, Favorite Healthcare Staffing, begins its website description of "Hot Jobs" by proclaiming: "Flexibility—Variety—Rewards." As a third national agency, Interim Nursing, says to interested nurses: "We recognize that you have many employer choices in health care staffing. That's why we value the opportunity to work for you—placing you where and when you want to work. You have the flexibility of choosing the job that's best for you."

One temp agency owner agreed and explained what really draws nurses into the temp business: "The nurses who work for agencies work for agencies because they want that flexibility." Family is usually a crucial factor on both ends: a spouse's income and health insurance make it possible to choose when to work and not work, and temp workers told us that they were not willing to commit to a fixed schedule that penalized them if they took off for family demands. A nurse who knew that she would often need to miss work might conclude that she would not be able to keep a regular position, but could keep a per diem or agency position.

Much of the literature and discussion about temp workers focuses on the costs to these "contingent workers."[20] But we note as well the costs to regularly scheduled workers, who often resent the irregular workers, sometimes for good reason. As one explained:

> A lot of [regular staff] people complain about having to work with agency staff. Everybody on the regular staff knows that they're making more money. They don't really see why they deserve more money. They have to be shown all the policies and procedures, have to be introduced to every resident.

This nurse suggested that the control gained by these temp workers (who say, "I don't want someone telling me what to do") came at the expense of the regular staff, who were "demoralized by them":

> When they [pool employees] hear something they don't like, a lot of them say, "Well, I don't care. I don't feel like doing that. It's not my responsibility. I'm just here to make all the money and get out of here. And I'll just go some-place else. The reason is I'm doing this because I don't want someone telling me what to do." That kind of thing. And so it's demoralizing.

For their part, temp workers stress that the system does not work quite the way the owner of the temp agency might suggest. Temp agency nurses' shifts are often canceled, sometimes just hours before they are scheduled to start work ("It happens every day"). It happens most often on holidays, especially because some organizations do what they call in the business "ghost booking"—that is, booking temp workers just in case one of their regular staff call out. As one pool nurse told us:

> You never know. It can be 5:00 in the morning, you can be canceled. . . . They're supposed to be able to call you up to four hours before, okay? But a lot of times they don't, or sometimes you go on the premises and they say, "Oh, you were canceled." . . . They did it to me Christmas, canceled me; New Year's, canceled me; Memorial Day, canceled me; now, they canceled me . . . when you get canceled, it's hard for the agency to find you another place to work. So you just eat that holiday.

Temp workers gain the flexibility *not* to work. What temp workers lose is health insurance and the ability to count on a stable income and stable hours.

Just as temp agency nurses cannot be sure they will work when sched-uled, hospital schedulers cannot be sure an agency nurse will be available when needed. A hospital administrator complained, "The agency, I don't have any kind of control . . . so I can be short, I can really need a nurse, and they're not obligated to do it." The schedulers at the well-run nursing homes we observed were reluctant to use pool nurses, in part because they cost significantly more and "demoralize regular staff," who earn less, and in part because "they don't know the residents."[21] This scheduler's opposition to pool nurses, however, was not based on these practical drawbacks:

> I don't like registry, period. I don't care whose it is. 'Cause you don't have any recourse. You can't put an attendance on 'em. You can't say, "You called out so many times when you picked this shift up and you canceled it." *It's . . . you have no control over that employee.*

Because of their desire to exert greater control, some employers deal with the "unexpected" need to fill slots by "floating" or reallocating labor internally. Instead of using temp agencies, organizations move nurses from adequately staffed units to those that are severely understaffed.[22]

Some hospitals have also developed another solution—what they call "flex teams" (something of a misnomer because these "teams" neither provide much flexibility for the employees nor are really teams). One large hospital created a 125-member flex team with staff they could send anywhere in the hospital "to fill holes." It hired a full-time consultant (who had set up similar teams at other hospitals) to organize this strategy. The internal team she developed was made up of "just-in-time" nurses and nursing assistants who were employed by hospitals to fill unexpected staffing holes. Flex team members—many of whom were people of color and immigrants—learned only from one hour to the next whether they would be working; if they did work, they received a higher rate of pay than regular staff in their positions.[23] After they were called in, the flex team members arrived and then were told where to go and when to move to another floor.

A senior vice president touted this flex plan as her "pet project." The system, as proudly reported by the consultant who became the director of workforce planning, allowed the hospital to cut back on expensive travelers and temps and to meet the growing "volatility in the census." But she also made it clear that this hiring strategy did not guarantee the flex team staff the protections available to the regular staff members; it was an inherently unstable system for those staff involved. And as the top manager noted, "I think that they're not always welcomed. . . . It wasn't, 'Wow, are we happy to have you tonight, you're really helping us out.'"

Overall, then, temp workers and the agencies that employ them serve as an important component of the collective web of time of advantaged employees and the organizations they work for (especially hospitals). On the one hand, these just-in-time workers and their organizations help regular workers and their organizations control and cope with normal unpredictability. On the other hand, this strategy comes at some cost, not only for the temp workers themselves but also for those advantaged workers they replace, and even for the managers who hire but cannot control them. Both employees and employers, as we shall see, prefer that holes be filled by coworkers rather than with temp workers.

Nursing Assistants' Official Basic Schedules

The story of nursing assistants' official schedules is a short one. These schedules are rigid, and CNAs have very little choice in them. In answer to the survey question "How many hours did you work last week?" nursing assistant responses averaged thirty-five, with an interquartile range of thirty-two to forty-six hours, about the same number of weekly hours as nurses. But in contrast to doctors and nurses, it is easy to describe the official basic schedules of nursing assistants who work in nursing homes: with limited exceptions, their basic job schedule is more or less fixed. They work a two-week rotation: for example, in week A they work the weekend plus two specified weekdays, and in week B they work four specified weekdays; then the schedule repeats until their job ends. They also must fit into one of three predefined rigid shifts: 7:00 AM to 3:00 PM, 3:00 PM to 11:00 PM, or 11:00 PM to 7:00 AM. They may request a change, and if another shift opens up, they may be able to move to it. This choice, however, is limited. Explaining why she worked the shift she did, one assistant put it simply: "I work when I do because they tell me to. I'd like to work something different; it's not my choice."

Two stories of how nursing assistants received their initial schedule assignments illustrate the rigid system. In the first example, a nursing assistant accepted a position from 3:00 to 11:00 PM, but was told to report at 11:00. Thinking there must have been a mistake, she asked the supervisor about it. "She goes, 'We overhired for 3:00 to 11:00, so 11:00 to 7:00's all we can give you.' I said, 'But I was hired for 3:00 to 11:00.' [She said,] 'Well, take it or leave it.'"

Another nursing assistant stood out because when we asked why she worked the schedule she did, she answered simply, "My choice." But a few minutes later, when explaining how she came to be hired, she offered this account:

> Well, when I applied here, I applied for a 6:00 to 2:30. So they put me up on Timberland, and then they called me back that morning that I was supposed to start, and they said, "No, we're gonna put you on Spring Creek at 6:00 to

2:30." And then they called me back like an hour later, and they said, "No, we're gonna put you on Spring Creek 3:00 to 11:00." And I'm like, make up my mind [*sic*]! So I had to change my whole body schedule to work a 3:00 to 11:00 'cause I've never worked 3:00 to 11:00 really.

There was a small bit of wiggle room. Nursing assistants who work in hospitals—where nurses predominate—are more often offered a wider range of schedules than the larger number of nursing assistants who work in nursing homes, again showing that organizations as well as occupations drive the scheduling choices.[24] But even in hospitals, schedulers reported that they offered more schedules to nurses, saying that most nursing assistants "have a set schedule." As they explained, nursing assistants "don't feel entitled the way nurses do. . . . They will not stir up trouble too much. They kind of like, you know, you gotta work," while nurses "know they can go anywhere and get paid, probably better than here, you know."

Emergency Medical Technicians' Official Basic Schedules

In our survey, EMTs self-reported the longest hours of any of the occupations: forty-six hours on their main job, with significant additional time in a second job; counting their second jobs, the interquartile range was forty-eight to sixty-six hours a week.[25] EMTs must work day and night shifts, weekdays and weekends, on a schedule that repeats itself from week to week. At the beginning of the year, firefighter EMTs receive several copies of the pocket calendar that lists exactly which crews will be working which shifts on every day for the entire year. The EMTs' official basic schedules for their main jobs are rigid and controlled, in large part, by others. Both of our working-class occupations thus had schedules that were set and, in principle, determined which days they would and would not work for the duration of their employment or until the contract changed it.

The type of organization they work for shapes the schedules they have. Firefighter schedules come in two variants, but in either case the basic official schedule is *totally* rigid. In one increasingly common variant, firefighters are on duty for twenty-four hours straight (typically beginning and ending at 8:00 AM), are off for twenty-four hours, work another twenty-four-hour stretch, and then have five days off. In the other variant, firefighters work a ten-hour day, another ten-hour day, and then two fourteen-hour night shifts, followed by four days off. In either case, firefighters work two day shifts and two night shifts, all work exactly the same number of weekends, and all operate on an eight-day rotation, so that each week their first day on duty comes one day later. There is no room for individual negotiation about this official basic schedule, which is built into union contracts.

Private-sector EMT companies do not have the same rigid official basic schedules as firefighters. But most of these EMTs are expected to work evening or night as well as day shifts, and weekends as well as weekdays. The largest private-sector EMT service in our area, EHS, covers two of the largest cities in the area and is fully unionized. The union contract provides that every six months the schedule is revised, and workers have no guarantee that they will keep the same schedule. If the company determines that it needs thirty paramedic positions, it arranges thirty packages of schedules; each package is likely to involve some shifts that the EMTs will like (Tuesday and Wednesday twelve-hour day shifts) and some that they will not want (Friday and Sunday eight-hour night shifts). Based on seniority, EMTs bid on these packages, and they must take the entire package, not pick and choose the pieces they want.

At other private-sector, non-unionized EMT companies, such as Medic-Route, an EMT can work with the scheduler more easily to devise the schedule he wants or needs. Nonetheless, almost all schedules involve evening, night, and/or weekend shifts, and the EMT has to persistently work with the scheduler ahead of time or be told, "Well, this is all I have. Take it or leave it." And even at Medic-Route the company's power is evident. When we asked one EMT whether the scheduler had ever asked him to change his schedule as a whole, he replied: "She has, yeah, she did it once, and she didn't even ask me, she just changed it." He did add that "usually she'll call you and ask you."

Overall, these working-class men, like the CNAs, had little variation in their rigid official schedules; they had less control over these schedules than both the nurses and the physicians had over theirs. They did not self-schedule. Note that their relative lack of control over scheduling was not primarily a result of a poor market position: EMT unemployment rates stood at about 3 percent over the last decade.[26] When we turn in chapter 7 to a discussion of time off and in chapter 9 to workers' families, we will see the ways in which EMTs expect and do exert some control. But we do not find it here in their official basic schedules, at least compared to the two more advantaged occupations.

OUT OF SYNCH: WEEKENDS, EVENINGS, AND NIGHTS

Because they all work in medical care that operates 24/7, every day of the year, the official basic schedules of all four occupations were often out of synch with the bounded nine-to-five, five-day-a-week routine that so many think of as the prevailing pattern. When asked what they liked least about their schedules, weekend work was often the first thing mentioned. Professionals did better than the working class at avoiding weekend work. In the survey, 45 percent of physicians and 52 percent of nurses reported working two or more weekends in the preceding month, but 82 percent of nursing assistants and 93 percent of EMTs had done so.

Almost twice as likely as the advantaged groups to work two or more weekends per month, EMTs and CNAs also disliked working weekends but accepted it as inevitable. A few EMTs argued that the schedule was an advantage, allowing them to go to places like Home Depot during the week when it was less crowded; one said, "I don't know if I could work five days a week again." For most of them, however, working weekends was what they liked least about their schedule. But as another noted about working weekends and Christmas, "you know that going into this field. You either have to accept that or you don't." A nursing assistant made the same point about inevitability:

> Some people grumble about working weekends, but you know, when you work in the medical field, basically anywhere you work, you have to work one weekend, at least. Unless you're working in a doctor's office where it's Monday through Friday, but if you're working in a nursing home or a hospital, there's no need for you to put an application in if you're going to complain about it.

The inevitability of working weekends, however, did not mean that nursing assistants liked it. Many took it for granted that, "you know, nobody wants to work weekends." Asked what an ideal schedule would be, one nursing assistant responded, "Well, the weekdays I work with no weekends!" and then laughed. Having to work Sundays, and consequently missing church, was an especially sore point. To control nursing assistants' reluctance to work weekends, both nursing homes had rules that required them to immediately make up any weekend they missed; one nursing home had also recently imposed a rule that if a nursing assistant wanted to take off a weekend day, she could do so only if she found her own replacement.

As we move to a 24/7 economy, a rising number of people are working not only weekends but also evenings and nights.[27] As is the case for the population at large, the out-of-synch work pattern associated with "nonstandard" hours varied among our four occupations. According to national data, nurses and nursing assistants are among the ten occupations with the highest number of people working nonstandard hours.[28] In our survey, nursing assistants and EMTs reported working 50 percent more nights than doctors and nurses did, but even doctors and nurses were much more likely to do so than most other professionals. Some nursing assistants and EMTs, and even some nurses, said that they found some benefit in working these hours, especially the night shift: with supervisors, visitors, case managers, therapists, and nutritionists gone, the evening and night shifts were more relaxed, informal, and friendly and less hectic than the day shift. At night, there were often fewer demands, giving workers time to hang around and chat. And those on the night shift often received an extra pay differential for working a nonday shift. Many, nonetheless, tried to avoid these out-of-synch shifts.

Most hospital physicians tried to avoid the night shift. At one hospital, the physician scheduler remarked that "a lot of scheduling is done based upon staff convenience, not upon patient care needs." Asked to elaborate, the physician said that the "night shift is understaffed and [is a] difficult-to-staff shift."

To reduce the demands on them during out-of-synch shifts, physicians sometimes behaved aggressively toward those they saw as subordinate staff. Listen to this exchange between two nurses on the night shift in a hospital. Just after midnight, one of them had called a doctor; she then related the conversation to the charge nurse:

NIGHT NURSE: I just got yelled at for waking the doctor.

CHARGE NURSE: Yeah, but you had to do it.

NIGHT NURSE: He said, "Why are you addressing this now?" And I said, "Because I just came on my shift and needed to know."

The night nurse concluded, sarcastically, "He's a doctor. He's getting paid. I'm only a nurse. I'm taking care of his patient." This doctor had tried to make the web of time he shared with this nurse operate more in his favor by limiting her pull.

Often nurses who work the evening or night shift choose that shift because of their family responsibilities. A nurse scheduler at a hospital reported: "I think evenings is a tough shift to recruit for. Because it's a busy shift, and plus, I think home life, you know, I think people like to be home in the evening with their families." But just as Anita Garey found among the nurses she studied, a number of the nurses we talked to could and did insist on working the night shift so that they could be visible and "regular mothers."[29] One said that working the night shift allowed her to be involved with her child: "I was always really involved in his school. What I told my husband, I said, 'cause I didn't want to work evenings, 'cause then I'd never see him [her son]. When you work evenings, you don't see your kids."

This choice comes with some cost. Just before a staff meeting, the night nurses talking among themselves shared war stories, with one remarking that she never slept because she was on nights and had kids. Another responded that she fell asleep for a nap in the middle of the day and her kids kept saying, "Mom, Mom, what's wrong?" These nurses shaped their schedules to meet their gender obligations, sometimes at their own expense.

Most EMTs have no choice and must work the night shift some of the time. Although working nights might be inevitable, that did not mean it was desirable. An exchange with an EMT working for a private-sector company captures this:

RESPONDENT: I would like it if it were a normal—it would be fun if it were a normal nine-to-five, you know, like a teacher's schedule.

INTERVIEWER: That seems to be difficult to find in EMS.

RESPONDENT: Yes, it's impossible. I'm sure that's a common theme that you hear from providers, that they would like a normal work schedule. Not happening. (*laughs*)

Structural Alternatives to Out-of-Synch Schedules

As we have seen, out-of-synch work was the part of their schedule that many in all four occupations disliked the most. But the doctors and nurses, the two advantaged occupations, not only individually negotiated ways out but also developed structural alternatives that helped them escape this onerous aspect of their jobs.

Most private practices limit physicians' weekend hours. Hospital-based physicians, like those in the ER, need to provide coverage at all times, so they do work nights and weekends, but even here, an effort is made to minimize nonstandard hours. As one nurse scheduler in an emergency room reported: "Physicians tend to discharge a lot of people Friday night or Saturday morning; they'll go in and discharge people because they don't want to come in on the weekend." Doctors explained this discharge decision by suggesting that it makes no sense for a patient to sit around the hospital waiting when radiologists will not be coming in and tests cannot be ordered. As one physician scheduler at a hospital reported: "A physician satisfier in a big way is about not making too much weekend time."

Physicians have also developed a structural alternative to deal with out-of-synch hours—the hospitalist, an entirely new category of employee. About three-quarters of hospitals now hire hospitalists.[30] Hospitalists emerged as a way for hospitals to deal with the reductions in weekly schedules that the Accreditation Council for Graduate Medical Education (ACGME) instituted in 2003 for accredited resident programs—thus transforming the web of time for hospital staff doctors.[31] Hospitalists also change the schedules of primary care physicians (PCPs) with private practices. Now an important part of PCPs' web of time, this emerging subgroup is slowly changing the demand on them to be on hospital call.[32] A hospitalist explained the first step in the process to reduce calls:

> So your old model is your physician got up in the morning, came in, and rounded on patients [in the hospital], and then went to the office and saw folks, and then, if there were any admissions in the evening, they came in or they were on call. Over the past, I don't know, twenty-five years or so, physicians have kind of banded together so that they have call groups so that they're not on call every night, and they don't round on their patients every morning, but rather there's one person who's sort of elected from their office or their group who rounds on the patients, usually for about a week.

A physician in a group practice reported that this was exactly what happened in his practice as it grew. As the practice expanded, each doctor worked in the hospital for a full week roughly once every three months. Even though "by the end of that week you're pretty burned out," he noted, the physicians did not have to visit hospital patients at other times. The group then decided to take the next step—switching to hospitalists.

Nurses also emphasized the benefits of having experienced doctors constantly available in the hospital. As one nurse remarked: "They [hospitalists] definitely make the nurse's job easier. In fact, I don't think we could do the things that we're doing at the hospital these days without having hospitalists. . . . Because the private physicians just aren't available enough."

Floating from patient to patient and often from floor to floor, and responsible for patients throughout their hospital stay, hospitalists—who work either a day, evening, or night shift—take over all hospital care of the patients. This reduces disruptions to the primary care physicians' home life caused by early morning, evening, night, or weekend hospital calls and visits. With a hospitalist system, PCPs "still take calls from home, that doesn't change, but they don't have to drive in like they used to not that long ago." The hospitalist system does not necessarily enable PCPs to work fewer hours, but it does make the schedule more predictable and increase physicians' control; moreover, "if that time that was scheduled as rounding time is now patient visit time, the physicians are reimbursed better."

The head of one private practice explained that his organization was moving to a hospitalist model (instead of being on call) because that was the way to attract new physicians to their practice. A director of hospitalists echoed this view:

> The reason why I think it's becoming the standard of care is that most primary care physicians in the office wouldn't even sign up to a particular practice unless they are confident or can be assured that they won't have to do hospital work . . . and I've seen this. . . . Dr. X wouldn't want to be in this office unless he knows that whenever his patient needs to be in the hospital, he wouldn't need to go to the hospital. So it kind of indirectly drives what has to become the standard, because otherwise the hospital would not be able to attract any primary care doctors. (*chuckles*)

To be sure, there are costs to this structural adaptation. Some primary care physicians mourn the loss of the skills and relationships associated with following really sick patients through the course of their illness.[33] One doctor we interviewed said that he "was very ambivalent about" the move to hospitalists for precisely this reason. Timothy Hoff, however, reports in his study of PCPs that "the biggest upside of not doing hospital medicine was the chance to attain this [lifestyle] balance without sacrificing income or devoting more time to work."[34] One of the physicians we interviewed, a mother of young children, emphasized this:

> If I'm on call over the weekend and one of my patients needs to get admitted to the hospital . . . prior to the hospitalist service, that would mean that I would need to go into the hospital and admit them and then take care of them through the weekend, which means with kids at home you'd always have to have a . . . you never know when you'd get called in and you'd have to have a backup plan, ya know, whether it's my husband or whether it's some backup child care. I can't bring the three kids in tow with me to the hospital.

Finally, the hospitalist system provides more predictable schedules not only for the doctors who no longer have to be on call but also for the hospitalists themselves. Like doctors in the ED or radiologists, hospitalists work standard shifts—sometimes an eight-hour, nine-to-five day, sometimes an evening or night eight-hour shift, and sometimes a twelve-hour shift for three days a week. One hospitalist, at forty-two the oldest in his group, reported a key attraction of the position, especially for younger physicians:

Because you're basically saying, "I work a limited number of hours, and I don't take any calls from home—when I'm home, I'm home." That, I think, is probably still key for the younger generation of folks. They really want a separation of work and life . . . and the older generation of doctors, we're all brainwashed to think that your life *is* your work. For the older folks of us, we still believe that your work, whether you like it or not, eventually it becomes your life. But the younger folks are very, very conscious that "I don't want that. I want my work, and I want my life. I don't want them to be mixed up. I want them to be very separate.". . . That's probably, in my experience, near the top, if not the top, reason [why people become and remain hospitalists].

The hospitalist system, another explained, "works better for people with families" (a benefit we will examine in chapter 9). And as this comment suggests, generational differences, along with gender and class divides, have important effects on the culture surrounding schedules. Not only doctors but also nurses talked about a generational divide: the older members of the occupational group claiming that their kind of strong commitment to work was less apparent among the younger members, while the younger members claim to have a greater commitment to a balanced life, which they feel is valued less by the older members of their occupation. Although we cannot be sure whether these differences arise from cohort or aging differences, we know that the hospitalist system provides a structural solution that allows a more balanced life among these professionals. When hospitalists are done with the job, they are truly done; the job does not follow them home.

Hospitalists provide a way of slowly advancing the privileges of doctors, both the hospitalists (who work a single shift, whether day, evening, or night) and the regular physicians (who no longer have to come into the hospital on evenings and weekends). The development of the hospitalist system has been a way to restore control to doctors, and it is uniquely designed to relieve scheduling burdens for members of an occupation rather than for organizations. But the emergence of hospitalists also relieves some staffing constraints on the hospitals that employ them, and as such, the system is part of the broad push by many organizations toward bureaucratic control of professionals.[35]

Nurses, like physicians, have also developed structural solutions to avoid or minimize out-of-synch work. Choosing where to work is one way: nurses who work in physicians' offices, schools, or insurance companies often do no weekend work. At nursing homes, it is almost impossible to escape working every other weekend, but some hospitals make it possible to do so. To help reduce the need for other nurses to work on weekends, hospitals have developed WIN (Weekend INcentive) systems and "Baylor plan" nurses. The general framework of both systems involves having nurses work only on weekends; these nurses put in two twelve-hour (sometimes sixteen-hour!) shifts every weekend, receive full benefits even though they work only twenty-four hours a week, and gain additional financial incentives. WIN nurses are, in some sense, structurally analogous to hospitalists, as well as an important part of nurses' web of time.

Both advantaged occupations—the nurses and the doctors—have used their class advantage to create systemwide alternatives that reduce out-of-synch hours for regular staff. Hospitals developed hospitalists for doctors and weekend plans for nurses as structural solutions to the scheduling part of the job that many of these professionals dislike. Nurses also hate mandatory overtime, as shown by their union contracts (which have numerous clauses outlawing its use except under very particular circumstances). Temp agencies, both local and national, and flex teams provide another way for employers to fill slots without mandating a regular staff nurse. At least in the area where we conducted our study, such structural solutions are rarely if ever used for CNAs or EMTs. Employers claimed that they have enough control to ensure that schedules are full and therefore no alternative solutions are needed.

CONCLUSION

Examining official schedules by occupational group highlights not only variation among the occupations and organizations but also the pervasiveness of the inequality among them. Employers decide what a staffing "hole" is, as well as how many workers they need for how many hours. Rather than emanating from a rational best practice calculated from research findings or even specific laws about how many workers an organization *must* employ to meet agreed-upon standards, these numbers are derived from a formula worked out in struggles between management and employees and vary from occupation to occupation. Sometimes these numbers are subject to policy and external institutional structures, but overall they are based on what come to prevail as the organizational parameters specified by management. Managers insist on their prerogative to distribute these schedules unequally.

Class (as manifested in occupation and organization), gender (expressed in the composition of an occupation and in work-family relations), and the intersection of class and gender shape official basic schedules. The two professional groups in our study not only clearly had more control over their basic schedules but were also able to use that control to gain greater variety in the schedules they were offered; moreover, these schedules were less rigid than those of either of the two working-class occupations. The doctors operated in a group where people were responsible to each other, and pressured each other, but were not supervised by any non-doctor. Moreover, they developed a structural solution, in the form of hospitalists, to fill the hours they did not want to work. Although nurses typically needed to fit within a structure set by administrators and organizational regulation, they too had many options within that structure, and sometimes those options were adjusted to meet their needs. They had developed structural solutions, whether in the form of a Baylor weekend plan or reliance on temporary workers, to fill the slots they could not fill or did not want to fill. In contrast, schedules for the two less-advantaged occupations, nursing assistants and EMTs, were typically presented as "take it or leave it."

Across occupations, the part of scheduling that people found most troubling was the out-of-synch schedule—having to work evenings, nights, and weekends. Although almost all health care workers are pressured to work some out-of-synch hours, class enables most doctors and many nurses, but not most EMTs and CNAs, to minimize or at least choose whether they want to do this work. Advantaged occupations gain the luxury of living life "in synch," or at least of being able to choose when to be out of synch; the disadvantaged experience no such luxury. These patterns can be generalized: doctors are like the other privileged workers identified around the world by Karen Lyness and her colleagues—they work long hours but control *when* they work far more than less-privileged workers do.[36]

Gender matters as well, and often pushes in unexpected ways against class advantage and disadvantage. Both male physicians and EMTs actively seek to work more than is required by the official schedule of their main job. Male physicians typically do so by putting in extra hours on their first (and typically only) job; EMTs do so by working a second job (which we address in chapter 6). Nursing assistants, disadvantaged by both class and gender (and frequently by race-ethnicity as well), are assigned more limited work hours but have little choice of when to work. Nurses, in a pattern that, as we will see in chapter 9, is also characteristic of many women doctors, seek to arrange work schedules that will not conflict with their family obligations. In contrast to the nursing assistants, nurses can thus deploy their class advantage in the service of gendered notions of work and family. Because of market conditions, organizational responsiveness, and family obligations, nurses, more than any of the other occupations we studied, push for and often obtain what work-life researchers conventionally mean by "family-friendly" flexibility in their basic job schedules. These women are able to use the cultural expectations associated with gender to gain workplace concessions.

The results reported in this chapter help us develop a more refined understanding of control over time: those with class advantage do not necessarily cut back on their hours but instead use their control to determine when they work, the fluidity and predictability of their schedules, and the extent to which and in what ways other responsibilities shape their scheduling choices.

PART II | The Forms of Unpredictability

Chapter 5 | Unpredictability and Churning: Is There a Fixed Schedule?

"Normal unpredictability" means that the schedules people actually work often do not match the schedules that are set in advance. Employers adjust staffing depending on the number and condition of the people seeking their services. Employees cannot work at some of the times specified by their schedules. Moreover, many workers put in extra hours, choosing from among the additional shifts that employers make available. For both employers and workers, the resulting unpredictability of schedules is both a matter of "objective necessity" dictated by external events and a struggle for control. The need to vary a schedule and the willingness to do so are both a source of vulnerability and a source of power.

To be sure, workers have some ability to vary their schedules within a framework established by management. Workers can and do use their willingness (or reluctance) to change their schedule as leverage. Workers both welcome the limited degree of schedule control they have been able to win, sometimes crediting management for its flexibility, and also resent the restrictions and penalties the system imposes. Employers might find it easier if they could just require workers to stay on the job (or to come in anytime the employer calls), but worker resistance to such demands is high.

"Churning," which we define as any variation from the official basic schedule set out in advance, thus poses an issue.[1] Who has the power to create variation—employers or employees? Does the schedule become what the employer wants or what the workers want? These questions are too simple, and almost all the evidence is open to multiple interpretations. Our basic answer is that schedules are shaped by a struggle, but in this struggle many managers at least sometimes side with workers, al-

89

most all workers sometimes agree with management, and many workers usually do.

Here as everywhere, class and gender are central. Strategies used to address unpredictable variation from the official basic schedule are less available but more important to the two working-class occupations, EMTs and nursing assistants, than they are to doctors and nurses. Even though doctors and nurses make changes in their schedules, they are better able to shape their initial schedules as well as make changes to them. In the two female-dominated occupations, churning is important (especially taking time off) but more difficult (especially adding time), in large part because of the more pressing family responsibilities that they—compared to most men, especially professional men—still assume. The varying needs and relative strength of employers and employees, and the history of past contestation, shape the rules and expectations about unpredictability that prevail in different organizations and among different groups of employees.

This chapter documents the extent and importance of unpredictability and churning, questioning the extent to which there *is* a fixed schedule. The chapter then asks how churning in these occupations can be explained and explores the question of who controls it. We use a number of different data sets to address these issues: the survey, observations, and, of special importance, a data set from the Berkman nursing home that includes both the official schedule that management hands out in advance and the schedule that employees actually work.

To start with the chapter's punch line: although the Berkman nursing home's official schedule was rigid and determined a year or more in advance, specifying exactly when each employee had to work, and although the nursing home had fairly draconian policies to enforce it, this official schedule was often misleading.[2] Both employer demand and worker resistance—which workers probably did not think of as resistance—led to all sorts of changes in that schedule. Even the most rigid and firmly set schedule cannot hold, it seems, in the face of even the most unorganized of struggles from the most vulnerable of workers. Things fall apart. Workers and their families have babies and surgery or get the flu. Teachers call in parents. The census of patients suddenly climbs or falls. Hurricanes wreak havoc or sunny days beckon. Life gets in the way. Schedules cannot hold.

Although our focus in this book is on direct care medical workers in four specific occupations, the issues raised here are much broader: similar concerns and processes operate in many other occupations. Take the one with which we are most familiar: university faculty may have predictable teaching schedules, but meetings, bad weather, and sickness can turn the best-planned schedule into chaos. People who work in construction and the trades have schedules that vary not only by the season and the weather, but also according to their employer's ability to keep getting jobs. Retail workers, the hospitality industry, hedge funds, food preparation, hairdressers, cosmetologists, waiters and waitresses, lawyers, social workers, truck drivers, tax preparers—all are likely to face churning in their schedules. Perhaps there is no better illustration of this than the iconic employer of our time, Walmart:

> When workers voted in a union in Quebec and they were actually forced to negotiate with a union, the union did not ask for wage or benefits increases. They simply wanted to give workers predictable shifts—to make it possible for workers to have lives. Instead of doing this, Walmart shut the store down. Walmart was saying, "We cannot operate when workers are sure of a regular shift."[3]

POSING THE PROBLEM

If this unpredictability and struggles over the control of schedules are so pervasive, why has so little research focused on this issue? When people think about work hours, they typically think about "usual weekly hours worked on the main job," and then they design large-scale surveys that use this approach and this question. The OECD, which reports the definitive data for some thirty-five relatively affluent countries, explains (in a footnote), "This table contains data on average usual weekly hours worked in the main job. . . . Actual hours of work instead of usual hours of work are only available in some countries (Mexico and Korea)."[4]

Many people assume that a Monday-to-Friday, nine-to-five schedule is the standard work schedule and that all other schedules are variations on it. Harriet Presser and others have made a significant intervention, pointing out that a large proportion of the workforce (including many people in our four occupations) work "nonstandard" hours—that is, routinely and as part of their standard workweek, they put in hours on weekends and outside of any nine-to-five framework.[5] These hours are not spillover from their regular schedule, but instead *are* their standard schedule. As Presser noted in 1999, schedules based on nonstandard days and hours are "disproportionately concentrated in jobs low in the occupational hierarchy."[6] That is precisely what we showed in chapter 4: nonstandard hours were most common among the EMTs and CNAs, the nonprofessionals among our occupations. Going beyond the first step of assuming a standard workweek schedule is Monday to Friday, nine to five, and beyond the second step of recognizing the pervasiveness of nonstandard hours, we introduce a third step that takes us into a dimension that has gone largely unremarked but is central to understanding the problems both people and organizations face in managing work schedules. Both the literature on standard hours and the literature on nonstandard hours assume, implicitly or explicitly, that there *are* fixed schedules, that people work at predictable hours on regular days scheduled in advance. Our data and analysis question that (usually unstated) assumption; we provide a case study for issues that need to receive much more attention.

In a series of important studies, a few other scholars have analyzed the absence of any standard schedule, most notably Susan Lambert, Julia Henly, and their collaborators. In her examination of four nonproduction industries—hospitality, retail, transportation, and financial services—Lambert finds that "last-minute adjustments to work schedules—adding or subtracting hours to the posted schedule a day or two in advance—were rampant in the jobs studied."[7] Julia Henly and her colleagues, working on the same large project as Lambert, report that in their interviews of low-income mothers, "almost 30 percent of workers report having schedules with variable start and end times. Ten percent report that their schedules fluctuate so much that they cannot provide a typical weekly schedule."[8] Lambert and Elaine Waxman argue that many low-level jobs involve not flexibility, but instability.[9]

Many of the jobs that these researchers have examined, however, are already known to be among the most unstable. Since hospitality and retail, for example, fluctuate in response to large, often seasonal, variations in the number of customers, it is not such a surprise that these workforces would have unstable schedules. When workers receive their schedules only days in advance of when they are told to work—as often happens in these industries—this is schedule instability, but not exactly churning as we use the term. That is, the problem for these workers—and the advantage, arguably, for their employers—is that workers do not *have* a set schedule known well in advance. In the occupations we studied, however, people had a fixed official schedule, but there were many departures from what appeared to be fixed. It is more surprising that we found unpredictable schedules in stable, full-time medical occupations than it is to find such schedules in retail sales; it is particularly surprising to get such results in a high-end nursing home like Berkman. Our findings, moreover, seem to depend at least as much on workers' decisions as on management's decisions; for example, the issue was *not* that workers were told to go home for the day because of a low census.

Those who are critical of the errors in survey data often urge that time diaries be used instead. Time diaries have their own problems, however, including the fact that they typically are kept for only one day; thus, the analyst is using one-day reports to project what a *usual* week would look like.[10] Even time diaries rely on self-reports, which are in some ways problematic. For example, D. Chase and Geoffrey Godbey, after asking the members of a swim and tennis club how often they had used the club in the last year, obtained the actual sign-in records. Almost half of their respondents overestimated their use of the club by more than 100 percent.[11] If the issue is the unpredictability of schedules—the variations from the "normal" schedule sought or imposed by workers or management—then it becomes particularly important to use a range of data that do not depend only on self-recall.

Observations and interviews provide both evidence and explanations for churning and unpredictability at a number of sites. The survey data help answer questions about frequency, the significance of differences among groups, and the generalizability of the patterns we uncover. For one of the two nursing homes where we observed, we had an additional unique data source that allowed us to specify the amount of churning, when it occurred, who did it, and why. For the Berkman nursing home, in addition to interview and observation data, we obtained the official schedules planned and handed out well in advance, as well as information showing who actually worked for a six-month period. Importantly, these data did not rely on self-recall. After we obtained these two sets of schedules, we sat down with the knowledgeable scheduler and asked her to give us information about each worker listed on the schedule—whether the worker was a nurse or nursing assistant, a mother, still working at the nursing home, and her race.[12]

Our survey asked, "In the last week, how many hours did you work at your main job?" and immediately followed that by asking, "Is this the number of hours that you usually work at your main job?" The fascinating finding was that many people reported that the last week was *not* usual, with a significant ($p < .05$) difference between the two professional occupations, on the one hand, and the two working-class occupations, on the other. Fifteen percent of doctors and 17 percent of nurses—that is, about one in six professionals—reported that they had not worked the "usual" hours the previous week, while 26 percent of EMTs and 28 percent of nursing assistants—one in four in the working-class occupations—reported not working the usual hours in the previous week. The class difference was substantial, but within class, gender differences (between nurses and doctors or between EMTs and CNAs) were rather small.

Even these results are likely to seriously understate total unpredictability, considering that our questions were open to some interpretation. If, for instance, an employee could not work Friday of the previous week (as scheduled) and had to work Saturday instead, that person would have worked the usual *hours* but not the usual *schedule* and might have had to cancel Saturday plans or scramble to make child care arrangements.

Showing not only the days and times people were originally scheduled to work but also when they actually worked, the Berkman data cover only work time, but they do so for both low-wage and professional employees for a full six months (187 days, 26.7 weeks), seven days a week, enabling us to determine the extent to which individuals varied their routines over this period.[13] Locating and obtaining these data so that we could combine them with our survey results was a stroke of particularly good luck. Recall that, using the survey data, we found a significant amount of churning across all four occupations, but also that the class differences were large while, within class, gender differences were small. The Berkman data allow us to further explore and specify those significant class differences because they contain detailed information on schedules and churning for both nurses and nursing assistants.

CHURNING: THE BASIC STORY

It is worth repeating how stable Berkman was. Most of the patients in this high-end, stand-alone, nonprofit nursing home were private pay, and many had private rooms. Workers received full benefits if they worked twenty-four hours a week; there was a 95 percent bed occupancy rate, so the demand for workers was constant; and there was low turnover among the staff, especially the nursing assistants, whose turnover rates were about one-fifth of the national average. If churning varies from employer to employer, we would expect Berkman to have a much lower level than many other places.

We use the word "churning" to cover *any* variation from a regular schedule that has been set out in advance. That is, we include not just the last-minute call-out when someone is sick, but also vacations and any other reason a worker takes time off. This definition may seem too expansive, but since we hope that by the end of the chapter it will be evident that even vacations are a problematic concept, we believe that the broadest possible definition of churning is the best starting point.

Each day at Berkman copies of the schedule for the day were made available. Consider a sample schedule, shown in figure 5.1. The typed-in names are those on the official schedule, set long in advance. A name crossed out—what we call a "cross-out"—indicates that someone did *not* work as originally scheduled. Where an employee's name is crossed out, a reason is usually recorded—such as "SK," for "sick." A name written in is that of a person who was not originally scheduled to work that day but *did* work; the nursing home called this a "pickup," and we use the same term. All the changes from the official schedule—all the cross-outs and pickups—are what we call "churning."

Figure 5.1   Sample Daily Schedule at Berkman Nursing Home

| Monday April 1 | | | | |
Unit 1	Unit 2	Unit 3	Unit 4	Unit 5
Supervisor: Karen	Supervisor: Imani	Supervisor: Jen	Supervisor: Michelle	Supervisor: Heather
Nurses:	Nurses:	Nurses:	Nurses:	Nurses:
Diane	Erica	Ligaya	Joanne	Olivia
Deborah	~~Rebecca~~ VAC *Lilly*	Cheryl	~~Aisha~~ HOL *Tiffany M*	Susan
CNAs:	CNAs:	CNAs: *Lauren*	CNAs:	CNAs:
Shakina C	Melvin	~~Shasta~~ SK	~~Sherita~~ SWAP	Ruth
Beyonce	Beatrice	Louise	Crystal	~~Tammy~~
Eve	Alice	~~Kayla~~ SK	Tiffany	Chloe
~~Zari~~ *off*	Laqueta	~~Brianna~~ SK	Wanda	Shamara
Sofia	Carmen	Aisha	Latoya	Tamika
Emma *Jasmine*	Jayla	Kimani *Keisha* *Lomai*	Edmaris *Amanda* SWAP	Ana *Naomi*
EVENING SHIFT (Supervisor Donna)				
Nurses:	Nurses:	Nurses:	Nurses:	Nurses:
Marianne	Julia	Theresa	Lynn	Jayla
Laura	Stephanie	~~Linda~~ SK *Jen*	Emily	Rebecca
CNAs:	CNAs:	CNAs:	CNAs:	CNAs:
Gertha	~~Sofia~~ VAC	Sheila	Melissa	~~Gina~~ ~~SK~~ VAC
Crystal	Nahir	Yvonne	Wendy	Laqueta
Angela	Jaynette	Nancy	~~Dawn~~ SK	Kanita
~~Veronica~~ HOL	Beth	Shalamar	Suheyrie	Ashley
Lenworth *Beyonce*	Yazmin *Thalia*	Annmarie	Betsy *Crystal*	Coleesha *Shakina T*
NIGHT SHIFT (Supervisor Jessica)				
Nurses:	Nurses:	Nurses:	Nurses:	Nurses:
~~Darlene~~ *Mary Ann (NF)*	Linda	Julie	Shaniqua	Jean
CNAs:	CNAs:	CNAs:	CNAs:	CNAs:
Musur	Mara	~~Valerie~~ SK	Melissa	Beth *Syleena*
Ayana	Nicole	Naderra *Shalamar*	Cecile	Marisol
Rachel				~~Denise~~ VAC

Source: Berkman daily schedule (names changed to protect confidentiality).

The key outcome (or dependent variable) is what we call the person-shift, by which we mean one person working one eight-hour shift. The simplest case is a single person working a single shift as scheduled; that would generate one person-shift entry. If someone "works a double"—that is, works two shifts in a row, or sixteen hours straight—that would be two person-shifts. If someone calls in sick, that generates a cross-out entry for the person who is sick and a pickup entry for the person who takes the shift instead—that is, two person-shifts are generated to fill one eight-hour time slot.[14]

At Berkman, when someone called in sick (in figure 5.1, see Valerie, on the night shift of unit 3), someone already at work (Shalamar, evening shift of unit 3) would often agree to work a double; when people did pick up extra shifts, about 40 percent of the time they did so by working a double (that is, by working sixteen hours straight). Covering the full work schedules for more than 150 workers for a six-month period, our data set for Berkman contains 19,902 person-shifts.[15]

Note that when one person calls out and another replaces them in the schedule, we count that as two person-shifts. When we first presented these data, an economist in the audience, thinking from the employer's perspective, wanted to count this as just one person-shift, since the issue, to the economist-employer, is the need to fill the shift. In this employer-oriented view, it is arguable that we are in effect doubling the level of churning. We are at least as interested, however, in the worker perspective as in the employer perspective, and in this case two people had their normal routines disrupted—one by not working when she normally would, and the other by working on a day she had not been scheduled to work.

Given this operationalization, we ask the following questions: How many of the person-shifts are worked according to the official schedule planned long in advance, and how many are not worked according to the official schedule? As figure 5.2 indicates, 34 percent of the shifts were not worked according to schedule, and 66 percent were.[16] That is, for every two person-shifts that were worked as planned well in advance, there was one person-shift that did not go according to schedule.

These are stunning results. Here we have a high-end employer in a highly stable industry, using benefited regular employees with a low rate of turnover, maintaining a steady 95 percent occupancy rate, and there is still a lot of churning. This instability is invisible in most studies of the workforce, which assume that the standard official schedule is the actual schedule. Some of this instability is even invisible in our own survey. For instance, asked whether the hours they worked "last week" were similar to the usual schedule, a worker might well answer on the basis of thinking: *Yeah, last week was about the usual. I worked four days I was scheduled to work, didn't work one of my regularly scheduled days, and had to make special child care arrangements when I picked up a shift I don't usually work. That's about the usual.* Analyzing this worker's response, we would easily miss that her "usual" schedule involved unpredictability—unexpected days added and scheduled days not worked.

Almost two out of three person-shifts were filled by regular employees

Figure 5.2   Person-Shifts Worked According to the Fixed Schedule

☐ Not Originally Scheduled Shifts   ■ Originally Scheduled Shifts

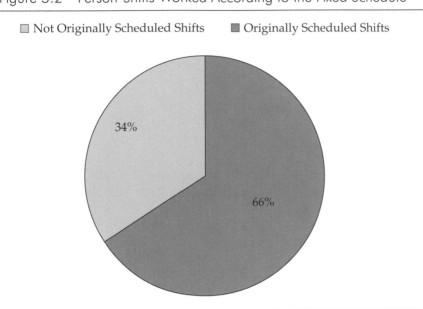

Source: Authors' calculations based on Berkman daily schedules.

working their regular schedules. Another substantial block of person-shifts were worked by per diem workers, who covered slightly more than one out of every twenty person-shifts; a much smaller number of person-shifts, about one out of two hundred, were covered by temp agency nurses.[17] About one out of nine shifts were cross-outs, which included vacations and holidays as well as call-outs for being sick. (Later in this chapter we break down some of the specific categories within cross-outs.) A little more than one in eight shifts were pickups.[18]

Unpredictability: Pervasive or Concentrated?

An alternative way of understanding churning is to determine whether cross-out and pickup shifts are concentrated among a limited subset of workers, or whether a substantial proportion of workers are significant participants in this process. For example, the literature suggests that less than 3 percent of the population is responsible for 75 percent of violent crime.[19] If 3 percent of the workforce are responsible for 75 percent of the churning, that changes how we think about the issue: It would mean unpredictability is not pervasive or diffuse but instead is concentrated.

Figure 5.3   Distribution of Disruptions to the Fixed Schedule

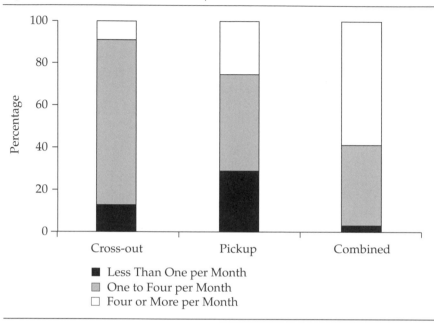

Source: Authors' calculations based on Berkman daily schedules.

How many of the people we observed did not participate at all in this churning? How many people showed up, worked their job, never took a day off, and never picked up a day? The answer is: *zero.* Not one employee did that over the course of six months. Churning is a significant part of the experience of just about every worker.

Just about everyone "crossed out" now and then, missing days they had been scheduled to work, and almost no one did a lot of it; about four out of five workers crossed out an average of one to four times a month—that is, somewhere between once a week and once a month (see figure 5.3). Remember, however, that cross-outs include vacation days as well as sick days, a point discussed later in this chapter and explored in more detail in chapter 7. There was much more of a spread when it came to picking up extra shifts.[20] A little over one-quarter of the employees we observed did so less than once a month, and a little over one-quarter did so more than four times a month—that is, on average they picked up at least one extra shift a week. And if we combine pickups and cross-outs, and ask how many people had less than once a month when they varied from the set schedule, the answer is less than 3 percent of the workforce (2.7 percent);

almost six out of ten people (58.9 percent) did so more than four times a month. Most people varied from the fixed schedule at least once a week.

We do not have equally detailed analyses of long-term data for any of the other employers, but an analysis of data for the Outercity hospital for a two-week period in September 2007 shows that in the emergency department 39 percent of the nurses picked up one or more shifts for which they had not been scheduled and on the medical floor 48 percent did so.[21] These data, combined with the survey results we presented earlier showing that one out of five times the previous week's hours were not "usual," suggest that Berkman's high levels of churning were by no means an anomaly.

Who Is Most (and Least) Likely to Not Work as Scheduled?

In most academic analyses, the primary focus is on variation—who is most and least likely to engage in the behavior. By far the most interesting and important point about churning is what we just discussed: the overall extent of it, and the extent to which such behavior is widespread. Nonetheless, we still want to know: Who is most and least likely to churn?

For the *overall* level of crossing out—not working when scheduled to do so, the surprising finding is that at least at the Berkman nursing home, none of the demographic variables available to us had a significant impact on the frequency with which people crossed out.[22] There is a tendency to think that null results are not interesting, but these are actually important results: for cross-outs overall, at least at the Berkman nursing home, it did not matter whether you were a well-paid nurse or a low-paid nursing assistant, whether or not you were the mother of a young child, or whether you were white or black or Latina. Members of every group had numerous days when they crossed out, and no category of worker was more (or less) likely to take off a day on which they had been scheduled to work.

This lack of a relationship between cross-outs and demographic group holds true only if we look at cross-outs as a whole. Explanations for why employees missed a shift were noted on the schedule sheets. The codes used were devised by the employer, of course, for the employer's own purposes; if employees could devise the reason codes, they might develop a different set (a day off taken for a child, taken for self, and so on). Although the codes enable us to begin to get at the reasons for variations from the schedule, we should note that, since these are employer codes, we have information only on why employees crossed out and failed to work as scheduled in advance. We do not have information on why employees chose to pick up extra shifts when they did (perhaps to pay a bill, to save for a car or vacation, or because child care was available that day).

The clearest contrast among these codes is between those times when an employee took the shift off with very little advance notice and those times when an employee took an extended vacation, which had to be requested at least a month in advance and during the summer had to be requested several months in advance. It is presumably easier for an employer to deal with a request submitted months in advance than it is to find a last-minute replacement.[23]

We can look at this same issue from an employee's point of view. The employee will be sanctioned if she takes the day off with only a day or two of advance notice, which usually happens because she or her child is sick or because of some other quasi-emergency. The employee can avoid this sanction by arranging for another employee to take her place through a schedule swap ("I'll work Friday for you if you'll work Tuesday for me"— see chapter 10). Swaps and call-outs (calling in to report being unable to work owing to their own illness, that of a child or family member, or other emergency) are all ways of dealing with the need for a day off that arises at the last minute, and together they constituted a little more than one out of four of the reasons listed why workers did not work as scheduled at Berkman.[24]

Although the overall number of cross-outs does not vary by the workers' demographic characteristics, there is variation when we look separately at call-outs and swaps. At the bivariate level, mothers are twice as likely as nonmothers to call out and swap, and nursing assistants are twice as likely as nurses to call out (even though, as we show later, they are more likely to face penalties when they do so). Motherhood is the driving factor here. It makes sense that, in our society, mothers of young children would be the ones who stay home with a sick child and who are more likely to get sick themselves from exposure to a sick child; mothers thus call in sick for both their own illnesses and their children's illnesses. Motherhood and occupation are correlated: the nursing assistants at Berkman were more likely to be mothers ($r = 0.40$).

At the other end of the spectrum of cross-outs, consider extended vacations planned well in advance. Vacation as a listed reason accounts for almost one-quarter of the shifts crossed out from the advance schedule.[25] Employers have trouble even with those, and we learned in our interviews about people being pressured not to take vacations, or not to take them when they wanted to. But we also need to deconstruct the category of vacations. For doctors, a typical vacation is a week or two off, at a destination resort, getting a real break from work. That is not the reality for nursing assistants, many of whom do not take vacations; one of their "benefits" is being able to skip a week or two of vacation and be paid extra for it.[26] Workers do this because they need the money. As one nursing assistant who was better off and owned and lived in a trailer told us, "When I buy my vacation time, I save it so I know I have the oil for the coming winter." Many others take their vacation a day at a time for family, using it, in effect, as extra sick leave. A day recorded by the employer as vacation may be used by the employee to take a child to a doctor's appointment. As one nursing assistant noted, "For years now, I haven't taken any vacation time. Not a vacation—I mean, I'll take my hours so I can take a day off, but I'm usually watching my kids or doing something like that." Normally Berkman administrators would impose a sanction if an employee took a single day off on short notice, but if the employee could persuade another employee who was not scheduled for that day to work it instead, then she would avoid any penalty. Thus, in the data available to us, a one-day "vacation" might actually have been a day spent at home with a sick child (see chapter 10).[27] That would be quite different from taking a week off to get a real break, and this is why we include vacation days in the broad definition of churning.

So how many Berkman nurses and nursing assistants took "extended vacations" if by that we mean that they took off at least three scheduled shifts in a row? If they took off three shifts in a row and carefully worked around their schedules, they could probably get a week off. Our data cover six months, not a full year, but the April-to-October period includes the summer, which is the most common time to take a vacation. During those six months, only 24 percent of the employees took off three or more shifts in a row, that is, took a one-week vacation. At the bivariate level, whites (mostly nurses) were twice as likely as nonwhites to take a week's vacation, and nonmothers were twice as likely as mothers (mostly CNAs) to do so. At least for these U.S. workers, taking an extended vacation was a race, class, and family privilege. For them, an "extended vacation" was extended only by comparison to the other Berkman employees—a European would be outraged at the notion that a week off should be considered an extended vacation.

What these results mean is that in order to keep their jobs these employees could not miss too many days of work. Therefore, whether a nurse or a nursing assistant, a mother or a nonmother, white or black or West Indian or Latina, one way or another the person will be at work a large majority of the time. Employees who missed too many days would have been fired and thus would not have remained in our study; the people still employed were able, one way or another, to operate within the constraints imposed by the employer.

Although this employer rule imposed one important sort of uniformity on all employees—how many total days could be missed—the circumstances of people's lives, of course, are not uniform. The mother of a young child misses work not only because of her own illness but sometimes because she has to stay home with a sick child. Thus, although all Berkman employees had roughly the same number of days when they did not work their regular shifts, how they spent their days off varied a great deal. A white nurse with grown children told us that she took a week or two off for a planned-in-advance vacation trip, while a black nursing assistant with young children told us that she missed days because of her children's illness and her cousin's court date. The nursing assistant's days off did not provide her with the same kind of break the nurse had; her time away from work did not serve to rest and rejuvenate her. Although the nurse and the nursing assistant took the same total number of days off when they did not work according to the fixed schedule, they did so in very different ways, and with different consequences for their sense of getting a break and being ready to return to work.

Who Picks Up Extra Hours?

Although there was relatively little variation in the total number of days that people crossed out, the story was very different when it came to picking up additional shifts. Berkman nursing home restricted the number of days a worker could miss regularly scheduled workdays, but there was no employer requirement that each worker had to pick up a certain number of additional shifts. The decision to do so was entirely up to the worker (unless it created overtime) and depended above all on financial compulsion.

The Berkman quantitative data show significant differences, based on employees' characteristics, when it came to choosing to work extra shifts. At the bivariate level, mothers picked up 50 percent more shifts than nonmothers, nursing assistants picked up 50 percent more shifts than nurses, and people of color picked up twice as many extra shifts as whites. On average, mothers picked up an extra shift almost once a week; nonmothers did so a little less than three weeks out of five. Evidently, for mothers— and, we might speculate, especially for the many single mothers in our database—the need for extra income overcame the complications of arranging child care. Whites picked up an extra shift in two weeks out of five, African Americans and Latinas in almost four weeks out of five, and West Indians more than once a week.

A random effects logistic regression, with controls for day of the week, shift worked (day, evening, or night), and whether the employee stayed at Berkman or left within the next two years, shows that people of color were more likely than whites to pick up shifts and that mothers were more likely than nonmothers to do so; once race and motherhood are in the equation, however, there is no longer a statistically significant relationship with occupation, that is, with whether someone is a nurse or nursing assistant. These findings pose serious challenges to the arguments of conservatives who suggest that low-wage workers are uncommitted, unmotivated, or even lazy and that it is flaws in their character that produce their low incomes.[28] The quantitative data from the Berkman nursing home show that nursing assistants, mothers, and people of color are *not* more likely to fail to work on a regularly scheduled day. They are more likely to need a day off with little advance notice—for their own illness or that of a child or for various other kinds of emergencies—but they make up these days off by taking fewer extended vacations; as a result, they work as scheduled as often as nurses, whites, and nonmothers do. When it comes to voluntarily picking up extra shifts, it is whites who, it could be said, do not "show a work ethic."

MAKING SENSE OF CHURNING

Churning is pervasive. Some qualifications and objections can be made to the basic Berkman statistics—it is only one nursing home, the figures include per diem and agency employees as well as vacations—but these data accurately summarize the problem that employers face in staffing and underscore the "weapons of the weak," that is, the extent to which ordinary workers are unwilling or unable to be tied to a rigid schedule.[29] Most of the literature on work and work hours either neglects churning or ghettoizes one piece of it to a study of temp agencies or only low-wage jobs. Although we have precise quantitative data only for the Berkman nursing home, we find unpredictability and churning to be pervasive at other employers as well. Overall, the survey data, limited quantitative data from two hospitals, and the interview data all provide reason to believe that schedule churning is widespread in other organizations and occupations and is likely to be so in many other parts of the economy. Moreover, the Berkman nursing home never sent employees home because of fluctuations in the census of patients; in many hospitals a major source of churning is employers canceling shifts. If we neglect the problem of schedule churning, we fail to provide a sense of the juggling act required to remain employed and still have a life outside of one's job.

It is time-consuming and difficult enough to create systematic data on unpredictability and churning even when an employer keeps such records, but sometimes no records are kept of exactly what is of most interest for these issues. We thought we were going to get the same kind of churning data on emergency room doctors; we did receive the schedule, but it provided no useful information. The scheduler explained that the schedule for July 31 and thereafter was set by June 20. We asked about changes made between June 20 and July 31. The answer was that no record was kept of such changes, which were rare, since people had the schedules they wanted. One doctor had forgotten his daughter's graduation,[30] and one's father had died; each of them arranged a switch with a colleague, but why keep a record of it? Similarly, when EMTs switched schedules to cover an hour or two, they often did so informally and kept no official record. The silence, the absence of a record, was perhaps the most telling indicator that these groups were not tightly and aggressively supervised.[31]

For the analysis here, since we define churning as any variation from the official basic schedule set out in advance, it could be argued that much of the churning at Berkman was a function of its schedule being set a year in advance. (The other nursing home we studied also set its schedule a year in advance, as did the fire station.) If the nursing home had announced its schedule a month ahead of time, or a week ahead of time, or a day ahead of time, there would have been less variation from the schedule set out in advance, but these shorter time frames might have made people's lives even more uncertain. At workplaces where schedules are posted only days ahead of time (which typically happens only for highly vulnerable low-wage workers), people are eager to have schedules set further in advance. Lambert reports that for the low-wage workers she studied, only three of the seventeen corporations posted schedules more than a week in advance.[32] Henly, Schaefer, and Waxman report that "there is a flurry of activity on the day schedules are posted" as workers try to learn their schedule "so that they can arrange or re-arrange child care and other family activities for the upcoming week."[33] Lambert, Haley-Lock, and Henly suggest that "one possibility for improving scheduling practices in low-level hourly jobs is to post schedules further in advance and to limit changes thereafter."[34] They report that "several public policy organizations, including The Center for Law and Social Policy (CLASP), Center for Work-Life Law, DEMOS, Workplace Flexibility 2010, and Women Employed, have recently made schedule predictability a core element of their policy recommendations," but elsewhere Lambert also notes the limits of voluntary employer action.[35]

If schedule instability is to be studied across a range of places, perhaps we need to refine our definition of churning to take into account the fact that workplaces vary dramatically in how far in advance they set their schedules.

Who Has the Power?

If unpredictability and schedule churning are so significant, what are we to make of them? When we have presented our findings, we are commonly asked, "Does churning serve managers' interests or workers' interests?" The simple answer: it serves both. But both the question and the answer are too simple.

Employers, it could reasonably be said, have the power, above all because of the wage system and people's need to work to earn a living. Karl Marx referred to the double freedom of the wage worker: free to work for whatever employer they choose, but also "free" of any means of support other than their wage and thus constrained to work for some employer.[36] The nursing assistants we studied felt that they had a choice, and almost without exception they felt an urgent need for more income; to a lesser extent the same was true of the EMTs and of some (although by no means all) nurses. Doctors too were clear that they worked the hours they did to earn the income they and their families had come to expect. Moreover, workers cannot pick and choose which additional shift to work; they have to take what management makes available, and the additional shift may be on an unfamiliar unit or at an inconvenient time. It may require that the worker arrange child care at a moment's notice. And then everything else about the worker's life must take second place to the job: any plans or social arrangements must be dropped if a shift becomes available. In these circumstances, to say that a worker has choice, power, and flexibility makes sense only understood as very limited choice within a system controlled by others.

But the flip side is also true: workers have gained a significant degree of leverage and have fought to preserve it. Through two centuries of struggle, workers have won and institutionalized the right to vacations and sick days (although, as chapter 7 will show, the use of a paid sick day may be penalized).[37] Some workers have won and regularized the right to switch schedules with other workers for a day or more. Workers in the 1930s won the right to time-and-a-half pay for overtime, even if they did not win the right to a minimum number of hours. Employers would find it simpler if they could require workers to stay on the job—and do so to a limited degree with EMTs—but many employers have found that if they make significant use of mandatory overtime they are unable to attract and retain top-quality employees. In practice, therefore, when a hospital or nursing home needs a shift filled, workers have and use leverage.

Nursing assistants reported that managers often begged them to work: "They'll call the unit and they'll say, 'Oh please, please, can somebody work?'" A Berkman nursing home scheduler reported that in order to fill holes in the schedule, she went around the floors and "begged" people to take the vacant shifts. "That's what I do. I go around, beg, say, 'Please can you work this weekend?'" Begging led to negotiations in which she often gave workers control over their future schedules. Asked if she ever cut deals with workers, she replied:

All the time! All the time. That's part of scheduling—you cut deals. I may say, "If you can work for me this day, I can give you this day off." Sometimes, you know, like, if they needed a day off and they weren't able to get that day off, and I know that they really need that day, I may say, "You know what, if you work this day, I'll give you that day off," and I'll find the replacement for them.

The Lucas Estates scheduler reported doing something similar when she desperately needed a nurse to fill a shift on the nursing home's most skilled unit:

I didn't have anybody to replace on Skylark, which is your rehab unit, which is . . . you need two three-to-eleven nurses. So I made a deal. I called one of the nurses that works down there regularly and asked her if she could work. She said no. I said, "Listen—I'll give you whatever you want. I'll give you a weekend off." So she did—she picked a weekend off. And I put her on the schedule. It was a Friday night, I'm sure she had plans with her husband. She canceled those plans and came in for us. So, you know, she did us a favor, we did her a favor back. And both were happy! (*laughs*)

These arrangements have a cascade effect; in a web of time, solving today's crisis creates next week's churning. Workers can use their leverage to gain (limited) control of (a small part of) their schedule—in this case winning a weekend off in exchange for being willing to work an unanticipated day.

Efforts to control the schedule are very important both to employers and to employees. Workers fight hard to win a measure of control within a system designed and dominated by employers. Although workers (usually) think about the issue of control in limited terms focused on specific decisions, often family-oriented ("I want to be at my daughter's soccer game," or "I need to take care of my son"), this jockeying for at least some control over their schedule has many of the elements of class struggle that Marx identified in his chapter on "The Working Day," what he called "a protracted civil war, more or less dissembled."[38] Total hours are important, but often the ability to control the work schedule is even more important, and workers will win at least skirmishes in this war, frequently by relying on one another, even if they sometimes do so at a considerable cost. Usually, however, workers pay only a modest cost for winning a temporary and limited instance of schedule control, since past struggles have institutionalized a culture that permits such control as well as structural mechanisms that enable it (whether in the law, the development of alternative occupations, or union contracts).

In the United States today most workers do not belong to a union. But the struggles between employers and unionized workers often provide a window into the issues that concern many other workers, even those with no way to engage in collective action. We see that here when a small local hospital with unionized nurses was taken over by a much larger non-union hospital. Two issues, both about unpredictability, stood out above all others in the contract negotiations. Management's intransigent line and nurses' unwillingness to capitulate led to a strike.

One issue was overtime pay: under the preexisting contract, if a twenty-four- or thirty-two-hour-a-week nurse agreed to stay past the end of her shift, she received overtime pay for the extra hours, even if her total for the week was less than forty hours; management wanted to eliminate this.[39] Second, management wanted to impose on nurses a variant of the Berkman "it's always your fault" sick leave policy for CNAs, the policy that said that an employee incurred a penalty anytime she missed work, for whatever reason, even if she had many unused sick days. The central issue of the struggle was how to respond to common unpredictability in schedules and the degree to which the employer could either reward employees for agreeing to do extra or penalize employees for not doing all that the official basic schedule required. The hospital was seeking to strengthen its control and impose harsher rules. Employees fought back because they wanted to maintain some freedom and power to respond to the normal unpredictability in their lives without paying harsh penalties when they did so.

Chapter 6 | Adding Time to the Official Schedule

Everybody talks about adding time to their official basic schedules—women and men, advantaged workers and disadvantaged workers—but workers have very different motives for wanting to add time, and they encounter very different responses from employers and the state. The issues associated with adding time play out as struggles over control, albeit struggles that are unequally shaped, fought, and won.

The addition of time to official schedules is a pervasive feature of the unpredictability of time and highlights the web of time: the hours and schedules people actually work are not the result of a set of isolated individual decisions or struggles, but rather are interconnected. Many researchers have shown that individuals decide to add (or cancel) shifts on the basis of their personal lives, especially their family situations. By looking at organizations and relations among workers within and across occupations, we show that these decisions cascade to alter choices and organizational requirements for other workers, affecting what happens in their families. People decide to stay late out of a concern for their patients (especially doctors) or their coworkers on the next shift (especially nurses); some of these decisions (especially doctors' decisions) then require that other staff stay as well. Decisions by per diem workers, who supposedly are at the bottom of the pecking order, lead institutions to cancel shifts for full-time regular CNAs. Such effects are missed in studies that simply aggregate individual responses and lack a view of the connections between workers and organizational contexts that shape the schedules of those within single occupations and across different occupations.

At the same time, when it comes to adding time to the official schedule, people usually have at least some choice, subject to the constraint of feeling a need for more money. In most cases, employers cannot compel employees to stay beyond their scheduled time if employees want to leave.

108

The exception is mandatory overtime, but that policy was rare for the nurses and nursing assistants in our study, and by no means routine for the EMTs. Paradoxically, doctors, who have the most control over setting their official schedule and almost never face "mandatory" overtime, probably feel least able to control the decision to add extra time.

Economic calculation influences both the ways in which workers supplement their official schedule and their reasons for doing it. It does so in two ways, but there is one surprising way it exerts less of an effect than we might expect: the employers in our study made little effort to avoid paying health care benefits. We expected employers to hire part-time workers to avoid paying benefits, and we expected workers to make decisions based on the need to have enough hours to protect their health care benefits. As far as we could tell, this issue was of minimal importance: our hospitals and nursing homes gave health care benefits to part-time employees (except per diems), and although the private-sector EMT companies required a forty-hour week to get benefits, EMTs routinely worked that much or more.[1]

Two particular economic calculations do, however, shape the issue of adding time. The amount of money people earn shapes how much and the ways in which they add time, as well as the control they have over that time, although not in a straightforward or linear fashion. Also important is the form of compensation people receive—in particular, whether they are paid by the hour. Being paid hourly changes how people think about time and money: research suggests that hourly wage work leads employees "to see time more like money, become more sensitive to the opportunity costs of their time and, therefore, prefer to trade more of their time for more money."[2] And as other research suggests, wage-earning men are more likely than wage-earning women to "prefer to trade their time for money."[3]

It is not just such personal preferences that distinguish hourly wage earners from those compensated in other ways. The 1938 Fair Labor Standards Act (FLSA) mandates a division between hourly and other workers; covered hourly wage earners must receive at least time and a half for time worked over forty hours in a workweek. Who is and is not covered, and whether private-sector workers should have the option of choosing paid time off instead of overtime wages, have been contested. But for now, as a result of the FLSA, time and money are tightly coupled for covered hourly workers and decoupled for those working under other payment systems, like salaries or partnerships.

Among the four occupations, only the doctors are legally exempt. Although health care organizations and nurses themselves debate whether they should switch to a salary rather than wage system, hourly wages still characterize the earnings of a large majority of staff nurses. This aligns them with the nursing assistants and EMTs, both of whom are paid an hourly wage. But the struggles around adding time play out in very different ways for these three occupational groups.[4] The most salient struggles over extra time occur in the occupational groups dominated by women. Some of this gender difference can be explained by the response of employers. Some can be explained by the position of unions. And some is rooted in men and women having a different sense of self and family responsibilities.

WORKING-CLASS EMPLOYEES ADDING TIME: THE EMERGENCY MEDICAL TECHNICIANS AND CERTIFIED NURSING ASSISTANTS

EMTs were the most enthusiastic of our four occupations about working overtime. Discussing overtime in a straightforward, instrumental way, they stressed the money they needed and wanted. And they often got it. There seemed to be little conflict, especially in the public sector, between the EMTs and their employers.

As one EMT explained, "We like the overtime. That's where we make all our money. We would die without our overtime." This was a common refrain among EMTs: "We choose to work a lot of overtime. It's good money." By and large, they were not deterred by institutional regulations, and they preferred companies that allowed it. A key advantage of one company, for instance, was that "there's as much overtime as we can possibly ever want." Conversely, one EMT explained the problem with his atypical employer: "There's not always the overtime here." Many EMTs loved the work, both the camaraderie with other EMTs and the opportunity to make a difference and (sometimes) save people's lives, but they emphasized that the chance to earn extra money was the reason they worked extra shifts:

> I don't turn down an overtime shift very often. Because I can't afford it. (*laughs*) Not because I just loooooove being here so much. The callback, I try to do them, you know, if I can, but like I said, you know, and it's—I hate it when I have something going on in five hours and I can't take a callback because of it. Because I'm thinking that's money I could be making, but I'm not.

Occasionally EMTs talked of working overtime as a decision driven by pressing financial constraints: "It's kind of hard to make do on a forty-hour job because we're not paid very well." But more often, EMTs did not talk about needing the money to get by; instead, they talked about overtime as a way to maintain the lifestyle to which their family had become accustomed. Emphasizing choice instead of constraint, one remarked: "I could be more careful about money and work less, but I choose to provide that. It's a good life at home, you know."

For nursing assistants—almost all women, and most of them women of color—there was more of a struggle and they were less able to exert control. On the one hand, the nursing assistants, like the EMTs, were hourly wage earners, and adding extra shifts loomed large in the consciousness of many of them, with money the main reason to work extra shifts. (They did occasionally also mention a desire to help out coworkers or help particular nursing home residents as a reason to add on hours.) Like the EMTs in our study, the nursing assistants were clear about why they worked extra time. As one put it, "We all work for the same reason—we all want the money." Another simply said: "Why do we work the hours we do? Poor, that's all there is to it. Just poor." In a group interview with three nursing assistants, the point was so obvious as to be a source of laughter (at the silly interviewer who would ask such questions):

INTERVIEWER: So why do you pick up the overtime?

RESPONDENT: Because we need the money. (*general laughter*) Because after forty hours you get time and a half, and we need the money.

INTERVIEWER: I know it's obvious, but that's the reason?

RESPONDENT: Right—that's the only reason. (*laughter*)

Somewhat paradoxically, the CNAs, like the EMTs, also worked extra hours not for the big financial reward but because their regular jobs didn't pay well: "The pay sucks. So I need the money. The pay is not good there. That's why I do it."

The CNAs differed from the EMTs, on the other hand, in talking about working additional shifts as a way, not to make "extra" money, but to get by—to pay rent, buy food, pay gas bills: "Sometimes you get behind with the bills, and you want to catch up with it, so you do overtime," and, "Like, if I know I've got a bill coming up and I know that the paycheck I'm getting today won't cover it, so I pick up that extra shift."

Family demands shape CNAs' need and preference for overtime. The scheduler at Lucas Estates described those who worked multiple overtime shifts, putting in sixty to seventy hours a week:

One-income houses. Yup. And they have no choice but to work these hours. It's not that they're not with somebody—the person they're with is not working. And it's hard. And I see their faces when I don't have the overtime. Or when I make them take the day off. "No, I'm workin'. I'll work straight through." I say, "You can't. You're gonna hurt yourself, burn yourself out. You can't." You know. And they don't like that sometimes, because they say . . . "My husband's not working." "My boyfriend's in trouble with the law." "I need the extra money." And I understand. I sympathize. Those will be the last ones that I would cancel.

At Lucas, the mega-overtime nursing assistants tended to be married but with out-of-work husbands; at Berkman they tended to be single mothers.

Even if many nursing assistants add extra hours and shifts, however, they often cannot get overtime pay. Organizations have developed strategies to prevent that. In recent years Berkman had offered nursing assistants only twenty-four- or thirty-two-hour-a-week positions—a pattern characteristic of low-wage workers in the service economy, for whom weekly hours have dropped slowly over time; as Annette Bernhardt, Laura Dresser, and Erin Hatton suggest: "Closely related to lean staffing is lean scheduling."[5] If such workers pick up an additional shift, employers need not offer them any overtime pay. One CNA explained that newly hired workers' official schedules were "always thirty-two, because they [management] don't want to pay overtime. I mean, overtime won't be if you make forty hours, overtime will be if you make more than forty hours. They're pretty smart." Not surprisingly, these lean-scheduled CNAs often wanted—or needed—more hours. In our survey, nursing assistants were the only occupation in which the number of people wanting more hours outnumbered the number wanting fewer hours. This need for additional hours contributed not only to stress and conflict but also to unpredictable scheduling—the kind of flexibility that employers seek and employees deplore. Our CNAs had a choice about whether to pick up additional shifts, but that choice was constrained by economic necessity; many felt compelled to pick up shifts if possible. "Like if I was to only make thirty-two hours, I'll be short of money." To get by, they had to show the "flexibility" to pick up any available shift—without receiving the extra overtime pay they so sorely needed.

PROFESSIONALS WORKING OVERTIME: THE NURSES

Americans associate wages with the working class and salaries with professionals. By and large, that association is correct (and is assumed in the FLSA). But the women professionals in our study were different. Indeed, a key difference between nurses and doctors is that most hospital and nursing home staff nurses are paid wages on an hourly basis instead of a salary. In our study, two nurse-midwives worked on salary. They sounded a lot like doctors. One nurse-midwife explained that on her days in the office she started at 8:30 AM. "I theoretically work till 5:00, but the truth is, I work till all the patients are seen and all the charting's done and all the phone calls have been returned." A nurse-midwife, like a nurse-practitioner, is similar to a doctor, not only because she is on salary, but also because she has the authority to determine how late she stays and she does not leave until patients are taken care of.

In contrast to those who earn a salary, for hourly workers money and time are tightly coupled, and that is true even for professionals like nurses who are paid an hourly wage. That coupling shapes their individual responses to the issue of adding time, as well as the organizational responses they encounter. Given their advantaged position, it comes as something of a surprise that the nurses in our study, like their working-class women counterparts, also engaged in considerable struggle over staying on the job for extra time, and they too often lost that struggle to their employer. But the reasons why nurses lost the struggle and the forms their loss took were different than for the CNAs.

Adding time for nurses often takes the form of remaining after a shift ends rather than adding a shift. Staying late frequently becomes a key source of tension between nurses and their supervisors: sometimes staying late results in overtime pay, but sometimes it means working for nothing.[6]

To most nurses, it is obvious that they should be responsible for finishing up the work from their shift on a regular basis, rather than passing it to the next shift; they want to make sure the nurse relieving them is aware of the situation for each patient. One hospital nurse explained:

> When nurses stay over, they're usually in the middle of something and they have to then, at the end of a shift, spend fifteen to twenty minutes turning over the patient and turning over the information—that's an essential part of the job, to give all the information to the next oncoming staff person. . . . You can't just leave the person there and say, "Guess what's going on there. (*laughs*) See if you can figure it out!" I would say that's a given everywhere—people stay.

Administrators try to restrict this practice. One administrator who was herself a nurse a couple of steps up in the hierarchy expressed indignation over staff nurses "wasting" time:

> I'm really getting annoyed with overtime. . . . If you have a system of documentation that allows you to put something somewhere, you don't have to put it again somewhere else, and that's what nurses do. They double-document. They create more work for themselves instead of just using a succinct tool to document blood pressure and pulse. They'll also write it in a narrative note. . . . Notes this long (*gestures*) that say, "He was peacefully sleeping." You're gonna take time to write "peacefully"? I was goin' nuts.

This administrator was aware that nurses often stayed extra time because they were caught in a web of commitments to both patients and coworkers that obligated them to do so:

> Nurses also feel that, if they haven't done everything they think they should've done for a patient, that they have to stay and do it because number one, they haven't done their job if they don't and somebody's gonna be pissed off because they've now dumped their work from their shift onto the next shift.

But she went on, exclaiming:

> Oh. Oh my God, I can't even tell you. This is age-old. So I'm starting to say to them, "Two minutes [per patient] to give report. I don't care how sick the patient is. I can give you a report in two minutes, no matter how sick that patient is. Stop giving me information that I can't do anything with. Give me what I need to know about the patient, and you have fifteen minutes [total] to give report and you're out of here." I'm really getting . . . I'm not obnoxious, but I'm getting obnoxious. (*laughs*) I was listening to a report the other day, and I said, "Would you guys move it along? We can hold on the valuables checklist for now." The look I got was probably deserved, but I've had it (*gestures*) up to here.

A top nursing home administrator expressed a similar concern over what she called "creep time"—people punching out late. If a nurse stayed late because a patient had fallen, that was okay, but when someone regularly stayed late, "We have taken it deep into the disciplinary level."

To maintain managerial control, hospitals and nursing homes have rules specifying that if a nurse is going to stay beyond her official schedule, she needs to get approval or face a potential reprimand. Sometimes the nurse is required to notify her supervisor well in advance so that efforts can be made to help her leave on time. Some nurses regard this as no big deal, but others resent the process because it challenges their commitment and, as they see it, their judgment as professionals. One nurse who worked at the same hospital as the outraged administrator matched the administrator's outrage, objecting to a new rule requiring nurses to get permission to stay late. Claiming professional privilege and dedication, she said: "I found it very insulting, and I know a lot of the other nurses did. . . . I mean, they can do that with the other employees in the hospital, but they can't do it with the nurses." In fact, she even expected managerial support for these privileges. "I think that there won't be any discipline, really, because there's no nurses that just stay late to get overtime. It just doesn't happen." Another nurse pointed to a catch-22 in the system: staying late "is only approved overtime if you told your supervisor like an hour before the end of the shift that you were going to be running late," and at that point, she added with some chagrin, "of course, you don't know."

When supervisors *do* hassle nurses, the pressure works—sort of. The work still needs to get done—there is no good way around that—but many nurses respond by punching out, then working off the clock. The hospital avoids paying for the time; the nurse avoids reprimands. This is wage theft of the sort Ruth Milkman, Ana Gonzalez, and Victor Narro have found to be so common among low-wage workers.[7] One nurse explained the thinking behind clocking out and then staying after the shift ended. Nurses do that, she said in response to our question, "just so that you don't have to listen to 'em. So you don't have to listen to the Susans and Cathy [supervisors, two of them named Susan]."

Nurses, unlike CNAs, not only think that they should have a right to choose but also think—or at least try to convince themselves—that they actually do have a choice about adding hours. One nurse, in explaining why she routinely worked through her unpaid half-hour lunch break, insisted that she had a choice: "No. I never put in for overtime for lunch. That's my choice. (*laughs*) I know, it's a little stupid, right? But it's my choice." At the same time, she recognized that her schedule was the result of constraints over which she felt little control. Asked why she did not put in for overtime, she responded:

> Well, because I could choose to go to lunch, and I *should* choose to go to lunch, but if I choose not to, it's not the hospital's responsibility to pay me, you know what I mean? That's an abuse of overtime. I choose not to go; if I choose not to go, I'm not going to say now you owe me. No, they'd say "go to lunch" of course.

When reminded that her choice was in part a result of the work she did, she said, "I suppose, but it's also because I truly want to be there. I do. It's a sick thing to say, isn't it?" (*laughs*).[8] This nurse, like others, used a "rhetoric of choice" to reassure herself that she was a professional who controlled her time.

There are important legal ramifications to working off the clock. If an employer requires nurses to work off the clock, that employer is liable not only for all back pay but also for triple damages. In a large facility with a regular practice of changing the punch-in time, pressuring employees not to ask to be paid for skipped lunches, or having employees work for an hour after punching out at the end of the day, the liability could quickly reach many millions of dollars. From the nurse's point of view, the situation is even more serious. One nurse explained that if there were an emergency and the nurse were to help out, "they're off the clock and yet they're doing patient care, so if anything happens, they're screwed. They're not covered by any insurance or anything because technically they weren't there."

THE HIRING OF PER DIEMS

One of the key sources of conflict, for both nurses and CNAs, is the employer practice of hiring per diems—workers hired, as needed, on a daily basis. Per diems are central to the web of time: their family circumstances determine when they can and cannot work, and their work choices affect the schedules of regular employees, who then struggle with employers who alter their schedules. Although national data are not available on CNAs, national data on nurses indicate that 4.7 percent of hospital nurses and 3.3 percent of nursing home nurses work per diem.[9] Some EMTs work on a basis that would be called "per diem" for CNAs or nurses, but for them it is framed as part-time employment, usually at a second job (which we discuss in a later section).

Managers are clear that hiring per diems for nurses and CNAs is an institutional strategy to fill holes left by regular staff and to reduce their overtime. Schedulers reported that their first priority is to use a per diem worker, the next priority is to use a twenty-four- or thirty-two-hour-a-week worker who will not receive overtime, and the last choice is to use regular staff who will receive overtime pay.[10] One scheduler stated the organizational rules simply: "Always use your per diem first." Administrators explicitly articulated such staffing practices as organizational rules, and staff were well aware of them.

The specifics of per diem hiring vary from one organization to another, but in general per diem workers are hired on an as-needed basis, do not have a fixed schedule but instead choose or are given (though they can refuse) their slots from among the openings in the schedule, are often required to work a minimum number of days per month but not specific times, and receive a slightly higher rate of pay but do not get any benefits (and thus in practice are the workers who cost employers the least). They work per diem by their own "choice" or within constraints imposed by their families and the jobs made available to them. Some per diem workers, especially nurses, have children and a spouse with health care benefits; the children make them reluctant to commit to a fixed schedule, and the spouse's health care benefits enable them to work limited hours. Others, in all occupations, have a full-time job and work per diem as a second job at another location. While per diems do not have to work prearranged regular schedules and are not formally penalized for calling out (which was a particular draw for the often penalized CNAs), they cannot be sure that they will get a particular shift, do not know in advance which floor they will be assigned to, and are typically not allowed to swap with other regular workers because "it's just not allowed." Explaining her schedule, one nursing assistant said: "I guess because I'm per diem, I have a lot of choice. Well, no, let me rephrase that. I can always say no, but they don't always need me on the days I'm available."

These staffing practices create a divide between regular and per diem staff. A scheduler told us what she said to the regular workers: "If a per diem picks up, I have to cancel you." She then explained: "They [regular staff] don't understand that concept [and think,] 'I was there first', [but] it goes by I have to slide in a per diem. You're overtime—I cancel your overtime. . . . I have to go to them that day sometimes and say I have to cancel your second half. And they don't like that."

At one heated hospital scheduling meeting that included both CNAs and nurses, the regular staff complained about the system in which per diems were getting their choice of days. Angrily, they said that the practice was unfair to regular staff. They expressed their resentment over per diems taking scheduled slots, depriving the regular workers of extra hours and overtime pay that they might choose (as in the case of nurses) or might need just to get by (as in the case of CNAs). The nurse manager tried to placate the staff, saying that the hospital would exert more control over per diems:

> We need to change it, and we will. We used to use them [per diems] in dire straits. Going forward, we will create a list of our holes and tell them [per diems] when they can work. We will no longer ask them when they want to work. That is not fair to our regular staff. We will call and say to per diems: "Here are the available days, when can you work?" Agreed?

There were numerous nods of assent from the regular nurses and nursing assistants attending the meeting. But several told us afterward that they had been promised this before and were not optimistic that the practice would actually change.

From the perspective of employers, per diem workers provide a nice buffer—they are obligated to work for the organization each month to fill holes in the schedule, and since they do not receive benefits, they are the lowest-cost workers. Managers develop practices to keep them—such as asking them when they want to work rather than telling them when they can work. Employers take the legal construction of overtime seriously but respond by developing systems that deprive their hourly employees of overtime. Those systems, in turn, create divisions and conflict among workers as well as between regular staff and management.

MANDATORY OVERTIME

One of the places where we expected to find the most conflict was over forced or mandatory overtime. Suzanne Gordon, a well-known journalist and author of numerous books on nurses, captures this position well:

> Every year, hospitals around the country observe "Nurses' Week," a national celebration. . . . Many registered nurses find themselves at catered lunches, listening to flowery speeches by hospital CEOs. . . . While the reality of deteriorating conditions awaits them back in the war zone of their hospital wards, overworked nurses can briefly enjoy free manicures and massages. . . . What's rarely addressed during Nurses' Week, however, are the workplace issues that are driving RNs away from the hospital bedside in huge numbers: of under-staffing, *forced overtime* and job dissatisfaction.[11]

According to national data for all occupations, 21 percent of full-timers work extra hours mandated by the employer; this is more common among men than women.[12] A gender divide in mandatory overtime can be found among the three groups of hourly wage earners in our study.

While all sometimes encountered mandatory overtime, EMTs—far more than nurses or nursing assistants—faced a significant amount. Although they objected to mandatory overtime, the EMTs—like working-class males in national surveys—were not nearly as upset by it as the women wage earners.[13] By far the most common form of mandatory overtime for these men are holdovers when an ambulance call is ongoing and the EMT stays until it is completed. An EMT might also be mandated to stay if the incoming shift was short one or more workers. In the fire service, such a mandate covered half a shift (five hours for a day shift, seven hours for a night shift), with the following crew mandated to bring someone on half a shift early. Although such mandates could make life difficult, coworkers provided some protection against being held over in this way. "If guys have got to be out of here at a certain time—'I've gotta be out at 6:00 today, Cap, because I've got something planned'—what we'll do is sometimes shuffle people around, so that they're not stuck in a situation where they might have to get held over." But in both the public and private sectors, mandatory overtime for these working-class men was significantly higher than for the two groups of women.

CNAs are rarely mandated to stay overtime. None of the nursing homes we observed used mandatory overtime except in highly unusual cases—typically snowstorms when management required staff to stay at work. The nursing homes did not need to use mandatory overtime because so many of their CNAs were now hired for twenty-four to thirty-two hours and were desperate to get extra hours.

According to the National Sample Survey of Registered Nurses, only 3.4 percent of employed nurses say they work mandatory overtime in a typical week.[14] Those who do work mandatory overtime are more likely to work in nursing homes, where fewer nurses work, than in hospitals, where nurses predominate.[15] Some locations make significant use of mandatory overtime, but management at the two hospitals and two nursing homes we observed made almost no use of mandatory overtime, despite the routine need for nurses to stay late. That is, the employers did not tell the employees to stay extra time; instead, as we have seen, they discouraged it. In interviews, we did ask about mandatory overtime, and people often wanted to talk about the difficulties they knew it imposed. That they occasionally experienced it, or their friends did, was a serious issue to them. But with two exceptions—and neither of them from the hospitals we observed—mandatory overtime was a minimal fraction of total nursing shifts. An emergency department administrator at Outercity told us, "I've done it [mandated overtime] once in eight years"; that was on a late night when "we had fourteen level-one traumas in four hours." She quickly added, "We wouldn't normally mandate people to stay. People offer to stay because they see the next shift coming on and they know how badly they're going to be hurting, so they'll say, 'I'll stay for a few hours.'"

As we have seen, much overtime is voluntary (although the divide between voluntary and mandatory is a bit slippery). Instead of mandating overtime, hospitals in a crisis use bonuses as an incentive to sway nurses to stay extra hours and shifts. At Outercity, for example, the bonus rate was $50 for each four hours. As an administrator noted, if a nurse who made $38 an hour agreed to do a twelve-hour overtime shift, with a bonus she would earn $57 an hour, plus $150, for a total of $834 for the twelve-hour shift, or $70 an hour. Two different administrators mentioned that they sometimes had to get a nursing shift filled by giving a double bonus (that is, paying an extra $100 for each four hours); one said that this happened "maybe once every three to six months." For the relatively advantaged employees eligible for these bonuses, organizations were paying significant sums to "incentivize" extra hours rather than mandate them.

THE VARIED PROTECTION OF UNION CONTRACTS

Although all three of our hourly wage groups worked extra hours, we have seen that they had different ways of confronting institutional regulations, responding to them, and exerting power to control them. Our analysis of the union contracts for these three groups of workers provides some more insight into these distinctive patterns of response and control. Union contracts are the product of struggles between workers and employers, and they indicate the points of stress, negotiation, and compromise that developed out of those struggles. Analysis of 105 contracts shows significant variation by both class and gender in the space that contracts devote to overtime and in the relative emphasis each occupation puts on one or another aspect of overtime.[16]

The contracts for all three occupations discuss the issue of overtime at some length. Moreover, overtime *pay* is the most prominent contract issue for all of the occupations, and there are no significant differences among the three in the amount of space devoted to it. This suggests that money is the key aspect of overtime for all of three occupations. But there are telling differences among them—differences that speak not only to gender but also to class struggles around time.[17]

Nurses' contracts, significantly more than those covering EMTs and CNAs, focus on ways to limit and avoid mandatory overtime. A nurses' contract typically stipulates that a committee be set up to monitor management to ensure that an organization lives up to its contractual commitments to avoid mandatory overtime. Moreover, if no nurse can be persuaded by management or coworkers to "volunteer" for mandatory overtime, the contract often says that mandatory overtime should be distributed among nurses in *inverse* order of seniority. Nurses dislike mandatory overtime, and unionized nurses use their leverage to restrict it. Their dislike may well originate in the gendered character of home life: the fact that they use their advantage to restrict mandatory overtime, and the irregularity it so often entails, more than the other two groups do may stem from their feeling that "they need to be home at a regular time to give care."[18]

By contrast, EMT contracts, reflecting the desire of most EMTs to work overtime, focus on the *right* to overtime by guaranteeing everyone an equal chance to do it. These contracts often stipulate that the most senior worker be given the right of first refusal—suggesting that EMTs seek and desire overtime work. One EMT contract, using a typical phrasing, emphasizes that right: "Any employee not receiving an overtime shift shall be placed first for overtime assignments for the following week." A union officer, asked about filed grievances, said, "The only thing that anyone bitches or complains about is—I got skipped on the overtime list." Just as nurses' resistance to overtime is probably tied to their responsibilities at home, so too the firefighters' push for overtime is likely tied to their need for income and their breadwinning role.

An analysis of CNAs' union contracts suggests the ways in which class and gender intersect. On the one hand, their contracts devote considerable space—about as much as in EMTs' contracts and significantly more than in nurses' contracts—to the right of access to overtime, an initial indication of class trumping gender. Nursing assistants need the money to support their families. On the other hand, their contracts provide neither the mandatory overtime protection that nurses (often) win nor the breadwinner boost to pay that EMT contracts (almost always) win. The nursing assistant contracts stand out in two other ways. First, they devote a great deal of space to provisions detailing the employer's right to avoid paying overtime. These provisions generally stipulate that no overtime can be worked without prior managerial approval and affirm the employer's right to give priority to a worker who could pick up a shift without accruing overtime. One such provision reads: "Overtime shall be offered on an equitable basis in rotating seniority order, except that management may elect to offer time to Employees who are able to work straight time before offering it to Employees who would earn overtime as a consequence." Second, indicating the limited power of nursing assistants, almost none (5 percent) of the CNA contracts discuss pay minimums for overtime (in comparison to 97 percent of EMT contracts and 74 percent of nursing contracts). Even in those limited cases where nursing assistants are unionized, employers insist that the contract emphasize management's power and its ability to limit extra pay to nursing assistants.

In one set of contract negotiations, nursing assistants encountered just this problem. A set of nursing homes were moving away from a norm of forty-hour-a-week schedules. Management had recently ended the routine forty-hour week and reduced workers' officially scheduled hours to twenty-four or thirty-two per week; that is, this unionized nursing home was moving to the situation that prevailed at the non-union nursing homes we observed. (The union filed a grievance, claiming that this was a violation of the contract; the case went to arbitration, and the arbitrator ruled in favor of management.) The lawyer for the management side insisted, "It's just not possible to have all forty-hour positions," and said that the new twenty-four- or thirty-two-hour schedule would reduce the use of overtime. More than one hundred union members attended the negotiations, and many yelled out in anger, "You turned people's lives upside down." One member said, and a dozen echoed, "You've moved us all to be twenty-four and thirty-two, but *every week* [*said emphatically, with strong emotion*] I make forty hours." Seemingly the great majority of members were still working forty hours, but with no predictability to their schedules. The members were prepared to strike over the issue, insisting that there were no circumstances under which they would agree to this arrangement.[19]

We see, then, both the ways in which CNAs are less protected by their contracts and, in this instance, their willingness to fight back to gain some right to forty-hour jobs and the control over overtime those jobs entail.

MALE PROFESSIONALS ADDING TIME: THE DOCTORS

Doctors look different from any of the other three groups. They are "exempt" workers, not covered by the Fair Labor Standards Act overtime provisions, whether they run a small business, are on straight salary, salary plus potential bonus or incentive add-ons (typical in health maintenance organizations, academic settings, and large corporate settings), or use a productivity-based compensation system (in which they are paid a percentage of all billings minus overhead costs).[20] The key distinction for doctors is between private practice physicians, whose earnings go up if they see more patients, and hospital-based physicians, who have little or no financial incentive to add time to their official schedule. Typically, a private practice physician has large fixed costs and may need to see about twenty patients a day to cover those costs. Beyond that point, the physician receives almost all of the revenue from additional patients; therefore, seeing thirty patients a day may bring in almost twice as much income as seeing twenty-five patients.

Although hospital physicians sometimes work an extra shift (rarely a double shift, however, except for interns and residents), by far the most common extra hours for physicians, both in and out of hospitals, come from arriving before the beginning of the workday or staying past its official end. An important reason cited by both private practitioners and hospitalists for this added time and the unpredictability it produces is patient need. A hospitalist noted: "We don't turn over on a very sick patient. . . . You're just expected to stay as long as it takes and you don't get paid any extra for doing so." The head of a group of hospitalists noted, however, that the unpredictability produced when a physician stays late to deal with a problem can have long-range negative consequences that doctors might not recognize:

> One of my frustrations, actually, is that I know that people will burn out by staying longer hours [to get to a completion point on a patient], and I need them to leave, so that they are enthusiastic about coming back again the next morning. And if they stayed way too late the night before, they won't be, and that's a challenge. I actually have to boot people out—it's tough.

For these hospital doctors, individual pay was clearly decoupled from the time they invested in patients.

In private practice, the extra time doctors put in is often not when they are seeing patients but when they are finishing the work associated with those patients. One doctor, pointing to the stack of papers on the table in his office, explained why he always left work late:

> At the end of the day, you know, I'm trying to finish the dictations, and I get all my dictations done and then I turn around and oh, there's a stack of things, and I don't want to leave them till tomorrow. . . . The ones that are prioritized, that say, "I'm out of my meds today," we usually take care of pretty quickly, and the others can usually wait until the next day. But then you've got patients calling in and want[ing] a call back, and you're trying to get to those, and then there's always a stack of labs that people need to be called, and the high-priority ones, the real worrisome ones, obviously those we take care of quickly. But, you know, almost every lab that comes back comes back with kind of a semi-abnormality.

Both hospital and private practice physicians talked about adding time for such work (and understating it) by saying, "If I'm working till five, I'd say I leave anywhere probably between six and seven."[21]

We might expect the private practice doctors to talk about controlling this extra time. In some sense they do: they can stay late or they can come early. They can do paperwork and much of their computer work at home or they can do it in the office. And they could control these actions far more than any of the other occupational groups, even if they did so at some financial cost. But that was not the primary way doctors talked about it. Many instead insisted that they could not plan their schedules because of the additional hours they "needed" to work. And they seemed routinely surprised by their inability to do so. Over and over, we had an exchange like this one:

INTERVIEWER: Is there usually much advance warning if you have to stay late?

RESPONDENT: No, no. Staying late is unpredictable, particularly when you're on call.

INTERVIEWER: How often do you usually end up staying later than you anticipate?

RESPONDENT: Every day, according to my family. (*laughs*)

Note that he said both that he worked late "every day" and that doing so was "unpredictable."

Paradoxically, in private practice, being paid by the number of patients rather than by the hour seems to reduce doctors' sense that they can predict—or control—that extra time. To be sure, they can decide to reduce the quality of care, and they do make decisions to spend less time with each patient. But often they make a decision that adds rather than reduces the time they spend working—they decide to increase the number of patients they see. Unless they are solo practitioners (of which there are fewer and fewer), they make these decisions on their own and in collaboration with the other doctors in their practice. Though physicians make these decisions, they can still be left feeling unsure about how long they have to stay at work. One private practice physician made an arrangement to play tennis with a friend every Tuesday an hour after the official end of the workday, but said: "That's been a joke. We've just never made it on time." Playing the joke on themselves, doctors manage to continue seeing these additional hours—or framing them for themselves, their families, and their peers—in terms of a taxing but unpredictable workload. They complain a lot about it. One doctor remarked, "We're supposed to be done at five, but we never are."

Doctors make a lot of money, and they want to continue to do so. (Recall that the average primary care practitioner—the lowest-paid of doctors—makes on average about eight times what an average nursing assistant earns.) At least for doctors in private practice, making more money may require that they come in early and stay late. But instead of talking about the money they make, these professionals, most of them men, make moral claims (to themselves and others) that they are dedicated and committed and therefore have no choice but to work such long hours.[22] Getting home late, they make those claims to their families. To be sure, they also make claims to privilege, like luxurious vacations and nice homes. But their struggles over extra time are essentially struggles with themselves (and sometimes with their families). As we have seen, this distin-

guishes these professionals, male doctors, from the other three occu[...]
tional groups.

SECOND JOBS: PREDICTABLE EXTRA HOURS

For primarily financial reasons, over seven million employees hold second jobs in the United States, and those who work in health and education have higher rates of multiple job holding than those in any other occupation.[23] The choice that workers make is often whether to work overtime or to take a second job. Overtime pays more per hour than a second job, but it is also more unpredictable.

On our survey, 17 percent of doctors and 22 percent of nurses reported some form of a second job. The second jobs for doctors were typically limited, however, and led to only a 9.4 percent increase in income for those who took these jobs. For nurses who worked second jobs—such as school nurses who worked at the summer camp attended by their kids—their pay increased by 17.1 percent. Nursing assistants were not much more likely than nurses to work second jobs, with 26 percent of nursing assistants doing so, but those jobs raised their incomes by 29.1 percent. Many of the nursing assistants who held second jobs worked not just a few extra hours but a second full-time job. As one nursing assistant who worked a second job explained quite simply, "I gotta pay my bills."[24]

EMTs were the standout second-job-holders among the four occupations. Although it was the exception in every other occupation, holding a second job was normative for the EMTs. On our survey, 62 percent of EMTs reported working a second job, more than double the rate for any other occupation. Interviews confirmed the survey findings: respondent estimates of the proportion of EMTs working a second job ranged from 50 to 80 percent, depending on the workplace.[25] Those who work a second job increase their income by 31.6 percent. Second jobs, then, are a routine aspect of EMT schedules.

One result of the large number of second-job-holders among the EMTs and the substantial increases in income for those with an extra job is to substantially raise average EMT incomes, bringing their total incomes close to those of nurses. We wondered why in our study the EMTs worked more hours than physicians, while other research has indicated that professionals work at their main job more hours than those who are less educated and skilled. The answer: second jobs. We wondered why the EMTs in our study made almost as much as our other professional group, the nurses. The answer: second jobs.

Not only do the majority of EMTs work a second job, but most work significant hours in those jobs. It is in working second jobs that EMTs gain some schedule control, which, as we have seen, they are much less likely to have in their regular jobs. They can decide whether to take second jobs. They often can decide when to work on the jobs they choose to take. We wondered why EMTs complained less about the unpredictability of their hours than did any other group. The answer: second jobs.

Bill, a private-sector EMT at Medic-Route, was one example of how EMTs sometimes load on the hours. On Wednesday, Thursday, and Friday he worked from 8:00 AM to midnight at Medic-Route. On Saturday and Sunday, he worked from 9:30 AM to 10:00 PM at Ride Heaven, a local amusement park. He tried to take off either Monday or Tuesday, working the other day at Ride Heaven, typically for fourteen hours or so. His total workweek came to eighty-seven hours. At Ride Heaven he tried to schedule himself only two weeks in advance, hoping that Medic-Route would know far in advance that it needed someone to work overtime; that way he could pick up the time-and-a-half overtime instead of working straight time at Ride Heaven. Bill had not always worked so many hours, but "right now," he said, "I'm in bill-pay mode." He had recently had medical problems that "racked up five grand in medical bills" and kept him from working for several weeks; during that time he had had no income.

Difficult as Bill's schedule was, he was not the person who logged the most hours. Melissa, a sixty-five-year-old African American nursing assistant, worked 104 hours a week, every week: she worked a full day shift at the nursing home, followed by a full evening shift at an assisted living facility. She worked that double shift, sixteen hours straight, six days a week; on Wednesdays she took the day shift off and worked only eight hours at the assisted living facility. Her husband, a truck driver, worked roughly as many hours as she did. They lived with her daughter (who told us that she worried about her mother's schedule) and grandchildren, so Melissa did not need to set aside time for laundry and housekeeping and meal preparation at home. Our guess is that she could work this schedule only because, as Melissa herself explained, the shift at the assisted living facility was less stressful. The residents at that facility "are not really sick; assisted living, they can do mostly everything for themselves. . . . You have time that you can walk them outside and sit out there and talk with them."

Typically, the second jobs of nursing assistants look different from those of EMTs. Nursing assistants' second jobs are often inflexible—the fixed-hours schedule of a second job can be as rigid as the schedule of the first job—whereas many EMTs pick up hours on their second jobs, scheduling themselves a week or two ahead of time, and can turn down hours in the second job if they want to work less. Thus, it is in overtime and second jobs that EMTs find control, while nursing assistants, even on second jobs, continue to have far less ability to control their time.

CONCLUSION

Adding time to the official schedule is sometimes planned long in advance, but it often arises unpredictably, whether at the last minute or a day or so ahead of time. Rarely, however, do we find that workers must add time. It is a choice, and as such they obtain some leverage in dealings with their employers, who have shifts that have to be filled *today* and thus are open to making deals with employees. The choice is shaped, of course, by economic constraints on both employees and employers, as well as by state regulation, the web of social relations on the job and at home, and cultural values—all of which vary by both gender and class.

On the one hand, the men in our study—both the EMTs and the doctors—worked the most "extra" time. The working-class men stated quite explicitly that they worked extra for the money: each hour added to their income. Many relished working this additional time that allowed them to purchase "extras" (a second car, a vacation trip) and, just as important, maintain their position as the primary breadwinner in their dual-earner families; for "old-school" EMTs, always being available for work was a sign of being a man. Although they had little control over their regular official schedule on their main job, on second jobs they were more likely to work per diem, with control over when they added time (as opposed to CNAs, whose second jobs were typically as inflexible as their first jobs). These men added a great deal of time to their official basic schedules, but as later chapters will show, they also shaped the additional hours around family activities and responsibilities.

The male doctors also worked a lot of extra time (though as we will see, they rarely shaped their hours around activities and responsibilities at home). But for doctors there seemed to be something of a paradox: male doctors controlled their official schedule, but decided that they had to extend their hours, and then they complained about it. Other researchers have noted this same paradox more generally for professionals, whether financial executives, academics, or lawyers. A number of social, economic, and psychological processes operate to coerce these professionals into that "choice." Not only do male doctors make a lot of money, but they come to believe that they need this money for themselves and their families and to attract other doctors to their practices. They travel in circles caught up in this "work and spend cycle" of status consumption.[26] Moreover, starting as interns and residents with 80-hour work weeks, they are socialized to work long hours.[27] Doctors also earn respect and honor from their peers and patients when they stay at work (or disrespect if they do not). As one physician described doctors, "The ones who work the most are looked up to. . . . You have to work harder; that gets respect. When you work more . . . that's a big badge." The male doctors in our study used cultural ideals of work and gender to collectively create organizational patterns that sustained their "badge" of masculinity. These patterns, along with the fact that typically they were their family's primary, even sole, breadwinner, made most of them choose to stay on the job for long hours, complain about it, and then make at least implicit claims about the virtue of their choices. Though they may have felt real pressure from patients who expected their personal attention, the struggle was in some sense internal. Or perhaps their choice to work long hours was sometimes also a way to do what they wanted (work the long hours that brought them rewards) while justifying their arduous schedule to their family as unavoidable and unanticipated.

In contrast, the two groups of women in our study struggled with their employers over extra time. Organizations developed strategies to get around paying overtime to them. Employers used per diem employees, an arrangement that created division among nurses. But the greatest source of contention was employer pressure on staff nurses *not* to put in additional hours *because* they worked for an hourly wage. The pressure often succeeded in its real goal—reducing the wages the employer paid—but did not do much to alter the time nurses actually worked; they just stayed for the extra time (though not as much as the doctors did) despite the fact that the hours were uncompensated. Nurses wanted to avoid mandatory overtime and often succeeded in prohibiting it in their union contracts, but often they voluntarily stayed at least a little while to finish the work on their shift. Although we might expect these advantaged female employees to use a cultural model of caregiving to explain working this additional time, they tended to explain their choices in terms of an obligation to help out coworkers on the next shift rather than in terms of an obligation to give care to particular patients (with whom, especially in hospitals with their shortened stays, nurses rarely developed much of a relationship). But whatever their rationale, these advantaged female professionals had to fight to give that extra time to their jobs.

For the other group of women, the nursing assistants, extra hours came primarily through working additional shifts (rather than adding on an hour or so at the end of the day, as the nurses did). Many chose to do double shifts, working sixteen hours straight. As one explained: "I work doubles so I don't have to work my days off. So I can see my kids, you know, at least sometimes. Because if I do just pick up every day off, I'm not really going to have much time for them." As a way to avoid paying time and a half for overtime for CNAs on the regular staff, employers hired per diems, who became central to the web of time: for example, the work schedule of a per diem's husband might end up determining whether the per diem picked up a shift and a full-time nursing assistant's overtime got canceled. In theory, the hours of regular workers are set first, and the remaining shifts then cascade down to the contingent workers; in practice, the per diem workers sometimes got first choice and the regular staff had to choose from the remaining options. This created divisions among nursing assistants.

Contestation over adding time was widespread. Employers, workers, and their unions wrangled over the state's definition of an "exempt" worker, that is, one who does not receive pay for overtime. EMTs fought to get and maximize their pay for extra hours. Doctors worked to earn more, gave what they thought was adequate care, and one-upped each other over who was most dedicated and hardworking. The struggles over scheduling were most apparent, however, in the two women-dominated occupations. Nurses and their supervisors had ongoing conflicts over staying past the official end of the workday, and nurses complained about working with agency nurses, who, they claimed, did not know what they were doing but got paid more than regular nurses. Probably the most common complaints we heard were from nursing assistants eager to get extra hours. Although their ability to choose whether to add time gave them some (minimal) leverage over their employers, it was a severely constrained choice and one that created significant unpredictability in their own lives. A thirty-two-hour-a-week nursing assistant earns a pretax $17,264 a year (including weekend bonus pay), which puts a single mother and her two children below the poverty line, making her feel that she must add hours whenever the employer makes them available, however disruptive to her own life.

This chapter has analyzed one side of churning: the processes that promote or deter extra work hours. In the next chapter, we turn to taking time off, the other side of churning. These two sides of churning—adding time worked and taking time off from work—are the components of normal unpredictability. But the effects of class and gender—and the ways they intersect—vary depending on which side of churning those organizations and employees create and confront.

Chapter 7 | Taking Time Off: Sick Leaves and Vacations

TIME OFF FROM WORK, whether for the pleasure of a vacation or the pain of an illness, is in some ways the defining example of normal unpredictability and a site of sharp inequality. The conditions under which people can take time off, or control their time off, are contested for every occupation.

CONTESTING WHAT IS NORMATIVE

The right to time off from work that many take for granted was contested and won for the most part in the last 150 years, with active skirmishing continuing today. Take the weekend. "The concept of the weekend, as we now understand it, didn't appear in the *Oxford English Dictionary* until 1879."[1] Moreover, "it wasn't until after World War I that the early [half-day] Saturday closing began to be common in America," spread by union insistence.[2] Henry Ford gave weekends a boost, and time off on Saturday and Sunday became even more common during the Great Depression, when efforts were made to spread the available work around. Thereafter, the weekend held sway at least until the twenty-first century; now it seems to be eroding. To this day issues of sick leave and vacations are central to union contracts, and are one of the first issues dealt with when workers organize.

Workers need to get these issues into a union contract, because, as with many other issues, U.S. law may prescribe some vague "duty of care" for patients but is notable in its lack of attention to any "duty of care" for workers. More than 60 percent of U.S. workers do get paid sick leave from their employers, on average about six days of it per year.[3] At the federal level, however, the United States does not guarantee paid (or, for that matter, unpaid) sick days.[4] Only one state—Connecticut—guarantees workers a legal right to *any* paid time off for themselves.[5] Most states make no

130

provisions for time off—not for vacations, not for public holidays, not for illness. A few U.S. cities provide workers with paid sick days for families, but only three states have guaranteed paid leaves to provide care for sick family members.[6] In the United States, only one piece of federal legislation provides (some) workers guaranteed time off: the Family and Medical Leave Act (FMLA), signed into law by President Bill Clinton in 1993 after an eight-year political struggle.[7] The FMLA guarantees covered workers twelve weeks of *unpaid* leave for the birth or adoption of a child and also provides that workers may take unpaid leave for their own qualifying medical condition or for the illness of a spouse, child, or parent. Leave for illness may be taken in one block (say, for a broken ankle) or intermittently a day or a few days at a time (say, for a child's seizures or asthma attacks).

The law is extremely useful to some workers but suffers from at least three significant limitations. First, only about half of the U.S. workforce is covered.[8] Second, the leave is unpaid, and a substantial number of workers cannot afford to take it except in dire circumstances. Other employees who use FMLA are paid for some or all of the time by using a combination of sick days and vacation time (which then is not available for other purposes). Third, whatever the law provides, in practice a substantial number of covered employers—by Amy Armenia, Naomi Gerstel, and Coady Wing's estimate, somewhere between one-quarter and one-half—do not fully obey the law.[9] A great many workers, moreover, have no awareness of their legal rights, or no ability to enforce them. These limitations, as we shall see, affected many of the workers we studied.

A worker in France, Germany, Italy, or much of the rest of Europe would be legally guaranteed not only paid sick days but paid vacations and holidays totaling five or six weeks.[10] There are no such legal mandates in the United States, although in practice the median U.S. worker receives ten days of paid vacation after one year on the job, fifteen days after five to ten years, and twenty days for those with twenty years at the same employer.[11] Not only do employees in the United States receive far less vacation time than workers in other countries, but they do not even take all the vacation time to which they are entitled. One survey found that the average respondent was entitled to 18.1 days of vacation but took only 13.4, leaving more than one-quarter of his or her vacation days unused.[12] The study also showed that those with incomes of $100,000 or more took almost twice as much vacation time as those with incomes of $50,000 or less.[13] In our study, we found much the same: the amount of vacation and, importantly, an employee's control over it are both shaped by the class and gender composition of occupations and organizations.

What the law provides and what happens in practice are not the same. Nevertheless, the creation in our laws of official categories for time spent away from work is a way of recognizing workers' (hard-fought) right to have at least limited release from the structure of the official schedule. And in recognizing that right, our laws also circumscribe it, set limits to it, and declare that even unpredictability must be bound by established rules. Meanwhile, in addition to efforts to enshrine rights in either laws or union contracts, employers and employees contest what happens in actual practice: how much time off there will be, and under what restrictions. The class and gender differences that manifest in this contestation are stark.

People have rights only to the extent that they are willing and able to avoid new restrictions and push to extend the boundaries of what they already have. EMTs have the clout to use their (paid) sick leave as additional vacation time; nursing assistants are vulnerable enough to need to use vacation days to cover illness. Sick leave is the most unpredictable kind of time off from work, hence the most troubling to employers, but employers try to restrict when employees can take *any* sort of time off. When a nurse indicated that she needed surgery, an administrator suggested that she wait and not have surgery until after the summer. More generally, although "sick leave" and "vacation" might seem quite different, the two categories overlap and blur, especially for the working-class occupations but to some degree for the professionals as well. This chapter therefore considers all time off together for each of the occupations.

PHYSICIANS

Sick Leave

Physicians stand out in two ways. First, their advantaged class position gives them by far the most control over their schedule, and this extends to time off as well as to hours worked. More than any of the other occupations we studied, a doctor who wants to take a day (or a week) off can do so without formal penalty, although there are variations depending on the doctor's organizational position (say, private practice versus hospital employee). Second, the advantaged gender position of male doctors combines with their class position to make it rarely, if ever, necessary to use their sick leave or vacation time to care for children or other family members. Related to this gender-class advantage, physicians have the sharpest contrast between sick time (which doctors take less often than any other occupation) and vacation time (which they take more often than any other occupation).

Doctors insist that they simply do not take sick days. When scheduled to work, the ethic is to work if at all possible. This obligation to work comes from group pressure and a sense of professionalism, not from accountability to a supervisor.

Some doctors had a hard time remembering when, or if, they took a sick day. Consider some of the responses to a question about sick leave:

- Sick days? Well, there aren't really sick days. (*What about sick days, if you're scheduled for a shift and you're not feeling well?*) You usually end up working it. You really have to be dying to not go to work.

- It's pretty rare that people call out sick. We have a very high threshold for calling out sick. (*Just how high is this threshold?*) I had pneumonia a number of years ago, and after I got on antibiotics I would see a patient, go into my office and lie down for a while, and see another patient and go into the office and lie down for a while.

- Well, I'm never sick enough to stay home. I honestly can't remember when I was sick enough to stay home. . . . About five months ago I fell and broke my pelvis. I was on vacation (*laughs*), so I had a whole week to recover. . . . I was on crutches. And I saw patients with my break, which was healing with no surgery, for three months, and then I had a cane for a month. I didn't take any time off, and I had my full schedule *and* my call schedule as though I hadn't broken my pelvis at all. But no, I can't remember the last time I called in sick.

Although most of the doctors we interviewed were men, the women doctors also had a very high threshold for taking time off—with two of them using their due date and labor as both reality and image to indicate that threshold:

- I operated all day and an hour after coming out of the OR [operating room] went into labor.

- I worked till my due date with both my children, with no time off beforehand. I never called in sick for either of my pregnancies. It's a very high standard.

Although the sanction for taking sick leave is "only" the possibility of losing the respect and support of colleagues and tarnishing one's sense of professionalism, clearly these forces operate to drastically reduce the use of sick leave among doctors. One explained: "If you call in sick, there's ten of us. You better be sick. And nobody calls in sick here." Doctors were reluctant to take sick leave wherever they worked, whether in ERs or private practices.

Male doctors differed from all the other groups, moreover, in a key way: with their stay-at-home spouses and ability to afford nannies (see chapter 9), their answers to questions about sick leave almost always focused on themselves. With every other occupation, answers focused at least as much on sick family members.

Vacations

Although doctors pressured each other not to take sick time and saw their willingness to work even when ill as a badge of their dedication, both to their patients and to fellow physicians, a completely different set of rules applied to vacations, which they expected and used extensively. Many saw little distinction between vacations per se and the continuing medical education (CME) needed to maintain their licenses, which might require them to attend a conference in Aspen during ski season:

> We get a fair amount of time off. It works out to somewhat on the order of nine to twelve weeks a year. . . . It's vacation and conferences. And we'll spend probably at least two weeks a year doing conferences. (*Have you ever not been able to take the vacation?*) No, I take that time, definitely, always.

Twelve weeks off was the top end, but four weeks was the bottom: "We have pretty good vacation time as a group. The shareholders, the people who were part of the group that [formed the initial practice], have six weeks of vacation and usually take six weeks of vacation. New people coming in have four weeks of vacation." One doctor who got four weeks of vacation and one week for continuing medical education gave a succinct answer to our question:

INTERVIEWER: Do you actually take all of your vacation time every year?

RESPONDENT: Yeah. Oh, I do—absolutely.

Physician vacations were most typically taken in one-week blocks and occasionally two weeks at a time; they rarely took vacations longer than two weeks, and they rarely took only a day or so scattered here and there. "It's hard to get away for more than seven or ten days, and so you're not going to go to India." Physicians did use vacation time, however, to go someplace, typically a resort, to have a break doing something very different from home life and to enjoy some luxury, which they came to see as a right—to their mind a need, at least for them:

Someone who has a very low-stress job may not consider a great vacation a need; they'll be happy going up to Maine for a week. I have a very high-stress job. Because I have a very high-stress job, I really need to get away, so for me, going out skiing to Utah two weeks out of a year, I consider that a really great escape.

Physicians stood out from our other occupations not only in their use of vacations as a "necessary" luxury and a break from the routine, but even more so in essentially never discussing vacation as a time to care for a sick child or to putter around the house.

Although some doctors were able to use careful scheduling to extend their vacations or get in extra vacations, even they, like other doctors, may in fact have done significant work during the time they were officially off.

[When I] go on vacation, I . . . come in the day before I [officially] come back, and I could be here six hours just going through the labs and things that have come in and trying to catch up for the week and a half. Because it doesn't stop while you're gone, and while my partners will take care of gross abnormalities, all the normals they leave for me to deal with.

One reason doctors insisted on taking weeklong vacations out of town was precisely to get away from the routine out-of-hours demands they would have faced if they were around and more or less available.

Although they had to schedule vacations in concert with their colleagues and many of them planned vacations enough in advance to avoid scheduling patients during that period (or to reschedule those already scheduled), doctors did largely feel that they were able to get vacation if and when they wanted. One doctor, a surgeon in a group practice, gave us a notable explanation of his hectic schedule. Contrasting his situation with that of others in his office, he said that when he decided not to come in one week, he "just canceled five days of appointments and went on vacation. *They* can't do that. They can't just decide not to come in. I can." If a doctor had a scheduling problem—including any he might have created himself by not checking his calendar—he did not worry about it, confident that it could and would be fixed by others.

The time doctors took off for holidays approximated that of other occupations, since almost everyone wanted the same holidays off. But even here, what was distinctive about physicians was the sense of control they had over these decisions. No one told them what to do; they (collectively) decided. Whether in hospitals or private practices, they often decided in group meetings. And they worried about imposing on their colleagues. Several said something similar to what this anesthesiologist said of his group: "Christmas week, we rotate it. . . . For the Christmas week, if you got it one year . . . then it's at least three years before [you get it again]." Or consider the words of the doctor in charge of the schedule at the largest and most bureaucratic of the units we observed:

> And I will likely take someone who is either single or who has expressed a willingness to work a Christian holiday in exchange for getting a Jewish holiday off. So those conversations happen. . . . It's a bit of a lottery, and if I can't satisfy everyone I'll have personal conversations and say, "I apologize, but I need you to work a Christmas shift. You haven't in six years; I hope you understand."

With their professional standing, the relatively flat occupational hierarchy, and their still especially good market position, doctors stood out. It is hard to imagine a member of any of our other occupations being told: "I apologize, but I need you to work a Christmas shift. I hope you understand."

NURSES

Sick Leave

Most nurses used their sick leave and in general felt able to do so without serious scrutiny or challenge to their right to it.[14] They seemed to be especially sensitive to what they did and did not have to say when reporting sick. One nurse we surveyed praised her workplace because, although "they really, really look down upon you calling in an hour before," nonetheless "nobody ever questions it" when people do call in. At one of the hospitals a nurse invoked the language of rights:

> I would be insulted if someone were to put me on the spot about me taking a day off, personally. I would not take it lightly; I'd be really upset. Because it's harassment; you can't do that, to anybody. . . . If you need to take a sick day the employer and employees you work with have no right to know why you were sick, why you called out. They have absolutely no right to know.

A nurse administrator agreed that it was all to the good that the reasons for call-outs were reported to human resources, not to her: "I don't need to know the specifics of your disease. It's probably not a good thing that I do, because it might be private."

At the unionized hospital, the contract provided for two personal days per year. When a personal day was used, it came out of the person's sick leave, so personal days could only be taken if the person had sick days available. According to one administrator, "A nurse calls up and says, 'I'm taking a personal day,' and the supervisor on the shift says, 'Okay.' And so, at the very last minute, they are granted a shift for a day off." When asked, "What is a legitimate personal day? Could it be anything?" the administrator's response was: "That's what the union says. It's none of your business. It's personal. . . . We've been told that we really can't deny them." This was the case even if the nurse slipped up and said something like she had "an opportunity to go to a concert." The union was not strong enough to increase the number of sick days in the contract, but it was strong enough to ensure that workers had two personal days to take off without guilt and without any concern about administrative pressure, penalty, or retaliation, something rarely found among our other employees.

Most nurses used their sick leave only for illness, their own or that of a family member, but some nurses felt that it was totally reasonable to take a mental health day when life was stressful.[15] One nurse elaborated:

> If you work a lot, if you're stressed out, if you have things going on at home, you take a mental health day, a sick day. Call in sick. You're sick, you know, you're losing your mind, you need to stay home. I personally think that's fine. Some people disagree and, you know, get upset about it.

Another nurse, at a different hospital, agreed, insisting that "I don't abuse it at all" and that she only called in if "it's good for my emotional well-being." She said that administrators never told her to come in and that her excuses were readily accepted. Typically, when she wanted a "mental health" day, she would make up an ailment: "And a good one is I have diarrhea, because they go, 'Ohhh! Diarrhea! Don't you dare come to this place with diarrhea.'"

Although these are examples of ways in which nurses usually avoided punitive scrutiny, the hospitals we observed did have policies in place to penalize people for calling out too often. At one, the first warning did not come until after the sixth call-out. At another, an administrator explained that when nurses were required to sign a "corrective action" statement, they did so willingly: "They tell me, 'Yeah, I've been sick six times. . . . Ya know, I was really sick.' And I go, 'Okay,' but it has nothing to do with credibility. It has nothing to do with believability. It has nothing to do with not trusting." The call-out was all that mattered to the hospital, which had little interest in the reasons a nurse was calling out. Another hospital was primarily concerned about the length of the advance notice given and had a policy to address this: "If you call out an hour before you're not getting paid. Two hours before you will get paid." At another hospital, managers were told, "It's at your discretion as to whether or not you count something as an unplanned event."

Nurses also took advantage of state-mandated leave policies for families. While those in the other occupations almost never mentioned the Family and Medical Leave Act, nurses mentioned and used it often. When a child, spouse, or parent required the kind of care covered by the FMLA, the nurses brought a note from their doctor to obtain official approval for time off from the human relations office, whose personnel knew the requirements. Then nurses called their schedulers, one of whom reported that they would say: "I am not coming in today because I'm taking an FMLA day." Hospital administrators were the ones who talked the most about the FMLA. At the hospital where the issue came up the most, Outercity, one nurse manager said, "I think it's good and appropriate for people who clearly need it, like if you have a child who has a chronic illness, if you have a chronic illness. It can be crippling to a unit, and I think there's a lot of room for abuse. . . . I don't think my staff abuse it." However, another nurse manager at Outercity told the story of a nurse who called her manager saying that she was taking an FMLA day—but then the nurse and the manager both attended the same wedding. As a result, the FMLA-abusing nurse was fired. This same manager reported that she had perhaps twelve people with FMLA certification, "and I'd say maybe out of the twelve, six abuse it maybe." A third manager commented: "I think when it works, it works well. I think there are people who abuse it and it's easily abused." In her unit she had perhaps ten people with FMLA certification.

> Most of them are intermittent, which means that they can call up today, and say, "I'm not coming in tonight, I'm taking an FMLA day." And there's not a thing I can say about it, it's already approved, it doesn't matter what the staffing is on the unit, it's "Okay, thank you for calling.". . . I have somebody who has a child who has seizures, so every time, so when she calls up to say, "I'm taking an FMLA day," I have to assume it's for her son, because that's the only reason she would be taking an FMLA day. Do I think that there are times that maybe it's not? Yes. But there's no way for me to prove it. So it is what it is. . . . If someone calls up and says, "Oh, I'm taking an FMLA day," the day before their vacation, you have to wonder.

Another nurse manager at Outercity reported that of her three people with FMLA certification, "one of them fortuitously has had them around the holidays, another one always has FMLA days near a weekend. So you really have to be vigilant." One administrator even turned FMLA into a verb, saying that nurses kept "FMLA-ing us."

The managers did not protest too loudly over what they saw as some of the nurses' overly frequent absences; they said the law silenced them, and they found that difficult. A nurse manager at a hospital said: "The challenge to staff this unit's been like trying to cover a hole with Swiss cheese—you get a piece patched and that falls through. And it's taken up probably eight out of [my] ten-hour days. [I spend] eight hours trying to fix the holes on a day-to-day basis." These problems were especially severe for nurses because, in order to attract staff, hospitals accept a wide range of nonstandard shifts; at the same time, it was harder to fill holes because nurses are less likely than EMTs or nursing assistants to seek overtime. Managers tried to figure out ways to obtain adequate staff "for relief"—helping regular staff swap with one another, hiring extra nurses, creating flex nurses within the hospital, and relying, reluctantly, on traveling nurses. Each of these strategies had its costs, as they saw it, but each also helped them deal with nursing shortages.

Vacations

The nurses in our study had far less success in getting and controlling vacations than the doctors did. First, nurses were the most likely to tell us that they wanted more vacation:

INTERVIEWER: Talk to me about days off, either vacation days . . . (*interrupted*)

RESPONDENT: They don't give me enough!

INTERVIEWER: (*laughs*)

RESPONDENT: I need more! (*laughs*) Which I think everybody says!

Another person reported: "I get three weeks' vacation, which is not a lot. A new person starting here only gets two weeks' vacation, which is, I think, ludicrous."

Although many nurses talked about wanting an extra week of vacation to go somewhere, a nontrivial number of nurses did not get as much as one week off for true vacation, a gendered pattern found even more among nursing assistants. Many nurses used their vacation to deal with illnesses, their own or those of family members. One explained, "I have cancer. I had cancer. Whatever. I have a lotta doctors' appointments, and I try to schedule those in a clump, so that's my vacation." Another nurse explained that she didn't take a block of vacation because "I usually use up all that time with kids' stuff and I'll call out." A third used her vacation for the year dealing with her daughter's surgery. Other nurses gave up part of their vacation and received extra pay instead: "They'll cash in one or two weeks of vacation to get the extra paychecks to kinda pay for their trip [the vacation they did take] instead of workin' extra hours."

The main issue for nurses, however, was the difficulty of scheduling vacations, a gender-linked issue that revolved above all around children: a high concentration of nurses wanted time off during school vacations, and the number of nurses willing to work extra at those times was limited. Management therefore restricted nurse vacation during school vacation periods. Not only did nurse vacations need to be scheduled months in advance, but even then they were subject to approval by management, and "prime-time" vacations (during the summers and during school vacation weeks during the school year) were restricted. One manager reported that her hospital was "fairly generous" about prime time because "we say to staff during that period of time [May 30 to September 8], 'You can have two weeks off.'" This was in fact the *most* generous policy we encountered for staff nurses; in many places nurses could schedule no more than a week of vacation during the summer. Vacation scheduling was a central concern in nurses' union contracts.

Similar issues came up around holidays, which nurses saw as a major problem. At one hospital there was no flexibility about Christmas and Thanksgiving, no matter how far in advance the request was made: "Why, if I get Christmas off, do I have to work the day after, so I can never ever go out of town for Christmas?. . . There's no way to go for like three days for Thanksgiving or that kind of thing. You'll never get that kind of time off, for any kind of a big holiday." Some nurses even took jobs—in schools, for example, or on particular floors in hospitals where only day surgery was performed—precisely because they would not be required to work on holidays:

> There's no weekends and no holidays in this job, so that's what I was look-
> ing for, being off weekends and holidays in a hospital. I paid my dues, and I
> wanted to have weekends off and holidays off, so I looked specifically for a
> job that would provide that.

Some nurses felt that their supervisors accommodated their requests, but holiday and vacation scheduling was often a point of stress, tension, scheming, elaborate arrangements, and outright resistance. Many nurses arranged schedule swaps with coworkers, doing so as much as six months in advance in order to be guaranteed the time off they wanted. A nurse reported that "when the summer vacation list comes up, there's always the hemming and hawing and scrambling, trying to find the people that can work for them." Nurses felt that in multiple ways they needed to push back against organizational pressures. One nurse reported that long in advance she told her supervisor: "'Well, I'm taking a vacation in September—I want to tell you now.' And she goes, 'That's an awful time!' I said, 'Well, that's when I like to go on vacation.'" And she took her September vacation.

EMTS

Sick Leave

The key fact for the EMTs, especially the firefighters, was how confident most of them were that individually and collectively they had enough clout that the rules about sick leaves often would not be enforced. A few of them sounded like the doctors, making remarks like, "I have to be deathly ill to call in sick." Most EMTs, however, assumed that they would use all their sick days, and many treated their sick leave as a form of entitlement. As one asserted: "Most of the time when I'm sick, I want to use those because we just need a mental health day. . . . People think that sick means that you're sick-sick—where a lot of times you just need to get out of there." In a lunchtime discussion, one noted that "Sean Fitzpatrick called out 'sick.'" Another asked, "Is one of his kids sick?" The response: "Nah, I think he just had stuff to do." Another EMT put it the most blatantly:

> We get two personal days a year; I use them all up. I am up to four weeks' vacation. I use every bit of it, and I will use all five sick days, and I am never sick when I call out sick. I'm very honest about that. The chief knows I'm never sick. I will call out sick when it's ninety-five and sunny on Saturday. (*laughs*)

Others had roughly the same approach: "Those are my mental health days," or, "It's prevalent for guys to just call out sick."

This approach was strongest among firefighters, but private-sector EMTs had a similar attitude: "If I can't get the day off, if I can't find someone to cover me for Saturday and I've tried—some people will try and find coverage, some people will just call out sick." EMTs, especially but not exclusively firefighter EMTs, saw themselves as having an almost unquestioned right to use their sick days as extra vacation. As one put it: "It's your sick time, and the thing is, don't give it to me if you don't want me to use it." Their supervisors de facto accepted this.

Despite their macho reputation, one of firefighters' most common reasons for using sick leave was to do the work involved in the "undoing of gender": unlike the doctors, the EMTs often used sick leave to take care of their children or grandchildren.[16] These working-class men expected and took sick leaves—for themselves and for their families. "They [management] understand that the ramifications are that if you don't have any family sick time left, you're just going to call it self-sick and you're going to take the time because you need the time."

Why do we find this pattern of sick leave among these working-class men? A number of factors probably contribute: EMTs' favorable market position (with unemployment rates at about 3 percent over the last decade), worker solidarity, the power of their unions, their cultural capital (as heroic masculine figures), and the fact that many of them were public-sector workers with some political leverage.[17] As a result, these working-class men had come to expect time off, and the organizations employing them tended to impose no penalties. Although committed to their jobs (especially the firefighters), these men did not think of themselves in the same way so many of the male doctors did—that they were irreplaceable professionals with ongoing relationships with patients who would suffer if they were not on the job. EMTs have no relationships with particular patients, and they are not employers but employees earning a wage. Our EMTs believed that they had won the right to use their sick leave—not because that right was inherent in the occupation or the institution they worked for, but because they had fought for it and continued to fight for it.

The EMTs were not only remarkably relaxed about this use of sick leave but often said that their organizations were too: "Unless you're a constant abuser of it, there's really no penalization for it." Managers agreed. They were bound, they said, by the rules: "Even though I know he's abusing the system, it's not up to me to figure that out." One manager said that in his town, if you called in when it was clear you weren't sick, "you get pulled in and get talked to. But once you've been on for twenty-something years, there's really nothing else they can do." Instead of *imposing penalties* for using sick leave, EMT employers, if they did anything at all, *provided rewards* for *not* using sick leave. At one fire department, "if you go an entire quarter of the year without taking a sick day, you get an incentive day or night, whatever you choose. And you can accumulate up to four of them."[18]

Again, organizational variation is clear. EMTs sometimes saw the use of their sick leave as a form of resistance, a way to get back at their employer—but that depended on their view of the organization and employer. One private-sector EMT noted that if management was "not being very understanding, if I get a call every hour and get pulled . . . I can get sick at 3:00 and go home. I don't do it very often, but if I've had a bad call and you made me mad and you just keep hammering me with calls, transfers, 9-1-1s—well, I'm going home." When an EMT called in sick when he was not really ill, it got more difficult not only for the employer but also for the workers who were left on the job—especially from the start of deer hunting season through the end of the year as workers used their sick leave because it would soon expire. "And now, because you want to stick it to 'the man,' now I've got to deal with that—you threw *my* day off." That friction passes, however: "As soon as my sick days are burned we're all like brothers."

Vacations

In some ways the working-class men resembled their more affluent male counterparts, the physicians, even more than they resembled the advantaged women, the nurses. Most EMTs took vacation time for granted, though they took less time than the doctors did. These working-class men casually mentioned taking two or three weeks, and occasionally four weeks, of vacation, which they simply expected and typically used. Note the language of this EMT's response to a question about his vacation—the word "probably" suggests that this was not an issue that worried him:

> Probably about three weeks a year overall on vacation time. . . . Yeah, about three weeks a year altogether on vacation probably, and I separate that and usually do one two-week and one one-week one. So I take two vacations a year. Time off, you know how it is, [given the basic schedule every week], I have five on, three off—that's about it.

Vacation time was an issue that at least some EMTs seemed not to have given a lot of thought to; they assumed a right to vacations.[19] The length of vacations depended on seniority; as one commented, "Seniority, seniority—it's all about seniority."

Although the EMTs recognized and accepted that those who had worked longer deserved more, they also asserted that they themselves controlled this process (within the accepted parameters). After reporting that "we get four weeks' vacation," one EMT went on to explain his sense of control: "But most of the bosses we have now are pretty lenient. I've never heard them really say to too many people, 'You can't have that day off.'" Vacation scheduling in EMS organizations is probably easier because, not only is the work male-dominated, but EMTs are men eager to work long hours. If someone is out, there are usually plenty of others who are available to work overtime (and who may be substituting overtime for what otherwise would have been hours on a second job), so managers can easily fill the slots when workers are on vacation.

The EMTs took vacations that were very different in location and luxury from the vacations the doctors took: "we go to a campground or something like that," said one, and a special trip that many of them talked about was going to Disney World. But like the doctors, "we spend at least a week out, just away." This kind of vacation was a pleasure and a privilege that these two groups of men simply took for granted, experiencing little of the stress that nurses experienced around vacation scheduling.

Although EMTs had to work holidays, most of them rarely saw this as a reason to complain; for key holidays like Christmas, most EMTs with young children were able to arrange swaps with coworkers. One remarked, for example, that he was off for Christmas that year, but had been on the previous year. He did not know about the year coming up, but as he saw it, "you take the good with the bad." His family creatively adjusted: "Last year we celebrated it—because I was working the day of—it was I think like the twentieth. Our holidays may not be spent on the holiday, but the family gets together." Then he concluded, with resignation and little complaint: "And it's just a day on the calendar; it doesn't really matter."

NURSING ASSISTANTS

Sick Leave

Of all the groups we studied, nursing assistants were the ones most likely to encounter policies that made it difficult to take a sick day, and the ones most likely to complain about those policies. Many of the nursing assistants told us that they were afraid to take a sick day off, even if they had paid days available: "Even if I'm sick, I will still go to work. (laughs) . . . Somehow I am going to make it."

At the time of our fieldwork, the Berkman nursing home—where 87 percent of the nursing assistants were black or Latino—had recently introduced a new sick leave policy. Under this policy, intended to limit the use and abuse of sick leave, workers received six paid sick days per year, but were penalized anytime they used one. This sort of policy is common for nursing assistants, and it is also used by Walmart.[20] If a person calls out sick for the day, they are paid, but they are also given a verbal warning. A second call-out within ninety days generates a written warning, a third call-out leads to a second and stronger written warning, and a fourth call-out is cause for termination.[21] The only leniency in this policy is for advance notice: if the employee knows a minimum of two days in advance that they will need a day off and requests a vacation day, *and* if the director of nursing authorizes it, then the day is not counted as a call-out.

A nursing assistant at another facility said that management told them in meetings that "we're not going to tolerate sickness." In sharp contrast to the nurse who told us that she was never challenged when she claimed to be suffering from diarrhea as a cover for her "mental health" day, a nursing assistant reported that, "if you've got diarrhea or vomiting, they still want you to come in."

> At our meetings, they say a sore throat is not really a sore throat. Lots of times they'll say to come in and do what you can, and if you can't stay, we'll let you go home. But lots of times they won't let you go home. The whole idea is to intimidate you so you won't call out. (*Have you ever talked to management about that?*) Others have and lost their jobs.

At Berkman, CNAs explained, "even if you have doctor's notes, emergency room letters, you're terminated. That's it—no ifs, ands, or buts, no explanations."

Although administrators agreed, they legitimated their sick leave policy by claiming, for example, that "there are times when people can't survive with this business." And these managers were quite certain that they could replace the nursing assistants if they did not "survive." (Nursing aides' unemployment rate was 9.2 percent in 2010, much higher than that for any of the other three groups.) These employers had the market power to impose harsh policies.

During our fieldwork, the Berkman policy was made even stricter. Previously, if a nursing assistant reported for work and was able to work through at least half her shift, but then had to go home sick (or to deal with a family emergency), she was paid only for the hours worked but was not penalized for a call-out. One day, at a 7:15 AM staff meeting attended by the just-off-duty night shift, management warned workers in vague terms about going home early, and to their surprise, the issue exploded with worker pushback. The rule that leaving early, at any point, would be counted as a call-out was developed during an exchange between administrators right after that staff meeting. In a discussion between three administrators, the director of nursing was crystal clear that the way to deal with early departures was through the imposition of a stricter rule:

> I don't care about their pay. Give them the sick pay, but it should count against them. They are doing it at the classic times, I'll bet. I'll bet it's at the end of a week, on Thursday or Friday nights. I'll bet this isn't happening on Wednesday night. . . . They've found another way to get around the rules.

Note that these claims were made in the absence of any data; none of the administrators knew which days of the week employees were most commonly leaving early. Other data suggest that there is reason to question these claims. One hospital administrator admitted to her own biased assumptions about who takes sick leave. Saying that she had been shocked when the hospital took a systematic look at who called out sick, she remarked, "I know who the nonperformers are." Thus, when she would hear that someone had called out—and that was usually all she heard, not the specific person who had done so—she would assume that the call-out was by a nonperformer. The systematic study showed her that "there's some great performers whose attendance is horrible, and I don't even know it . . . 'cause I haven't been looking for it." She herself concluded: "What a bias I have."

The Berkman managerial response to any perceived problem was to impose a new rule; they viewed the situation as a constant struggle between workers and management, with workers trying to find ways around the rules and managers imposing new rules to stymie workers' responses to the rules. In a the conversation after the staff meeting, the director of nursing said, "How can they be sick at 3:00 AM and not sick at 2:00 AM? That's ridiculous." The scheduler, who was closer to the workers, said, "They say they are staying and completing their duties, and then going home sick." This pattern could be viewed—as the scheduler did—as workers showing a commitment to the collective enterprise, staying through the most demanding and important part of the shift and then leaving at the point when the work was in hand and their coworkers could manage without them.[22] The director of nursing's response was to say, "That's unacceptable." What was needed, she asserted, was a new penalty—having it count as a call-out when nursing assistants left early. "I bet that puts a stop to it pretty quickly."

Shortly after the post-meeting conversation in which the new rule modification was developed, the director of nursing said: "They were all worked up about floats and sick days and call-outs. There are rules about those things. They say, 'Well, they didn't used to enforce this.' Well, I'm sorry, but I do enforce the rules." Later she reinforced these views:

> You'd be amazed, you'd be amazed at the call-outs. And that's why we've had to get really tough. What people were doing is going home halfway through the shift: "I'm not feeling well!" "Alas and alack, I have a headache, I need to go home." So we've changed the policy now that if you leave early it counts against you in your attendance.

The director of nursing's claim that the rule had always existed and she was just enforcing it when others had not was accepted as truth by the nursing assistants. Perhaps the rule had always existed—but when we began fieldwork we were given a full set of written policies, and we could not find this policy anywhere in the more than one hundred pages of material.

The new modification generated worker hostility. In one nursing assistant's view, "basically what they're saying, [is] you're screwed. Once you get in the building, you punch in, you can't leave. And if you do leave, it's a call-out." Her friend chimed in: "It's bullshit. It doesn't make any sense." One part of the policy generated especially strong hostility: "You can have a doctor's note too, but you'll still get a write-up." To avoid a penalty, one nursing assistant said, "basically you'd have to tell them, 'I'm going to be sick next week, here's my two weeks' notice.'" In an exchange between two nursing assistants, one complained about what happened after she caught a communicable skin disease from one of the residents she cared for:

RESPONDENT 1: So the deal went, she [the supervisor] came over to me and she says, "You know what, Jane? We're just going to count this as one call-out." I said, "It shouldn't be counted as *anything*, because I got sick *here* on the job!" What she did was, she was "understanding"; she let me use some of my vacation time, some of my holiday time, and some of my sick time to make my forty hours so I got a decent paycheck two weeks ago. (*very sarcastic*) So I thought that was really nice of her, you know what I'm saying?

RESPONDENT 2: Oh, she's a decent person. (*equally sarcastic*)

Many nursing assistants complained about the policy, its irrationality, and its destructive consequences for them, their families, and their patients, saying, "It's terrible," "It's not fair," "I don't think that's right," and, "They add on as much as they want, but when you go to say something they don't give a crap about you." They were angry, even furious, about the policy, but at this non-unionized workplace they did not think it could be changed.[23] It was not that they were incapable of conceiving better alternatives; rather, they were sure (based on a lifetime of experience as low-income women, mostly of color) that they had no hope of changing policy. Just as doctors knew that their power was such that they could control conditions, nursing assistants knew that they had no such power and had to accept what was imposed on them:

No, you're not gonna change the policy there. (*laughs*) Never. I mean, people can go and complain, but once the rule is made there, it's just, that's it.

> Everyone thinks it's crazy, or that it doesn't make sense, but what are you going to do? You're not going to be able to really change it. They do what they want, basically. I've been here four years, and I know that. They change the rules when they want to change them and stuff, so, you just gotta sit back and deal with it.

Although most of their hostility was directed at management, occasionally Berkman nursing assistants pointed fingers at each other. One nursing assistant said, "I know people have abused their sick days, they keep calling out, keep calling out. Until they had to come up with this. Because they really had to look into it." Another nursing assistant strongly condemned some of her coworkers, saying that, in her view, "the other staff members—some of them are lazy, some of them, they get paid on Thursday, they do, and they drink and they party, okay." Some of them, she said, "they tell you, like, a day before, you know, 'I'm going to call out, because I'm going to party tonight.' You know, so you know what to expect. So, you know, they call out, you have to work short, it's not nice, you know." In contrast to nurses and EMTs, only one nursing assistant explicitly endorsed calling out sick in order to get a break from work, to relax. Some Berkman nursing assistants used the language of "abuse" of sick leave— that is, someone calling out when she could have worked. These workers were less likely to condemn management for leaving the floor short-staffed when a worker called out.[24]

No nursing assistant liked being left to work short-handed, but most nursing assistants were understanding about it:

> Everyone has their moments where they call out, because, you know, people have different things going on in their lives and stuff, so you might have on the floor one person calling out all the time during a certain time. And you're like, oh, they call out so much. But then, it could be you during the next couple months.

The Family and Medical Leave Act is of no help to these workers, even though the nursing homes are covered by the act. In contrast to hospital nurses, a number of nursing assistants described situations that legally were covered by the FMLA but for which they incurred penalties; as one said, "There's no excused absences." Another nursing assistant described her nursing home's policy: "I think if you bring a doctor's note, you know, they shouldn't be like, 'Okay, if you be absent one more time, you're gonna be fired.'" The rarity of the FMLA's use by the low-wage nursing assistants becomes even clearer in looking at schedules from one of the nursing homes: over a six-month period, the schedule shows that only one CNA changed her work hours because of the FMLA. Some of the women had children with recurring medical conditions, such as seizures or asthma, that led to periodic hospitalizations—exactly the kind of situation that the FMLA was designed to cover. Not one of these women had heard of the act (which was discussed, however minimally and legalistically, in the more than one hundred pages of written materials given to new employees), and all reported that management penalized them for any day they were out, even if they had evidence of being in the hospital with their child.

The organizational response probably reduced the number of call-outs at this nursing home, but the "penalize, penalize" policy has at least three costs. First, it creates hostility and resentment among workers. Second, and related, it fails to enlist worker cooperation and in fact creates a reverse effect of motivating workers to get even. One West Indian nursing assistant who worked two jobs, putting in more than seventy hours every week, and whose kids were upwardly mobile, had suggested to the director of nursing that the nursing home offer some reward to those employees who did not call out, a policy actually followed at another nursing home and at many fire departments. The director's response: "So what? Do you want us to pay you to come in?" This response angered the CNA, who concluded: "Forget it, I call out after. I call out. I say I'm due now to call out. Everybody that's on the floor, they call out. Everybody else, they call out, so I just call out. Yeah."

The third cost of reducing the number of allowable call-outs is apparently an intended effect of the policy: as one nursing assistant in our study reported, "Even if I'm sick, I will still go to work. (*laughs*) Like, I think it's been two days that I call out in all the time that I've been there.[25] . . . Somehow I am going to make it. Even sick, I'll make it out there." This is a major impact of this sick leave policy, and it has perverse consequences:

> You know, you work in a health care facility, and somebody has a real bad cold. But they still have to come anyway. In the book they give us, the handbook they give us for us, it says, when you're sick you're not supposed to be coming in. Because, you know, more people will get the cold or something. But then, the only thing they are afraid of is the pink eye. But the rest of the stuff, they don't care. You still have to come in.

Is it a benefit for a nursing assistant with a bad cold (or worse) to come in to work and feed, bathe, dress, and toilet a frail ninety-year-old suffering from assorted ailments? Such a policy runs a nontrivial risk of damaging the health of at least some residents on at least some occasions. (Of course, this is also true for doctors who come in sick, though they do not make note of this potential ill effect of their resistance to taking time off; indeed, even though the potential spread of contagion is rarely remarked upon in discussions of sick leave policies, a wide range of service workers who have contact with clients, both in and out of the medical system, run this risk.)

Not all nursing homes are as punitive as this one. And the differences between the more and less punitive organizations are telling. Some of the employers offer paid-time-off (PTO, also occasionally referred to as ETO, or earned-time-off) systems in place of separate sick days and vacation days. Employees who would have had eight sick days and fifteen days of vacation might instead receive twenty PTO days. Such systems are increasingly common: 51 percent of employers now offer such plans to at least some employees.[26] Though these plans may add some time off for some workers, they also reinforce inequalities at the workplace: employees who need to take off more days for their own or their children's illnesses have fewer days available for vacation. Lucas Estates, with different official policies on sick leave than Berkman and a different organizational culture, used such a PTO plan. Its effects were evident in one nursing assistant's explanation that "I hate using my sick time—'cause I'm saving up for a vacation!"

Calling out at Lucas could also lead to penalties, but the penalties did not kick in until the third call-out within a given period, rather than at the first call-out. Lucas nursing assistants were thus subject to a policy that was halfway between the Berkman policy and the policy of six call-outs before imposing a penalty, which was the policy applied to some nurses, discussed earlier (in the section on nurses' sick leave). Lucas management regretted enforcing the policy and tried to avoid doing so. The nursing home administrator went the extra mile to avoid penalizing an employee:

> We enforce the absenteeism policy. But we also try to give people outs. If you need a day off, let us know the day before. We'll take you off the schedule, we'll cover you, and then it's not a call-out. Even though it's last minute, it's not considered a call-out. Because they called at one o'clock.[27]

In theory, Lucas had a "no excuses" policy, but one member of the management team (in addition to the administrator) reported actively interceding on employees' behalf, and some absences were in fact excused. Management made every effort to keep the place fully staffed if they could do so: "Oh God, yes. I don't wanna see them workin' short! These are like my children, a lot of them." The administrator would make exceptions for good employees, even if they reached the point where, according to the policy, they should be terminated: "We set up some probationary periods for those people. The next step would've been termination, but I put 'em on a probationary period because I really wanted to see them successful."

Similarly, whereas at Berkman the director of nursing reportedly scorned giving rewards for good attendance, at Lucas workers with perfect attendance for a year were recognized with an award certificate and their names were posted in the break room. (We observed other employees looking at these certificates.) At Lucas, where rules were less punitive, no workers complained of "abuse" by other workers. People were reluctant to take days off because of a sense of responsibility to their coworkers: "I don't like cuttin' my floor short." If someone did call out a lot, "it becomes an issue." Other workers "won't tell on 'em"; instead, "they'll talk to the person and say, 'Hey, you know, it's really not cool that you've been calling out. We know you're not really sick, and you have to be responsible. If the job isn't working out for you, then let someone else have it.'" At Lucas coworkers were thus both a reason not to call out and a method of dealing with problem workers who did. A system that addresses such problems not only with management rules but through coworker culture not only is more effective but also creates less resentment.

This exemplifies a more general contrast between the two nursing homes and illustrates the importance of examining organizations in combination with occupations. Both nursing homes dealt with the same sorts of elderly patients, needed to provide continuous care, used roughly the same mix of direct care personnel, and paid roughly the same wages. But in the less punitive home's organizational culture, employees were valued and motivated through recognition and support and the culture was for everyone (from the administrator on down) to pitch in to help. No activity was beneath anyone, at least as a culture and often as a practice. Every effort was made *not* to penalize nursing assistants, and as a consequence nursing assistants themselves developed a culture that enforced a work ethic and responsibility to coworkers. At the other nursing home, by contrast, the organizational culture was one of keeping staff under control through punitive policies imposed from the top. A large majority of the nursing assistants employed there, seeing the policies as unjust and irrational, had no desire to assist management in its goals—in this case, enforcing absence policies. Workers were angry at management, but they also blamed their coworkers for the punitive and dysfunctional system, objecting to "abuse" by others. The system seemed less successful at achieving its goals (of continuous staffing without excessive call-outs), and it certainly generated worker hostility.

It is difficult to determine the extent to which these organizational differences simply reflected choices made by the administrator of each nursing home or were "determined" (within a U.S. context) by managerial responses to the racial composition of the workforces—87 percent of nursing assistants at the more punitive nursing home were people of color, and 80 percent at the other were white.

Vacations

As with so many other aspects of work hours and schedules, the nursing assistants got less vacation than any other occupation. They received fewer days of paid vacation and had even less control than any other group. The contrast was most dramatic with the doctors: while physicians really took their vacations, usually as weeklong breaks in resort locations, at the Berkman home, over a six-month period including the summer, fewer than one-quarter of the nursing assistants took a vacation of a week or longer. If a nursing assistant wanted to take an entire two weeks off at once, that had to be approved by the director of nursing. One nursing assistant, a single parent, had an even more limited notion of what constituted a vacation. Asked, "When you say you're on vacation, you mean you aren't coming in at all?" she replied: "No, vacation means a vacation from doing the doubles back to back, you know."

The CNAs also often organized their vacations around their families, but this took a very different form from the nurses' vacations. First, many CNAs' key family responsibility was being the family's major (or sole) breadwinner—as a result, they took very short vacations, if any at all. Second, "family" meant something different to CNAs than what it meant to affluent professionals: because extended kin were far more central to these low-wage women workers, their vacations often took the form of organizing holidays and long weekends around relatives rather than just spouses and children. When nursing assistants did take a week or more off, often it was to visit relatives. "I have a brother that lives in Denver, and I'm planning on using my time to go out there . . . at least a week or so to see him. That's what I did last summer."

Nursing assistants' vacations were limited not just in the number of days they could take but also in the scheduling of those days. For nursing assistants, as for nurses, vacations had to be planned long in advance. At a nursing home we observed, a vacation of two days or more required a minimum of one month's notice; summer vacation requests had to be submitted by mid-March. The scheduler was clear about this: "Vacations—you can definitely say that those were settled months in advance." There is a major gender difference among the occupations, then, in the amount of advance notice required to schedule a vacation and in the stress and unhappiness this induces.

Nursing assistants got less vacation than those in the occupations dominated by males; they were far more likely to take their vacation a day at a time, and they had less choice or "flexibility" in when they could take vacations. In addition to all these differences, many nursing assistants simply took no vacation at all, driven by economic necessity to cash in the time to help pay their bills. A nursing assistant presented being able to do this as one of the generous benefits of her job.[28] Another said, "All of it I cash in. Might as well—it's there, might as well use it, right?" One CNA explained that if she had twenty-four hours of vacation built up over and above the amount she was required to leave in her vacation earned-time bank, "I could tell [the payroll person], I wanna cash in twenty-four hours. The following week, on that Friday, I would get my check plus a check for twenty-four hours. So I'd have extra money." She did this, she reported, "around Christmas, and stuff like that. Or when I'm in debt or somethin', you know?"

With the accumulation of debt, vacations disappear. The United States looks bad when we compare our vacation policies to those of other nations, but it looks even worse when we compare the haves and the have-nots in this country.

CONCLUSION

Gender and class, and their intersection, dramatically shape the experiences of our four occupations with respect to sick leave and vacations in a number of ways: how much time is taken off, the purposes for which the time is taken, who controls that time, and who monitors it. There is essentially no overlap between the vacation experiences of doctors and nursing assistants. All but a handful of doctors took four or more weeks of vacation each year and used it to go to luxury resorts. One doctor's vision of an unacceptably low-end vacation was a week in Maine. Most nursing assistants rarely took a week of vacation, and if they did, it was to sleep on the couch in the apartment of a relative they were visiting; for them, a week in Maine might have been a once-in-a-decade experience. EMTs took vacations, spending a week or two at a campground or, for a treat, taking a trip to Disney. For nurses, scheduling a week off was stressful and uncertain, requiring as much as six months of advance notice; even then, some nurses had to arrange a swap with a coworker in order to get a week off approved, and getting two weeks off at a stretch might require approval from a higher-level supervisor. For nurses, vacations—experienced as significant leisure time to relax and recharge—remained a privilege, and for all of our occupations something of a masculine privilege.

Very few of the doctors or EMTs reported stress, anxiety, or frustration about their vacations. They might have had to plan ahead, and they might not have gotten their ideal week, but they assumed that any vacation issue would get worked out and not be much of a problem. This is a clear expression of gender privilege, both at work and in the family, and it is all the more remarkable given that some of the doctors—and some of the EMTs as well—were married to nurses. (None of the nursing assistants were married to a doctor or EMT.) At least much of the time, the doctors and EMTs with nurse-wives were taking vacations with their families, including their wife, but to them the vacation scheduling was not a major concern. To their nurse-wife, it was. We saw this especially around the summer months, when children (and often other family members) get time off. These patterns show quite clearly the ways in which gender and class act as institutional locations and collective relations—rooted in occupations, organizations, and families—rather than simply as personal attributes or individual choices.

This difference emerges clearly in a comparison of the union contracts for nurses and firefighters: every nurse contract addressed vacation scheduling, but one-third of firefighter contracts did not; more than 95 percent of nurse contracts, but fewer than half of firefighter contracts, specified a "prime time" when the ability to take vacation was restricted, and 40 percent of nurse contracts, as opposed to fewer than 5 percent of firefighter contracts, specifically framed this restriction in terms of school vacations. While the EMTs were relaxed about their vacation options, these professional women were often frustrated because they had to plan far in advance and collectively allocate vacations in ways that took into account family responsibilities that remain gendered.

This is particularly difficult for women because not only are responsibilities at home gender-segregated, but so too are occupations. Employers seek to restrict nurse vacations because, in a woman-dominated occupation, many workers seek time off around children's schedules. There are two reasons this is less likely to become an issue for EMTs. First, although EMT fathers may want to take off a week to be with their kids, they are more likely than nurse mothers to take days off for themselves (say, to go deer hunting) and less likely to take a week off just to do child care during a gap in summer coverage. Second, for EMTs far more than for nurses, coworkers are likely to be eager to pick up the overtime made available by their absence. The *joint* family-work pattern of segregation intensifies difficulties around time off for many women even as it eases them for many men.

The specifics of sick leave policies are different, but the impact of class and gender and their interaction are just as clear. The two groups at opposite poles—the male professional doctors and the women working-class nursing assistants—try hard not to take sick leave. Doctors do so out of a sense of professionalism and commitment to their coworkers and patients; those reasons matter to nursing assistants as well, but at least as important to them are the harsh and rigid sanctions they face for using sick leave. Doctors are much more successful in always being at work because of their ability to control not only the terms of the workplace (say, deciding that they will lie down between patients) but also their families. It is reasonable to ask: What is cause and what is effect here? Are there so few external controls over doctors because they take so few sick days? Or do doctors take so few sick days because they have control over their own schedules?

Despite their best efforts, nursing assistants take many more sick days than doctors do, partly because their own health is not good (from hard lives, suspect diets, and limits on their ability to get exercise outside of work), but mostly because they have primary, often sole, responsibility for sick family members and often need to stay home to take care of them, while doctors (at least male doctors) rarely do so. Their extended family may help take care of a sick child, but these same family members may themselves demand the nursing assistant's help. The punitive rules nursing assistants face often endanger their jobs. If a nursing assistant has two children, and an illness is going around, she stays home first with one child and then with the other, and then she herself catches the illness, she is—as Joan Williams notes—one sick child away from being fired.[29] But such punitive rules may also endanger the workplace: workers respond favorably to a supportive workplace, but are more likely to find ways to resist the demands of a punitive organization. This is true for both nursing assistants and EMTs.

EMTs receive more sick days than nursing assistants, but the key difference is that they are not penalized for using them. To the contrary, it is clear to all that EMTs—certainly the firefighters, but to a considerable degree those in the private sector as well—treat sick days as extra vacation of the one-day-at-a-time variety. For whatever reason—their cultural support (as heroic figures), their political muscle, their public-sector location, their strong union, or maybe just their male privilege—EMTs work in an environment where this attitude toward sick leave is de facto accepted, even by their supervisors.

Nurses are much less restricted than nursing assistants, and much less entitled than EMTs. The most notable feature of nurse sick leave is their active use of the Family and Medical Leave Act—a major factor in their sick leaves that is rarely mentioned by those in the other occupations. Broadly, when a nurse needs sick leave for herself or a family member, she finds protection from the state and typically does not face much penalty from her employer (but, ironically in this context, only if she brings in a note from her doctor). The opposite is true of nursing assistants, even though they often have more family responsibilities: these low-wage women are much less likely to get protection from the state and are more likely to face penalties from their employer. Here, at least, class (and perhaps race) trumps gender, in some ways resembling earlier historical periods; the rights and responsibilities of conventional womanhood are protected and legitimate for middle-class women but not for low-wage women.

"Unpredictable" events like sick days might seem like an invariant, externally imposed natural force, and vacation time might seem to be just a matter of the number of days someone gets (or takes). In fact, both sick days and vacations are shaped by social context and vary by class and gender. A sick child is not a work problem for a male doctor who has a stay-at-home wife. A worker does not return from a vacation day feeling refreshed if the "vacation" was spent taking care of a sick child or appearing in court for a cousin. Lean staffing and changes in the family can turn unpredictable events into serious threats. Whether they are sick themselves or one of their family members is sick, how workers respond, how well they are able to respond, the degree of protection they receive from the state, and, most importantly, their ability to control normal unpredictability not only vary by gender *or* class but rest on the joint effect of gender *and* class.

PART III | Families and Jobs: Creating and Responding to Unpredictability

Chapter 8 | Unequal Families: Class Shapes Women's Responses to Unpredictability

BOTH EMPLOYERS AND EMPLOYEES in our study said that families drive unpredictability and the struggle over schedules. Talking about hours and schedules, a human resources administrator reported that when she talked to nurses about their schedules, "the *key* issue is family." "Family is your responsibility, and it's your first responsibility," was how a nursing assistant with two children phrased it. A fire chief who supervised EMTs told us, "Family comes first." Even a middle-aged doctor with a couple of kids insisted: "Family, then work, then anything else. That's all. You have to prioritize." Very similar formulations, it seems. Very different realities.

In their analysis of paid work hours, Jerry Jacobs and Kathleen Gerson show that the key change over the last few decades has not been the number of hours that *individuals* work but rather the number of hours that spouses jointly devote to paid work.[1] Because so many wives and mothers entered the labor force in the last few decades, and because the economic well-being of both adults and children has come increasingly to depend on the paid work of women, the United States has witnessed a dramatic increase in the working time of families. This change has produced new conflicts and new opportunities for both women and men, but it has also produced more routine unpredictability.

In a family with a male breadwinner and a stay-at-home wife, there is a built-in way of adapting to schedule unpredictability. In a family with children and two full-time wage-earners, or a family with a single parent (both are family types that have increased dramatically in recent years), how to respond to unexpected events is much less obvious.

Much of the literature on the modern family emphasizes the centrality of companionate marriage, the desire of partners to be "soul mates," and

159

the importance of intimacy between them. Given this view, it is in some ways stunning how little impact, both across occupations and across different types of families, spouses (or partners) have on each other's schedules. For example, we might have expected to hear spouses in dual-earner families talking of their need to be home to see one another, or wives saying that they needed to be home to fix dinner for their husbands; these concerns, however, rarely came up in our interviews. Instead, it was another aspect of family that shaped job hours and was absolutely central in the lives of these modern families: children. It was above all for women that children figured so centrally, but this was the case for many men as well. Not only were children the central factor shaping job schedules for all our occupations (except for male physicians), but the unpredictability of job hours was a defining concern for those who were parents, specifically because of their children.

It is not just nuclear families that create and respond to unpredictable events, but also extended families, and especially with the rise of single parents, extended family ties and dependencies have also increased in recent years. These kin create new demands and unpredictability at the same time as they are sometimes crucial in any effort to respond to unpredictable events.

Families have made an appearance in preceding chapters, but this chapter and the next will focus on them. Together, chapters 8 and 9 show that families' responses to the growing unpredictability of hours and schedules are shaped by class interacting with gender. Advantaged male and female employees use their class privilege to uphold conventional gender expectations. In contrast, class disadvantage pushes men and women to weaken gender expectations. More specifically, the two class-advantaged groups—nurses and doctors, one almost exclusively women and the other mostly men—have a series of choices about work hours. They use those choices in gendered ways: male physicians tend to prioritize careers, and female nurses tend to balance families and careers. The two class-disadvantaged groups—female nursing assistants and male EMTs—face greater constraints and have more difficulty meeting gendered expectations. To some extent, both of these disadvantaged groups "undo gender," even as both sometimes resist or at least have reservations about doing so.

A focus on occupations rather than scattered individuals makes it possible to see that cultural schemas are not simply individual choices, but rather are built into occupational cultures and organizational arrangements. In turn, this perspective allows us to highlight the ways in which cultures and arrangements are shaped by pressure from groups of employees in those occupations and organizations.

If these two chapters show the ways in which jobs shape families, they also show the ways in which families shape jobs. The former—the view that jobs shape families—has been the standard view. Researchers have analyzed a number of different ways in which spouses' job schedules shape and limit families, including the number of hours and shifts that spouses work, the division of domestic labor, the level of stress in the marriage, and connections to kin networks.[2] The reverse view—that families (especially nuclear families) influence hours and schedules—is also widely held and widely reported, especially for wives and mothers but increasingly for husbands and fathers as well. These two chapters not only reinforce but twist both standard arguments in two new directions.[3]

First, these chapters show that one important way to understand family is not simply as an influence on jobs but as a key *source of resistance* to job hours and schedules. There is a certain irony or paradox here: given the combination over the last thirty years of increases in women's participation in the labor market and the march toward a polarization of good and bad jobs, professional women's insistence on shaping job schedules to respond to family becomes simultaneously an act of conformity with conventional gender prescriptions and a major form of resistance to job demands.[4] Working-class men also resist the demands of the job in order to respond to family, but in doing so they are violating gender prescriptions. Second, what the standard view does not reveal is the unusual class and gender combinations—and the exaggerated inequalities—produced by these causal pathways. This chapter and the next highlight both of these outcomes.

This chapter focuses on the two occupations dominated by women—nurses and nursing assistants, one advantaged and one disadvantaged. The next chapter turns to the two male occupations—doctors and EMTs, again, one advantaged and one disadvantaged. Although this ordering may seem to emphasize class differences, the two chapters together are focused on clarifying the interaction of gender and class.

NURSING ASSISTANTS

Diluting gender conventions, women nursing assistants often give priority to job hours and schedules, in part because of the structure of their families. According to our survey, while the majority of those in the three other occupations were married, fewer than half of the CNAs were.[5] And the husbands of married nursing assistants rarely made enough to allow them to live on one income. Because their household income was low, women nursing assistants, whether single or married, were often their family's primary breadwinner and felt compelled to work additional and unpredictable hours beyond their official basic schedules, despite the problems this created in attending to domestic concerns. Class disadvantage then often coerced these women to violate gender expectations— some of which they wanted to meet (though they also occasionally sought to escape them).

This process could be seen clearly in our observation of a nursing home scheduler. She asked us to explain our research to someone who had just taken on another shift. Saying that we wanted to know "why you work so much," the worker responded: "Number one, I'm single. Number two, I got two kids. Number three, the rent is $750. So I have no choice; you can see it, right?" Another single mom, whose child had cerebral palsy, joined the conversation and described a conversation they had at home: "I'll be like, 'If mommy don't go to work, what am I going to do?' I was like, 'You won't have no money.' But she's three, so it's—she just wants her mom. She doesn't want me to go, but, you know." She then expressed her own fears about mothering and her need to abandon traditional gender schemas: "I do feel like I'm neglecting at times, but just like she said, 'Where's the money going to come in from?'" Then comes this mother's sense of injustice: "If it grew on trees, everybody would be all right. And that's if people didn't cut down the trees," she added, laughing, "and just take it themselves." Still another CNA succinctly explained why she picked up an extra twelve-hour shift every week: "I gotta pay my bills. I gotta support my family. I'm a single mom."

Some married mothers used similar rationales, typically because their husbands were unemployed or had limited earnings: "I'm more of the breadwinner in the family, so I have to pick up extra [shifts]. You know, if my daughter needs stuff for school, where's it gonna come from? I have to work." And still another explained that she not only worked her regular shift but did doubles in private care for six weeks straight because, as she told her kids and husband, "I *have* to do this; it will help us so much." She could pay bills that she was usually unable to pay; she "even paid her parents' oil bill."

This logic—and the institutional uses to which it is put—was revealed with particular clarity in a discussion of the nursing assistants' family pictures, which were around the office desk of a sympathetic scheduler in a nursing home. Asked about the dozens of pictures on the bulletin board next to her desk, the scheduler said that she put them there because the CNAs were not allowed to post pictures anywhere near where they worked, so "this way they can put up pictures of their family someplace." A nursing assistant listening to the conversation piped up: "She has them up so when you come in and say, 'I quit,' she can point to the pictures and say, 'You remember why you are working?'" This exchange made clear three points: first, the organizational disregard for, or even insistence on the invisibility of, nursing assistant families; second, the informal disruption of that disregard by a floor-level supervisor who, like lower-level supervisors studied by others, was more responsive to assistants' familial needs than were those higher up in the managerial ranks; and third, and perhaps most important, the necessity these disadvantaged CNAs felt to reject conventional gender conventions by serving as their families' primary breadwinner and—to come full circle—the organizational use of that necessity.[6]

The abandonment of conventional views of motherhood came with additional costs for these women who were paid so little. Doctors spoke of taking their children skiing at resorts; nurses spoke of taking orchestra bus trips and going to beach cottages; an EMT talked proudly of taking his kid to Disney World every year. But listen to Maria, a CNA, sadly recounting that she could not always afford to buy her kids an ice cream sundae once a month:

> And what I do now with them is that my first two paychecks from my first two weeks of the month go to bills and rent, and then my other bills. I try to stretch out my money as far as it can go. And I treat them at least once a month, or if that's a bad month, then I talk to them, like, well, "This month I can't take you to Friendly's for sundaes," or whatever it is that they were looking forward to. And I hate having to say that to them, but, you know, when you're having a bad month and things are not going your way, then sometimes you just don't have control of that.

Carmen, a single mother, had a television (as so many conservative commentators often note about poor mothers) but could not afford cable:

> I don't receive child support, and this is for both kids because they're different fathers, so like, if I was to only make thirty-two hours, I'll be short of money. I won't have . . . you know, and I don't have no big Comcast cable, uh-uh, because anyways, my kids only need to see cartoons. There's a channel, a local channel, they give cartoons, that's what they watch, and they're fine with that! (*laughs*) So I try to keep my bills [down], you know.

The limited income from their jobs—Maria and Carmen each earned less than $10 an hour and had official basic schedules of thirty-two hours a week—forced these single mothers to negotiate the difficult terrain of persuading their children that they were loved and cherished even though they would not (that is, could not) give them the goods and opportunities that many others take for granted and that have become markers of love, bonding, and belonging.[7]

The pressure to earn money to support their families, in combination with their low wages, little power, and even less control, made it difficult for these nursing assistants to resist schedule demands, even if they wanted to do so. When three nursing assistants were talking during their break about how one of the younger aides needed to control her "attitude," one of them asserted, "When you have to feed your kids, you have to behave differently just to keep the job." The entire group agreed that they could not afford to lose their jobs. One CNA added that often, when one of "them" (management) told her to do something, "I want to be like, 'What did you say? (rolling her eyes, turning her head) Psshh.' But instead, I'm like, 'What did you say? (singsongy and cheerful) I'm coming!'" She reiterated: "You gotta think about your kids."

Indifference and Resistance

Sometimes pervasive organizational indifference and insensitivity led CNAs to express resentment and try to make changes in their jobs. One nursing assistant who worked two jobs so that she could support her young kids expected a lot of them but wanted to be able to ensure their safety. Her nine-year-old son got himself to school every morning after she had to leave for her job, and she would say to him: "'Just make sure you call me to say you're heading off.' . . . "That way," she said, "at least I can know he's on his way to school." This single mother described her panic when she did not get a call one morning. Finally, she called her son. He had called and nobody had told her. "He said, 'Mommy, I've been waiting for fifteen minutes, they just found you.' And I said, 'Nobody told me you were on the phone, honey, I'm very sorry.' . . . And he was very upset"—in part because there was no longer a crossing guard to help him across the busy street he needed to cross to get to school. Angry, she went to her supervisor, a nurse, and asked her why no one had told her about her son's call. "I said to her, I said, 'I can't understand.' I said, 'You have your kids, and whenever a call come in, whether your husband or your kids, I always come and find you. And you did that to me.'" She concluded: "That's not right." Her response to the incident showed both her wish to make changes and her limited ability to do so: "And I was very upset . . . I said, 'Well, I have to fix this problem.' And my only way of fixing the problem, I changed my shift" (which was itself often difficult for a CNA to do).

Nursing assistants clearly saw their children as a reason *not* to resist the job, but their children sometimes also became a reason to do just that, even if resistance could be particularly costly for all CNAs. One nursing assistant expressed defiance toward an institution that was unresponsive to her family:

RESPONDENT: If my son is really sick, I feel that it's not my mother's responsibility to take care of him, I'll stay home with him. And my attitude is, with work, is, my son comes first. He's more important to me than any job.

INTERVIEWER: And how are they [the nursing home] about that?

RESPONDENT: They're understanding, but they're not understanding. Because, you know what I mean? They feel that I have a responsibility to my residents.

She concluded, with some indignation, "But I also have a responsibility to a child that I gave birth to."

Although hospital nurses routinely made use of the FMLA, nursing assistants often could not get their employers to comply with the law. As one CNA said, "There's no excused absences":

I think that the administration needs to be more understanding of the fact that we have families; some of us don't have the healthiest families. I mean, my daughter has a seizure disorder. The baby has real bad asthma. So there's times where I have to stay home or whatever because he can't breathe, she's having seizures, whatever the case. I think that if we come in with a doctor's note it should be considered an excused absence—it's not. There's no excused absences. So it's not fair to us as parents. Basically they want us to put our jobs ahead of our families. But they want to pay us chump change.

The CNAs in our study did not devalue families or work, as some recent commentators have proposed about low-wage workers.[8] Quite the reverse. The nursing assistants occasionally reported that their family obligations made it necessary to resist what they saw as unfair scheduling demands from their managers. Giving care became a potent but difficult source of resistance in the face of economic deprivation. Some insisted that they did call out, not only when their child was sick (which fit within the official sick leave policy), but also to attend important events at their child's school. Instead of being defensive, one nursing home worker just asserted: "You gotta understand about the little kids, they're kids, you know? You can't come to work if your kids are sick. . . . I understand work is your responsibility, but truthfully, family is your responsibility, and it's your first responsibility."

Workers sometimes asserted the superiority of their own morality and values over management's, condemning employers for any attempt to challenge the priority of families. One mother reported that, after learning of a schedule change only slightly in advance of an important event at her young son's school, she angrily castigated her boss for saying, "Well, I'm sorry, but you have to find your own replacement, or if you call out you'll get wrote up." This nursing assistant was furious, and she noted and accepted the negative consequences she was likely to face: "I'm like *what?!* Well, you're going to have to write me up because this is very important. This is something to do with my child's school."

Such defiance on the floor was usually a response to the needs of their children, but not always. One CNA received a call at work from her sister, who was so hysterical that it was hard to make sense of what she was trying to say. But the nursing assistant finally understood that her sister was saying that their father was "deathly dying in the hospital." In response, she quickly called the supervisor and told her, "I have to *go.*" Reporting the conversation that led to her angry defiance, she told us: "You know what she said to me? 'Are your residents done?' Then, I said to her, 'I'm sorry, but my father is in the hospital deathly dying, and it doesn't fucking matter if my patients are done or not. I don't give a shit if they're done or not—I'm going.'"

Nursing assistants are driven to this level of anger precisely because of their recognition that their employers refuse to alter the organizational policies or culture to be more accommodating to their families. As a rule, the employers of nursing assistants, in contrast to employers of every other occupation in the study, are *not* family-friendly and do not attempt to accommodate families. Nursing assistant employers mete out strong penalties to CNAs who put family first. As a result, most of the time nursing assistants put the job first, but crisis and mini-crisis situations change that dynamic, and family is the leading reason why people call out. According to the nursing home's scheduler: "The majority of the call-outs are babysitting issues. . . . More in the wintertime, it's transportation and sick; summertime it's always babysitting."

Occasionally a lower-level supervisor or scheduler helps nursing assistants resist. Lisa Dodson describes a "moral underground" of lower-level supervisors who are mandated to enforce punitive and unfair policies but try, at least sometimes and in limited ways, to humanize their organizations and occasionally make exceptions to the rules.[9] We also encountered first-level supervisors trying to make exceptions for workers when they could do so without attracting the attention (and disapproval) of higher management:

> I've done favors for a lot of CNAs in this place because of family issues, ta-kin' them off the schedule without management knowing. Um . . . if they need a certain day off to see their child in a play and they don't have a two-week notice, I knew I could fill it, so I gave it to them. I say, 'Shhh, it's be-tween you and me, don't be telling anyone,' but of course they do. Um, they have a lot of family issues. You've got to remember, a lot of these people are working for not much money and that's why they're doin' the overtime. . . . Their family comes first as far as I'm concerned. I've always thought that family comes first, job is second. And that's my standards, but that may not be their [management's] standards. And what they don't know is not gonna hurt them.

This supervisor was correct: upper-level management usually did not ac-cept lower-level supervisors' attempts to accommodate workers' families. According to a nursing home director of nursing:

> At my staff meetings over this past four-month period, I have been remind-ing people that I'd like to do away with the deals. There are a lot of deals. People, not for the benefit of the organization. So I've given them about six months' notice to say we can't continue to do that.

At least some nursing assistants did not believe the deals would end. As one said when a group gathered, "Yeah, they said that, but . . . they can't, because half of us are mothers." Even the director of nursing acknowl-edged imposing strong penalties and cracking down on all "deals" would not, however, mean that family issues would no longer have an impact on CNAs' jobs.

> More often than not, if we lose a nurse, we lose her to a hospital setting, to an acute care setting, or we lose [her] to moving, relocating geographically. I can't think of a single nurse—and I've only been here nine months—that has left because they were discontent. . . . We sometimes lose people because . . . very rarely geography with CNAs, but we sometimes lose them because of personal reasons: "I have a sick child," "I have no babysitter," "I'm preg-nant," "I can't leave my other children"—it's usually personal and confiden-tial. That is the biggest reason why we lose CNAs. Nurses, I think it's career development; CNAs, I think it's personal reasons.

"Personal reasons" were, to her, unacceptable: "There are times when people can't survive with this business."

Managers are quite certain that they can replace the nursing assistants if they do not "survive." Their inferior market position makes "personal reasons" or family concerns less powerful. One human resources staff member told us that the larger "population," or "pool," of available nursing assistants, compared to that for nurses, helped explain why family issues for CNAs were less of an organizational concern:

> I think the population of aides in general is a greater population that we can source from, and nurses is a harder population to source from—there just aren't as many. When it comes to CNAs, you . . . I don't want to say you can pick from a pool, but you have a bigger pool to pick from. So you're not necessarily going to have the same family issues.

Family concerns led nursing assistants to push against the employer's scheduling rules, to seek accommodations, to call out sick—but nursing assistants had comparatively little leverage. Even if they succeeded in making a deal with their immediate manager for a minor change in their schedule, or were forgiven for a specific, even well-justified, call-out, top management would often push to end that deal. Nursing assistants resisted, but their victories were few.

How Do They Care for Their Children? The Place of Extended Kin

Given their need to act as primary breadwinners and the family-unfriendly organizations that most of them worked for, how did these low-wage workers take care of their families, especially their children? A limited subset—those who worked the day shift and had public vouchers (certificates that allow families to get state subsidies that pay part of the cost of child care)—relied on day care centers as the first option. Day care centers, however, were not available on the every-other-weekend schedule that nursing assistants had to work, and they were not available when a CNA had an opportunity to pick up an evening or night shift. In some cases the children's father provided care, whether or not the mother and father were still together. More than any of the other occupational groups, however, the nursing assistants depended on extended kin.

Three-quarters of the CNAs told us that they relied on their (non-spouse) relatives for an important fraction of their child care. Even though she had a voucher for day care, one explained, "The problem is, in the nursing field you *have* to—it's a *must*—you have to work every other weekend." As a result, she, like so many other nursing assistants, relied on her mother, her sister, and the father of her children (who did not live with them) to help:

Unfortunately I have to depend on my mom for that, or the baby's father for my son. We kind of stood together, and he comes. He helps out as far as that, but because he's a plumber, then it's kind of like, "Well, there's a call. (*snaps her fingers*) It needs to be done." So it's kind of like I can't really count on him. . . . I mean, the good thing is that we both have A plan, which is him, then B plan, which is my mom. . . . If they call you for a job call, [I call] my mom to come over here and stay with the kids or whatever, my sister. So that's how we do it. . . . It's either my mom or my sister. I guess I spend more time with my sister than what I do with my mom.

Many said things like: "I don't know what I would do without my sister," or, as another insisted, "[My mother] is my rock. She is my life." The CNAs also talked about getting help from their grandmothers, brothers, aunts and uncles, cousins and nieces, as well as their own older daughters and sons. Some nursing assistants lived with relatives, and many others lived near one another. Listen to how filled with kin their lives could be:

Well, I'm a single parent. That's my aunt [pointing to another person who worked in the same nursing home], so I stay with her. . . . Usually, if both of us have to work that same day, that guy that you just saw in here, that's my cousin, and that's his girlfriend. So if we all have to work, I'll stay here till 8:00 and bring the kids to their house, which is the next block over. Right, we all kind of work together to make it happen.

Their relatives were key to nursing assistants' survival—both material and emotional. When asked, "How does your family influence your work hours?" a nursing assistant with a live-in boyfriend and a young son answered: "I don't actually have family out here. My family's in Philly."

Nursing assistants both gave help to and got help from relatives, in part because of the frequency of health problems (which are more common in low-wage populations), not only their children's but also other relatives':

I have to take my mother to doctors' appointments. . . . We own one car, my husband and myself, but all of his sisters and brothers, nobody owns a car. But they all medically need rides here, need rides there, doctors' appointments every day, you know. So I sleep as long as I can, which usually is three to four hours. Oh my God. I have a sister-in-law who's had two lung surgeries in the past year, so she depends on me.

Some CNAs said that their work schedules required them to rely on extended kin, but made it difficult to provide care for relatives who needed it, adding another layer of stress to their already complicated lives. One married nursing assistant whose mother-in-law had moved in with them about four months earlier remarked, with almost saintly aspirations, "I hope that makes me an even better [nursing assistant] because I realize how much responsibility this is." But then she trailed off: "My mother-in-law lost her husband. Today she is home alone by herself. And I am worried about: will she maintain her food restrictions? I cry in the car every day about her."

The reason these nursing assistants relied so much on relatives had to do at least as much with their work conditions as with the needs of their families. To arrange care on the weekends, and at all the unpredictable times they worked to pick up extra shifts, most nursing assistants needed to piece care together. A thirty-seven-year-old married mother, a nursing assistant who regularly worked thirty-two hours on evening shifts, sometimes alternated shifts with her husband but still needed to rely on her sister and mother. "Sometimes it's hard to find a babysitter from three to eleven, 'cause people got lives, like my sister, she got two other kids, and it's hard so . . . she just goes, pick him up in school, then she drops him off at my mom's house. That's what she does. He sleeps with my mom." Talking about the time when she first started working as a nursing assistant, she continued by discussing a common complaint among low-wage workers: "Before, I didn't have a car, he had to stay, he stayed for months at my sister's house, 'cause I didn't have a car." Another CNA, still in her midtwenties, pulled together help from a day care center (run by her aunt), her children's father (whom she did not live with), her mother, and her aunt. She noted how hard weekends could be: "On the weekends, my day care is closed, so on the weekends they're either with their dad, their grandmother, or my aunt. So I have those three people, so whenever I have to work on the weekend, I know they're with one of those three people."

Such arrangements may provide extended kin with the pleasure of taking care of a young relative, but the unpredictable arrangements also impose burdens on them. When a nursing assistant lost her day care voucher, she needed to rely even more heavily on her mother. This CNA regularly worked the evening shift (3:00 PM to 11:00 PM), but if somebody called out on the night shift, she would say, "Oh, I'll stay till 6:00 [AM]." How did she do that? This nursing assistant called her disabled mother, who was available because her bad back made it difficult for her to work outside the home. Asking her mother if she could watch her son overnight was not so easy: "You know, of course, here she is watchin' him three to eleven. And now she's gonna stay with him overnight and then have to get up with him in the morning and then watch him all day."

Nursing assistants themselves occasionally complained or expressed ambivalence about their need to rely on and care for relatives. One explained her feelings in terms of her desire to be independent:

> I *hate* asking for help. I'm very independent. That's why it's so unfortunate I have to depend on my mom, because I really don't like to depend on anybody. So I have to have their help; I've got to wait for them to help me because they're busy with something else. My mom barely will take care of my kids. It's usually my sister.

It was not always so easy for their children either. The nursing assistant whose son had to stay at her sister's when she herself did not own a car noted how hard it was: she would experience anxiety attacks and depression "because [her son] used to cry—he doesn't like my sister."

If extended kin were unavailable or unreliable or caused too much tension, nursing assistants might rely on their own kids, who would become, in the language of Lisa Dodson and Jillian Dickert, "mini-moms" (and occasionally mini-dads).[10] Some of these mini-moms were adults: "My daughter doesn't work, so she's there to pick up any slack, which is a blessing. Then, when she's not there, then it's like I've got double the work." Sometimes, the mini-moms were teenagers. Working a double day, one CNA explained that she had a thirteen-year-old who could get herself and her younger siblings home from school and could cook for them (that is, she could use the microwave). Another with twins said: "The thirteen-year-olds, they watch [the younger ones] for eight hours." Researchers have expressed concern about the costs to the development and social lives of young teens who take care of their siblings.[11] And some of our CNAs agreed: they spoke of their uneasiness about asking their young children to watch other children. But again, they felt that they had little choice.

No other group in the study came close to the nursing assistants in the degree to which they talked of giving and getting from kin. The contrast between the value the nursing assistants placed on kinship versus the value professionals put on the nuclear family became particularly clear during a union negotiation between CNAs and their nursing homes. At the bargaining session, six "bosses" (as the workers called them), including a white lawyer and the management of the nursing home, sat at the front. Facing them across the table were fifteen people who were the union negotiating committee (union staff and worker representatives), with an additional fifteen or so workers in the audience in the hotel conference room where the negotiations took place. There were, of course, various points of contention, but the lawyer and managers seemed genuinely surprised or taken aback when the talk turned to family. The topic was bereavement leave, and it became clear that the professionals and managers thought the distinction between the nuclear family and the extended family was simple: nuclear families were more important. The CNAs they were bargaining with suggested otherwise.

The contract they were negotiating contained two clauses on bereavement leave:

> (1) Up to 3 days will be allowed for death of an Employee's: (a) Spouse / Partner (b) Parent or (c) Child. (2) Up to 2 days will be allowed for the death of an Employee's (a) Brother, (b) Sister, (c) Grandparent, (d) Grandchild, (e) Stepchild, or (h) Parent-in-law.

The workers launched an attack. One worker at the table said: "They're telling me I can only take two days for my grandmother. Only two days for my grandmother. No way. And then you gonna tell me I can take three for my partner. Don't tell me that they didn't love their grandmother and don't need three days for her. At least three days, oh no." Then heated remarks arose from workers in the audience, who before this exchange had been sitting rather quietly. One worker member yelled, "I need a week for my grandmother." There was some indignant muttering in the crowd about how their grandmothers took care of them. Another spoke up: "And only two days for my sister?" The worker at the table then jumped back into the discussion, criticizing the distinction these clauses made between partners and other relatives. "At least, say not a difference in number of days for these."

This conversation revealed the relationship between class and family. For poor and near-poor women like the nursing assistants, "family" means extended family in a way it does not for the other groups. Lack of power leads not only to unconventional gender behavior but also to more expansive kinship forms.

NURSES

The experience of the relatively advantaged nurses was different from the CNAs' experience. In the small room at a hospital where nurses changed into their uniforms, about one-quarter of their lockers were covered with family portraits—some wedding pictures, occasional photos of husbands or family dogs, lots of prints of smiling children as well as some children's paintings (of what often appeared to be happy families). These pictures symbolized the draw of family ties and domestic responsibilities for nurses and their intrusion into the workplace. For nurses, the family came to work, but very differently from the way it did for CNAs. The nurses' pictures seemed to symbolize their domestic attractions and responsibilities—a reason to go home rather than to stay additional hours. The nurses had control over the placement of their pictures, which thus symbolized their leverage, at least compared to the situation for the CNAs who worked in nursing homes. It was nurses especially who said that they could and did use their families to resist demands to work schedules that interfered with what they viewed as their primary responsibility to give care at home.

Some of the basic facts about nurses help us understand how and why their families were often the central reason they chose to resist what they saw as unwieldy hours or schedules and why they were able to win changes. Nurses enjoy a favorable labor market position, especially compared to nursing assistants, and the consequences are highly visible on the floor—schedulers make what seem like endless calls to find nurses to come in to replace those who say, "My daughter is sick, so sorry, but I can't come in today."

Not only their favorable labor market position but also the nurses' marital status shape their job hours and schedules. Most nurses are married (71 percent in our survey), and most are members of dual-earner couples. Among our respondents, nurses and their husbands together typically earned an income considerably higher than the national average (a household median of $90,000 at a time when the national median was half that). A significant fraction of these married nurses made comments like, "We had plenty of money to play with, to pay our bills, to live," and, "I'm sure no one could really have enough money, even though money doesn't buy happiness, because it doesn't. But I live comfortably, and it's not just because of my income, it's my husband's too." They emphasized the importance of their *dual* incomes, while the small number of divorced nurses, especially mothers, more often emphasized the difficulties they faced going it alone.

The majority of the nurses had children; 43 percent had children still at home (though only 5 percent were single mothers). Others had adult children for whom they still provided considerable care—whether babysitting for their grandchildren, helping with housing, or running errands for them.[12] These kids cost money and time, which the nurses routinely connected in their conversations. Nurses talking in a hospital's break room told stories that linked their hours and schedules to the expense of kids—the cost of college, the cost of orchestra trips to Washington, or the cost of taking a family vacation at a beach cottage. Paying for college came up especially often in their conversations. The frame, at least implicitly, was that these women needed to work hard *and* rely on their husbands to make middle-class experiences available for their children. These women were neither working to make pin money for "extras" nor working to put food on the table; their talk about time centered on the reproduction of class position and, even more important, class mobility for their children. This kind of talk is typical of professionals (whether women or men), but much less common among low-wage workers.

Their families, and their "comfortable" household incomes, along with what is an undeniably favorable labor market position, are important in shaping nurses' work schedules. There is one more "fact" that is key to understanding why nurses use their families to influence, even resist, unpredictable hours on the job: a set of gendered cultural conventions that promote the expectation that these middle-class women bear primary responsibility for care on the domestic front.

Nurses made claims in the name of family, and that worked. Individually, they obtained the right to take care of their families. Collectively, they helped create institutional and organizational practices that supported families in what we might call feminized organizations, which contrast with the masculine organizations that Joan Acker and others have so clearly described.[13]

Many nurses told us stories of official basic schedules individually tailored to meet their family's needs. Recounting their personal histories, nurses spoke again and again about how they and their coworkers had shaped their hours to coincide with the kind of child care they wanted and needed at various stages of their life course. Talking about changes in her schedule, one said: "When my son was two weeks old, I went back to work. I was only able to do that because I could get in all of my hours working evenings or weekends or being flexible when I knew that I had child care [her husband] available." Another nurse explained that "my one day off was when [her children] had a half-day [of school]." Still another told us that she changed her work schedule to coordinate with her husband's work schedule and with what she saw as the needs of her developing children. "I started at two nights a week." A couple of years later, after her son was born, she had difficulty sleeping because he was not a "good sleeper," so she decided to change shifts again: "[I] got a babysitter, worked the evening shift. Then I had a second child, and my kids hated a babysitter, so I worked twelve-hour nights on the weekend, because it worked for me." Correctly assuming that her narrative was a common one, at least among advantaged women like herself, she remarked: "I'm your story right here, okay?" She continued by describing how she and her husband divided child care: "Twelve-hour nights on the weekend worked out for me, because my husband worked Monday through Friday. During the day I took care of the children, he took care of them on the weekend." Sounding vastly different from the nursing assistants, she concluded: "So it was perfect."

Adapting schedules was not always for children. An older nurse talked about taking off a year to care for her mother, "who was really sick." Still another told us that she moved often to follow her husband's career, but that "one of the great things about being in nursing is you can almost name where and when you want to work."[14]

Nurse schedulers and managers corroborate these stories. An evening shift supervisor in a hospital recounted her "flexibility" in response to the family needs of nurses: "If somebody came to me tomorrow and said, 'My husband's sick and he needs to have an appointment with his doctor tomorrow and I need to go,' we'll fix it or we'll try and fix it." Asked what determined nurses' shifts, a nurse manager did not hesitate:

> Family. I would say family rises to the top for people who have concerns. A lot of people have, like I said, older children or grown children, but there are a number who, when they speak to me about certain days that they want to work or not work, it's directly related to child, husband, father, child care. Yeah. (*What do you say to them?*) "We'll figure it out." No guarantees. I say, "No guarantees, but we'll figure it out."

In all occupations, managers sometimes arranged a day (or days) off for employees dealing with a family illness or issue, but nurse managers were typically (although not invariably) comparatively friendly and understanding about such issues, especially in contrast to many of the managers of nursing assistants.

Nursing is the only occupation in which managers routinely adapt the official basic schedule itself to meet employees' family needs, offering shifts that would not otherwise be available. Recall that hospitals offer different basic shifts of varying length—six, eight, ten, and twelve hours for three days a week. A nurse manager on a hospital's medical floor quite casually reported the power of children: "People will come in, take a full-time job, they have children, and they'll go for a part-time job." (*And do you have available positions for full time and part-time?*) Oh, we've always got them, yup."

Not only do nurses need to meet the weekday schedules for which they are hired, but most hospital and nursing home nurses also have to work weekends and holidays. But in many circumstances, nursing supervisors shape official basic schedules around nurses' family needs, rather than requiring nurses to adapt to the hospital's preset schedule options. A manager who was head of human resources said that her hospital was a good place to work because "it understood that the key issue is family: that nurses want schedules that allow them to take care of their families." Because nurses fought for, and won, a position of power, it is often employers, rather than nurses' families, that must adapt and revise their positions.

Some supervisors (typically also women), wrestling with similar issues in their own lives, said that they were happy to adapt the schedule; others were more reluctant to do so. One recurring theme was that efforts to offer nurses a range of options and thus induce them to work a schedule that fit with the rest of their lives involved costs to the hospital. One administrator explained: "I cannot tell you how much time it takes me. . . . This is such a waste of my time."

Although nurse managers prioritize making accommodations for children, this sometimes created divisions among nurses. At one hospital, nurses who had no children insisted on holding a staff meeting as a forum to express their concern that only nurses with children received special scheduling treatment. The meeting was called. The room was crowded, and some nurses brought their children. The nurses who had asked for the meeting complained that "the worst schedules fall to those without children," or as one said, "Everyone else gets screwed. . . . If we are going to do preferences, we need to ask everyone. If school, child, or whatever." Another piped up: "It isn't fair. I don't have kids, but I have preferences. Why can't I get my preferences? It really isn't fair." The director of nursing replied to these three by simply warning, "Stop it," and then moving on.

The hospital managers remained responsive to family needs—especially the needs of children—not only because so many nurses insisted on it and had the market power to resist, but also because it fit their own assumptions about women, work, and family. When we were setting up an interview with this director, she called to change the time, explaining that she had to go help her daughter take care of her baby. In presuming that we would understand, this administrator was assuming that we shared her beliefs and expectations about the force and meaning of family.

Gender, Housework, and Child Care

Thirty-five percent of nurses reported that they at least sometimes disagreed with their husbands about job hours. Nonetheless, nurses typically adapt their schedules to their husbands' job schedules and do significantly more of the chores on the home front, even though they report that they earn, on average, 57 percent of the family income. This is a gender divide, then, but not one based primarily on exchange or money. Nurses demand schedule adaptations because they typically have—and believe they should have—primary responsibility not only for children but also for housework.

This inequality is apparent in various aspects of housework, whether cooking, cleaning, or shopping. One nurse first described her husband as "an easygoing guy who never had a problem with my working. He wanted me to work. So whatever I had to do to work." But then she revealed that when she worked evenings, "I just cook the meal" and her husband would come home to a family dinner she had prepared. Another nurse whose husband was a self-employed consultant commented dramatically and sarcastically: "My husband's hands would disintegrate if they hit dishwater!" Some reported that they shared household work, but then, when probed, said things like: "He does a lot. He's better than the average guy. He does suppers, laundry, baths. He doesn't do a lot of cleaning-cleaning, like, he wouldn't clean the bathroom and vacuum, dust and all that, but he'll do the dishes, he'll pick up after supper, he'll keep the house as tidy as he knows how." A number of nurses employed an economy of gratitude: husbands who "helped," their wives exclaimed, were "rare," "better than the average guy," not only "wonderful" but even "a luxury."[15]

One unusual nurse who was married to a real estate broker said that she and her husband made the choice to give more of the domestic work to him. Asked if this bothered her at all, she smiled and responded: "No. Are you kidding? I have never cleaned the bathroom! I wouldn't even be able to tell you what he uses—I have no clue!" But then she expressed some chagrin: "I think it's hard for him sometimes, because I make more money than him, so I think ego-wise that that's hard for him sometimes."

Some nurses were even more explicit about housework being their work—as prescribed by their understanding of what gender frames are and should be. In a break room, nurses were sitting around the table, eating the lunches they had brought from home, and talking about their shifts. One talked of switching to nights and commented, when asked why, "My daughter is now in first grade, and if I did not switch, I would never see her. She needs a mom. My husband can't do that. It's a mother thing." Others nodded in assent. Using the words "responsibility" and "burden" in quick succession, one nurse commented: "One thing, I don't know if you are addressing this, especially as a woman's perspective—even though I have a great, great partner, as most women do, I think women still have the responsibility for the meal planning. As helpful as I think people are who both work, I think the mother always gets the burden."

As much research has shown, this gendered division also prevails in the care of sick family members, including elderly parents. But the claims and the gendered division were especially clear with regard to children, who were the main focus of the nurses' break-room discussions about why they insisted on particular hours and schedules.

Even though they subscribed to conventional gender expectations, nurses sometimes resented the division of labor. As one nurse, married to a physician, explained her greater role in the household's division of labor: "I just can't imagine anything . . . unless he were to negotiate to cut back his practice, which I can't imagine him doing. . . . I mean, he's the primary breadwinner." She described her work as wearing "so many hats in my family. Financially, I do all the bill paying, I do all the grocery shopping, the meal planning. I think that's a female thing." As she continued, this nurse's comments showed that she understood the division in terms of individual choice, as an obvious way for her to proceed herself, rather than as part of a broader and externally driven gender divide: "That's just a personal bias. Now, it could have been the other way, *it just happens* to be the way it is in our family. It has always been—that's always been on my shoulders."[16] Although she admitted, when asked, feeling some resentment, she quickly normalized it: "Sure, absolutely. That's normal. But then after a while you realize—that's my job. That's actually one of the many other hats that you wear. That's my job, and thankfully I can do it." Her comments about the division of labor echoed the comments of the male doctors (whom we discuss in the next chapter).

These women were not simply responding to external constraints or to husbands who earned a living but resisted doing their share of the daily work of the home. Some nurses told us that they preferred having additional time with their children, that caring for their children provided an appealing contrast to the intensity of their jobs, and that the nursing shifts and hours, along with their partners' incomes, allowed them to design the schedules they preferred. As one explained: "Well, the big thing is that I like to be home with my kids." Such preferences, together with the constraints they faced at home, pushed them to demand flexible schedules from their employers. In this sense, they used family as a way to resist what they saw as the unwieldy demands of paid work and to do so in such a way as to meet traditional gender expectations.

This kind of resistance had its costs. On the one hand, these professional women paid an economic penalty for resisting and for using their power to demand the flexibility to be with their children.[17] On the other hand, they were able to "balance work and family" in a way that is unavailable to many other women as well as men. They had fought to get some work-life balance, and these advantaged women had often managed to win that fight.

CONCLUSION

This chapter provides a view of the families of two groups, the CNAs and the nurses, who take different approaches to gender conventions. Low-wage nursing assistants usually do not have the opportunity to form the kind of nuclear family that promotes traditional feminine expectations—including intensive mothering and lowered job involvement—even if, as Cameron Macdonald and others have argued, they are subject to the same cultural models of family, mothering, and jobs that affect more advantaged women.[18] Although nursing assistants push back against the scheduling rules and practices imposed on them, most are unable to change the rules of the game. Occasionally a lower-level supervisor provides an accommodation, and coworkers frequently help provide a solution to the worst scheduling problems (as chapter 10 will show). But the nursing assistants have not (so far) been able to change organizational structures and rigid scheduling practices. To put food on the table for their families, breadwinning takes priority and their families must adapt—including adapting to the unpredictable hours and shifts.

In contrast, nurses use their conventional ideas about family responsibility to resist and reshape work schedules. Managers and organizations often comply with nurses' requests and preferences in this woman-dominated occupation. Family-friendly policies for nurses develop out of the labor market power they hold, the division of labor they construct at home, and to some extent even the administrators' assumptions that these advantaged women (and only the advantaged women) should be responsive to their responsibilities at home. Many nurses feel some ambivalence about organizing their family and work lives this way, but many also feel that doing so allows them to have the relationships they want at home, especially with their children.

These advantaged women are quite explicit that balancing work and family requires a struggle for control. Balancing does not just happen, and nurses do not just react: they push their supervisors and organizations. A particularly telling discussion occurred at the central desk of a hospital medical floor when shifts were changing. One nurse asked what our research was about, and we explained that it was about hours and shifts. Another nurse standing nearby jumped in: "I want mother's hours. I saw the movie *Nine to Five*. That's how you get mother's hours. Have to push very hard. They had to do a lot to get those hours." The group of listening nurses laughed and nodded in agreement. Several points emerged from this conversation. First, the nurses understood that to balance family and work they had to insist—both as individuals and collectively—on their right to do so. Second, the nurses were very different from the low-wage nursing assistants: not only did they make these claims about the importance of family in shaping work hours and schedules, but they also could insist that these were legitimate claims. They knew that organizational administrators would listen, even agree. Finally, these claims rested on inequality not only across occupations but also inside families.

The next chapter focuses on the other two occupational groups, those dominated by men—EMTs and physicians—to look further into families and untangle the ways in which gender and class operate jointly to create complex inequalities.

Chapter 9 | Unequal Families: Class Shapes Men's Responses to Unpredictability

AN EXAMINATION of emergency medical technicians and doctors—the two occupations dominated by men—suggests a process parallel to that for nursing assistants and nurses: those with class advantage promote gender conventions, while those with less class advantage "undo gender." That is, professional men "do" gender convention and working-class men undo it.

Cecilia Ridgeway argues: "The rigid structure of work time that the traditional workweek involves implicitly assumes that ideal workers cannot have direct responsibility for the daily care of dependent children."[1] In our study that aptly describes one group and only one group—the male physicians. They look very different not only from the low-wage CNAs and professional women nurses but also from the working-class male EMTs. The EMTs revise their schedules, especially their overtime and second jobs, in the name of family in ways that doctors do not.

EMERGENCY MEDICAL TECHNICIANS

EMTs work long hours and rigid basic schedules, but they also try to organize their time around caregiving for their families—and in doing so they revise standard notions of masculinity. Certainly the firefighters, and often the private-sector EMTs, have very little control over their basic official schedules. And across organizations, EMTs work substantial overtime and, more than any other occupation, put in time at second jobs. For overtime and second job hours, however, most EMTs try to pick up only those hours and shifts that allow them to take unpredictable time off to take care of sick family members or attend special events, intermittent time off to

181

run household errands, special time to just enjoy their wives and children, and more routine time for regular parenting activities.[2] For working-class EMTs, these family roles entail a reversal of what both the popular press and academic research suggest is conventionally expected of men (probably in part because neither looks very often at working-class men). In stark contrast to nurses, EMTs' involvement in family, especially fathering, entails a kind of resistance to the normative family—to the conventional "ideal male worker" who turns out to be a professional man.[3]

Although they usually could not alter the official basic schedules that were handed out months in advance, the male EMTs in our study talked not only about refusing callbacks and overtime but also about leaving early or arriving a little late because of family responsibilities.[4] Without hesitation, one EMT described how he and his wife had divided their schedules:

> Like when my wife—when we first had Sara [their daughter], my schedule needed to match hers. It was so I could be off when she was on and needed to be on when she was off—so I did. That was a major schedule change for the family. [I] modified my schedule to accommodate the family.

The EMTs talked of picking children up from school, feeding them dinner, or staying home with them when they got sick. The EMTs saw this work as their responsibility—shared with their wives. One described his schedule: "My son's out of school at 2:30 in the afternoon. That means that I have to leave here about 2:15 to make sure I'm at the school to pick him up." Another described his willingness to take callbacks: "When my daughters are in school, I come in a lot during the day. Weekends, that's a rarity unless it is late at night or early in the morning. I'll come in from midnight on." Or as another explained the general pattern: "The reason that for the most part scheduling gets changed around and stuff, it's, it's, 98 percent of the time it has to do with the kids." Especially when their children got sick, many of the EMT fathers took it for granted that "of course that's a reason to stay home." These working-class men produced schedule unpredictability in response to what they saw as their children's needs.

It was not always easy for these EMT fathers to change their hours when they felt that they were needed at home. One emphasized that by prioritizing his family, he might, under some conditions, be forced to accept penalties at work: "If there was a family emergency, the good thing about where we work, I'd leave. . . . So I would get up and leave, because it's family and friends first. I have no problem, and you can dock me a day's pay."[5] Others talked about having to "jump through the hoops" with managers and coworkers in order to get the time with their kids that they saw as necessary. Asked how his work hours related to his ability to take care of his children in the way that he liked, one EMT responded:

> In some aspects, it works out great because you've got days off, the time off during the day, so school vacations, summer vacation, you tend to be there with the kids more. There are times, though, that you're scheduled to work for some big school event, and now you have to start jumping through hoops to get the time off to go attend those and things like that. But by and large, everybody's found a way to make it work for them. Unfortunately, there's just some things, you can't make it, and there's no two ways around it.

But then he concluded: "But by and large, I think the majority of time we find some way to accommodate it." By "we" he was including both co-workers and supervisors.

Although EMTs were the most likely of the four occupation groups to work second jobs and also to put in lots of overtime, some of these working-class men scoffed at materialistic goals and desires. As one EMT commented:

> You just have to live with what you make. . . . Well, the way I figure it, my kids have everything they need; there's foolish things they don't need, so they don't get it. More would be better, but it just seems if you made this much, you live with that much; but if you make more, now you spend up to that much. So if you didn't have it, you'd still have everything you want, but now your goal gets bigger, what you want, the more money you make—I want that, I want that, I want that.

This EMT used this antimaterialist argument to legitimate family involvement. As we will see, the opposite happens with some doctors: materialism leads them to give less hands-on care to their families.

Even those EMTs who spoke about wanting more put it in terms of their children and the contributions of their wives. Standing around the dispatch center, we asked a private-sector EMT whether the company's financial incentive to work holidays worked for him. Generally, he said, it did not: "Time with my family is more important." Commenting that "life is expensive, you know," one EMT told us that he took his kids to Disney World every year. He went on to explain: "My wife, she matches my income. If I didn't work the hours I work, I wouldn't be matching her. Yeah, so money is really—it's important, you know. It rules." But even this EMT concluded: "I'm making just what I need."

Many EMTs emphasized how easy it was for them to get their employers and coworkers to help them make schedule accommodations for their families. When the son of one EMT supervisor was born, "I did alter the hours to accommodate, I guess, my wife and my son . . . if my wife can't take care of the baby because she's feeling ill, or she just needs extra time in the morning, I can essentially come in a little later in the morning, and, you know, and adjust my hours, so it works out well." We asked whether the ease with which he could adjust his schedule meant that he had a lot of autonomy. "Yes. Yep, I mean, in the afternoon, if there's an appointment or the baby needs to be out and she needs assistance, I have the liberty . . . pretty much I can go in and assist with that and step away from work without much repercussions happening here."

This EMT—who, to be sure, was a supervisor—resembled many of the nurses whose employers would adapt their hours to meet their gendered family responsibilities. Both were very different from the nursing assistants and doctors.

One EMT reported that, although most of the time the company did permit workers to shape hours to fit family needs, at one point a new manager changed the schedule options, eliminating the shifts that ended at 6:00 AM and offering only shifts that ended at 8:00 AM; since the company often had mandatory holdover, EMTs might not get out until 9:00 AM. When that schedule change was introduced, according to one male EMT, "I would say we lost at least ten to fifteen people in a very short period of time. They said, 'We cannot do this with our children,' and they had to go to another ambulance service." We asked whether there were more women than men among the people who left, or whether both women and men had quit. "It was women and men. . . . These days it seems like both men and women, and both mothers and fathers, have their full-time jobs, so either one . . . it affects the family just the same nowadays. Just from my perspective."

Workers' anger, combined with the high number of people who quit and went to other companies, led the company to transfer the offending supervisor to another city. The manager's forced transfer did not necessarily come from upper management's abstract commitment to family-friendly policy. The company already had enough trouble recruiting personnel; an EMT reported that, at this company, "there's as much overtime as you want." Whatever the company thought about families, it apparently did not want to lose qualified workers; a supervisor who exacerbated a labor shortage had to go.

EMT fathers took considerable pleasure in being able to manipulate their schedules for their kids. As one remarked, "My time going with my kids like that is irreplaceable. That's kind of how I feel about it." Another felt good when he compared his situation with others': "I love the fact that I can be home with my kids a lot, because it's long hours at times, but honestly, I get four days off in a row with my kids. How many people get that much?" Still another echoed this sentiment by describing how he changed his ideas about work time when children came into his life: "I was working eighty hours a week, and I loved it, [but then,] the idea of having kids? That helped me scale back hours, because I love being a dad."

The basic facts about EMTs' families again help explain why they could shape their families this way. Like doctors and nurses, most EMTs in our study were married (60 percent), and 52 percent had children under eighteen; one-quarter had kids less than six years old, and many of the remaining had grown kids whom they helped out or who were the reason they sympathized with and wanted to help other EMTs whose kids were still young. Though few of the EMTs were divorced, those who were consistently talked about being involved in their children's lives. One talked about moving a great distance and changing jobs to be near his children when his ex-wife moved away with them. A few pushed for and obtained joint custody, which they took very seriously—insisting on time off so they could be with their children.

A majority of these working-class men who were married had employed wives (90 percent), most of whom worked full-time. Their wives contributed on average, according to our survey, almost one-third of the family income (average family income was $76,000), and a number of their wives contributed a significantly higher proportion of family income. As one EMT summed up the pattern: "There's only one guy I know in my department that his wife doesn't work, and he works and they have three kids and a house, and he doesn't know how he makes it, but every week, by the skin of his teeth."

Tag Team Parenting

Almost half of the EMTs with children alternated shifts with their employed wives so that they could share parenting. These working-class men preferred making this arrangement and relying on relatives so that they did not have to rely on "strangers"—a derogatory term that a number of them used to describe those paid to take care of children. One spoke of juggling: "My wife and I have juggled our schedules so that there's always a parent home. . . . and we've done that since the time the kids were born. There was always a parent home, and we could adjust our schedules for that reason, so the flexibility allowed by our schedule for me was perfect because I wanted to raise my kids." Though he said that "it gets a little hectic," he went on to muse about the result: "It gives me what I want: time with my family, good pay—well, reasonable pay."

Although many EMTs said that they preferred alternating shifts as a way to care for their children, doing so was not always easy. According to the survey, 51 percent of these EMTs said that they often or sometimes had disagreements with their spouse about their job hours. A number talked of the marital conflict that such alternate-shift parenting sometimes caused, saying that there was "a lot of tension, it puts a lot of strain on marriage," or that "sometimes it's a screaming match." As other research shows, "tag-teamers" have three to six times the national divorce rate.[6] Concentrated in the working class, this form of parenting may solve some problems, but it clearly also has costs.

Moreover, alternating shifts often does not provide adequate child care coverage; given the insistent and often unpredictable demands of two jobs, the EMTs and their wives often had to rely on other relatives. One whose work hours overlapped with his wife's remarked: "My folks or her folks watch the kids from six to midnight, which is, you know, where would I get day care to do that? We're fortunate we have family support; if we didn't, I don't know how we'd make it work." But even being able to count on the grandparents did not always work out so well; he described the patchwork coverage that he and his wife, like so many others, pulled together:

> The world works on 8:00 to 5:00, you know. Even for day care. I ran into trouble this summer because my folks couldn't watch the kids. I had a heck of a time, and I couldn't find a day care that would take my kids on a rotating basis. Okay, it's a Tuesday this week, it's a Wednesday next week, how about a Thursday? No. You either commit to a whole week or . . . they won't do that because they can only take so many kids. It's hard. The world doesn't work on a rotating schedule, even though our schedule does.

Even a job that has relatively few restrictions on time off and also enables workers to swap schedules does not and cannot guarantee that an EMT will be able to manage the full range of unpredictable events. As another EMT noted:

> "Daddy, I need a ride here," "Daddy, I need a ride there." "Well, honey, I'm going to be locked into the station, I can't help you. You have to work it out with your mother." And if my wife is busy, well, guess what? You're not going here, you're not going there, and there's nothing we can do about it.

The Influence of Wives

Their wives cannot alter EMTs' basic job schedules, but they can and do influence if and when their husbands pick up overtime or extra jobs. Listening and responding to their wives, the EMTs routinely turned down overtime as well as per diem work in their secondary jobs in exchange for spending time with their families: "There's been a lot of times that I have turned down overtime because I knew it would be on a day that, say, my wife would have off, and making the extra money wouldn't offset that loss of time with her."

Listening to their wives often led to doing a considerable amount of domestic work. A firefighter whose wife was also a firefighter believed that housework was his job as much as hers. This shaped his job hours and schedules: "I stopped working in a second job, so when she's at the fire station I'm home, and a lot of times I'll try to get the dusting and stuff, like that, laundry, done. That way, when we are home together, we aren't doing stupid things in the house. So I take those days to try to get [a] little [bit of] housework done." Another EMT remarked, "We kind of share responsibilities."

The women EMTs, a small number of whom we interviewed, sounded very much like the men when it came to discussions of the division of labor in and out of the home. (And as we shall see, they were, in this sense, very different from the female physicians, who sounded so different from their male counterparts.) These working-class women, who, like the working-class men, had rigid basic schedules but contributed a significant part of their family's income, talked of making adjustments where they could for their family, especially when it came to parenting responsibilities and sharing these responsibilities with their husbands. The husband of one woman EMT, who owned an auto repair business, scheduled his work around her schedule. Coordinating their calendars, he would ask her, "Can I do two days this week?" In part because she had also "learned to let things go," she believed that "working has made our relationship more equal."

Spousal influence ranged from subtle signals to outright demands. While eating lunch at work with a number of his fellow EMTs, one man responded to the question, "Do your families ever ask you to not come in?" by laughing and saying, "No, they tell you: you're not going in." The other EMTs sitting around joined in the laughter and nodded in agreement. Others said that sometimes they would wait to see what their wives thought before agreeing to go to work:

> So there is that conflict where the phone will ring, and we have the caller ID, she'll look at it, and she'll be like, "It's Longford [his job site], what do you want to do?" So sometimes we just let it ring. And that's our agreement. I'm able to read her now; I know where she's *Don't do this to us.* But there'll be times where she's like, "Hey, it's Longford—do you want me to get it?" She'll let me know she's okay with it.

Then he made the kind of remark we were more likely to hear from the nurses: "But I feel guilty, because my girls are only going to be this age once."

Another male EMT emphatically described the power of wives to shape their husbands' refusal to work extra hours:

> They don't like you leaving at nighttime for a night shift . . . but the extra hours, the overtime. There are guys there who feel it's their obligation. You don't have to do thirty or forty [extra hours], but you've got to do at least some of it to help out [coworkers]. And if they're getting up and leaving right after dinner, you know, there are some guys there who, their wives will tell them, "You're not going in," "You do not go in," "You can only go in if I'm not home, and you better be home before I get home." (*Does it really work in an emergency-type [situation] . . .?*) They won't come in.

Still another summed up his experience and that of others: "I was telling you about the fire a couple of nights ago when they called people in. They had to actually call me in, my wife says, 'You're working?'" He concluded by telling us: "So obviously I couldn't go in."

Overall, then, these working-class men worked long hours and in many ways their schedules were as rigid as the CNAs' schedules. Because of employer demands, many alternated rigid basic schedules with their wives, which meant that these spouses saw relatively little of each other. That was a cost, many told us, of their schedules. But both the structure and culture of their families and jobs led these working-class men to revise conventional gender expectations, especially those concerning parenting.

PHYSICIANS

The male physicians in our study used the power of their jobs to shape their nuclear families but did little to revise their jobs. As earlier chapters showed, male doctors often insisted that they needed to be available for long, sometimes unpredictable, stretches when their job demanded it. They felt as though they had too much to do and not enough time in which to do it—a classic case of what Leslie Perlow has called a "time famine."[7] But it was not just the pull of work conditions: many said that they worked long hours because they wanted the lifestyle they had developed as successful breadwinners for their families. Many doctors and their families embraced the consumer revolution, or as one doctor carefully put it, "We have gotten used to a particular way of living. I have to work the hours I do to get what we now think we need."

While other occupations often turned to extended kin, the male doctors turned to their spouses: they expected their wives to take care of the household and the children, to reduce their own job schedules, and, if necessary, to quit their jobs. It was these men, then, who enacted the "ideal-worker norm" as described by Joan Williams: the ideal worker is made possible by the availability of a counterpart at home who supports his availability at work.[8]

The male doctors, almost without exception, were their family's primary breadwinner. Like most of the EMTs and nurses, most of the physicians were married (77 percent according to our survey), and most (59 percent) had minor children still living at home. But that was where the similarity stopped: not only did they earn significantly more than any of the other groups, but the doctors also earned, on average, a higher proportion (87 percent) of their family's income. Forty percent of the men surveyed had a stay-at-home wife.[9] Some of the wives quit working because their husbands worked such long hours and brought in a good income; as Youngjoo Cha's analysis of national data shows, this pattern of quitting their jobs is common among women married to affluent men who work very long hours.[10]

Of the remaining physicians with employed wives, 40 percent of the wives worked part-time (less than forty hours a week), and when employed, the wives often worked in jobs with flexible hours that they could use to assume domestic responsibilities. Serving as their family's primary breadwinner, these men normalized their greedy jobs—both by pointing to the nobility of the work they did and by saying that their wives got something in return. Many had beautiful homes and new cars and took, as we have seen, lengthy and pricey family vacations. That is, many of them talked of this division as being rooted in the moral economy of the workplace and the material economy of their marriage. But just as clearly, the family economy was rooted in cultural models of marriage, family, and gender (shared by their supervisors, when they had them).

None of the male physicians with children did more of the child care than their wives, and none even shared it equally. Many remarked that this arrangement just made common sense. For example, consider this doctor, who had three kids, aged thirteen, sixteen, and seventeen, and earned about $200,000 a year: "My wife doesn't work, because she takes care of the children, since my youngest one. She used to work part-time— she was a nurse. She used to work maybe one or two days a week, but then my youngest one, when she was five—she's thirteen now—had an illness, and she stopped working." His conclusion: "It's much better. I don't know how you could work and take care of children."

As some doctors saw it, or at least claimed to see it, this division was rooted in occupational choices that they and their wives made jointly.

One doctor with four children—three in their twenties and a fourth who had been "an accident" and was not yet a teenager—was married to a physical therapist who worked in the same office where he was a physician. He often took his son to school at 7:30 AM before going to his office but found it hard to get home before 7:00 or even 8:00 PM. Working part-time, his wife often insisted that he stop work and come home to join the family: "Well, I mean, I have conversations with my wife all the time. She says, 'You need to restrict it, you've got to come home.'" He tried, but often found it very difficult because he felt an obligation to do his fair share with his colleagues, to fill out all the paperwork, and to help his patients. (At the end of each day there would be patients who might need a prescription filled or want a callback because of a high-priority lab test—the ones he called the "really worrisome ones.") In his office, he ran from appointment to appointment. At the end of the day, the first time he would sit down for any extended time, he would point to the high stacks of papers on his desk, which he dealt with until 7:30 or 8:00 every night, much to the annoyance of his wife. Even on his days off, he relied on his wife: "In terms of work, the days I'm off typically I have to go see nursing home patients on those days, so that usually my wife and the kids go off. I've usually managed to get there for the vast majority of their major events," he noted, then added with a laugh, "but they know I walk in late." Such laughter may have concealed a fear that his job created pressures at home. As he concluded: "It's gotten worse, I think, over the last five years."

Another doctor, whose wife was also a professional, answered our questions more succinctly:

INTERVIEWER: Have you ever changed your hours, shifts, or jobs in response to your family or family responsibilities?

RESPONDENT: No.

INTERVIEWER: Is this something you've ever considered?

RESPONDENT: Ah, I've considered it, but I haven't changed anything.

INTERVIEWER: Has your spouse ever changed her hours, jobs, or shifts in response to the family?

RESPONDENT: Yeah, she has; she's working less now. And I think she saw a need, so she did it from that perspective.

His formulation suggests his wife sees "the need," but he does not see—or at least does not imagine—that he might be the one obligated to fill that need.

To make possible their complicated schedules and long hours, the doctors with children whose wives were employed often combined the help of two women: a wife and a nanny. Many talked of relying on their wives working part-time—as therapists and nurses as well as physicians and lawyers—and on nannies to "pick up the slack." One surgeon, married to another surgeon, had two little daughters, aged two and four. He described his wife's part-time schedule: "She's home for the weekend . . . for four days, for Saturday, Sunday, Monday, and Tuesday, and the nanny's there for the other days." Like so many of the other male doctors, he explained (to us and probably to himself) their division of paid work, household labor, and parenting in biological and economic terms, even if that division was also driven by a set of norms about gender. The explanation was based in part on his wife's internal predispositions: "Well, you know, she took time off . . . to have the babies and took time off afterward, several months after, and knew that she only wanted to work part-time because she wanted to be an active participant in the raising of the kids." He paused, then said: "And I, of course, do too." Then he went on to explain the gendered division in terms of external constraints: "But I . . . you know, the way the practice runs and the earning potential for my practice is greater than hers, so we set it up so that she works the half-time and I work full-time." On the three days his wife went to work, he "helped" the help by getting up around 6:30, or "sometimes seven, depending on what I have in the morning." He explained their "division" of child care:

RESPONDENT: My wife works Wednesday, Thursday, Fridays, so on Monday, Tuesday, we don't have our nanny; my wife takes care of the kids on those days. But on other days, sometimes my wife . . . the days my wife works, she always leaves (*laughs*), so I have to see off the nanny.

INTERVIEWER: And when you say "see off the nanny," the nanny comes and picks up the kids and takes them someplace?

RESPONDENT: No, no.

INTERVIEWER: You just mean . . .

RESPONDENT: Yeah, she's . . . sometimes the kids will be awake, and I will get them started with breakfast, and she'll kind of take over.

The power of economic concerns came home perhaps most forcefully when another doctor talked about his wife's decision to quit her job as an attorney. Seeming to at least implicitly recognize the monetary value of her unpaid family work, he explained (without cracking a smile): "Now I pay her to be at home."

Physicians' incomes enable those without a stay-at-home spouse to purchase a family-substitute who provides (but does not get) flexibility.

They were the only occupational group who routinely hired nannies—someone who came into their home and was, they said, "flexible" in her hours. Nannies were expected to be available for unpredictable hours on demand. For the male physicians, flexible wives and flexible nannies made their schedules possible. Unlike the other groups, they almost never talked about staying home to care for sick children, alternating shifts, or relying on extended kin for help. When asked if he ever stayed home with his kids when they were sick, maybe canceling patients or even surgeries, the surgeon married to a surgeon replied, "I haven't. My wife has."

> I even had one of my staff go to my house and watch the kids (*laughs*) so I didn't have to cancel a day. Because my schedule is so booked in such a way that to take twenty-five patients—where do you put them? Well, you know, it's either waiting six weeks or double-booking everything for the next three weeks, which is a nightmare for all the other patients too. So it's really hard. So she has a little more of a lighter schedule in that regard and can move patients around a little easier, so she's been the one who has to do a lot of that moving around. I don't know if she's ever actually canceled surgeries because of it. We've been lucky to be able to accommodate those days.

Surprised by this story, given that his wife was a surgeon who worked with cancer patients, we probed by asking, "This is just from an ignorant patient's perspective, but if I were scheduled for surgery for cancer, and it had to be canceled because somebody's kid was sick, I mean. . . ." He interrupted, not answering why his (non-lifesaving) surgeries should have priority over his wife's cancer surgeries, but instead explaining how hard it was and how his wife adapted:

> You're right—it sucks. But the reality is that what most people fail to realize is that, you know, you look at a doctor and say, well, you know, they're there to just take care of me, but you realize that we're . . . as human beings, you know, we've got to make sure our kids are taken care of and make sure that we're, you know, ourselves are taken care of and everything. And how things in our lives affect our patients is a big deal, but there's also family emergencies and things that you can't overcome.

But then he switched and asserted, without hesitation and perhaps with no awareness that he had done so, that his wife was the one who had to make sure their kids were taken care of and handle those family emergencies: "And obviously if, for instance, she would have to cancel a case, well, then she might work on her day off to accommodate that, so it's never like you say, well, that lady's got cancer, she can wait another six weeks, it's fine. It just doesn't happen that way." Clearly this physician felt pressed by his obligation to care for his patients, an obligation that took precedence over staying home with his children when they were sick. The structure of his job and family life led him to organize his time so that he took care of patients and his wife took care of their kids.

Another physician's family went so far as to ensure the priority of his job hours and schedules by home-schooling their kids. Though when they first met she had planned to attend law school, his wife now stayed home and did the schooling. He began explaining this choice by saying: "The idea was that because I could make my own schedule and take vacation anytime I want." But midsentence, he too switched logic to explain that his wife needed to put aside her career to home-school their kids and take them on vacation when he could go: "If kids are in school, then you're kind of tied to their vacation schedule, but if I want to take a vacation in the middle of March, we go the middle of March." Note his choice of pronouns: "if *I* want to take a vacation," not, "if *we* want to take a vacation."

Doctors often made claims about the differences between women and men, and these differences legitimated for them the ways they had set up their lives. Another physician's wife—again, a physician herself—worked part-time so their children could have a "more available" parent. Though this father perceived himself as equally involved, he admitted that, "quite honestly, on a day-to-day basis, kids need Mom more than they need Dad, and I honestly think that's true. . . . I don't know whether . . . it's not meant to be a sexist statement or anything like that, but we both share in the house . . . I mean, I'll do stuff for the kids just as much as she will, just not as frequently."

This doctor was not alone, as became particularly apparent with regard to sick leaves. As chapter 7 showed, the minimal impact of physicians' families on their hours and schedules is perhaps most visible with regard to sick leaves. For all the other groups, a question about sick days was often answered in relation to sick family members, but this was something that physicians rarely mentioned.

This gender ideology—allowed by their class advantage—sustained physicians' way of life, made them feel better about their jobs, and shaped their families. Another doctor, a young guy whose wife quit her job as a doctor over the course of the study, tried hard to engage with his kids but found himself, as he saw it, in a world organized around gender. He said that he "allowed" his wife to work part-time, then quickly caught himself and recast his explanation:

> If she [his wife] wanted to work full-time, fine. But I allowed, I mean, not allowed her, but I was okay with her, not because life was better in a way. Life was better. . . . She works plenty outside, and she does a ton of other

stuff in terms of relationship and family and house. But she was happy as a clam. And I wanted her to be happy. And we can do it. We're very lucky we could do it. We're very lucky. So I take advantage of that fact.

He then went on to generalize her situation to other women they knew:

We have multiple women colleagues who . . . one's a plastic surgeon. These are women. One's a plastic surgeon, one's an endocrinologist, one's an ob/gyn. They're all obviously smart and very successful and so on. Once you get married and once you have kids, things change dramatically and always . . . well, I shouldn't say always, but 80 percent of the time they want to work less. It's always the main topic of discussion and a comparison about what kind of schedule do you work. Guys don't do that. We don't . . . if anything, there's this more . . . that if you don't work at least fifty hours, you're not working enough . . . with guys I would say.

Male physicians are able to work long (and often unpredictable) hours because they think they should, because they are the only group able to decide to stay late without the permission of a supervisor, because they can afford it, and because their wives and children are willing to adapt—say, to eat dinner (or at least sit at the table) at the time these work hours dictate. When asked whether he usually got home for dinner, one physician said, "Yeah, but we eat dinner at 9:00 at night. My kids, you know, they've already eaten, but we'll always, while we're eating, we'll always sit at the table and talk. . . . It's like a great time for us."

The male physicians stood out in our study: they were the only group for whom daily family responsibilities and unpredictable events exerted barely any influence on job hours and schedules.

Male Physicians as Public Fathers

This division of labor does not mean that the male doctors were not involved in their home lives. They were involved—but as "public" fathers rather than as "private" fathers, the latter being more involved, as many EMTs were, in the daily and less publicly visible work of family.[11] As public fathers, physicians tended to highlight their participation in or presence at public events, which made their participation in parenting visible to others in the community. For example, one doctor explained that "I don't work around the house," but he did work as an assistant coach (and a couple of times as a head coach) for his children's softball and soccer teams. Coaching kids' teams "could be very tough—you're always rushing from one place to the other." In season, it might involve four or five hours a week; watching games added another two to four hours.

A number of doctors emphasized their concerted attempts—even given their long hours and unpredictable schedules—to attend important athletic events, music performances, and dance recitals. "I have a family of three kids, preteens and teenagers, and they're all into sports, they're in three different schools and three different sports teams, and there's a lot of driving I need to get done. My wife and I, she does most of it, but I have to pitch in when I can." Not just a sports metaphor, "pitching in" also implies that he *helped* his wife, who had the major responsibility for even these public events. But participation in such public activities often requires a significant financial outlay. This kind of fathering is thus reinforced by the income associated with an advantaged class position: being a good father means attending these events and making them possible by being a good breadwinner.

One surgeon told us that he balanced multiple obligations by sticking to his priorities. From our observations, our field notes report:

> I asked what these priorities were and he replied curtly: "Family first. Family, then work, then anything else. That's all. You have to prioritize." I asked about how he felt he got to the position where he could balance as well as he feels he does, to which he replied simply, "I own the place. Everyone here works for me. Everyone." I asked if that meant he didn't feel pressure to accommodate patients or pay bills and he said, "Look. Yeah, of course I do. But we make plenty—more than enough to pay the bills. Of course there is pressure there, but it's family first. These patients, I could die tomorrow and they won't care. Really, they won't. Family absolutely comes first. If one of my kids has an event, non-negotiable. When I was coaching their teams [when they were younger] and had to be out of here by 3:00, non-negotiable. If there is a parent-teacher conference, non-negotiable. You have to prioritize.

For the record, all of this doctor's examples of "non-negotiable" family priorities were instances of "public" parenting. He added: "Family understands the expectations of the profession. I mean, if it's life or death, I have to take care of it. That's just the way it is. If it is something that I can control, I have to. That's why I went into medicine. My family understands that."

An Easy Family Bargain?

Although male doctors complained often about their crazy schedules, they only occasionally talked about their wives' resistance to them. One doctor described the demanding hours and insisted that he never felt undue pressure from his colleagues, as when he agreed to be on call for two weekends in a row. Instead, the pressure—which failed to sway him—came from home:

> Where we do tend to feel the pressure a little bit is on the other side—not here, but at home. My son's got a lacrosse game at Williams. [My wife is] like, "*Why* are you *doing* that?!" I said, "Well, you know what, that's just the way it worked out." And I think our families have to be a little flexible in how we do things as well.

However, in our survey, fewer than 5 percent of physicians reported that they and their spouse often disagreed about job hours, and only another 35 percent sometimes did so.[12] While their wives might not have been so keen about the greediness of their husband's job, they relented and even made it possible.

Although they might not have had explicit disagreements about the issue, leaving most of the care of the children to their wives did not always feel like an easy bargain for the male physicians. They expressed regret about their children. Occasionally, a doctor would emphasize the loss and pain of the reduced parenting they felt they had to practice—the kind in which mothers spend far more time with the children than fathers do. Tears rolled down the cheek of one doctor as he described his need to be in the hospital caring for patients while his wife was bathing and putting their children to bed. An emergency doctor with two young children whose wife stayed home said of his children: "So they've learned that I'm away a lot, and I feel a little . . . I guess a tiny little bit remorseful about that, because one of the reasons that I chose emergency medicine was that I thought that I would be able to have a bit more livable schedule."

At least some of the doctors also realized that it was not such an easy bargain for their wives:

> I mean, when I'm not home, especially for a prolonged period of time, her stress goes up dramatically, because she's working, she's taking care of the kids, she's trying . . . she's the primary person for keeping the house in order, you know, calling repair people and stuff. God, if I were to pick up a screwdriver or something, I might explode. And then, you know, she's taken over, over the past several years, paying the bills as well. . . . She has an incredibly busy schedule herself, and it's stressful. So anyways, me not being home, or spending too many hours here and not enough hours at home, adds to the stress.

Another gave a powerful account of the pressure that the sick place not only on him but also on his family:

I think that to a certain extent the families of physicians, of some physicians anyway, get screwed because they take second place to people that the doctor has no relationship to—do you know what I mean? It's so hard for somebody that doesn't bear that responsibility to see why. . . . How can you justify being late for the kids' graduation ceremony to see somebody else's child in the emergency room? But that happens every day, or you end up looking at those choices every day. And the only way I could deal with that was to see the [sick] kid. I couldn't stand sitting there wondering if I'd made the right decision about taking care of it over the phone or asking them to wait a little bit longer and see what happens and stuff, when I knew that with one look you could be pretty certain whether or not the child is in any danger. So I just couldn't not do that.

Even though doctors and their spouses recognized the importance, even the necessity and worthiness, of their demanding work, there were often marital costs: "My wife puts up with a lot. It's better now, but the first, say, ten or fifteen years of practice was really kind of hard—for her. Doing it the way I did it made it a lot easier on me, but it turned out that she and my children were the ones that paid the price to a certain extent. It's a hard thing."

Completely involved in his practice, this doctor was much less involved as a father, a trade-off that he now struggled to legitimate, even to himself:

I was a distant father. I wasn't necessarily distant emotionally, but I was not home very often in those days, and oftentimes I was either exhausted or worried about somebody, so there was something. But I think that they had enough family overall that they didn't suffer, at least that's what they tell me. Of course, they just may be saying that to make me feel better.

Recognizing the costs, doctors legitimated their decisions by insisting that they had little choice. But these male doctors chose not to resist what they saw as the demands of their jobs. Instead, they used their class advantage to maintain and legitimate their enactment of conventional gender expectations, even if that entailed some personal losses.

A Rhetoric of Constraint and a Reality of Choice?— Atypical Men, Typical Women

When we look at some atypical male physicians and some female physicians, the male doctors' response that they had little choice but to give priority to their jobs begins to seem more like a "rhetoric of constraint."

The comparison suggests that the male doctors had a "reality of choice," even if they did not see it (or denied it).

A very small minority of male doctors reported that they had reduced their hours or shifts, often in response to their wives' pleas. One doctor who divided his time between patients and research told us that he shortened his workday at his wife's insistence: "My wife said I needed to [come home], essentially, and I agreed with her." Hinting at serious marital conflicts resulting from his earlier schedule, he added: "I didn't have the insight to see the impact of what not being home was having on people."

If our study included only male doctors, we might conclude that the choices most of them made were necessitated by occupational demands; we might think that if they were to remain doctors, these were not really choices at all.[13] Our study also included, however, a small number of women doctors. Most of them were married to professionals who earned good incomes.[14] They demonstrated that these outcomes were not simply a result of external occupational demands. Instead, such actions involve choices—perhaps difficult choices, but choices nonetheless.

Many of the women doctors organized their work and family lives quite differently from the men.[15] Of the eleven women physicians with whom we did intensive interviews, four worked part-time, four worked full-time and had primary responsibility for their children and household, and three had a stay-at-home partner—a very small group of women doctors, and a revealing one.

One doctor, married to another doctor, decided to go half-time when she had her second child. She explained that "it was a huge paradigm shift for me." However, "I love what I'm doing. But particularly in having this second child, it just became clear to me that I wanted to be at home and with our children and enjoy the things . . . not that it's not possible to work full-time, it absolutely is, but to enjoy sort of the littler . . . the smaller things." Although she said that she loved her work, she had paid a motherhood penalty and expressed some ambivalence about her choice:

> I still work more than my hours state. There are weeks that are really busy, and I don't feel part-time like I want to. I don't get compensated for any of this extra time that I'm talking about. None of it. I'm not a partner. Being a partner does happen in practices. I'm not sure what I want. I'm not sure whether I want that or not. I definitely get compensated less. Absolutely. For equal work even.

This doctor could take the economic hit, however, because she lived in a dual-career family in which, by their calculation, her husband was the "primary breadwinner":

I'm fortunate that I'm not the primary breadwinner. My income is additional to our family, so we can afford it. And that can be frustrating, so you just have to decide what's more important and right now . . . I like what I do, but it isn't . . . it's a constant thing that you struggle with. Definitely. So my income is added income. When I say "added income," it's not like it's our vacation money, it's our retirement money, it's our school savings money.

As she saw it, the "additional" money she earned was earmarked money—a view tied to gender that constrains her and advantages her breadwinning husband. She insisted that both she and her husband chose this division:

Now he really likes it because . . . as a woman, you just tend to do more at home, even in this supposedly equal professional marriage, you still do. He sees the benefit that it has both for our household functioning and just for the children as well. (*Did he ever consider working half-time?*) He has joked that he would. I personally don't think it's his character that he could do it.

Commenting on what she seemed to think might raise eyebrows, but which was in accord with what we heard from the male doctors about their wives, she stopped herself and said: "I'm being honest 'cause you're doing this. . . . I wouldn't be happy with, on a personal level, with me working full-time and him working half-time." She went on to insist that this was her own choice, though her words twisted and turned:

I want to be the one that knows what's going on with the children and that sort of thing. But I also don't think that it's really his . . . ultimately his character that he could do it. Just honestly, the vast majority of the burden of the household is on me, and if I were to work more it would just mean I work more and still have that burden. It just would, so I want to be there to experience what my kids do.

She concluded: "So I'm happy with that." But as Youngjoo Cha concludes in her national study of those who have spouses who work long hours: "Overwork is a gendered process that results in women's exclusion from the labor market."[16]

Another woman physician who went part-time did so because "we just seemed to be running all over the place" and because "kids need structure." "I think that we are in a fortunate situation," she said. "My husband works [as a school administrator], and I took a 20 percent pay cut [upon going part-time]; I didn't take an 80 percent." She commended her colleagues for letting her cut back at work: "I feel incredibly fortunate that the people I work with are good people and have treated me incredibly fairly. So I feel very fortunate about that. I think that's one of the reasons why I can stay there." But noting that her male colleagues made other "choices," she went on to list, quickly and succinctly, the options:

> I also have a lot of colleagues who don't have working spouses. (*laughs*) That's the difference. I think a lot of the people who do what I do as a physician, you either have somebody who stays home all the time or you have somebody who has a job that might be more flexible, or you have family members that are in the area who can back you up, or you pay an awful lot of money for day care and babysitting.

In contrast, another married woman physician in private practice, who had three kids and earned an income of $160,000, was typical of the four women physicians who worked full-time and had primary responsibility for children and housework. In her office, she raced from office to examination room with her laptop computer open and in hand while her daughter and dog sat waiting in her office. One day her teenage son sailed into the office after she had gone out for a few minutes; he took aim with rubber bands at various items on a desk, picked up the tennis clothes she had left for him, and called her on his cell phone, saying impatiently, "I was wondering when you were going to pick me up." She described how, in her hectic life, she, her husband, and her babysitter divided up the chore of transporting the kids:

> Mondays and Thursdays the babysitter brings them, Wednesdays my husband does, and Tuesdays and Fridays I do. And so it means we never know who's got the homework, the backpack, the lunch boxes, the note that was sent home that was really important that had to be signed for some field trip or, ya know, where things go is . . . ya know . . . I invariably forget someone's cupcakes for their birthday or don't have a field trip note signed or, I mean, that's the kind of thing that happens. I drive the teachers crazy because somebody hasn't turned in whatever they needed turned in.

This woman doctor also made a "choice" that was one the news media—or her mother—might report if she were a low-wage worker:

> I leave the little ones being guarded by [the family dog] for ten minutes while I drive them, which my mother thinks is really shameful. Technically they are too young to be at home. Um, but it's ten minutes, and if something happened it would be awful. I make [the dog] their guardian, though.

More explicitly than was expressed by most of the male physicians, hers was a story of self-blame and guilt for being an inadequate parent. The persistence of a cultural model of intensive mothering but not intensive fathering has created a guilt divide: "I get the mother guilt thing 'cause I'm not there enough for them." She interpreted her children's behavior through its lens (even though her husband, commuting about an hour for his job as an architect, was away as much as or more than she was):

> And honestly when I'm around more, their behavior gets better. The interesting thing . . . when my daughter started middle school, which is right next door, she started coming to my office after school a lot and hanging out here and big things changed. She stopped biting her fingernails. And at first I was thinking it was 'cause she was happier at school, and then I realized, or I think, my conclusion is that she was seeing a lot more of me and she seemed less anxious.

Both blaming herself and elevating her role, she concluded: "Guilt, guilt, guilt."

In yet another pattern, three women physicians had a version of the stay-at-home partner to take care of the children. Two of the three were lesbians, with women partners staying home. The third woman, a hospitalist—the only woman physician in our study whose career had priority over a husband's career—referred to her husband as "Mr. Mom"; when she arrived home from work each day, "my lovely husband has usually got supper ready or almost ready," she said with a laugh. "He works his schedule around mine." Like her male counterparts, she insisted that the hours and schedules of her job made it difficult to have a second job in the family, but in her case there was some regret, or at least worry. "I think he would like to get going a little bit more career-wise and feel good about that. But I don't know if he'll be able to do that, you know, with the kind of schedule that I'm working."

Conventional gender expectations were salient, pervasive, and explicit in the talk not only of most women and men doctors but also of many physician administrators. It was perhaps most common (and powerful) when these administrators talked about women colleagues who sometimes resisted the job demands in order to give hands-on care to their families:

> We have one employee, who's a part-time employee, and she's a working mother, and I think we weren't considerate to start and we've had to learn how to be that way. And she snapped us in shape pretty quickly. (*So talk to*

me about that.) Well, it was wonderful! I mean, you know, we always have been of the mind-set that you stay and do the work until the work is done, and if I'm here until 8:00, you're here till 8:00—we just stay and do it. At 5:00 she needs to leave, and within a week she said, "I can't do this, I can't work for you guys." And we had no idea why. And so we needed to become considerate and understand what *her* pressures were as a working mother, and we've had to make contingencies.

Another physician administrator—a vice president who managed a large floor in a hospital—insisted that families should shape doctors' work schedules:

I personally put them [family concerns] at the highest level of importance. A stable doc comes to work as a stable doc. Doesn't bring baggage, knows that his home life is valued and is supported. Everybody that comes in this service for the past twenty years has gotten the same prioritization from me. Patient first, your peers second, you're third, and, overriding all that, and not even in the same solar system, is your family. You take care of that obligation. And if you need support, this is a big department—all the resources of the department will support you to make sure that's working. Because today it's you that needs the support, tomorrow it's me, tomorrow it's the next guy. And they've gotten that same story forever.

But then, when probed about the kind of family issues that could shape physicians' schedules, he talked about crises rather than routine domestic events.

INTERVIEWER: Give me some examples of how this works out.

RESPONDENT: Oh, sure. You know, a sick child. And I don't mean like an otitis media [the most common middle ear infection]. A child that has leukemia. A death of a parent.

INTERVIEWER: Give me some real people coming in to see you and your response.

RESPONDENT: I had one exactly like that. One family was going to lose a kid with leukemia. I don't want that doc to have to worry about anything going on here. And so how that translates is, they'll come in, they'll say, "I'm scheduled to work the next two weeks, and here's my shifts." Then I put out a memo to the service and say Dr. X needs these shifts covered because his child's ill. And they pick up the extra shifts.

INTERVIEWER: These are crisis situations. Have there been any requests more broadly for shifts in hours?

RESPONDENT: Sure. Like, "I'm going to adopt a baby and I need to be able to go to China," or whatever.

For the far more numerous unpredictable events that are not crises—like a child with an ear infection—the male doctors were significantly less likely to adjust their schedules, and this administrator was much less likely to expect (or want) them to do so.

Instead, when talking about the need to be responsive to family concerns, administrators would often switch the discussion—without hesitation, and seemingly without quite realizing they were doing so—to talk about women doctors rather than men. Take this administrator's comment:

> People who have families want to work less. You know, one of our partners came and just had a baby, and, you know, took a couple months off. That's fine. . . . One of our partners, we want to have kids. You know, *she's* moved into the community with her husband, and once we get help, we love to see people have kids, raise families, and be part of the group.[17]

This physician administrator concluded by using "family" as a metaphor for the work organization: "We want people—in our group, we want people to come, and stay, and be part of the hospital family."

An administrator who oversaw scheduling for his department showed the limits of the support for family:

RESPONDENT: Yeah. (*chuckles*) Say "bias," but it's mainly females that don't want to work.

INTERVIEWER: But why?

RESPONDENT: I don't know, because of commitments. They always have commitments, something . . .

INTERVIEWER: Like?

RESPONDENT: Family things, you know.

INTERVIEWER: Is it usually family things?

RESPONDENT: Oh yeah, at least that's what I hear.

He concluded by restating, with a little sarcasm, even mistrust: "That's the excuse I hear. Family things, babysitting."

The difference between men and women physicians is striking—more striking than in any other occupation. Our analyses of these patterns emphasize the persistent power of the cultural expectations that divide women and men. If it were simply structural demands—realities of constraint—in play, the women doctors would look like their male counterparts. But they do not.

CONCLUSION

Family members—across gender and class—are key parts of the web of time. Husbands and wives, extended kin, and especially children routinely increase unpredictability. But family members also help solve the issues posed by unpredictability. The form that these pushes and pulls take varies at the intersection of gender and class. By comparing the four occupations, this chapter and the last have shown the ways in which these pushes and pulls play out: class advantage promotes gender convention, while class disadvantage promotes the undoing of those conventions—for both women and men.

This chapter shows that, for professional men, the flexibility to put in long and what they see as unpredictable hours on the job—thus fulfilling traditional masculine dictates—typically depends on having a wife who takes care of family matters. Male physicians often said that they had no choice. But the experience of women doctors suggests that physicians' schedules are not simply set by organizational and occupational structures; instead, male doctors choose to enact masculine privilege. That is, class advantage for *both* female and male doctors promotes gender conventions, but constructs them as opposites. The women doctors who quit or reduced their hours said what Pamela Stone heard from women executives: they used a rhetoric of choice.[18] It is rhetoric, Stone argues, because the structure of their lives—whether it includes an unhelpful husband, a rigid career path and demanding clients, or an unresponsive workplace—drastically constrains their choices. For most of the small number of women doctors we spoke to, this was at least in part what we heard—a rhetoric of choice and a reality of constraint. The male doctors used the reverse: what might be called a "rhetoric of constraint" and, in some very broad sense, a "reality of choice." Looking at the women illuminates the alternatives that might be available for the men. This divide between rhetoric and reality, however, misses the ways in which cultural models and institutional constraints are mutually constituted and sustaining. What we find is that male doctors use cultural ideals of work and gender, along with the income, power, prestige, and moral claims associated with their work, to create or reinforce organizational patterns that sustain these ideals. Both they and their families then confront, or are constrained by, these very patterns and ideals, and it becomes increasingly difficult for the family to change course.

The EMTs constructed a very different kind of masculinity. Although they worked long hours and often had second jobs, they used family to resist and reshape work schedules. They were able to do so because of responsive employers and cooperative coworkers, and they felt a need to do so because of the income and insistence of their wives. Limited income, the family's dependence on a wife's income, and the wife's preferences all encouraged male EMTs to do significant domestic work. Although they sometimes felt ambivalent, many of these working-class men also spoke of the ways in which this refashioning of their jobs and families allowed them to develop relations at home that they valued—again, especially (but not only) with their children. Unlike doctors, who provided most of their family's income, EMTs were in families that relied considerably more on the wives' earnings. Prioritizing the man's career was less common among EMTs than among more advantaged professionals; other studies suggest that this is true for working-class men more generally.[19] The EMTs sometimes made fun of one another for doing so much work at home even as they and their supervisors justified that involvement in domestic work. As one private-sector EMT said, "These are going to be the only children I'm ever going to have. I wanted to be able to raise them myself without palming them off and not seeing them." The lives and choices of EMTs showed not only the flexibility of gender but also how that occurs.

Much recent work on the relationship of masculinity to the practice of paid work and domestic life draws on the now-classic theoretical formulation of R. W. Connell.[20] Developing the concept of "hegemonic masculinity," she argues that much older literature used a categorical model of gender that treated men as an undifferentiated group, but contemporary research documents a considerable range of masculinities. Firefighters are a fascinating group: on the one hand, they are iconic examples of hegemonic masculinity, macho figures who brave all dangers, rushing into burning buildings to save people's lives; on the other hand, they embrace major responsibility for the day-to-day care of their families. While prior scholarship tended to conflate sex and gender, Connell offers a counterview: she suggests that diverse masculinities can be traced to the "social dynamics generated within gender relations" and through other structures that vary across social locations. In fact, class is a social location, Connell emphasizes, although she criticizes work on masculinity for being "class-bound."[21] That is precisely what we find. The practices of class-based masculinities are tied to the *relational* character of the gender order—not only are the relationships among men in each of these occupations important, but their relationships with their wives and children are essential components of their performance of a refashioned masculinity. Not only family but also work obligations play a very different role in the lives of the men in the two class contexts.

Together, chapters 8 and 9 have shown that it is at the two ends of the class-by-gender continuum—among male physicians and female nursing assistants—that the family becomes less powerful in its call to come home. Nursing assistants are overwhelmingly women. They may sometimes wish to fashion the same lives the nurses have, but they rarely have the option to do so. Family leads them to occasionally resist work's demands, but they pay a price—sometimes a heavy price—for such resistance. Because they must, these working-class women, many of whom are women of color, redo conventional expectations of gender both on the job and at home. Physicians, in contrast, have the class advantage to shape their work schedules, and here we see a clear gender divide. It is male physicians who use their advantage to make their jobs a priority, in the expectation that their nuclear families will conform to what they need to advance their careers and incomes.

Both CNAs and doctors suffer in some ways. For CNAs, these ways are especially obvious—they miss the time with their children, and they worry about their needy relatives.[22] The demands and attractions of family are the most important factor leading them to protest job conditions and seek changes in their schedule. But institutional insensitivity and low wages make it difficult to protest too much. Less obviously, male doctors and their families also suffer: the relationship between family and work creates hardships, contradictions, and reduced family time for them. Male doctors talked of the value of daily family participation and recognized that they "should," even wanted to, do more at home. At the same time, they felt the need to stay long hours at work to earn money for their families, thereby distancing themselves from those very families. And the women doctors faced a different sort of penalty: though they said that they preferred it this way, these professional women faced the economic penalties associated with choosing motherhood over all-involving careers.

Neither nurses nor EMTs talked nearly so much about the ways jobs shape families. The issue came up, of course, but it did not feature to the same degree as it did for physicians and nursing assistants. Instead, these professional women and working-class men both used their families to more clearly reshape and resist work demands. Balancing work and family requires just such resistance—sometimes in the name of gender expectations and sometimes in opposition to them.

Overall, professionals used class advantage to reinforce the gender order: women nurses and women physicians prioritized family, while men physicians prioritized careers. Women nursing assistants and men emergency medical technicians had more difficulty meeting conventional gendered expectations. So the low-wage women's work-family balance was, in some sense, more like that of the men physicians than that of the women nurses, but the low-wage women lacked the power and respect to control the conflicts between work and family.

There are always conflicts and contradictions between work and family, but how these are resolved is a function of the operation of class and gender in particular contexts. This leads to exaggerated inequalities as advantaged occupations "do gender" in conventional ways while disadvantaged occupations "undo gender."

PART IV | Strategies to Address Unpredictability

Chapter 10 | Finding Solutions in the Web of Time: Coworkers

THE WEB OF TIME, which often creates unpredictability and causes schedule problems, can also provide the solutions to these problems and turn what might have been a major difficulty into a minor complication. With help from coworkers, people can take a sick day without being charged with one, and they can get vacation days or an extra shift at times that the scheduler says are not available. By swapping hours and schedules with one another, employees themselves, not the managers, take charge of a key aspect of scheduling decisions and solve the toughest problems, the ones that managers cannot or will not solve. Initiated by employees to serve their own purposes, these problem-solving actions provide highly valued employee control over crucial scheduling challenges. Coworker-initiated scheduling of this sort is unequivocally a win for workers.

In many ways this form of employee control is also a win for managers, who set the parameters for what is acceptable and who also benefit when workers solve what would otherwise be tough problems. In one respect, however, coworker schedule swaps are not a win for management. A prevailing theme in labor history, labor studies, and sociology generally is that those with power maintain their control in part by creating or exacerbating divisions among workers, divisions often based on race or gender. Some employers seek to have employees identify with the employer (think the Walmart cheer) and to eliminate practices that create solidarity among them. Nevertheless, employees often identify primarily with their coworkers, who may rely on one another to develop a joint critique of the organization's rules and policies and to protect one another from the negative effects of punitive policies.[1] The practice of switching work hours with coworkers is a case in point: it sometimes increases resentment of management and almost always provides both a reason to get to know coworkers and a material underpinning to their solidarity.

211

The practice of swapping hours as a way to gain control over unpredictability differs by class and gender, but it happens to a significant degree in every occupation. Our survey shows how widespread the practice is and how it varies from one occupation to another. In every occupation, a large majority of workers used schedule swaps: 93 percent of EMTs, 88 percent of physicians, 83 percent of nursing assistants, and 72 percent of nurses. As these figures show, while just about everyone swapped, men were more likely than women to swap, and those in working-class jobs were more likely to do so than professionals. Nurses were the least likely to swap—but even so, more than two out of three sometimes did so.

Across all four occupations, coworkers were both a source of emotional and practical support (or stress) and a central resource in managing the web of time, but the challenges that workers faced, the relations they formed, and the swaps these produced differed by class and gender. The two working-class occupations, nursing assistants and EMTs, faced rigid schedules; swapping with coworkers was a vital way to gain some control over what was otherwise fixed and unalterable. This control was especially important for nursing assistants, who frequently needed a way to escape the punitive consequences of their employer's sick leave policies. The two professional occupations, nurses and doctors, were better able to shape their official basic schedules, so although they also relied on coworkers, being able to switch with coworkers was only one of several means of addressing a scheduling problem at their disposal.

The two male-dominated occupations, doctors and EMTs, were not constrained by overtime laws—the doctors because they were exempt from the laws, and EMTs because many of them were public-sector workers (with somewhat more flexible rules) and almost all were already working overtime. Moreover, although taking care of children was a responsibility that many male EMTs accepted, women were more likely than men to be responsible for family matters. Family was both a reason women wanted to switch schedules and a constraint making it difficult to do so. But for women too, swapping schedules was subject to the intersection of gender and class: nurses, who swapped the least of any group, had class advantage but were also laboring under the familial constraints associated with womanhood. They were able to gain a significant degree of control over their work schedules and often had the financial wherewithal to use that control to accommodate their family schedules, but this made it more difficult for them to accommodate their coworkers. Although nursing assistants also faced family demands, financial constraints often led them to put the job first and made them willing to swap shifts with others so that they would be able in turn to call on coworker support and use the web of time to their own (and their family's) advantage. Coworkers, then, make it possible to weave together work and family—albeit in ways that are responsive to the intersecting claims of gender and class.

The recent literature on work time has devoted surprisingly little attention to the importance of coworkers, though for many years this issue was central to both scholarship and practical management, from Frederick Taylor to the Hawthorne studies to discussions of quality circles.[2] Today's analyses instead stress the importance of frontline supervisors and managers. For example, discussions of the ability of women executives to balance a career and a family often emphasize that only the approval of a sympathetic supervisor enables them to work less than the typical executive schedule (eighty hours a week and available at all times). Although Pamela Stone reports that very few women have been able to reduce their hours and remain in a high-powered career, the experience of one of the few who has done so highlights the "moral" for women: "flexibility was only as good as your last manager."[3] Erin Ryan and her colleagues note the flip side of the same coin: "An employee may expect that s/he will be able to work flextime when a policy is announced but then find s/he cannot because . . . a lack of supervisor support makes it difficult to carry out."[4]

Given this prior work, Susan Lambert and Julia Henly began with the hypothesis that "manager agency may also make a great deal of difference" to the low-income employees whom they studied. But their results led them to conclude otherwise: "Although frontline managers may find 'discretionary spaces' in the face of tight accountability practices, their discretion is limited in scope and impact."[5] Like most other researchers, however, they did not discuss coworkers.

In our study, coworkers came up all the time, and relations with coworkers could be emotionally and personally powerful, for good or ill. Coworkers influenced whether people wanted to be at work at all, but they had even more impact on whether people were willing to pick up extra shifts and able to get time off. Coworkers shaped the breaks that workers took (or did not take) during the day.[6] Above all, coworkers and the arrangements they made with one another were the most important sources of worker-controlled schedule flexibility in the face of unpredictability. Only a supervisor could approve a regular, ongoing, special arrangement that a worker might want to make—say, not arriving until 7:15 or 7:30 because the day care center did not open until 7:00. But if the problem was unusual or unpredictable, then the solution was more likely to come from coworkers than supervisors.

Building relationships with coworkers, through interacting face to face and helping each other with work tasks, makes it possible for workers to meet with their child's teacher over a discipline problem, attend a cousin's wedding, or even take vacation when they want, while avoiding any penalty for missing work. For these unpredictable events—and many more—they do not need a supervisor's approval (except in a perfunctory way, signing off on routine paperwork); all they need is to be able to find a coworker willing and able to swap days or work an extra day for them, allowing them to take a day off without the advance notice that would normally be required. Although some aspects of the web of time may "just happen"—that is, they result from external shocks (from employers, from families) over which workers have no control—workers can actively construct this part of the web of time, albeit within a framework imposed by management. Workers are able to solve schedule problems precisely because they and their coworkers are often willing to do more for each other than they are willing to do for management. If management asks an employee to work on Wednesday instead of Tuesday, the answer is likely to be no; if a friend asks the same worker to work Wednesday so that she can see her daughter's band concert, the answer is likely to be yes. Management may object and intervene if, for example, the switch creates overtime for the employee who agrees to the extra work. Otherwise, management usually accepts—often even promotes—coworker switches.

THE BASE: COMMITMENT, CONNECTION, TRUST, AND AFFECTION FOR COWORKERS

To take many kinds of action, and certainly to arrange a schedule modification, workers depend on at least some level of backing from their coworkers. The grounding for most forms of worker activism is the face-to-face small group of workers who know and interact with each other on a daily basis.[7] In the same way, in all four of the occupations in our study, the greater the positive connections between workers, the more they were committed to and trusted each other, the more they liked each other, then the more likely they were to be willing to do schedule favors for each other. In most workplaces, there is deep bonding between at least some workers (although, for some people, tensions and animosities sometimes arise).

Across occupations, a number of people talked of their coworkers as sources of identity and emotional support; in those cases it was obvious why people would help each other out. These statements were most eloquent from those in jobs that had low turnover and lots of time spent together. Listen to a nurse-midwife:

> I would go to hell and back for my partners, and to be able to go to work with your best friends every day is another kind of compensation that's very

valuable to me. And I love my work—I love what I do. . . . We work very
hard to help each other live human lives.

Or this EMT:

> [During your days at work] you do everything together—you eat together,
> you drink coffee together, you hang out together, you discuss calls together,
> you talk about your homes, you talk about fixing your cars, whatever. It is
> like being in a family. And this sounds really weird for me to be saying, es-
> pecially at this age, because it totally sounds like it's a gang of kids and we
> have a fort in the backyard, but when it comes time to leave I really feel sad-
> dened by it. I used to have a hard time, like at the end of my night shift, my
> last night shift, you'd leave and you're like, I'm not going to see these guys
> for four days. And they are a great bunch of guys, and . . . you feel like
> you're truly a part of a team. . . . You go to the grocery store to buy your
> groceries and you're just another face in the crowd. Everything you do,
> you're just another face in the crowd. But you go to work and you're some-
> body. You matter to somebody. Guys, they feel your absence, when guys go
> on vacation or if they call out sick, their absence is almost palpable. The crew
> is always kind of off; it throws your timing off. I love being a part of that. . . .
> I think it gives me my identity. If I had to boil it down to something, that's
> what it is.

A nursing assistant felt much the same:

> Staff I work with are the best. They are wonderful. . . . We all are in the same
> boat—we all help, we all know we're there, we're all hurting here or there,
> so our backs are hurting or our whatever. So we're there for one another, and
> it's wonderful.

Some people had chosen to work in one place rather than another specifically because of their coworkers, as was the case with this physician in
choosing a residency:

> Everybody was so . . . just nice. That sounds kind of lame, but it wasn't an
> intimidating program. Nobody put you down. . . . It was very nurturing and
> . . . like I said before, they all look out for one another. They're very protec-
> tive of one another. There's like a camaraderie here, and I'm really, really
> appreciative about it.

Workers who have these kinds of relationships with their coworkers
want to come to work and are in a strong position to support each other

should they want to rearrange schedules. But obviously not everyone loves all of their coworkers. Some workplaces are filled with mistrust and bad feelings; in others, although most feel a sense of solidarity and mutual support, a minority find their coworkers difficult, unpleasant, and unreliable. One physician in private practice insisted on the importance of coworkers, a lesson learned through tension with a partner. "We just were polar opposite, but in like the worst ways." In fact, "I've learned that picking your partner is more important than picking your spouse because you spend more time with them."

Working with the same people all the time can create problems, an issue that is most pronounced for firefighters. Asked whether people said things about workers who chose not to accept callbacks and do overtime, one firefighter answered:

> Behind their backs. For whatever reason. Now, I don't—I don't know if they say it to their face, but you hear scuttle, and there's cliques no matter—it's like high school, I swear to God. . . . Oh my Lord. Backbiting, backbiting. I'm like, "You guys"—but, I guess it's just human nature, is what I think it is. And I think that the quieter it is [the fewer fires and ambulance calls there are], the worse it gets.

Another firefighter explained that "if you have a weakness, don't let them know it because then they pick on you." He went on to make another "kid" analogy: "We're like big kids. It changed a little because girls came in, but it's just like big kids, so if you say, 'I don't like to be called that,' guess what? You're going to be called that."[8] Note two stereotypes he easily invoked: first, it is kids (rather than adults) who bully people; and second, tense social relations and bullying depend, to a large extent, on a homosocial world—that is, one consisting primarily of men. This formulation was invoked in a somewhat different way by one of the relatively few women EMTs at a private-sector company; she had previously worked as a day care teacher. "When I started working here, I realized it really wasn't much different than doing day care. Except for the fact I'm not changing diapers. You know, you've still got your same conflicts, you've still got your same personality differences."

Both the sense of bonding and the petty bickering seemed to be most common among male EMTs, especially firefighters, who spend considerable time with each other without much to do. One person who did trainings that took him to many fire departments said that, at some, "I'm amazed at what a great setup they have." But at other places, he continued, "I go in and I shake my head wondering how they survive day to day, because they've got guys literally at each other's throats."

The conflict that sociologists might expect most would be men creating a hostile environment for women coworkers.[9] Such tensions are surely present, but most of this conflict takes place among white men, especially between paramedics and old-line firefighters. The "old-school" firefighters are older, heavier, not as fit but more macho, and proud of *not* using safety equipment; they also resent taking orders from low-seniority paramedics, which happens in any medical crisis. At fires the young medics all put on hoods and "go on air," as one told us, because

> we're taught that in the academy. In the academy they're like, "You want to live long enough to collect your retirement, and the only time you should not be on air at a fire scene is when there is no fire." . . . The old guys are kind of making fun of you because they're breathing all this crap. You're pulling down plaster, and all this junk is just mushroom-clouding around you, and these guys are laughing at it.

On his crew, this EMT insisted, "it's good-natured, a lot of good-natured ribbing," but in other situations such teasing led to open contempt and conflict.

Although conflicts among white male firefighters were the most evident, one nursing assistant argued that at her nursing home the older Jamaican workers bullied and harassed the newer Latino workers and that the interactions were explicitly racial: "Calling me a bitch, a spic, a Puerto Rican dummy . . . saying that Puerto Rican people don't know what they're doing, that we're the majority of the crime rate . . . grabbing up one of the paperwork books and throwing it at me." These problems, she noted, were specific to the first shift: "When you go up to the cafeteria, you see there's a table for all the white people, there's a table for all the Puerto Rican, there's a table for all the black. You only see that from the first shift. Now, if you go in there to the second shift, it's all mixed up." Even on first shift, although they sit separately, in the other units "I notice that they all get along with each other, they all respect each other, they work as a team. But with my floor I don't see that."

Although this nursing assistant reported open conflict, tensions and conflicts among nursing assistants were generally quasi-covert and most evident in decisions about whether or not to work an extra shift. One nursing assistant contrasted two opportunities for extra hours, one she turned down and one she embraced, based on her coworkers:

> Those aides are lazy, 'cause I once worked with them and it was hell. And I said, you know what, I'm exhausted, it's not even worth it to come in order to deal with that. I said, I need the money, but you know what, I'll survive

without it. Yeah, definitely, you definitely look at that, and you see a few girls that you like, that you know they're gonna be there for you, you say, "Oh yeah, I'll work, go 'head, put me to 11:00 too." Definitely, that's a big thing.

Other nursing assistants concurred on the importance of coworkers to schedule issues. "I like to see who's in the schedule," said one. "If I see it's not a reliable team, there's some names that if I see their name over there, I don't go." Another said, "I think that if I'm goin' to work and I'm gonna be agitated and I hate a few of the girls, not worth it. . . . That's why I don't do mornings." One nursing home scheduler reported that coworkers were a major factor influencing whether or not nursing assistants would agree to work extra:

I mean, when I call and ask, "Can you work this day?" and then they say, "Who's working?" I tell them who's on the schedule, and they'll say, "No, I don't want to work that day." Then I'll say, "Well, can you work on *this* unit?" And then I'll tell them who's on that unit. They may say, "Oh yeah, okay, I'll work that one." But yeah, it depends on who's working because, again, some people don't get along with certain people. (*And how often do you think that is?*) That's all the time.

Not getting along with some people may have been the part of coworker relations that was most visible to this scheduler; she bumped up against the reality that coworkers were often the reason why people refused to work extra when she asked them to do so.

Such refusals indicate the power of workers—in this case, low-wage workers. Coworkers are not just a problem, and they are not just a factor complicating the schedule and making it harder to fill holes. On the contrary, the willingness of workers to do favors for each other that they are often not willing to do for the employer is the key to managing the most difficult scheduling problems, such as being given short notice or settling a vacation conflict.

WORKERS TAKING CHARGE OF THE SCHEDULE

Coworkers provide a way for people to evade the rigidity and harshness of employer-imposed rules about time off, whether for vacation time, sick leave, or personal days. Consider a common situation. It is Thursday afternoon before a worker learns that her daughter will have a solo in Tuesday's band concert. The employer requires a minimum of one week's notice to schedule a vacation day. (Managers say that they need that much notice, and often more, to find another worker to fill a shift.) If she misses the band concert her daughter will be hurt and she herself will be disappointed, and if she calls in sick she risks being fired for abusing sick days, if she is found out. Her problem is solved, however, if a coworker agrees to switch shifts with her.

Schedule swaps and last-minute pickups for coworkers become the way to handle pressing, unpredictable scheduling problems. Especially in the two working-class occupations, but sometimes for nurses as well, being able to make these arrangements sometimes spells the difference between holding down a job and being fired, between being with children at key moments and feeling like an absentee parent, between attending a wedding and missing it. Sometimes such arrangements with coworkers make it possible to take vacation in the desired week. Physicians also switch schedules with their coworkers, and count on being able to do so, but many physicians have other ways as well to handle schedule problems that arise, such as changing patient appointments.

Most of the time people found it easy to arrange schedule swaps:

A physician: (*And you can always find somebody to swap with?*) Almost always. The only time it gets difficult are some of the more undesirable shifts. . . . If it's something that's very important almost always someone will step up and offer to swap with you. . . . There's swaps being asked on a weekly basis. . . . I'd say at least once a month I'm swapping a shift to help someone else out.

A nurse: We do that all the time. . . . We bend over backwards to help each other cover what needs to be covered.

A nursing assistant: (*Was it easy for you to find another aide to cover?*) Yeah, it was. I, you know, I didn't even have to ask her. She just, I was just telling her, "Oh, they're not gonna give it to me." And she went to the office, and she said, "I'll work for her, that's not a problem." So, that was very nice.

In some cases, however, it is difficult to arrange a switch. Although EMTs more than any other occupation treat switches as routine, not even all of them find it easy: "Ugh, swapping is a pain in the ass. It's kind of like you have to beg people to swap." A nursing assistant reported what happened when, early in her scheduled sixteen-hour shift, her mother had a heart attack: "I had to do the sixteen hours, nonstop, just like worried and what's going on, and I can't call out, 'cause I get fired . . . you know, and I'm like, damn, you can never find somebody at the last minute." One nursing assistant said that winter was easier: "In the summer you better best believe you ain't gonna get nobody come work for you on no weekend." A nurse noted that "sometimes it can be hard to find somebody to switch hours with, but people try to—they really do try to."

Although sometimes it is hard to make arrangements, other times co-workers take charge of the schedule and make impressive commitments to help out one of their own. One firefighter who was still two years away from retirement developed a debilitating disease that made it impossible to work. The other firefighters organized themselves and voluntarily covered his shifts, for free, for two years, so that he and his family could continue to receive benefits and ultimately qualify for a pension. As one said, "It really is like a family. We take care of each other. It's what I love about this job. I know that if something happens to me, that my kids will be taken care of."

FACILITATING CONDITIONS AND RESTRICTING RULES

Certain structural conditions make schedule swaps possible, but some rules restrict them. Schedule swaps would not be possible if everyone worked the same nine-to-five, Monday-to-Friday schedule. In health care, people are needed seven days a week, and most work four or fewer days a week so that they have open days available for switching. If people are willing to work a double, as many nursing assistants and EMTs are, then even on one of their regular days of work they can cover for someone on another shift.

Structural factors other than schedules also either facilitate or discourage worker-initiated changes to the schedule. Because people can only switch with those who have the same skills that they do, swaps must always be arranged within the same occupation, but beyond that a paramedic can swap shifts with a paramedic, but not with a basic-level EMT, and an emergency department nurse can switch with another ED nurse, but not with an ICU nurse. Switching might not be possible in workplaces where each person has a separate specialized skill. Switching in direct care medicine is possible because the work involves discrete tasks, but switching might not be possible for a long-range project.[10] Switching is facilitated by flat hierarchies, in which there are many people at the same level and with little prospect of promotion; to the extent that coworkers are competing to move the next step up the ladder (as is true for many in managerial careers), they might be less willing to help each other out. It is easier to switch if there is a substantial pool of people to draw from: nurses at hospitals (where nurses predominate) have more people they can ask than do nurses at nursing homes (where nursing assistants predominate). Switching is also easier in low-turnover workplaces, where people work together long enough to get to know each other. Given all this, switching with coworkers may not be important everywhere, but it probably takes place in large segments of the economy: restaurants, hotels, retail sales, police, prison guards, utility workers, bus drivers, any specialty that has to be on call at unpredictable times (from plumbers to computer maintenance), and a range of nonmedical direct care operations.

Many of these structural factors operate across all four of our occupations, but gender and class also appear to jointly shape switching. This becomes especially visible among nurses: in our study, they were the least likely to use switches. Although, as indicated earlier, more than two-thirds (72 percent) of nurses reported some switching, the percentage of those who did was substantially lower than for any other occupation, and interview responses reinforced these survey findings. Although some nurses reported that nurses switch with each other "all the time," when others were asked how often they switched, they responded as one nurse did: "Not very often. It's been a while. I'd say it's probably been five, six months." Two hospital nurse administrators noted—one with approval and one with disapproval—that the nurses in their units did not switch much. The first said, "The fortunate thing is, most of my experienced nurses don't switch shifts. . . . The younger ones tend to do that more. They haven't got their life as set around their schedule." The second administrator regretted the paucity of switches; when asked, "Do they swap with each other?" she answered, "Not as much as they should be. Sometimes they do, but they're not very good at swapping." In response to the question "Do people swap shifts?" a nurse at a nursing home said, "Not that often. I see it more, like, with the nurses' aides. There's a lot of nurses that don't wanna change their days off, their shifts, you know."

Two factors rooted in the intersection of class and gender may explain nurses' less frequent use of schedule switches. First, nurses are better able to shape their official basic schedules and less likely to face harsh penalties for calling out, so they have less need to switch. Second, entering the culture of switches requires not just a wish to get out of a required shift but also the ability to reciprocate by working on another day. To the extent that nurses have a full schedule of family obligations, they may have less room to reciprocate.

One worker-initiated schedule arrangement is apparently permitted only for EMTs, especially but not exclusively firefighters: swapping part of a shift when there is a need to arrive late or leave early. These working-class men typically make such swaps, interestingly enough, to spend time with their children. It is a kind of swap that makes these men's lives easier and reduces stress. It also probably reinforces (or results from) the class divide we saw among men in parenting: the EMTs were far more involved in the daily care of their children than were the male doctors.

How do these informal swaps work? Instead of changing an entire shift, one person covers for another for a couple of hours at the beginning or end of the day. While switching an entire shift requires paperwork and supervisor approval, that is not necessary when EMTs arrange to swap parts of shifts. One firefighter EMT gave a typical example:

RESPONDENT: If I call up and say I'm going to be late, normally they know it's because [my wife, a nurse] is held over at work, and people are really cool about it. Somebody will stay. . . . We do this on my crew all the time. . . . We cover for each other, and so I've had good success that way.

INTERVIEWER: When you do that, is it done formally or informally?

RESPONDENT: Informally. No paperwork is generated.

INTERVIEWER: What are the rules on that, or how do you work that out?

RESPONDENT: If it's going to be over an hour, officially the department wants paperwork on it. But I can tell you that usually guys will say, "Hey, I'll be forty-five minutes late (wink-wink, nudge-nudge)." No problem.

Being able to make this kind of swap, EMTs find it easy to solve a range of scheduling challenges that sometimes confound nurses and CNAs. A variety of factors may facilitate EMTs' ability to do these swaps: the reduced (or absent) constraint of overtime laws, the strong solidarity that comes from stable crews and extremely low turnover, and the more tolerant approach of public-sector employers, as well as the recognition among EMTs that they have to or want to share in parenting.

Interestingly, this state has a statute that is intended to permit workers to take off a couple of hours for a school conference or for the medical appointments of family members. This statute is in effect a formal and legally mandated equivalent to what EMTs create informally. Such a law might in practice be of special help to women across the nation. In practice, however, the Small Necessities Act seems to play almost no role in the working lives of those it was intended to help; not only CNAs but nurses as well made essentially no use of it and typically did not even know about it.

WHY MANAGEMENT AGREES TO WORKER-CONTROLLED SCHEDULING

Schedule switches are initiated by workers and serve the purposes of workers. For the most part, managers approve of the practice because it also serves management's purposes: at the same time that management learns of a potential problem (a worker calling out), it is presented with the solution—and a solution, moreover, that does not increase overtime. (If managers have to find solutions to a call-out, at least some of the time they have to approve overtime to cover the slot.)

It is remarkable that we did not hear of a single employer—in any of the occupations—that prohibited schedule swaps. Officially, management approval of swaps is required, but this is almost never an issue. Management tends to routinely grant approval, with two provisos. First, as noted earlier, the person filling in has to have the equivalent skill set. Employees accept this rule as reasonable; in only one or two cases did we hear even a hint of objection to it. Second, and generally more consequential, the schedule switch (or pickup) cannot require the use of overtime; this primarily affected the women, both the nurses and the CNAs. As one nursing assistant explained to us, "The nursing home can put you into overtime, but your friends can't." Workers generally accept the fact that management will not approve a schedule change if it generates overtime, although there is some tension over this, since there is often room for debate about whether a change would increase the total overtime the employer would in any case be paying.[11] For people working exactly forty hours a week (a minority of those we studied), that means that the switch has to take place within the week.

On balance, the system is a clear plus for managers, but it comes with at least some drawbacks for them. First, if swaps were impossible, some workers would take the shift (and miss the band concert); if a switch takes place, that creates some paperwork and some possibility of confusion. Second, and more important, the switch might restrict management freedom by reducing the number of workers available to fill in for a call-out. For example, after the schedule switch, a thirty-two-hour-a-week employee might have forty hours, so if she is needed to fill another slot she will get overtime pay. Moreover, in the summer, for vacations, switching reduces the number of available workers of any kind.

There is a reason why management wants to permit, say, only two people at a time to be on vacation in any given unit. With schedule switching, two people are on vacation and one additional person is precommitted, reducing the labor pool available for managers to tap. At Outercity hospital, for example, a nurse wanted to get two weeks of vacation to go out of the country. The hospital approved only one week of vacation, so the nurse arranged coverage for her second week by getting a per diem nurse to agree to cover her shifts. The scheduler reported that "I've sort of put the nix on that." She felt that "per diems are supposed to meet the unit needs—they're not your own personal access to having additional time off."[12] Although the manager's new rule applied only to per diem workers, the principle was the same: schedule switches to get around the limits on the number of people on vacation are likely to make it hard for managers to fill slots in July and August.

WHY WORKERS AGREE TO SWITCH SHIFTS

It is easy to see why the worker initiating a switch would want to do so, but why does another worker agree to the switch? That person is likely to be making a sacrifice by agreeing to work at a time he or she would not otherwise want. If workers were eager to fill these holes, management could easily get them to do so and would not create rules penalizing the use of sick days or requiring substantial advance notice for vacations. Management has trouble addressing the schedule problem because many workers are not willing to go out of their way to help management.

There were at least three reasons why workers who would be reluctant to accept a management request might agree to switch when asked by a coworker: reciprocity, the relationship between the two workers, and the reason for the particular switch. Money is a fourth reason to accept a switch, though it seemed to operate only with nursing assistants.

Reciprocity

A norm of reciprocity is key for shaping schedules. People agree to switch with others because they expect to need someone to cover for them in the future and want to build up credit and a reputation that will lead others to cover for them if they get in a jam. A nursing assistant explained that a key reason to agree to swaps was "'cause you never know when you're gonna need them to work for you." A swap can be looked at as a gift or favor to a coworker. As Marcel Mauss indicated in his classic study, a gift creates a more enduring relationship than does an economic exchange, because an exchange immediately restores balance but a gift relation endures over time until it is reciprocated; relations may endure indefinitely because no clear balance point of "no one owes anyone anything" is reached.[13]

This sense that everyone faces the same difficulties and anyone might need help tomorrow is probably an important factor across occupations. It does not operate on a one-to-one model of banking a credit for future spending. Rather, workers have a notion of generalized reciprocity: if they maintain a reputation of being willing to help others out, others (not necessarily the person they are helping at present) will help them out when the need arises.[14] Here we see little class and gender difference. An EMT reported: "People are usually willing to help out. It's kind of a rare thing if someone says, 'No, I just don't want to.' It's like, you know, 'Come on, you help me, I'll help you; you scratch my back, I'll scratch your back.'" A nurse stated even more clearly how this "norm of reciprocity" becomes generalized: "People are pretty much cooperative.... For the most part, people are very helpful because they know if they can't help you, nobody's going to help them—what goes around comes around."[15] A nurse supervisor saw variation in this principle based on reciprocity:

> I think if you're a person who is willing to switch time with people, you will not have a hard time finding somebody to switch, because you're doing favors for people so people will do favors for you. If you're somebody who is never willing to help out your coworkers, then, yeah, you're going to have a little bit more difficult time.

A sense of all being in it together and needing to help each other meet complicated and demanding schedules was at least as strong among doctors as in the other occupations, a finding that is somewhat surprising since doctors have more control over their own schedules. Since overtime pay is not an issue and doctors often have enough control of their lives to make switches possible, swaps are common for them. According to one doctor, "It's very informal, and nobody even asks why." Asked whether swaps happened often among doctors, he replied: "Oh yeah.... It's almost never an issue.... We're very supportive of each other in that group, in that sense."

Although some doctors rarely initiated swaps, no doctor reported that he or she could not make swaps, and a number of them said that they did so several times a month. The ethic of reciprocity includes the view that a doctor should offer a shift that is at least as desirable as the shift he or she is asking someone to take: "When I swap, I try to do equitable swaps, so if it's a day shift, it's a day shift, if it's an evening shift, it's an evening shift, if it's an overnight shift, it's an overnight shift, if it's a weekend shift, it's a weekend shift."

The Relationship Between the Two Workers

The second factor influencing worker-arranged schedule switches is the relationship between the two workers. Although generalized reciprocity is a significant factor, people do not accept every request, and they do not necessarily agree to a swap with every person who asks. Across class and gender, people are especially willing to make accommodations if the request comes from someone they know and like. One EMT made decisions about swaps according to how much he liked the person and the urgency of the request: "If there was someone I really liked and they really needed it, I would do it." And a nurse reported:

> It's nice in a small facility because we tend to be friends. We like each other, that's part of the reason we're there, that we like each other. And so you want to help out your friends. So it works out okay. Like this weekend, one of the nurses' daughters is getting married. Very unexpectedly! Like, she decided yesterday and she's getting married this weekend! . . . So she [the nurse/mother] has to take off. So one of the other nurses from the day shift is actually gonna work a double to cover for her. So it's not too difficult, you know, if you are friendly with people.

To the extent that swaps are more likely to take place between friends, we would expect social homogeneity to influence the process—that is, for West Indians to be more likely to switch with other West Indians, mothers with other mothers, women with other women—especially in those settings large enough to allow such selection. In the nursing home unit where there were racial tensions, swaps took place primarily within race; in other units, swaps were often cross-race. Of course, most of our workplaces were largely gender and class homogenous. Such homogeneity presumably promotes swapping.

The Reason for the Switch

A third factor influencing the willingness to make a schedule accommodation to help out a coworker is the reason for the switch. People switch shifts for a variety of reasons, but family-related reasons are generally key, across gender and class, as one male EMT noted: "We swap a lot. In order to meet our needs. (*What are some of the reasons that you swap, generally?*) Oh, let's see, four kids, from a soccer game, to guitar practice, to figure skating, to conferences, to—(*laughs*)—I could probably go on. Majority of it has to do with the kids."

Many workers see switching shifts as something that no one wants to do and that people do so only to help someone out; for them, the willingness to mess up their own schedule in order to help someone else depends on the validity and urgency of the other person's need, as noted by this nursing assistant:

> Like Saturday, I'm working for this lady, I feel sorry for her because she lost her sister. So, I'm gonna work for that lady. . . . For that one, whether I needed time or not, I would have worked for her. But if somebody's going like to the beach or whatever and they don't need overtime,[16] mmmnnn, I don't wanna do it.

The willingness to help people out for what are seen as valid reasons and the expectation that the person will then be available to reciprocate are both related to the finding reported in chapter 5: mothers swapped shifts significantly more often than nonmothers. Nursing assistants sometimes came in because of a coworker's last-minute call to their home:

> Like one day, I remember one of the girls ask me, her son had an accident and she wanted to take him to the dentist. And she called me, I was home, it was my day off, and she requested me to work for her, and I tell her, there's no problem. Sometimes you have to come instead, get out of your comfort zone and just do what you need to do. Because if you see somebody asking you to work for them, they really need that day off.

For most nursing assistants, covering a shift for a coworker was something they did in order to help a coworker in trouble. Doing so was a kind of favor, but a favor based not only on friendship but on a sense of solidarity (which is often tied to friendship), a sense that someone was having a crisis or facing an urgent need in a world where life was tough and employers were often punitive and inflexible. As one CNA noted, if a coworker has "to take a child to school, I'll work it for you. But not for you to go partying, no, I'm not gonna do that." The drawback to these judgments about reasons is that sometimes a worker feels compelled to provide more details about her private life than she would normally want to share. But sharing those details is likely to create or solidify a sense of connection.

We saw this same solidarity among the EMTs. A specific instance of "having a good reason to need the day off" is Christmas, which looms large in EMT accounts of swapping. One single-father firefighter explained that when his daughter was little,

> my biggest thing on Christmas was seeing my daughter open her presents in the morning. Beyond that I could care less about Christmas, so Bill used to, if I was working, if I was coming in Christmas Day, Bill was working the night before. So he would stay a couple of extra hours for me, so Jasmine could get up, we could have breakfast together, she would open up her presents, and I would come into work, instead of for 8:00, I would come in 10:00 or 10:30.

His daughter was now much older, "so I'm to that point where I can do that for the younger guys or girls that have the kids." The ethic is for people without young kids to offer to cover Christmas for those with kids. "I've worked most Christmases," another firefighter said. "I've swapped with people who have kids, because I figure they probably wanted to be home with their kids or whatever. I don't have any kids right now, so I figured I'd give them the opportunity to take the day off."

Stages of the life course figure into the web of connections, both in terms of identifying who is likely to offer to help and who needs and receives it. Reciprocity over the life course is a form of generalized reciprocity that is not limited to particular moments or particular individuals but rather is sustained over time, reinforcing a broad sense of solidarity.

Money

The fourth factor influencing whether a coworker will agree to a swap—money—came into play almost exclusively for the nursing assistants. The kind of straightforward switches common to all occupations—two workers exchanging equivalent time on and off—has no financial consequences for either worker. With other kinds of switches, and above all for nursing assistants, one person gives up a day of work and another person takes it, gaining an extra day's pay. The person who gives up a day of work almost always uses a vacation day in order to receive a normal paycheck. Normally, two weeks' advance notice is necessary to have a vacation authorized, but no advance notice is necessary if the person arranges for a replacement.[17]

Nursing assistants varied in what they were willing to do for money. Many set limits; one said, "I don't see myself [going to another floor]. I'll stick with a crappy paycheck." But many nursing assistants eagerly sought extra hours. One said that she had agreed to work the Fourth of July for a coworker because "I want the extra money." This eagerness for extra time was new for her: "I never felt like that when my kids were younger. . . . I never picked up extra. Never." Things changed because her husband had been laid off from his job at a warehouse. Before that happened, "I really was working just to help my husband pay the bills," she said. "Now, I'm more of the breadwinner in the family, so I have to pick up extra."

Some did not passively wait for opportunities, but instead badgered others to give them a day:

> She was just, she was like, "Come on, you don't need it. You know you wanna stay home and relax." That's what she'll tell you, just to convince you to give her the day. She's so funny. And I was like, "Let me tell you something. I need the day too." "No, you don't need it, Deborah. Come on, you got vacation time. You haven't taken vacation, you got holiday, you got all your days here." (*laughs*) (*So, Anna's always looking for time?*) Yes, she's always looking for time. She will hunt you down, all day, all night. She'll be there, asking, "Listen, I know you don't need it. I know you need to rest.

Your face, you look tired, you need to stay home." (*laughs*) . . . Until you be like, "You know what, fine, let me get the paper and let me sign it. Okay, you can take the day!"

Other workers, however, were not amused by this worker's constant importuning and angrily told her to leave them alone. But while her pushiness and insistence were unusual, her desire for extra hours and pay by covering others' shifts was not.

WHO BENEFITS? EMPLOYERS OR WORKERS?

Swapping arrangements made by workers can be viewed in a variety of ways. An argument can be made that they fit Michael Burawoy's model of "manufacturing consent" in that they are an instance of what he calls a "game" and, as such, co-opt resistance, providing an individualized solution that serves the worker's purposes but also serves the purposes of the employer.[18] As a result of worker-arranged schedule swaps, the organization works better and workers solve management's problem of how to provide adequate staffing on short notice or at times when management cannot get people to (voluntarily) work. The burden of these difficult arrangements is taken off of management and placed on the worker with a problem and on her or his coworkers. Although management refuses to solve the problem, or is unable to do so, management avoids responsibility as well as workers' resentment because it is willing to accept a worker-arranged solution (as long as it stays within management's quite restrictive rules). If workers become unhappy, their ire, it might be expected, is directed at coworkers ("Why won't you help me out?") rather than at management.

In some ways, and in some cases, this is true. But more striking is the other side of the coin: worker-arranged swaps increase resentment of management, which workers feel should be willing, able, or required to itself arrange to cover the slot, at the same time as it increases a sense of solidarity among coworkers. When workers feel that management is unreasonable, they resent having to arrange a switch, and if they can get away with it they will just call out sick. For EMTs, this was most evident in their dealings with EHS, the private-sector company that many EMTs despised:

I think people's attitude towards the company made them call in sick instead of finding coverage. I think if they felt a little better about the place that they worked, I think they would look harder to find coverage for themselves, but mostly they would just call in sick because they don't care.

After leaving EHS, this EMT explicitly contrasted it with his new employer: "I wouldn't leave this place hanging because I respect that they do things for me. People don't mind leaving EHS hanging because EHS has left them hanging hundreds of times."

But the most widespread and pronounced resentment of management arises from those times when workers provide enough advance notice that they feel management should be able to make arrangements. Workers feel that management is simply unwilling to do what it takes to accommodate workers, in particular concerning weekends and vacations, some of the toughest scheduling problems. The only way workers can get time off, they come to feel, is to arrange it themselves.

For the growing number of organizations that operate seven days a week, weekends have become a special sticking point. As with much else, this is particularly an issue at nursing homes, above all for nursing assistants. At Lucas Estates, a de facto policy was emerging that workers could not take off a weekend day unless they arranged their own replacement:

> A lot of people do that. It's the easiest way to, you know, pretty much guarantee you'll get the time off that you want. Sometimes the scheduler, if you ask for a weekend day in particular, even if it's a month from now, they may tell you that they'll really appreciate it if you find someone to switch with.

A nurse at Berkman reported that the policy there was shifting to put more of the burden on employees. She said: "Weekends are hard to get off . . . 'cause their policy now is like, you basically have to find a replacement for any time you want off." A hospital scheduler was clear on this point: "Our rule says you have to find coverage for your weekends." In these ways, management makes use, for its own ends, of a system that workers began, pushing off onto workers changes that management might once have arranged.

Nurses and nursing assistants complained that the time-off policy was shifting. Lucas had a long-standing policy of "find your own replacement for weekends"; Berkman developed this policy during the period we were observing. In these nursing homes, the pattern seemed to be that if the hole in the schedule came at a time when many people would want to work, and it would not be difficult to find volunteers, then management would find the needed worker. But if the hole in the schedule came at a difficult time—on a weekend, on a holiday, or during a peak vacation period—then management was not willing or able to fill the hole and workers had to cooperate with their coworkers to get the shift covered.

In other words, management handles the easy and routine parts of running the workplace but cannot solve difficult problems, so direct worker action is not only needed but proves capable of taking care of the problem situations. The constant effort to push ever more of the difficult scheduling problems onto workers may make life easier for management in the short term, and this might seem an ideal arrangement from management's perspective. But the tightening policy increases both workers' resentment and their solidarity. Instead of the official scheduler doing her job, workers feel that they are forced to find their own replacement, something that management should do. As one nursing assistant said, "I think they [managers] have to take that responsibility and find the people themselves. Because they know more who'd like to pick up time than you do." A nursing home assistant said, "To me, I feel, and I'm sure other people feel, like, why should I have to find somebody?" The response was to create a need for more solidarity, as one nursing assistant pointed out to her coworkers when the new weekend policy was introduced: "Like I had said to them in January, if this is gonna be the policy, we have to help each other out. Pretty much everyone's good with that if you ask them, they'll work, 'cause they know they might need it."

Gender and Swaps: The Case of Vacations

As we saw in chapter 7, workers in the women-dominated occupations found it particularly difficult to get vacation when they wanted it, even if they made their requests long in advance, thus increasing the importance of swaps. For the male-dominated occupations, doctors and EMTs, getting the vacation they wanted was less of an issue. Sometimes they swapped shifts with someone to get the vacation they wanted, but this did not produce resentment of management. For EMTs especially, swaps produced extended vacations without the use of any official vacation time. A firefighter working twenty-four-hour shifts works only two days out of every eight, so if other workers are willing to swap to cover two shifts, the firefighter can be off for twelve days without using a single vacation day.

The nurses and nursing assistants, on the other hand, often bumped up against the fact that a conflict for just one day could lead the scheduler to turn down an entire week's vacation request, even if the request was made months in advance. Workers might solve this problem through schedule swaps, but the need to do so frequently generated hostility directed toward management, as with this nursing assistant:

> I know one girl asked for a vacation off in August, and because I'm off the same week, she got denied for one day, 'cause we would overlap one day. She was denied her whole vacation because of one day. So now she has to find someone to work that one day or they won't give her the week off.

Another angrily described a similar situation, explaining that she had to rely on several coworkers to get six days of vacation: "Well, for instance, I put in six vacations, and I was refused for four or them. So, in February, I had to get Ligaya and Tiffany and Wanda each to work a day for me so I could have February vacation off with the kids." She not only felt solidarity with her coworkers but also felt and expressed resentment toward management: "So, you get aggravated when you've worked there for thirteen years and they deny your vacations." But then she concluded on a note of resignation: "But what can you do? You can't do anything about it."

The scheduler at Lucas Estates tried to be helpful: she identified for workers the day or days that had caused their vacation requests to be denied. Bound by rules about how many people could be off on any given day, the scheduler could not solve the problem. If the nursing assistant could find people to cover those days, the vacation could be approved. The scheduler was trying to be helpful to the extent that she could within restrictive rules set by upper-level management, but that did not mean workers accepted the rules. These non-unionized nursing assistants might have said, in resignation, that there was nothing they could do, but they still resented management.

Nurses are more accustomed to managers responding to their requests and may feel especially resentful if they themselves have to arrange coverage—which may be one factor explaining why nurses make the least use of schedule switches. One angry hospital nurse refused to arrange a switch:

> I didn't even try to find anybody because I said, "That's my vacation, I'm leaving Friday night." . . . I just called in sick! Hey, it was *my* vacation. It's ridiculous. To me that's very unfair. And they should be able, management should be able to let you have your vacation, especially if you don't abuse it.

This is hardly an example of a system that "manufactures consent" or that leads workers to blame each other for problems. This nurse's action may have been unusual, but in a milder form her attitude was representative of the widespread reaction of workers to managers refusing their requests for time off, then inviting workers to make the arrangements themselves.

CONCLUSION

As a central component of the web of time, coworker ties become especially consequential when they swap shifts and days to fill holes in official schedules created by normal unpredictability. In fact, making schedules functional *depends* on the control and collaboration of coworkers. The fact that swaps occur points to the need among workers to rely on one another, to do so in quite visible ways, and to do so routinely. Every week in a year's official schedule offers examples of workers solving schedule problems themselves and specifically finding solutions in those cases where management says that it cannot or will not make an accommodation and thus confronts the worker with a difficult and painful choice. These practices depend on, even as they create, solidarity among coworkers as well as conflict between coworkers and management.

The practice of swapping makes clear workers' priorities and value systems: many workers are willing to inconvenience themselves for coworkers but are less likely to do so for management. At least occasionally, this reverse power dynamic frustrates the schedulers, who are exasperated by the fact that workers will not pick up a shift to help the administration but will pick up shifts to help each other out. A nursing assistant told one such story of the Berkman scheduler, who was almost always good-humored and understanding. This CNA reported that the scheduler was so mad one day, "'cause she was desperate looking for people to work, and they all refused. So one day she's like, 'No, I'm not gonna give it to you. 'Cause one, you get people to work for you, but when I ask them to work, they don't wanna work for me, so I'm not gonna give it to her.'"

Gender and class solidarities shape the frequency, conditions, and logic of coworker swaps (and are reinforced in the process). But differences among the four occupations are less visible here than in other aspects of scheduling. Advantaged and disadvantaged, men and women—they all swap. In significant ways, whether they are EMTs, nurses, or nursing assistants, workers are taking control of one piece of the scheduling process and establishing in a limited way—for pressing problems—a variant of the worker-controlled scheduling that is routine for doctors setting their own official basic schedules. Workers are going beyond resistance to create an alternative, to run the system, albeit within a framework imposed by management.[19] Day-to-day life reminds workers, especially the low-wage CNAs, that management is inflexible, that it is coworkers who help them out and enable them to deal with unexpected difficulties. Management is, or professes itself to be, completely unable to solve a problem, but workers can solve it—further proof of management incompetence or lack of concern. The potential need to switch shifts is a reason to get to know coworkers, to help them out, and to be friendly with them, since the web of connections—the friendships and trust that coworkers build—will, at some point in the future, be crucial to their ability to keep their jobs and take care of their families. When workers swap shifts to cover for each other, this does not manufacture consent but rather establishes (or reestablishes) that the employer (not necessarily the immediate supervisor, but the "big boss" somewhere up there) does not care about workers and their families and always puts the bottom line first and foremost. Coworkers, on the other hand, are the people who can be depended on, who make it possible to get by.

Chapter 11 | The Push of the Family and the Pull of the Job

MANY SAY THAT THE FAMILY is a haven in a heartless world—and it is the job that *is* the heartless world. This chapter reverses that understanding. Here we show the ways in which workers often use the metaphor of "family" to describe the relationships they develop at work at the same time as they reject the view that their own family is a haven or an escape from the job. Paid work becomes the escape, and family the source of stress. As a result, workers sometimes seek extra hours on the job and do not always want to take full advantage of "family-friendly" work policies.

Corporate managers and executives also use the language of "family" to describe the workplace; they use it to draw in workers, boost the bottom line, and control work hours. For example, the president and CEO of Walmart recently said at a shareholders' meeting: "The fact is we aren't just associates and customers in our stores. We're people who grew up together, worship together, and live on the same streets. . . . At Walmart, we are family."[1] McDonald's presents itself as "a family" where "happy time is family time" and its executive center is a "home office." It is not just those corporations serving the less affluent that sell themselves as family. Explaining the success of her upscale clothing company in an interview, Eileen Fisher said, "I think it comes out of a family model."[2] Larry Page, cofounder and chief executive of Google, remarked: "It's important that the company be a family, that people feel that they're part of the company, and that the company is like a family to them."[3] George Lakoff defines metaphor as "understanding one kind of thing or experience in terms of another"; thus understood, the use of metaphor "not only helps make sense of activities but also structures them."[4] The metaphor of family helps shape expectations, actions, and relationships in the workplace.

For workers to conceptualize jobs as families depends on the conditions of their families and the conditions of their jobs, both of which vary by gender and class. It was the relatively disadvantaged women workers, the CNAs, who were most likely to speak of their relations at work as "family"; they did so more than members of any of the other groups, whether the two groups of professionals or the male working-class EMTs. Not only were the low-wage women caregivers more likely to talk of their relations at work (or at least some of those relations) as family, but they were also more likely to think of these work relations as an escape from home.

This may seem a paradox. As we have seen, nursing assistants often work under difficult conditions—not only do they earn low wages, but their jobs entail intense activity, frequent injuries, unpredictable hours, and little authority or control over their tasks or schedules. Even though nursing assistants recognized, sometimes complained about, and sometimes protested these job conditions, we will show here that they also turned those very jobs into "family"—finding attachment and connection with both coworkers and patients (or "residents," as they are called in some nursing "homes").[5] We argue that this seeming paradox can be explained at least in part by the recursive relationship between paid work and family. That is, jobs with unpredictable schedules that cause injury and provide few material benefits often produce stresses at home, and these tensions sometimes send workers back to the job as an escape from their homes.

This chapter examines three factors that lead nursing assistants to choose work over home and to use the language of family to describe their jobs. First, the residents whom nursing assistants care for become either children or parents to them. Second, their coworkers become partners and siblings. And finally, these two attractions of work are often combined for nursing assistants with a third factor—the stress of the actual family at home, which can lead to the job becoming an escape. We conclude by showing that this combination of factors is associated with gender and class: nursing assistants' experience of work as family does not apply, or applies with diminished force, to the other occupations we studied.

FAMILY: HAVEN IN A HEARTLESS WORLD?

Perhaps the most common popular and academic understanding of the family is as a haven, a bedrock of support in a tough world.[6] According to this argument, if people could afford to do so, they would prefer to spend time at home rather than on the job. In this dominant view, the impersonal workplace is the site of strife, control, and exploitation, and the family is the place where people look for warmth, meaning, and emotional support.

In *The Time Bind,* Arlie Hochschild challenged this conventional view of the family as a haven.[7] She made the provocative argument that employees flee the pressures of home for the relief provided by their jobs. Hochschild reminded us that much stress and conflict, even exploitation, occur at home, while much support and personal reward occur in the workplace. She argued that because employees look to paid work as an escape from the stresses of family life, many do not take advantage of institutional policies that allow them time off to be with their families. Based on her intense observations at one family-friendly corporation, Hochschild argued that such companies make it possible to take time off, but employees prefer to work long hours on the job instead of going home. In her words, few employees are "time dissidents"; consequently, they do not forge a "culture of resistance" on the job.[8] However, Hochschild looked at only one workplace, and devoted little attention to variation by gender and class.

Hochschild's book generated much controversy. Criticizing her for studying only one organization, a number of researchers used survey data of employees and found that only a small proportion agreed that they preferred time at work to time at home.[9] Hochschild could reasonably respond that survey preferences are likely to reflect cultural expectations— what people believe they should say.[10] In practice, people might choose to work longer hours, even while saying in a survey that they prefer shorter hours. Using intensive interviews and observations with employees at multiple organizations, we argue that Hochschild was on to something important that too many have rebutted or ignored.

We refine her argument by suggesting that the understanding of work as family is shaped by gender, race, and class, distinctions that Hochschild mostly ignores. With respect to gender, Reed Larson, Maryse Richards, and Maureen Perry-Jenkins, in a much-cited and fascinating study, compared the emotional states experienced by mothers and fathers during daily activities both at home and on the job by asking participants to report on these states at random times on the pagers they carried.[11] Mothers reported more positive emotions on the job (because they faced more burdens at home). Fathers reported more positive emotion in the home sphere, "partly because they spent more of this time in personal and recreational activities and partly because they experienced more choice, even during family work."[12] Thus, we might expect that Hochschild's thesis would apply to women more than men. And as this chapter shows, it does.

What of class? We might expect that, compared to less-advantaged workers, more-advantaged workers would be drawn to the job and want to work longer hours, given their greater control over their work hours and their more favorable job conditions. But what we find is that class and gender interact: the low-wage women in our study were more likely to turn to the workplace as an escape from their homes. This accords with what Lillian Rubin found in her study of the working class a generation ago: "For the [working-class] men in such jobs, bitterness, alienation, resignation, and boredom are the defining features of the work experience. For them . . . work is a requirement of life, hours to be gotten through until you can go home." In contrast, women's "attitudes toward their work are varied, but most find the work world a satisfying place—at least when compared to the world of the housewife. . . . There is, perhaps, no greater testimony to the deadening and deadly quality of the tasks of the housewife than the fact that so many women find pleasure in working at jobs that by almost any definition would be called alienated labor."[13] This chapter shows that the situation Rubin describes still holds today—even as women are far less likely to be housewives.

Finally, these class variations in families are likely to be deeply tied to race, in part because race is so highly correlated with class. For many professionals, often white, "the family" usually means spouse and children. As we saw in chapter 9, "family" for low-wage workers is far more likely to include siblings, grandparents, aunts, uncles, nieces, nephews, cousins, and even non-kin. With this more expansive view of what family means, nursing assistants, many of whom were black and Latina, were particularly open to using the language of family for patients and coworkers.

NURSING ASSISTANTS AND PATIENTS: FAMILY AS METAPHOR AND WORK AS ESCAPE

When nursing assistants were asked: "Some people tell us that they use work as a way to get away from their families. Do you ever feel that way?" the response was overwhelming: 77 percent of the CNAs agreed. The view of work as an escape also spontaneously came up often among CNAs: 40 percent of them brought it up in other parts of their interviews when we were not asking about it directly (compared to 25 percent for female nurses, 19 percent for male EMTs, and 7 percent for male doctors—a difference discussed later in the chapter).

For CNAs, work is an escape from their families at home in part because they become attached to nursing home residents as "family."[14] In the national survey of nursing assistants, when asked about the main reason they stayed in their current job, the two top reasons they provided were "caring for others" (chosen by 49.1 percent, far more than any other reason) and "kind of work that feels good" (coming in second, but chosen by only 8.6 percent).[15] Walking away at the end of her interview, a Latina nursing assistant mused about the residents she cared for: "They're my babies—my people. I would do anything for them." She compared their relations to her real family: "You come there every day and you see them, some of them they get so happy when they see you," she said with a laugh. "You be like, 'Okay, not even my momma gets so happy when she sees me.'" Another Latina assistant, a single mother with a young child at home, seemed wise for her age even though she was only twenty-five years old: "When they [residents] end up leavin', if they goin' back home, trust me, you're gonna miss them. You be like, 'Oh, okay, I miss this person,' you get like attach, I get attach with somebody, you know." The nursing assistants used the metaphor of family to describe the people they cared for, and they used these relationships to explain why they might sometimes want to escape their real family.

For these women, the meaning of family they find with patients comes not only from giving much-needed care but also from gaining appreciation, sometimes from those who come from very different walks of life. Another Latina single mother, with two young children, said, "We're not strangers, we're the people that take care of them, we're like their family. They're my family." What did she mean? She could talk to them: "You wanna know, I love to talk to them." She also admired and learned from them: "I learn so much from these elderly people, it's not even funny. I know what they used to do. I love to ask all that. So, that's something I always do." Her job sometimes made it hard, however, to talk to residents because, as she saw it, the nursing home wanted to limit these relationships. "Sometimes you don't have the time," she said, but added that she sometimes defied the organization's schedules and rules to be with the residents. "Nah, everybody not going really by the books." Then she explained why: "I love to communicate with the residents and talk to them. Even Jerry [a resident she cared for], I sit there and ask him how he was a lawyer. And you know, you learn a lot from them, from talking to them and asking about their lives."

Personal bonds with residents led CNAs to value their job over other jobs they had held and sometimes to contrast their jobs favorably to jobs that paid much higher wages. One white nursing assistant favorably compared working in a nursing home to working in a factory, where she had previously made significantly more money. "I love doing what I do, I like being with the residents, I really do. You know, I could have stayed at the factory and made double what I make now, but I wasn't happy there. I was working in the office at that point too. I just, I didn't like doing that type of work, to me it wasn't fulfilling." Asked what she found more fulfilling about her nursing home work, she immediately replied: "Just the caring and the compassion that you can give to someone. . . . There's people there, who love us as much as they love their own family. . . . It's nice when you see a certain resident, (*gasps*) they're so happy to see you when you come in."

One of the few male CNAs, a Latino, first emphasized: "This is not an easy job. I don't care what anybody tells you, we have a lot to do as aides. A lot. Dealin' with a lot of people. A lot of your time is sacrificed doin' this stuff, you know. And, uh, there's a lot of times even when people are passin' away, you're there talkin' to 'em right when they go." Constantly using the colloquial phrase "you know"—which implies (and promotes) a shared understanding—he said: "You know, I spend more time with these people than I do with my own children. You know, my kids are in school eight hours a day. You know, I'd be lucky to spend eight hours with my kids." Then he went on to favorably contrast his job as a nursing assistant to that of physicians; as he put it, "Doctors might be the ones who, like, go in there and fix everything, but, we're family to these people. We spend more time with 'em, we're family. We treat them like family." Asked what he meant by "family," he said that residents confided in him: "Like, I have people talk to me about things that they probably never told anybody else. But because they confide in me and things like that, just sit there and listen to 'em . . . it's, it's an experience for both." And they argued with him: "They can get mad at us, just like a family does. They can do all the crazy . . . they argue with us, just like a family member does." Though this male CNA was in his early forties, he recounted how these cross-class relations with residents socialized him, teaching him about a world to which he would not otherwise have had access:

> I'm learning because I'm still young. . . . I'm still learning about, you know, everything they've gone through and I'm like, wow, it's amazing. It's, like I said, we're their family. I remember them, like, a resident who talked to me about her whole life story. And when she passed away, I knew who she was. I mean, she told me everything. How she was born, how she came from Italy. How she heard her father and mother had nothing, and owned a small piece of land which grew . . . and now today, the land is actually, uh, Mountain Community College. You know? (*laughs*)

In conclusion, he used an affectionate phrase more often heard in the context of old-fashioned affairs of the heart: "She was just a sweetheart," he said, emphasizing the care he gave her until her death forced a parting of ways: "When it comes down to it, we're here to take care of them. And every day we're here to make sure they're happy, and, you know, when their time is . . . well, time to pass on, we made it comfortable for 'em."

Occasionally, nursing assistants came in on their days off to check on residents.[16] Some cried about the pain or death of residents. Although facing frequent deaths among those they cared for, these nursing assistants did not develop—and did not think they should develop—the kind of "detached concern," or emotional distance, that Harold Leif and Renée Fox thought to be important for doctors, who see so much death and dying.[17]

On the one hand, nursing assistants would sometimes say, "We're just ass-wipers, that's all we are," but on the other hand, the job of taking care of human beings was one that they felt good about and that mattered to them. As a number of scholars have argued, the relationships that CNAs form at work may have a paradoxically adverse effect on them: employers can pay them low wages not only because hands-on care work is generally devalued but also because the personal relations they develop can substitute for financial compensation.[18] Note that CNAs themselves often come to naturalize the emotional pleasures and connections of the job rather than emphasizing the special skills the job requires; they highlight emotional connection as a natural outcome (much as wives and mothers make natural—and in some ways devalue—the skills they use to do unpaid domestic work).[19]

Some organizations regularly pair particular residents with particular CNAs, which probably encourages these emotional ties.[20] Other institutions, however, discourage such relationships; at least some organizations, it seems, may not rely on emotional rewards as a substitute for higher wages. Some managers warn nursing assistants *not* to get too involved with the residents and sometimes tell them not to develop favorites among the residents in the fear that those relationships would take priority over the organization and management. When nursing assistants are moved around to different residents, many managers believe that the residents will be less likely to have high expectations or to become too demanding of—or on behalf of—the staff.[21] One African American nursing assistant reiterated what a number of them told us: "They [management] tell you not to get emotionally involved, but that's nonsense. The residents are like your family; you spend more time with them than with your own family. If you've been here a year, you know everything about a resident."

These emotional ties are reciprocal. Just as CNAs become attached to residents, residents also get attached to CNAs. They sometimes insist that only a particular nursing assistant is acceptable as someone who can take them to the toilet, help them dress, or adjust their bed.[22] This suggests that policies that separate CNAs and residents may have negative consequences, not only for the workers but also for the residents to whom they give care.

Although data on more organizations are necessary to systematically assess the distribution of these institutional strategies and their consequences, it is already clear that institutions try to use different, sometimes contradictory, strategies to bolster the bottom line. Sometimes they promote relations between CNAs and residents, and sometimes they undermine these relations. The residents and nursing assistants work around the institutional strategies. When asked, "So why do you like it here?" one white married CNA responded: "I dunno. I like the people. I love the residents. I mean, the residents . . . they're just . . . they're like family. You know?" She described the ways in which the organization had sought to deter these personal relationships with residents: "When I first became a CNA, they always told us, 'Don't get too attached to the residents.' But I was talkin' to a nurse last night, and I'm like, 'How can you not get attached to them?' We're with them sometimes more than their family is. And they know us. And we know their daily routines and everything. I love these residents."

Coworkers as Family

For CNAs, coworkers also become family. Recall the intense ties to coworkers that some described in chapter 10, sometimes using the metaphor of family. Speaking of her coworkers, one white nursing assistant said: "Pretty much it's more like a family sort of thing, you know, we're all together." Explicitly contrasting the "family" she found with coworkers to the family she had at home, a black nursing assistant said: "What I think about my coworkers, more of a family, because we spend more hours with them than even our families." She explained how her work affected her experiences at home. "By the time, you know, that I work seven to three, by the time I go home, I'm tired, I want to rest. You don't even have much time for your family, like you do have . . . you spend more time with those girls there, and the nurses, than you spend at home." When time spent on the job reduces involvement at home, creating tensions and exhaustion there, people at work become more attractive.

The likelihood of workers referring to family-like relations with their coworkers varies from one location to another and appears to be associated with particular structural conditions that CNAs encounter on the job. The shift matters: some told us that there was more companionship on the night shift, when fewer managers, supervisors, and residents' family members were around. There is also more downtime on the night shift, which allows personal relations among coworkers to develop: while most patients were asleep, we observed hospital and nursing home personnel sharing details about their personal lives. They were less likely to have time to do so during the more hectic hours of the day shifts.

Some said that particular floors, and not others, became like family: "With the girls on the Baker unit on 3:00 to 11:00, we all know pretty much everything about everyone in everyone's family. We seem more like we are a family." Just as is true more generally in social life, the nursing assistants often formed friendships and alliances with others who were similar to them, whether in race-ethnicity, generation, or occupation.[23] They usually used "family" to refer to coworkers who were at roughly their same level, not in reference to supervisors or bosses (although bosses sometimes used the word to refer to subordinates). Organizational context further shaped ties between coworkers: the CNAs who worked in nursing homes were more likely to form ties with coworkers than CNAs who worked in hospitals, perhaps because nursing homes provide a considerably larger pool of nursing assistants to draw from and larger groups can meet up in the break rooms to relax and chat about their lives.

Whatever the structural forces and personal attractions shaping them, relations with coworkers were important substitutes or supplements for the relationships the nursing assistants had at home.

Escaping the Family

In addition to the attractions of patients and coworkers, nursing assistants also focus on the other side—on the stress they face *at home* that leads them to turn to their jobs. That stress came in part from the material circumstances these low-wage women faced at home. A nursing home scheduler noted, "I've had people in here when we have a heat wave— everybody shows up. . . . They don't have air conditioning at home."

Nursing assistants themselves contrasted their family-like relations at work to their real families at home and offered a number of explanations—some related to their job, some related to their family—for why they saw work as an escape from home. Some simply emphasized the appeal of being engaged in paid work over staying at home. A married African American nursing assistant who earned $25,000 a year used the evocative image of a tasty dessert to contrast her job to her less appealing home. This nursing assistant, whom we interviewed in her apartment, spoke evocatively of her job as an "ice cream cone," reporting, "I feel better when I'm at work. I feel, you know how some people, they drown theirself in the bottle because sometimes they'd be so miserable and unhappy? That's me. To me at work is . . . it's like a big old ice cream cone." When we asked why, she replied, motioning around her dark apartment, "Sometimes I just don't want to be here."

The nursing assistants also talked of their paid-work relationships in terms of time: while their jobs sometimes made it difficult to spend predictable time with their real families, the fact that they spent a lot of time with coworkers and residents turned work, they said, into "family."

More often, the nursing assistants talked of the emotional void or the burdens they encountered at home. The reason they volunteered for an unpredicted, suddenly available extra shift was not just that they needed the money, but the fact that relations at work offered relief from those at home. A number of those who talked this way were single mothers, who sometimes mentioned the loneliness they faced at home to explain the pull of the job. One unmarried Puerto Rican mother with two children under twelve pointed to her small, crowded apartment and said, "I really, you see my apartment, it's very lonely here, it is very lonely."

Some single mothers highlighted their appreciation for the distraction from the stresses of home that work could provide. A twenty-one-year-old Latina nursing assistant who earned less than $20,000 a year addressed this issue:

> Like any other person at the house, sometimes you need to get away, and I feel like, you know, when I work, you're just busy working so you don't focus on whatever's going at home or whatever problem you have, you don't focus on it, you're focusing at your job. That's the reason why I like to work, because your mind is off of things that you're so worried about at home.

An African American single mother said that she would cut back on her hours if she could, "if money wasn't an issue," so that she could have more time with her children. Her long hours made it difficult to raise her kids the way she wanted to. But after talking about the stresses of home, she quickly switched her focus and discussed her desire to escape from home and the draw of her job: "I still would pick up [extra hours], because you need that adult environment, you know. Because when you're around your kids all the time, sometimes you do get a little stressed out. . . . You just need that outlet to get out, or either—you know, even when you come to work and it's a little stressful at times, you're around other adults, so it passes by a little better." This single mother concluded, capturing what so many told us even while expressing confusion about its legitimacy, "I don't know if it makes any sense . . . work as an escape."

A Jamaican single mother was particularly emphatic about the stress of children as a reason her work was more appealing. She even cut short her sick leave because of it:

INTERVIEWER: So for a fractured ankle and a broken toe you missed a week? Only a week?

RESPONDENT: Yeah, I should have been out longer, but sometimes it's depressing when you're at home. You know when you're home you should be homely, and it's like it's not. . . . It's like everybody's yelling at me, everybody's wanting things done; it's more peaceful if I go into work. Do you ever feel that way sometimes?. . . Because sometimes when I'm here [the interview took place in her apartment] on my days off, it's like everything is just caving in, and when I'm at work I feel that peace.

When we began examining nursing assistants' talk of escaping their homes to go to their jobs, we hypothesized it was because so many were single mothers. But further analysis proved this initial assumption wrong. In fact, the *married* nursing assistants also emphasized the pull of the job as an escape from the home. A married African American nursing assistant with one teenager still at home mentioned both her nagging husband and her son:

INTERVIEWER: Some people say that they go to work as a way to escape from their families. Have you ever felt that way?

RESPONDENT: Mmm, do I ever feel like that? Yes, once in a while.

INTERVIEWER: Yeah. Tell me.

RESPONDENT: Sometimes my, my husband, he been nagging me. And my son will be giving me a lot of talking. I just want to get out, and even if I don't go to work, I just get outta there. Sometimes, I enjoy going to work.

A married white nursing assistant also emphasized her escape from her teenager and her husband:

INTERVIEWER: Sometimes people tell us that they use work as a way to get away from their families. Have you ever felt that way?

RESPONDENT: Oh, sometimes I feel like that, especially with teenagers. Definitely. Sometimes it's nice just to go to work. Definitely.

INTERVIEWER: Tell me more.

RESPONDENT: Ohh, I think, too, when we go to work, we can just vent with our friends and it makes you feel better, and makes things easier to adjust to at home. Sometimes when I'm aggravated with my husband, I can't wait to get outta there! 'Cause I think if I stayed home, I'd be nitpicking more and arguing more, so it's better that I just leave for eight hours and things seem to resolve themselves. At least with the kids, maybe not so much with my husband.

Other married women spoke of work as a way to escape from their husbands. An African American nursing assistant whose two children were grown held two full-time jobs. She suggested that such long hours helped her marriage. "Even though me and my husband don't see each other," she said with a laugh, "so we can get along better that way." We pursued this line of thought by asking: "Sometimes people have told us in these interviews that they worked in part as a way to get away. . ." Before we could finish the sentence, she interrupted by saying: "Sometimes with my husband. He's a clean-freak-maniac." A married white nursing assistant whose children were grown denied the pull of work at first, but changed her mind in the middle of a sentence:

INTERVIEWER: Sometimes people have told us that they go to work as a way to get away from their families.

RESPONDENT: Really?

INTERVIEWER: Is that anything that, I mean sometimes . . .

RESPONDENT: No, no, I never. That's never crossed my mind (*laughs*), except for now, that my husband is, you know, his back operation and everything, and he's always sittin' in that kitchen saying, "Ohh, ohh." (*laughs*)

Another nursing assistant took a similar position. Asked, "How does your husband feel about your working nights?" she answered: "Oh, it's perfect! At this rate our marriage will last forever, because we never see each other," she said, laughing. "So it works out good!"

Like single mothers, the married mothers also talked of their teenagers as the reason for conflict at home. A young Latina who was married and had only one teenage child spoke about how lonely it was at home and the companionship she found with residents: "I am always home by myself, and my son. So, it is stressing, it gets depressing when you just doing nothing. So, I just wanna work." Again, we probed: "But it definitely feels sometimes like you'd rather be there [at work] than here [her apartment, where the interview took place]?" She continued with the same line of thought:

Yeah, but because it's like, sometimes you're stressed, and if you stay in the house, it gets more stressing. So, but when you're working, like the residents can make you laugh or, you know, you can make them laugh, you could have a better day over there than in your house. . . . I just rather just go to work.

Agreeing with her was a white married mother with teenage kids who was hired to work thirty-two hours on the day shift but picked up about an extra shift a week. She explained: "Sometimes I say I should have stayed at work and did a double because it's more stress going home."

Sometimes it is a young child from whom married nursing assistants seek relief. One twenty-five-year-old married mother who worked the day shift reported why she cut short her leave:

I had my son, and then I'm like, I cannot wait to go back to work, because with him I think sometimes I work more even being at home than here, with him, because he is—he's nonstop. He's into everything. He's so curious. So, there's days when I'm just like, oh, I can't wait until I get to work. At least I'm not chasing someone around, you know, 24/7.

As others have argued, a life-course approach helps us understand the particular tensions from which employees seek relief.[24] Many CNAs who talked of work as a draw were escaping the demands of parenting—both young children and teenagers. But as we have seen, some also sought an escape from the demands of marriage. Many nursing assistants, married or not, with children or without, told us that they sought additional hours and sometimes picked up unpredictable hours not only for the money, which many of them did very much need, but also because they found the job more appealing than their home (in part because of their low wages). Ironically, they wanted to escape the very family relationships that so many commentators describe as "the haven in a heartless world." These low-wage workers in dead-end jobs, many of whom were given unpredictable hours and denied leaves while working under intense pressure with little control, came to describe (at least some aspects of) their workplaces as like family at the same time as they used those workplaces to avoid their at-home families.

WHO ESCAPES? COMPARING CNAS TO DOCTORS, EMTS, AND NURSES

Nursing assistants were substantially more likely than those in the other occupations to talk about sometimes preferring work to home. The three factors we have identified—the pull of patients, the pull of coworkers, and the push to escape home—help explain these differences.

The Pull of Patients

CNAs in nursing homes have long-term relations with residents. Those relations sometimes last for years, are conducted in stretches of at least eight hours, and involve intimate personal care and repeated interactions. Nursing assistants themselves noted that in hospitals (where there are many nurses but few nursing assistants) they did not get to know the patients. One day in a hospital, a nursing assistant commented: "I used to work in a nursing home as a CNA. I made less money. But at least there, you got to know the patients, what we call the residents. You had a personal relationship with them." A nursing assistant standing nearby joined in, saying: "I was sixteen years at a nursing home and ten years here. I will always see the nursing home as my real job. I miss the long-term attachment to the patients."

None of the other occupations came close to having the kind of relationships with the people they served that the CNAs in nursing homes had with patients. Nurses care for patients for eight or twelve hours at a stretch, but the average hospital stay in the United States has decreased substantially and is now less than five days.[25] EMTs deal with people in crisis situations, and the entire encounter is typically over within an hour; most of those patients they never see again. Primary care practitioners may have long-term relations with patients, but they are an ever-smaller fraction of all doctors. They generally see patients for relatively short visits and rely on hospitalists for the hospital care of their patients; as a result, primary care practitioners spend less time with their patients than they did a generation ago.

To be sure, some doctors talked about being drawn to their jobs, and as we have seen, they often worked long hours and almost never took sick leaves. Their explanations for their sense of commitment to their jobs, however, tended to be very different from those of the CNAs. Using a "rhetoric of constraint" (see chapter 10), physicians often asserted that they had to stay long hours at work; they often presented this as inevitable, a result of duty or peer pressure but not because of close (never mind family-like) relations with patients.

One EMT used a love metaphor to talk about the attraction of work, but it was the work itself, not the patients, that exerted the pull:

> I've always said this: EMS is a jealous lover. In many different ways, it's a jealous lover. Like an old flame, it's always in the back of my mind. . . . I'm married and I have a respectable life, but I have this naughty girl on the side, and that's what EMS is like. It's like my dirty little secret. I'll take my girls to

the park, I'll teach them how to ride their bikes, and in the back of my mind I'm thinking, *Tomorrow night I go back to work, tomorrow night's my first night, I wonder what that's going to bring.* It's always back there.

In his eyes, work was more like an illicit love affair than a family.

The Pull of Coworkers

Of the three forces that led nursing assistants to sometimes prefer work over family, the one that exerted the most significant impact on the other occupations was coworkers. Doctors, nurses, and EMTs all found co-workers to be one of the attractions of work. And some used the language of family to evoke the closeness of these coworker ties. One EMT explained that, "if I were on a call and any one of my teammates got hurt or worse, I'd be devastated, because it's a family group." Another EMT used the language of family to describe the shared holidays and domestic work they did: "It's like a second family. I actually look forward to going into work because you get real close with the people that you work with. Yesterday was a holiday, so we knew it would probably be slow and we didn't have any inspections, so we actually cooked a big like Thanksgiving dinner." Another EMT said, "You work. . . . It is like being in a family" because "you do everything together." EMTs, more than any other occupation, also noted the downside of their work "family": "There can be some pretty good arguments amongst each other, because if I'm doing forty hours [of overtime], you're not doing any, I feel like I'm taking more of the workload on, and you're not doing anything . . . there's personality differences, big ones, inside the firehouses. It's not the big happy family that . . . [is] portrayed on TV." He concluded: "It's just like any family, there's brothers and sisters fighting." Another developed this same theme, again drawing on images from television and contrasting the pull of the "dysfunctional" workplace "family" to that of the home-based family:

> We [firefighters] are like a big dysfunctional family. We're like brothers and sisters, we talk about each other, fights like a soap opera. So you'd say so-and-so's an idiot for not doing his part of the deal [by working extra hours]. And he may have had a great family reason for not having to stay.

These men seemed to have a less romantic view of families than the nursing assistants. One EMT, talking about the ease of finding another EMT to swap hours with him, first described work relations as being like family—saying, "It's a family group"—but then went on to combine the metaphor of family with another metaphor—that of a team, which is at least implicitly masculine and also often used by employers: "Like I say, it's a team effort."

The pull of coworkers was powerful for some nurses. A midwife went back and forth between the language of family and the language of deep friendship when she spoke of the companionship she found at work: "We're family. To be able to go to work with your best friends every day is another kind of compensation that's very valuable to me." This sort of statement was much less common, however, for nurses (and EMTs) than for CNAs, and not a single physician talked this way.

The Push to Escape Home

To be sure, many people—across class and gender divides—see the workplace as an important supplement to, if not a substitute for, relations at home. Yet there are important distinctions. Because of their higher incomes, those in the other occupations may have been less likely than the CNAs to talk about the ways in which conditions at home pushed them toward their jobs.

Doctors   Although they worked long hours because, they said, they had to, doctors were the least likely to bring up the draw of work over home. Only one doctor used the term "family" to describe work. This was a woman doctor with a small private practice who said that she and the staff regularly had lunch together, and that "we look forward to that, we have fun. We have fun as a group. At this point I feel like some of these people are more like my family than my family."

Not a single male doctor used family as a metaphor for the job. One male doctor did talk about being more drawn to his home than to his job. He told us that he had changed jobs, moving to a less lucrative job in a clinic (where he earned *only* $175,000 a year), because he developed heart problems and came to "hate part of [his job]—the paperwork, the millions of phone calls, the on-call at night." He contrasted his job and his home with an evocative story about using his workplace elevator as symbol and motor of both return and escape that quite dramatically reversed the CNAs' (and Hochschild's) story:

> I had a thing where our elevator in my office building was a bad elevator, and it broke down a lot. And so I would stand . . . before I'd go into my office at the bottom, when no patients of mine were there, and I'd wait, and when the elevator would come I'd take it up, and I would stand in the elevator and go, *You know, if it broke, I'd be stuck here and I wouldn't have to go to the office, and*

it would be okay. But going home, I never took the elevator because there was no way on the earth I would want to get stuck in the elevator on my way home. So I always walked down the stairs and I always took the elevator up.

Using the reverse formulation, another male doctor reported, with some sadness, that he felt pushed to work by the absence of his family. He had no children still at home; his wife, who had stayed home until the kids were grown, now had a job she liked and sometimes came home late. Because he had come to think of home as boring, he signed up for extra time in the hospital: "Today was supposed to be my day off, and I signed up for it because it was open. And this is . . . you know, this is going to be forty-eight hours for me this week." His wife, he said, "laughs, she can't believe it [and asks,] 'What's going on?'" He explained the boredom he felt in the house that was now emptied of all but their pets: "I'm all by myself at the house, with the dogs. And [it's] kind of boring! (*laughs*) I mean, I'd rather work!" This wealthy, middle-aged physician with no children still around, but a family income over $250,000 a year, could not find much to do at home. In contrast to the nursing assistants, his rationale for feeling the pull of his job was the monotony rather than the stress he encountered at home.

Another explanation for the pull of work came from a woman doctor who was critical of some of her male colleagues. Coming closest to suggesting that doctors work long hours because they want to escape their home, she suggested that male doctors want to stay at work because of the power they enjoy there:

[They] want to be at work because they are the top of the heap there. People do whatever they say. But [they feel,] "When I go home my wife's grumpy." They have power at home, but the contrast is substantial. At the office, when they say, "Bring me a cup of coffee," somebody hops up to do it. At home, that is not so clear. When they go home, their wife says: "Take out the garbage. What should we do about Billy's school? You need to talk to Billy. You forgot we are going out to dinner tonight."

The male doctors themselves, however, rarely talked about having a desire to escape their homes. Perhaps male doctors just do not give as much thought to tasks at home, which are all but invisible for many of them because they have spouses who typically take care of most of these tasks. One fifty-year-old white doctor, with a perfectly trimmed black mustache and spotless large office, headed a hospital unit. Earning about $400,000 a year while his wife stayed home with their three kids (one eleven years old, the other two teenagers), he described the long hours he worked and then referred to his family as a "hobby"—a characterization it would be hard to imagine coming from the women, or even most men, in the three other occupational groups.

> Obviously, my family likes having me around, I enjoy being around them, and they are my hobby. When people ask me, "What is your hobby?" the answer is, "My family." My family is my hobby. So time that is not work-related, they are the focus of that time. Yes, they would like to have more of me around them, but at the same time they also have developed good, busy, and productive schedules between schoolwork and after-school activities. The two older ones are also self-sufficient.

This rendering would be less likely to come from a woman—few mothers describe their teenagers as "self-sufficient" (or their family as a "hobby"). Certainly no nursing assistants did. Overall, then, the male doctors did not talk or think of work as the "family" that provides an escape from home.

Emergency Medical Technicians   The EMTs, like the doctors, had relatively little to say about escaping their families to spend more time at work, even if they talked of the tight bonds they had with their coworkers. A few, but only a few, of the EMTs spoke of their job as an escape and their workplace as family:

> There are days that I am thankful I'm coming to work. Sure, I would be lying if I said different. There are days like *arg!*—when you are walking out of the house and it's like you're going nuts. It's "I'm going to work now, see ya." As you're walking out of the door, you're turning off the cell phone because you don't want to hear it.

For many EMTs, the reverse imagery—the draw of the home—is more powerful. One full-time EMT with a wife who also worked full-time explained why he would not go in for overtime money:

> If I haven't been home with my wife for a bit, and maybe I was gone all day and we just both get home and we just had dinner, and I'm going to open a nice bottle of wine. . . . I would never go in [for an overtime call] if she just walked through the door and I haven't seen her all day, there's no way I'm going to get up and say, "Yeah, I'll be back in an hour and a half."

It is notable that so few EMTs spoke of trying to escape their homes because, as we have seen, these working-class men did considerably more domestic work than the male doctors did. Perhaps it is because they divide or share that work and believe that they themselves made the choice to do so that the EMTs did not experience the home—and its associated labor—as a constraint or burden they looked to escape.

Nurses Recall that a significantly higher proportion of the female nurses than the male EMTs or doctors (but not as a high a proportion as the CNAs) said that they went to work to escape the demands they faced at home—they talked of not wanting to face dishes, bathrooms that needed cleaning, demanding children, difficult husbands. One nurse who talked this way was divorced. Now in her late thirties, she remembered her abusive husband and remarked: "I had a husband that became extremely controlling, extremely controlling. So work was a good way to get away." It was not, however, only abused nurses who talked about work as an escape from family. A nursing home nurse, a married mother of two teenage kids, said: "My home life has been no picnic, believe me . . . my husband's a pain in the ass. My kids they . . . give me trouble too." She described the nursing home residents as "my second family." But she was one of only two currently married nurses who used the language of family in reference to her job.

Though relatively few nurses used the family metaphor to describe their work, some nonetheless spoke of their jobs as an escape. One nurse, like many respondents in Hochschild's study, explained that she did not take full advantage of family-friendly policies because she was drawn to work.

> I never took a four-month leave of absence. Because I went nuts at home. I had to have more in my life than that. I made arrangements to take a four-month leave of absence when I had my first child, and I went back in six weeks. . . . And when my youngest one was born, I took two weeks off and I went back.

Although nurses insisted that they wanted to escape to work more often than those in either of the male occupations, this formulation came up spontaneously in only about one-quarter of the nurse interviews (compared to 40 percent of the CNA interviews).[26] The nurses were not simply women responding to external constraints or dealing with husbands who earned a living but refused to do their share in the daily work of the home. Some nurses talked about how much they liked cooking family meals and gardening and how much they wanted to take the time to see their elderly parents and especially to have time to care for their children. As one explained: "Well, the big thing is that I like to be home with my kids." And as we have seen, the nurses, unlike the CNAs, often could take advantage of policies at work that allowed them to take the time away from work to care for their families. They could afford to do so, and they did.

CONCLUSION

Dichotomous thinking is often misleading, and certainly when dealing with work and family. Presumably no one would defend a simple dichotomy of "work bad, family good," but in practice such a view often shapes the thinking of both ordinary people and academics. Barbara Garson wrote: "Real work is a human need, perhaps right after the need for food and the need for love. It feels good to work well."[27] It should not surprise us that people seek balance and that they value work. If work becomes too demanding, it can only be resisted by a powerful alternative force, and often that force is family. But neither do people want their lives to be totally dominated by family demands or to have their social and intellectual limits set by a child, a teenager, or even a spouse. Many people look to the workplace as a source of personal connection. The pull of the web of time depends not just on external demands but also on individual choices and preferences. Work provides a sense of accomplishment and meaning and—at least in care work occupations—a set of social connections, both with those to whom care is given and with other caregivers. That is one of the reasons people agree to work so many hours, not simply as part of their set-in-advance schedules but also to pick up shifts at unpredictable times not scheduled in advance. Choosing to add hours at work is, in some ways, a decision to introduce some unpredictability into their lives themselves, rather than simply being subject to management's power to impose unpredictability on them.

This is a story of inequality, however, not just in the workplace but also at home. More than the men, women—nursing assistants as well as nurses—are likely to talk of their jobs as offering an escape. Others have found that many women who are mothers or housewives speak of feeling isolated at home and seeking jobs as a way to find adult companionship.[28] But that broad view, like Hochschild's, tends to be insensitive to class variation. In our study, it was most often the low-wage (frequently black and Latina) nursing assistants who explicitly stated that they looked to their jobs for an escape from their often stressful families, and they were also the ones who used "family" as a metaphor for their relations at work. Though this finding might at first seem startling given nursing assistants' difficult job experience, it underscores two points.

First, family means something different to low-wage women workers than it does to the affluent. As we argue elsewhere, low-wage women workers' view of family outside of the workplace is extended rather than nuclear.[29] That is to say, family is broader for them, and more inclusive. Extending that idea of family to the workplace may be less of a stretch for low-wage women workers. So, too, nursing assistants sometimes used their relationships with the residents to speak ill of the residents' actual families. Much like the African American men in Michele Lamont's *The Dignity of Working Men,* these low-wage women (often women of color) criticized affluent (often white) families for providing inadequate care for their family member—sending him or her to a nursing home, not visiting enough, or visiting but misunderstanding the resident's needs.[30] Affluent families, the nursing assistants thought, had a narrow vision of family and just did not take care of their own.[31] That made the work of nursing assistants all the more important—because residents, in their opinion, needed family, they themselves, the CNAs, became that family.

Second, family and work are not separate. Difficult work conditions are associated with, and contribute to, difficult conditions at home. Their job hours and pay often make it hard for low-wage women to take care of their families and lead them to seek meaningful relationships outside their families. At the same time, adding hours or shifts brings in more money, which is likely to make life at home a little easier for them. This exposes the ambiguity of their daily choices.

Two sets of relations underpin these feelings and choices. CNAs described residents in terms often used for spouses or partners—as sweethearts, confidants, or adults with whom to discuss intimate matters. They sometimes described the residents as good parents, those who were teaching the CNAs about life. Sometimes CNAs also described them as lovable children: "They're my babies." Whether talking about coworkers or residents, the nursing assistants, especially in nursing homes, talked in terms of emotional attachment and companionship—the hallmarks, historians argue, of the modern family.[32] These nursing assistants also talked of knowledge and practical care—the indicators emphasized by many work and family scholars—when they spoke of why people at their worksites were "family." They did not use the metaphor of family to talk about unequal relationships; the metaphors they used invoked an idealized modern family rather than the hierarchical or patriarchal family of old. Ironically, the workplace became the place where they sought those equal relations.

Workers' use of family as a metaphor for relations on the job has several consequences. First, as George Lakoff and Mark Johnson suggest, "the very systematicity that allows us to comprehend one aspect of a concept in terms of another ... will necessarily hide other aspects of that concept."[33] Using "family" to describe the workplace may help workers accommodate to devalued jobs and conceal or at least assuage problems with them. Workers' experience of "family" in the workplace may even help employers substitute personal relations formed at work for financial compensation. But we saw the flip side of this benefit for employers: they also sometimes view employees' personal relations as problematic and try to deter them; they fear that these ties may compete with employees' loyalty to the organization, or come at the expense of the organization.

Second, these patterns probably appear in other occupations. Rachel Sherman, in *Class Acts,* examined the relations between service workers and patrons in luxury hotels—relations that are in many ways parallel to those between nursing assistants and residents in nursing homes.[34] Sherman argues, on the one hand, that scholars of work should "take positive interactions seriously rather than dismiss them as only performative, forced or instrumental."[35] That surely applies to nursing assistants who seek additional job hours. On the other hand, Sherman's research suggests that such relations between clients and low-wage workers powerfully reinforce broader class inequality. These relations normalize class entitlements and, we would add, class disadvantage.

Third, this pattern helps create a form of resistance, in this case to the family, not the job. These health care workers use jobs that they conceptualize as family to escape their real families, which they also experience, at least sometimes, as oppressive. Not all workers use jobs this way; doing so depends on both the conditions of their families and the conditions of their jobs—both of which are tied to race as well as gender and class.

It comes as no surprise that class matters to family life. A growing number of qualitative researchers who study families have demonstrated the power of class.[36] The surprise is not that class matters to family life but that class matters to the meaning of family and the uses to which "family" is put. It is no surprise that gender matters to family life, but what is particularly striking here, especially as a specification of Hochschild's argument, is the interaction of class and gender as well as race. In some sense, understanding the two groups of men is relatively simple. Even if EMTs did significantly more domestic work than physicians did, neither group of men did most of that work. They had it relatively easy at home and had no need to escape. Men are probably also less likely than women to use family as a metaphor for cultural reasons; some EMTs substituted the metaphors of an "illicit love affair" and, more often, a "team"—perhaps masculinized versions of connection. A more serious puzzle is nurses, who might enjoy more power at work than they do at home, but who do not see their coworkers as "family." It may well be the nurses' greater power to reshape organizations to meet their family demands that leads them to seek more time at home. Moreover, as we saw in chapter 9, the nurses in our study were focused on "doing gender" in ways that called attention to the pull toward family and motherhood. Thinking that they were responsible for most domestic work, the nurses could use their relative power in the workplace to meet cultural schemas about motherhood, and they could afford this position, while the low-wage nursing assistants could not.

Note some potential caveats that may limit the generalizability of the argument. In asking, "Some people tell us that they use work as a way to get away from their families. Do you ever feel that way?" we recognize that a "yes" answer, which so many nursing assistants gave us, does not mean that the respondent always felt that way—only that they sometimes felt that way. Moreover, in some sense, we sampled on the dependent variable: the people we studied were employed, and they had not quit their jobs.[37] We expect that some workers would quit—say, when unpredictable hours made it impossible to care for a sick child. Those employees might have expressed less of a draw to work. It is possible that for either patients or coworkers to be seen as family requires (and in turn helps to create) long tenure at a workplace. But if this were all that was operating, we would not expect to find the kind of class divide that we uncovered.

As Arlie Hochschild predicted, the differential responses to our question have consequences for applications of family policies in the workplace. The CNAs got the least benefit from them, in large part because they were less likely to be offered those benefits—say, for FMLA days or paid sick days. They were also less likely to know about these policies.[38] But as we see here, they also sometimes wanted to be away from home— even when they had a broken ankle or a young child. This should come as no surprise given the standard—now even old-fashioned—feminist critique that families are not the "havens in a heartless world" (especially for women) that some have romanticized. At the same time, the experiences described here serve as a critique of the all-too-common argument that poor people do not value work or that welfare should be cut because it reinforces the resistance of the disadvantaged to hard work. What we find here is quite the reverse—a willingness to work, often an attraction to work, even under difficult conditions.

Finally, a grand theme of sociologists and economists is that the market increasingly intrudes on personal life, in many different ways.[39] The analysis here is an extension of that theme: Many write of the "outsourcing" of family tasks to commercial entities—for example, restaurants cook, cleaning services do housework, and nursing homes care for parents; as the family metaphors they use imply, corporations strategize to replace personal ties with the services that they sell. The workplace becomes like the family. The "family" that provides companionship and support is the workplace, and this is affirmed not only by employers but also by employees. Research has made clear that marriage and family can be stressful, especially for women. That is what makes the negative response to Hochschild's work so partial. It is as if the scholars forgot their critiques of marriage when faced with what they saw as a critique of family-friendly policies that release employees from their jobs.

PART V | Conclusion

Chapter 12 | Inequality and the Normal Unpredictability of Time

CONVENTIONAL WISDOM holds that work policies about time are too rigid. This book shows that for many Americans the problem with work policies is too much flexibility as often as it is too much rigidity. Not only do supposedly "flexible" work policies often force employees to adapt to unpredictability, but these policies are unequally distributed, as are the stresses they produce.

Inequalities of power organized around gender and class shape how time and normal unpredictability play out—who controls time and who pays the costs. Control over time is negotiated and contested, in ways both direct and hidden, between workers and employers, between husbands and wives and other relatives, and among coworkers. Together all these actors create a web of time—pushing and pulling, supporting, substituting for, or struggling as they try to get the time to do what they want or need to do. The struggle over time does not simply occur at the point when someone is hired and the official basic schedule is set (although it does sometimes occur there). It is far more ubiquitous, involving an ongoing set of conflicts, strategies, and negotiations about the daily, weekly, and yearly events that are not predicted at the moment of hiring: Will you work extra (and under what conditions)? Will you stay home for a child with a bad cold? For one with pneumonia? For a mother-in-law who moved in with you because she just lost her husband? If you need to stay extra hours at work, will you be compensated for that, and how much? These decisions shape the micropolitics of the labor process. Literature on the labor process focuses, for the most part, on skill, autonomy, and money. This book analyzes time and who controls it. After all, what labor sells is first and foremost time.

Unpredictability in hours and schedules is not just pervasive and is not

261

simply a fact of nature; there is good reason to believe (even if we do not have good historical data supporting this view) that unpredictability has grown over the last few decades. Part of the growth in temporal unpredictability is tied to macro changes in the economic system and labor market. Committed to precarious employment, increasingly organizations are lean-staffed and hire temporary or contingent workers to fill some of the holes created by their lean staffing. Occupations that demand night and weekend hours are growing. New technologies add to the sway of unpredictability. Alongside such economic changes, broad-based trends in the family have made normal unpredictability more common. More women are in the labor force, many as part of dual-earner couples, and are thus less able to cover for the unpredictability that routinely occurs at their husbands' jobs. Increasing numbers of adult children are moving back home, disrupting their parents' routines. With delayed marriage, the high rates of divorce, and the increase in babies born outside of marriage, many more people are single parents, especially single mothers, who must cope with unexpected events; often single parents rely on extended kin, whose own lives then become less predictable.

These related trends in both the economy and the family create events that are predictable in the aggregate but unpredictable from the perspective of the individuals coping with them. Without understanding the social or collective character of these larger conditions, people who encounter them come to think that something is wrong with them personally. They often think that it is their own fault that they struggle to manage their crazy schedules.

Focusing on unpredictability and control—and the inequalities underpinning them—leads us in a direction left largely unexplored by the growing number of researchers who study work time. With a limited number of important exceptions, such studies tend to focus on whether people work and on the official listings of hours that managers or workers report on a survey for a "typical day."[1] We find that the usual categories of full-time and part-time and even nonstandard hours—that is, the entire notion of a fixed schedule—are all problematic across a range of organizations and in both advantaged and disadvantaged occupations.

When the work-family literature considers the situation of a worker needing an exception to the normally required schedule, it primarily looks at managers and supervisors, who may make special arrangements for valued workers. So, too, even as organizational sociologists explore the roles of a range of actors, they often focus on the vertical hierarchy rather than the horizontal relations among coworkers. In our own work, we have been more struck by how coworkers help each other deal with unpredictability through "swapping"—a strategy that prior research has neglected but that we find to be important across gender and class. Only a manager can change a worker's basic schedule, but coworkers are often the solution to problems created by unpredictable changes, whether it's needing to meet with a child's teacher at school, an illness in the family, or a boyfriend's court date. And there are collective consequences of these coworker relations: while reliance on managers for assistance separates workers from one another, coworker help in these situations builds worker solidarity and sometimes fosters resentment toward organizational unresponsiveness.

Not only have many researchers overlooked coworkers, but many have also misunderstood families. Although it is families that make workers reluctant to challenge their employers, we find that children—whether babies, teenagers, or adults—are the main reason workers resist employer-imposed schedules and hours. The needs of their families—for both relatively advantaged women and less-advantaged women and men—lead many workers to restrict their hours, push for nonstandard schedules, and call out. When workers do face unexpected familial demands, their employers often refuse to make accommodations for them. Workers are frequently prepared to put their families above their jobs, even if they (all too often) face a penalty for doing so.

Understanding this unpredictability and collective responses to it requires a perspective that is both horizontal (looking at linked organizations and occupations, coworkers, regular and "irregular" workers, and spouses and partners) and vertical (looking at hierarchies in the workplace and in families). Many organizational theorists have moved from an entity-based to a process-based view that places fluid personal relations, culture, and networks, rather than atomized actors or technically neutral decisions, at the heart of organizational premises and practices.[2] They have emphasized the importance of examining local processes—internal routines, divisions of labor, employee groups, and the practice of policy within organizations—to understand the generation of inequality.[3] Although rarely used to analyze time, organizational theories help illuminate not only internal vertical influence and internal horizontal influence but also external environmental impacts (from the state and from families). Together, these provide a useful framework for understanding why organizations schedule the way they do and the processes shaping job hours.

The web of time operates across individuals, as well as within and across occupations, organizations, and families. This is most obvious within organizational and familial units: if a child is sick, the odds are that some family member (mother, father, grandmother, aunt, cousin) must stay home, and if an EMT calls out, another EMT must take his place. But the web also operates across occupations: the doctor's decision to stay late has implications not only for his family but also for those in other occupations, such as the nurse working under his control. And the web of time operates across organizations as they slough off various functions and components to others: today hospitals send patients to nursing homes earlier and rely on EMTs to take them there, private physicians rely on hospitalists instead of visiting their patients in hospitals, and hospitals hire nurses from temp agencies to fill the holes left by regular staff. This is how the web of time works within the medical system, but it probably operates in a similar fashion in other occupations and other organizations.

The components or strands of the web of time are by no means equal, a point made evident when we note who must wait for whom: patients and nurses wait for doctors, and EMTs and nursing assistants wait for nurses. Within families, we see the inequality in decisions about whose schedule takes precedence (usually husbands' over wives', especially among professionals). The strands of the web reinforce inequality even as they create solidarity.

Discovering the operation of a web of time requires data that are multilevel (for different occupations and different organizations) and multiple methods (including fieldwork, intensive interviews, a survey, documents, and schedules). If we had studied only one occupational group (say, just doctors or just nursing assistants), if we had studied only one organization (just a hospital, for instance), or if we had collected only one kind of data (only a survey, for example, or only face-to-face interviews), we would not have been able to understand the collective nature of time, the pervasiveness of normal unpredictability, or the unequal negotiation and contestation of control.

CONTROLLING UNPREDICTABILITY: THE JOINT OPERATION OF CLASS AND GENDER

We argue that unpredictability is structured in predictable ways. That is, class and gender jointly shape the meaning, the experience, and, most important, the control of unpredictability as well as the stresses associated with it. Many have argued, correctly, that gender shapes the hours that people work. Many have insisted, quite rightly, that class is key to understanding the struggle over the working day. But neither acts alone: gender and class operate jointly.

This interaction of gender and class is negotiated by employers, employees, and their families in a process that both is shaped by and in turn shapes organizational rules and cultural schemas. Those with class advantage tend to reinforce the gender order (as we see in the hours and schedules of male doctors, female nurses, and female doctors); those at a class disadvantage undo gendered conventions (as we see in the hours and schedules of EMTs and nursing assistants).

In advantaged occupations, both women and men obtain the flexibility to control unpredictability—but flexibility of very different sorts. Men doctors find the flexibility to put in long hours on the job that they come to see or present as unpredictable and inflexible (a situation they describe using a rhetoric of constraint). The experience of women doctors suggests that schedule (in)flexibility is not simply set by rigid organizational and occupational structures. Women doctors are often the "beneficiaries" of the idealized flexibility found in the work-family literature. Their advantaged position gives them the power to gain this flexibility, but doing so also has the negative consequence of devaluing their work and perpetuating inequality in the home (in the name of "it was her choice"). Comparisons of advantaged women and men show that women pay an economic "flexibility penalty" for enacting the cultural mandate associated with womanhood.[4] That is, women pay a very real material price, and this "preserves positional inequalities between men and women in work organizations."[5] And women do more of the work of the home, which fuels these positional inequalities both at home and on the job.[6] Perhaps professional men also pay a flexibility penalty, one that is social or emotional rather than pecuniary—that is, they pay a penalty in their relationships with their children and spouses.

At the other end of the class-by-gender divide are low-wage women workers—often women of color—who cannot get enough hours. They are hired to work twenty-four or thirty-two hours a week; for many, being able to pick up extra shifts is the difference between getting by or being cold in the winter. This creates another paradox: it is nursing assistants, more than any other group, who turn the workplace into "family," perhaps in part because their more exploitative job conditions create greater stress at home.

The inequalities of time come into play not just with respect to disagreeable events—such as overwork or underwork—but also to pleasurable ones, such as whether workers can take vacations at times that work for them and their families rather than at the convenience of the employer. No surprise, vacations are easier to schedule for those with class advantage. But that class advantage, like class disadvantage, interacts with and sometimes is trumped by gender. Taking vacations when they want to, or taking one at all, is far more difficult for women employees than for men— even for advantaged women employees like nurses, whose workplace includes so many others like themselves (other women) that they all face the same family demands to take the same vacations. The gender segregation of jobs, then, has consequences both time on and time off.

Organizations help construct inequality; they create processes whereby class advantage allies with gender convention and class disadvantage reduces gender convention. Within hospitals, nursing homes, and doctors' offices, both employers and employees find that unpredictability is both a burden and the object of strategy. How do organizations respond? For their advantaged workers, they create alternative structures and institutional systems, like hospitalists for doctors and weekend-only work for nurses. For advantaged women (women doctors and nurses) with good labor market positions and low rates of unemployment, organizations adapt, responding to the cultural schemas that uphold women's responsibility to families. Culture matters less to organizations when it comes to disadvantaged workers. Employers often insist that working-class and low-wage workers overcome the unpredictable difficulties they face outside of work and learn to put the job first. In general, employers seek to fill their schedules, but at the lowest possible cost, and they may be willing to create unstable schedules as long as that does not risk patient safety (too much) and does not lead (hard-to-replace) workers to resign. Unemployment rates—which are much higher among the working-class and low-wage occupations—make that easier for employers to do.

Many have written of masculine (or masculinized) organizations. We also find the opposite—"feminized" organizations. Discussions of so-called semiprofessionals, such as teachers, in the scholarly literature of the 1960s and 1970s occasionally analyzed the ways in which educated women obtained reduced schedules (not individually but as a group) but were rarely granted the income or status of the professions, dominated then as now by men.[7] Today we find that it is advantaged women who most clearly resist *and change* the allocation of time. Nurses feminize organizations by using flexibility for their own and their families' ends—whether by insisting on and getting a range of schedules and shifts, taking advantage of the FMLA, or switching to temp agencies rather than stay in regular employment. Although less successful in changing the organizations they work for (in part, because there are fewer of them), women doctors individually feminize medicine for themselves—by working fewer hours and insisting that they must take care of their families. Many do not want to, or come to believe that they cannot, "lean in" if they want jobs and families.[8] This indicates the limits of organizational rules when they are countered by cultural expectations. To be sure, there are some costs of such feminization: job segregation, in particular the concentration of women in particular jobs, makes it difficult even for advantaged women to obtain vacations when they want them (because so many want the same time off). Moreover, those very "feminized" organizations and their advantaged workers reinforce gender inequality outside the workplace as women continue to do far more domestic work at home than do their husbands. But theories that stress workplace discrimination and victimization of women are limited if they do not pay attention to the ways in which those with class advantage can use gendered conventions to transform organizations.

We might expect men to follow suit. EMTs—at least in some sense—"undo gender" by doing not only "public" but also "private" parenting.[9] Most male doctors, however, do not use their schedule control to undo gender. Seasoned physicians insist that they have to work long hours to be the primary breadwinner in accord with the conventions of masculinity, even if they sometimes feel sad that they must miss their own child's development while they give care to someone else's child.

THE LIMITS OF THE STUDY

There are, of course, limitations to the study, things we did not do and wish we could have done. It is both a strength and a limit that the occupations and organizations we studied are "good jobs" (by today's standards in the United States) with comparatively low turnover, solid benefits, and job stability. Had we studied Walmart or the day labor industry, the situation for workers would have looked much worse. And although we made a considered decision to study four linked occupations in one system—medical care—we cannot know to what extent our findings generalize to other occupations and organizations. We suspect that many of them do.

We originally intended to interview the spouses of a substantial proportion of our respondents because, as Jessie Bernard so convincingly suggested, every (heterosexual) marriage contains two distinct views of the relationship—a "his" and a "hers."[10] We did only a few such interviews.

Our study focused on a particular geographic area in the Northeast; if we had studied another region, then some of the findings might have looked different. For example, a California-based study would probably have included more nurses of color and a stronger nurses' union—both of which might well shape organizations and workers' control over hours and schedules.

More generally, we wished we had more racial variation within each occupation in our study. In the only organizational cases where we were able to capture significant racial variation—in the two nursing homes—we found striking differences, with a punitive approach at the home with a workforce comprising mostly people of color and a (largely) supportive approach at the home with a mostly-white workforce. Within the nursing home where a high percentage of the nursing assistants were people of color, they picked up significantly more shifts than white workers did. Although class and race are so highly correlated that it is difficult to design a study that fully separates them, a study specifically designed around racial difference would be likely to yield useful findings about the racial dynamics that shape unequal time and control over it. We would certainly like to see the results of such a study.

We compared gendered occupations. The women's occupations were more gender segregated than the men's. But there was a cost to this research design: we could not make gender comparisons within women-dominated occupations, and although we made some gender comparisons in the male-dominated occupations, we found significant gender differences for doctors but not for EMTs—suggestive again of the power of the advantaged.

Finally, our study participants were all people who, in one way or another, and at whatever cost to themselves and their families, were (at least for the time being) managing the unpredictability of their hours and schedules. Somewhat unintentionally, we sampled on a key dependent variable—those who could not handle unpredictability were no longer employed or had switched to jobs with different scheduling constraints. Thus, we cannot compare those who are managing unpredictability and those who are not; we can only compare those who do so with relatively little strain to those who experience constant stress.

REGAINING CONTROL OF TIME AND MAKING IT MORE EQUAL

The control of time is one of the most pervasive—and most unrecognized—issues in our society. People often experience the (seemingly) neutral demands of "the job" as a natural necessity to which they and their families must adapt. Their problems, they think, are personal, not, as C. Wright Mills wrote in The Sociological Imagination, "public issues of social structure."[11]

In analyzing extensive evidence for multiple occupations and organizations, this book has raised a question: If time matters, if unpredictability is pervasive, and if we should be concerned about the schedules and hours that people work and about their ability to both control their work hours and be present for their families, what are ways to approach the problems posed by these realities?

Some scholars would appeal to employers and try to persuade them that "family-friendly" policies and "flexibility" are good for business. Unfortunately, however, employers that introduce family-friendly policies that de facto are for professionals and managers, and only for them, are probably making sensible bottom-line calculations: turnover among managers and professionals is much more costly than among low-wage workers. But the broader moral and political question is whether we want to focus energy on winning additional benefits only for those at the top, and only within the limits set by the need to boost corporate profits. By looking at the changes that some professional women insist on, we can see the changes in hours and schedules that are possible not only for women but also for men—possible, that is, if they not only want but insist on those changes. By looking at professionals and the work time policies developed for them (not only here but in many other countries), we see more generally that worker power can effectively address unpredictability in hours and schedules—even if the solutions arrived at come at some cost to employers. For example, nurses routinely benefit from "participatory scheduling," a range of shifts, weekend-only jobs, and the ability to take their legally guaranteed FMLA leaves. Why not offer these benefits to nursing assistants?

A crucial first step is to recognize the full dimensions of the problem as it is experienced by ordinary workers as well as by the affluent, and to see the connections among the various pieces, which are often seen as separate. When gender was "the problem that has no name," when women were aware of one or another inequality they confronted but did not have a language or a framework through which to understand the larger issue and see these inequalities as injustices, it was hard to develop a movement.[12] Having a language with which to discuss issues of work hours and schedules and thinking of sick leave, vacations, mandatory (or coerced) overtime, cancelation of shifts, nonstandard shifts, temporary workers, and short-staffing as part of a larger complex pattern would make it more possible to develop a movement—and the rise of a movement would lead to an increase in consciousness. Academics tend to believe that consciousness precedes action (as in some ways and at some times it does), but the reverse is just as true: workers' consciousness often develops after an employer sanctions them for taking care of a child's pressing need for hot soup, aspirin, and emotional comfort.

The struggle over the working day has been a defining feature of capitalism from its beginning; this struggle has been concerned with both the total hours at the workplace and the ability to set the pace and take breaks during the day, and it has involved both individual acts and organized collective activity, political and otherwise. The struggle had been in process for decades before Marx wrote; almost the last change Marx made to volume 1 of *Capital* in 1866 was to add a chapter on the struggle over the working day. Time struggles in the United States continued with legislation in 1867 instituting an eight-hour day, the 1886 Haymarket Square bombing and the beginning of May Day, and with the rise of the weekend. Today's time struggles are less about total hours worked than about a variety of what might seem to be unconnected specifics that nevertheless are manifestations of normal unpredictability. Work-family activists address family and medical leave (will it be paid or unpaid?), the right to paid sick days (can they be taken without penalty?), child care, elder care, school schedules, and the right to take time off for "small necessities." They and others address limits on mandatory overtime and the right to vacations and defend people who actually use their vacation time.[13] A range of people and organizations are trying to think about a problem that is typically most pressing for professionals (as for some of our doctors), the problem of being expected to answer emails and phone calls (and maybe take follow-up action) at night and on weekends—the problem, in other words, of rarely if ever being truly off-duty.

Also failing to recognize these issues as related, and significantly so, are most union activists today. On the one hand, it is remarkable how central hours and schedule issues are to labor-management negotiations—they take up the majority of the space in union contracts for nurses (61 percent), nursing assistants (56 percent), and EMTs (53 percent). On the other hand, union leaders often do not recognize the centrality of these issues and have not thought about how to address them systematically. On more than one occasion, we arrived to observe union negotiations, only to be told by union staff that the session about to begin would be boring for us because it would focus on minor details and would not address our issues of workers' hours and schedules. Then, when negotiations would begin, attention would be almost entirely on what we had come to understand as issues of time. In one notable case, the focus was on management's move to end guaranteed forty-hour-a-week schedules and to guarantee only schedules of twenty-four or thirty-two hours a week, while making available additional shifts at unpredictable times. Workers' refusal to accept the deal brokered during days of behind-the-scenes negotiating between union staff and employer representatives led to a strike threat and a final contract that left the issue unresolved; both sides retained the right to continue fighting on a point each considered vital. Note that, despite the union's limited power and the staff's limited initial recognition of the problem, this highly democratic union brought workers together, gave them a voice, enabled them to articulate what they considered central and crucial, and settled on terms chosen by the workers. If all workplaces offered such options, the terms of contestation would change dramatically.

To develop alternative policies, a primary focus should be on winning everyone basic protections in the face of temporal unpredictability. "Basic protections" should include:

1. The right to paid sick days—as offered in most other countries (127 provide a week or more annually)—that the worker can use for personal reasons or to care for a family member, whether a child, a spouse, a cousin, or a grandmother, with no penalty of any kind for using the days

2. The right to the levels of paid vacation offered in many other countries, and the right to take at least a significant part of their vacation in the summer[14]

3. Paid family leave for large and small necessities, such as meetings with teachers or kids' dentist appointments

4. Overtime pay for any hours beyond the originally scheduled shift (even if the worker has less than forty hours in the week)

5. Participatory scheduling in which all workers, not only the advantaged, have significant influence over the schedules initially offered and changes made to them.

6. Effective mechanisms and movements to be sure that these mandates are enforced[15]

We could think in more ambitious terms: a single-payer health care system so that people are not constrained to work enough hours to qualify for health care; double time for overtime so that employers face a more significant economic penalty for relying on it; and—dare we say it—a guaranteed right to a job that pays a living wage for an adequate number of hours per week.

These and other policy changes that many others have suggested are well worthwhile.[16] But as the analyses offered here suggest, many who address policy do not address the pervasive inequality in our society and the power that employers have over their employees—especially nonprofessionals—together with the inequalities not only between but inside families that shape the forms that policies can and should take.[17] The most important changes will not come from the top down. Change will come from workers' self-activity, the actions they take when employers make demands that create dilemmas, when keeping the job is at odds with having a life or caring for their family and dearest friends. Change will come from struggles inside families to achieve an equality that is based not just on women taking on paid work but also on men embracing, valuing, and doing child care, elder care, and housework, and men and women insisting that their jobs provide the schedules and accommodations that enable them to do so. Resisting the grind of the job, some workers assert their rights by taking off a "mental health day." Many workers assert that their needs should take priority, whether it is for children, partners, extended kin, or close friends who need care. A fundamental change in the current system will come only from movement struggles that change the balance of power, giving people not only new policies but also changed cultural understandings and collective organizations of representation.

Notes

CHAPTER 1

1. Jacobs and Gerson (2004), 35.
2. Recent survey data from Lawrence Mishel (2013) also confirms that there is a time divide across class, with those at the bottom of the income distribution struggling to work enough hours to get by. Above that threshold, however, as Mishel shows, people at the top work fewer hours than those at the middle or above. In our mail survey of people in the four occupations, only the low-income nursing assistants said they were eager for more hours. Working-class EMTs, however, because they were more likely to take second jobs, reported fractionally more hours than doctors did, and nursing assistants worked as much as nurses—a finding we develop in the coming chapters.
3. As we discuss in the next chapter, race also matters, but race is less important to this study because in the area of the country we studied, three out of the four occupations were overwhelmingly white; only nursing assistants included a substantial number of people of color.
4. On schedule unpredictability in low-wage jobs, see Henly, Shaefer, and Waxman (2006), Lambert (2012), Lambert, Haley-Lock, and Henly (2012), and Watson and Swanberg (2011).
5. See, for example, Lyness et al. (2012).
6. Milkman (2009).
7. Stone (2007).
8. Or at least a white professional woman's job. As discussed later, there is a contrasting policy for nursing assistants, most of whom are people of color and almost none of whom are college graduates.
9. On gendered-male schedule practices, see Acker (1990).
10. Hochschild (1997).
11. Although heart attacks are likely to happen more often and at earlier ages in low-wage workers (Marmot 2005).
12. Appelbaum et al. (2003) and Gordon (2006b).

13. All names used are pseudonyms. On occasion we have altered minor details to help preserve informant confidentiality.

14. Perlow (2012).

15. Steven Greenhouse, "A Part-Time Life, as Hours Shrink and Shift," *New York Times,* October 28, 2012. Available at: http://www.nytimes.com/2012/10/28/business/a-part-time-life-as-hours-shrink-and-shift-for-american-workers.html (accessed May 15, 2014).

16. Jacobs and Gerson (2004). Americans work many more hours than Western Europeans—an average of 1,787 hours a year, which is 200, 300, and even 400 hours a year more than in some Western European countries. The difference amounts to what would be five to ten weeks a year of additional vacation. The book that revived interest in this issue was Juliet Schor's *The Overworked American* (1992), in which she argued that over the previous two decades working hours in the United States had increased and the compulsive commitment to jobs and the conspicuous consumption it allowed led Americans to work longer than people in other nations. According to the Organisation for Economic Cooperation and Development (OECD, 2012), however, U.S. (paid) work hours are not the longest in the world and in fact are only about average for the (mostly) affluent countries of the OECD.

17. Tim Kreider, "The 'Busy' Trap," *New York Times,* July 1, 2012. Available at: http://opinionator.blogs.nytimes.com/2012/06/30/the-busy-trap (accessed May 15, 2014).

18. Zerubavel (1979), 106. See also Zerubavel (1981).

19. Stone (2007), Ryan and Kossek (2008), and Lambert and Henly (2012).

CHAPTER 2

1. Centers for Medicare & Medicaid Services (2012).

2. Reis (2012).

3. McKinlay and Marceau (2002), Mechanic (2006), Relman (2007), Joyce (2008), and Gawande (2009).

4. See website figure 2.1 for the national data at https://www.russellsage.org/publications/unequal-time.

5. See website table 2.1 for a comparison of data for our area to national data.

6. See website table 2.2 footnote for response rates for each occupation.

7. See website table 2.2 for data on the number of people interviewed in each occupation by gender and organization.

8. See website table 2.2 for the distribution of interviews by source, occupation, organization, gender, and race.

9. The two of us did most of the observations and interviews ourselves. Graduate students did the main observations at the EMT sites and at one of the

doctors' offices and did observations at one of the nursing homes where we also observed.

10. There were eight local hospitals excluding those with restricted admission, such as veterans' and soldiers' hospitals.

11. Zerubavel (1979).

12. For comparisons of men and women in the same occupation, see Blair-Loy (2003), Epstein (1993), Moccio (2009), Pierce (1995), Stone (2007), and Williams (1992). For studies of men and women working in occupations dominated by their gender group, see Charles and Grusky (2004), Hegewisch et al. (2010), and Stainback and Tomaskovic-Devey (2012).

13. Acker (2006), Lorber (2005), and Ridgeway (2011).

14. Blair-Loy (2003).

15. U.S. Census Bureau (2012), table 703. Among full-time, year-round workers, women with an associate's degree earn $42,307 and men with a high school degree earn $43,140; women with a bachelor's degree earn $53,449 and men with an associate's degree earn $55,631.

16. U.S. Bureau of the Census. Available at: http://www.census.gov/hhes/www/income/data/earnings/call2usboth.html (accessed May 21, 2014).

17. England (2010, 2013).

18. However, if the term "working-class" is added to the choices (which is less commonly done), only fractionally fewer respondents choose that label (45.6 percent) as choose "middle-class" (46.2 percent). See Pope (2012), citing the NORC General Social Survey (GSS) for 2006; see also Hout (2008).

19. See the critique of this view in Wright (1979).

20. Bourdieu (1984).

21. See, for example, Giddens (1973) and Tilly (1998).

22. Zweig (2000), 11.

23. Wright (2008), 341.

24. Thompson (1964), 9. Thompson's 1964 prefeminist text uses "men" where we have substituted "people" (in brackets).

25. David Johnson, Chief of the Social, Economic, and Housing Statistics Division, U.S. Census Bureau, personal communication with the author, January 2012. These figures should be treated with caution because the Bureau of Labor Statistics (BLS) sample size for any given occupation is small.

26. Marital status varied among the occupations to this extent despite the fact that the average age of interview respondents in all the occupations was quite close: the median age for nurses and CNAs was thirty-eight, and for physicians and EMTs it was forty-two.

27. Clawson (2003).

28. An EMT paramedic directs the work of a basic-level EMT, but not the members of any other occupation.

29. Other factors do not receive the same attention: age, for example, is much less likely to be considered important.
30. See website table 2.2 for racial distribution for each occupation.
31. Stainback and Tomaskovic-Devey (2010).
32. Lambert and Waxman (2005).

CHAPTER 3

1. Institute of Medicine (2007), 139.
2. Ibid., 42. Brown, Dawson, and Levine (2003) is cited, so these figures are not current; they do, however, indicate the magnitude of the difference.
3. Nationally, 45 percent of EMT service is fire-department-based (Institute of Medicine 2007, 55).
4. The best available data indicate that in 2003, nationwide, 86 percent of EMTs were non-Hispanic white; almost half were thirty-five or younger. On "heroic masculinity," see Carol Chetkovich's (1997) study of firefighters.
5. See Centers for Disease Control and Prevention (CDC), "National Nursing Home Survey: National Nursing Assistant Survey," tables 1 and 15, available at: http://www.cdc.gov/nchs/nnas.htm (accessed June 10, 2010).
6. Lopez (2006).
7. Diamond (1992), 130–67.
8. Lisa Dodson and Rebekah Zincavage (2007) also observed CNAs coming in on their days off to check on residents.
9. Leif and Fox (1963).
10. On this shift of duties, see Appelbaum et al. (2003).
11. At hospitals where we observed, almost all the nurses were RNs. In nursing homes, although nurses make up a much smaller part of the staff, more nurses are LPNs than in hospitals. At nursing homes, the two nurse categories are largely interchangeable; the key difference is that only RNs are allowed to assess patients.
12. The racial composition of the nursing profession varies by region; these are figures for nurses in New England, where we did our study (U.S. Department of Health and Human Services 2010).
13. A charge nurse is the nurse responsible for the immediate operation of a unit, like an emergency department or a medical floor, during a particular shift (day, night, or evening).
14. See website table 3.1 for a detailed report on a full hour of this nurse's time.
15. Gordon, Buchanan, and Bretherton (2008), 31.
16. Kletke, Emmon, and Gillis (1996).
17. See website table 3.2 for a detailed report on an hour spent with this doctor.
18. Fuchs (2012).
19. Precisely because moving between floors takes so much of the hospitalist's

time, some hospitals are now moving to what they call "geographic systems"—assigning patients on contiguous floors to a single hospitalist on each shift, so that the doctors can remain in one area.

20. All of these organizations also employ other staff. Hospitals, for example, have receptionists, administrative assistants, social workers, custodians, dietary and housekeeping workers, phlebotomists, X-ray technicians, respiratory therapists, and a range of others. Our focus is only on these organizations' employment of people in the occupations we studied.

21. Data are from the *AHA Guide 2009* (American Hospital Association 2008), supplemented by the hospital and nursing home profiles available from Hospital-Data.com (www.hospital-data.com).

22. Despite the common usage, not to mention the popular TV show *ER*, for medical personnel these days "ER" has been replaced by "ED," indicating an entire department for emergencies.

23. Over the last fifteen years, emergency rooms have served a growing number of patients who come not only for true emergencies but also for regular medical care, often for chronic conditions, especially if they do not have private insurance (but do have public insurance like Medicare and Medicaid), if they cannot afford private physicians, or if their physicians are not available 24/7 (Peppe et al. 2007; Cunningham 2011). Largely as a result of the 1986 Emergency Medical Treatment and Labor Act (EMTALA), hospitals are required to provide emergency services regardless of patients' ability to pay.

24. A 2009 Massachusetts law specified that no more ambulances could be diverted, and as a report on this change notes: "Some of the key changes needed in hospitals in order to accommodate the new role involve reworking of schedules and workflows" (Harlow 2009).

25. Zussman (1992), 68.

26. We use the term "nursing assistants" to cover a range of unlicensed assistive personnel who worked with, and under the direction of, nurses. In nursing homes these personnel were almost exclusively certified nursing assistants; in hospitals they were sometimes medical assistants or technical assistants, who have more training, can undertake more tasks, and earn higher incomes.

27. The medical floor at each hospital had a break room for staff. The one at Outercity was a separate room with a large table where staff sat and had meals, took breaks, or held meetings. Occasionally looking at the TV that was left on, they would chat about their lives both on and off the job—vacations, mistreatment by doctors, distressed or sad patients, sweet or nasty patients, switching shifts (something we heard a lot was: "If you can take mine, I will take yours"), and their exhaustion after long shifts. This room was split off from a locker room where pictures of family members decorated over two hundred lockers. In the break room at Countryside, a much smaller locker room was in the same space as the table, and there was no TV, but here too

staff took breaks, sat and chatted, often about the same subjects that the nurses and nursing assistants discussed at Outercity. A number of staff at Countryside got a little upset when an official meeting would occasionally be held in the break room because that took away the space for the valued breaks they expected. They also came to the break room before going home to change at their lockers—which illustrated, quite literally, their transition out of the workday because so many were decorated with pictures of family members (typically children and pets).

28. Centers for Disease Control and Prevention (CDC), "National Nursing Home Survey: National Nursing Assistant Survey," table 45, available at: http://www.cdc.gov/nchs/data/nnhsd/Estimates/nnas/Estimates_InjVac_Tables.pdf#45 (accessed September 2, 2010).

29. Registered nurses at the nursing homes in this area earned an average of $26.04 an hour; LPNs earned an average of $22.29.

30. Kocher and Sahni (2011).

31. In 1977 there were 1,236,000 building fires and 6,357 fire deaths in the United States (U.S. Census Bureau, 1980, tables 121 and 925). In 2007 there were 531,000 structure fires and 3,430 civilian fire deaths (U.S. Census Bureau, 2010, table 345). The change is a result of better preventive measures, the development of flame-resistant or -retardant materials, better building codes, and the use of smoke detectors.

32. Appelbaum et al. (2003).

33. Zussman (1992), 65.

CHAPTER 4

1. Zerubavel (1979), 117. We would note, however, that the degree of emphasis on this varies from one occupation to another. For firefighter EMTs, the defining scheduling principle is to assign each person exactly the same official schedule; for nurses, there are large differences between the schedules of, say, weekend-only nurses and nurses who work in doctors' offices.

2. West and Zimmerman (1987).

3. Gordon, Buchanan, and Bretherton (2008), 3, 38.

4. Editorial, *Boston Globe*, May 22, 2006.

5. Massachusetts Hospital Association flyer dated September 11, 2003, trifold for NSR hearing.pdf. Available at: http://www.google.com/url?sa=t&rct=j&q=&esrc=s&source=web&cd=1&ved=0CCsQFjAA&url=http%3A%2F%2Fwww.mhalink.org%2FAM%2FTemplate.cfm%3FSection%3DNSR%26template%3D%2FCM%2FContentDisplay.cfm%26ContentID%3D8864&ei=gnh1U_SQOLGysAS174CADg&usg=AFQjCNH90V7dB7Pn_4-gqvNyuI9XlmrW2A&sig2=63WDiMNe21-eo-sNW0AhCQ&bvm=bv.66699033,d.cWc (accessed May 21, 2014).

6. Another indication of managerial prerogative is the fact that the number of nurses per 100,000 people has tripled since 1950, with more than a 50 percent increase since 1980, but a nursing shortage continues to be widely reported. The number of physicians per 100,000 people in our home state of Massachusetts is more than double the rate found in twenty-one other states (U.S. Census Bureau 1983, table 162, and U.S. Census Bureau 2012, table 165).

7. Maguire (2009).

8. Americans for Effective Law Enforcement (2010).

9. Tilly et al. (2003).

10. Lopez (2006), 55.

11. Zerubavel (1979, 1981).

12. Zerubavel (1979), 106–7.

13. The number of hours worked varied by specialty; see Goldin and Katz (2011).

14. What does and does not get counted as work on a closed-ended quantitative survey is a problem for research that uses surveys to estimate work time. Professionals probably underreport work from home, and working-class respondents probably underreport second jobs, especially if they are off the books (Perry-Jenkins 2005).

15. Lyness et al. (2012), 21.

16. Barker (1999).

17. Manias et al. (2003), 457.

18. On the use of temporary nurses in hospitals, see American Hospital Association (2001); on temporary hires in hospitals, see Aiken et al. (2007).

19. Although most temp agencies are close to the hospital they serve, another less common type of temp is the "traveler"—a nurse employed by a national agency and sent to various locales around the country, usually on one- to three-month contracts. The hospital pays the traveler nurse a salary and provides transportation and board. According to the professional association for travelers, an estimated 25,500 RNs work in travel nursing jobs in the United States, which means they are about 1 percent of all nurses. (Note that these numbers are from the traveling nurses' own professional association, so we cannot be certain of their validity.) The advantage of a traveler is that she is sure to be available, as one manager explained:

> I call the [local temp] agency and I say, "I need a nurse, do you have anybody available?" They call their nurses who are ER nurses that have been oriented to here: "Can you work tomorrow night?" They say no, they call me back—I don't have anybody for you. And that's it. I have guaranteed hours with a traveler, but you're paying a lot of money for them. And you may not need [all of those guaranteed hours].

Most organizations try not to hire too many travelers because they are expensive, with an hourly charge considerably higher than pay for staff nurses.

Some research suggests that there may be another cost of traveling nurses—agency staffing is associated with reduced quality for patients and residents (Castle, Engberg, and Men 2008). Another problem with using travelers, hospital administrators reported, was that even though the hospital had a rule that it would not employ any traveler who lived within a fifty-mile radius, some nurses managed to avoid these rules. The result was that instead of hiring someone as a staff nurse, the hospital ended up hiring the same person as a traveler at higher expense. Finally, a number of regular nurses talked to us about tensions with traveling nurses, and one traveler said that the staff "kind of look down on the travelers," adding, "You've kind of got to make your bones . . . they're thinking, 'Yeah, this is a traveler, they're coming in here making all these big bucks, why should I bust my ass when they should be doing it?'"

20. See Burgoon and Dekker (2010), Cummings and Kreiss (2008), Golden (1996), Golden and Appelbaum (1992), Kalleberg (2009), Piore (1986), Smith and Neuwirth (2008), and Standing (2011).

21. A fair amount of research would seem to support this worry about quality, especially when a significant proportion of the staff is from such agencies (Castle, Engberg, and Men 2008; Phibbs et al. 2009), although there is still some debate about whether it is the temporary nursing staff or other characteristics of the organizations they work for that cause the ill effects (see, for example, Aiken et al. 2007).

22. It is not just managers who count on this strategy. At one unionized hospital, nurses told us that such a practice was an important part of their contract because it protected them from being sent home in times of low patient census (a practice that the union contract severely restricted while it accepted floating as a way to avoid layoffs).

23. Although we do not have exact numbers, all of the staff who came in during our observations of the flex team were people of color, and many of those the administrator talked to had "strong accents."

24. Nursing assistants who work in hospitals are often more educated and are called medical or technical associates (TAs).

25. Note that these were *self-reported* hours. We believe that the EMT hours reported were probably fairly accurate, as were those for CNAs and nurses, but as suggested earlier, doctors seem to have consistently underreported their hours.

26. U.S. Bureau of Labor Statistics (2010).

27. Presser (2003).

28. Ibid.

29. Garey (1999).

30. Wachter and Bell (2012). The first statement about hospitalists appeared in 1996 in a "Sounding Board" piece in the *New England Journal of Medicine* in

which Robert Wachter and Derek Goldman coined the term to refer to a "new breed of physicians we call hospitalists—specialists in inpatient medicine" (514). Since then, the number of hospitalists has expanded rapidly (Wachter and Bell 2012).

31. Brotman and Nelson (2011) and Wachter and Bell (2012). The rise of hospitalists has been attributed to a number of factors, ranging from the regulations of the Accreditation Council for Graduate Medical Education (ACGME), the use of diagnosis-related groups (DRGs) rather than length-of-stay payment, and the growing desire among younger physicians to have more "balanced" and "flexible" lifestyles, as well as system caps on residents' hours. In addition to Brotman and Nelson (2011) and Wachter and Bell (2012), see also Hoff (2010).

32. It would be interesting for someone to explore the issue of how generalizable this is: to what extent do new sub-occupations emerge in order to deal with the parts of the job (such as the hours and schedules) that privileged professionals try to avoid? For example, has the number of non-tenure-system faculty and professionals increased not only because they are cheaper but also because tenure-system faculty want to teach less and may not even want to advise undergraduate students?

33. Hoff (2010).

34. Ibid., 72.

35. McKinlay and Marceau (2002) and Relman (2007).

36. Lyness et al. (2012).

CHAPTER 5

1. The term "churning"—the act of agitating and shaking cream in order to turn it into butter—has been applied in numerous other ways: stockbrokers constantly buying and selling stocks in order to generate commissions, people acquiring new credit cards in order to gain bonus miles, and switching from one job to another (without ever being unemployed) in order to get a better job. Our usage here—keeping a job but not sticking to the official schedule—has something in common with these other usages, but also differs from them. There is no other existing term for what we are analyzing because scholars, with exceptions noted later in the chapter, have not previously recognized the phenomenon, much less analyzed it.

2. The same sort of invariant schedule, fixed for the present as well as the future, was used at the other nursing home and at all the fire stations. The hospitals and private-sector EMT services, by contrast, typically scheduled in six-week to six-month blocks.

3. Nelson Lichtenstein, interviewed by Micah Uetricht, "Why Walmart, Why Now?" *In These Times*, October 10, 2012, available at: http://inthesetimes

.com/article/13979/why_walmart_why_now (accessed October 14, 2012). See also *Grounding Globalization* by Eddie Webster, Rob Lambert, and Andries Bezuidenhout (2008), who note that "unevenness and growing insecurity is the central theme of our book" (1). The three factories they studied—in South Africa, Korea, and Australia—were similar in that they "not only manufacture refrigerators, they actively manufacture insecurity as the key source of discipline over workers" (77).

4. See OECDStatExtracts, "Average Usual Weekly Hours Worked on the Main Job," available at: http://stats.oecd.org/Index.aspx?DatasetCode=AVE_HRS (accessed April 29, 2014). Nathaniel Baum-Snow and Derek Neal (2009) argue that "the data on usual hours from long form [U.S. census] respondents appear to contain significant and systematic errors."

5. Presser (2003); see also Golden (2001) and Gornick, Presser, and Batzdorf (2009).

6. Presser (1999), 1778.

7. Lambert (2008, 1218).

8. Henly, Shaefer, and Waxman (2006), 610.

9. Lambert and Waxman (2005).

10. Bianchi, Robinson, and Milkie (2006). Suzanne Bianchi and her colleagues, noting the limitations of one-day diaries, argue that one of the strengths of their study is their use of one-week diaries from dual-earner, middle-class respondents.

11. Chase and Godbey (1983). Others also focus on the problems of various sorts of self-reported time data; see Chang and Krosnick (2003), Jacobs (1998), Juster, Ono, and Stafford (2003), and Todd et al. (2009).

12. There were some questions we did not ask either because we were reluctant to do so or because the scheduler, in answering them, would not have been uniformly clear about current conditions. For example, although we know whether each worker on the schedule was a mother, asking whether she was partnered or single would not always have elicited a clear-cut answer.

13. The data covered the period from April 1, 2007, to October 6, 2007.

14. One for the person who "crossed out," one for the person who "picked up."

15. See website table 5.1 for data on person-shifts over the six-month period.

16. See website table 5.1 for an explanation of the calculation.

17. There were fourteen employees who took long-term leaves of absence during this time for unspecified reasons—perhaps for the birth of a child, perhaps to recover from a major accident or illness. We exclude these workers from most of our subsequent analyses of who was more or less likely to engage in churning, since their behavior might be anomalous: for example, if one of these fourteen took a lot of vacation days, was that separate from the long-term leave or were those days taken to deal with the medical problem that ultimately required the long-term leave?

18. There were more pickups than cross-outs because sometimes the facility was short-staffed; for example, if a worker had just resigned and had not yet been replaced, management would have decided that their shifts needed to be covered.
19. Braga, Papachristos, and Hureau (2010) and Lipsey and Wilson (1998).
20. The Berkman nursing home did not use mandatory overtime.
21. Because the Outercity hospital and Berkman nursing home used differing systems for basic scheduling and data maintenance, the analyses are not strictly comparable, but are suggestive.
22. We did not attempt to analyze gender since there is almost no variance: nursing assistants and nurses are overwhelmingly women.
23. See website table 5.2.
24. The number of shifts listed as call-outs was twice as large as the number listed as swaps, but many shifts not identified as swaps may have much of that character. Swaps for vacations might have been arranged months in advance and did not appear in the records as swaps.
25. Almost half of the crossed-out shifts were for a variety of not so easily interpreted reasons that included: no reason of any kind, a reason that seemed holiday-related, or the code "off" or "health," indicating that the day had been arranged sufficiently in advance to avoid sick leave sanctions.
26. Workers cannot cash in all of their vacation days and must leave some unused, presumably to provide for contingencies.
27. When this employee took what was actually a sick day but was counted as a vacation day, she got the same paycheck as if she had worked that day; the employee who covered for her worked an extra day and got an extra day's pay. This was arranged by the two employees themselves, rather than by the nursing home's scheduler.
28. See, for example, Gilder (1981), Murray (1984, 2012), and Steele (1991).
29. Scott (1985).
30. And what does that say?
31. DeVault (1999).
32. Lambert (2008).
33. Henly, Schaefer, and Waxman (2006), 621.
34. Lambert et al. (2012), 309.
35. Lambert (2014).
36. Marx (1867).
37. For discussions of similar processes in the creation of cultures and institutions to protect working-class interests, see Thompson (1964) and Fields (1990), among others.
38. Marx (1867), 283.
39. This was also the policy at Countryside, the unionized hospital we studied, and at Lucas Estates, a non-union but comparatively beneficent nursing home.

CHAPTER 6

1. Perhaps these policies with respect to health care benefits stemmed from our employers being health care organizations themselves.
2. Devoe, Lee, and Pffeffer (2010), 639.
3. Golden and Gebreselassie (2007).
4. Nationally, two-thirds of workers report working overtime (Smith et al. 2013). According to the latest GSS data, a significantly higher proportion of men (70 percent) than women (60 percent) work overtime hours, and men do so more frequently (almost two more days per month on average). Blue-collar workers are the most likely to work mandatory overtime (Stein 2012).
5. Bernhardt, Dresser, and Hatton (2003), 44.
6. The National Sample Survey of Registered Nurses (U.S. Department of Health and Human Services 2010, table 22) estimates that only 15 percent of nurses earn paid overtime; the percentage is higher in hospitals (19.9 percent) than in nursing homes (13.5 percent). Note that Berney et al. (2005), using data from New York State, found significant variation (from almost none to 16 percent) in the amount that nurses worked overtime and showed that the amount of overtime varied by a number of hospital characteristics (including for example size, location, and unionization).
7. Milkman, Gonzalez, and Narro (2010).
8. This nurse's practice of not taking a lunch break is not unusual. Perhaps as a result, a 2013 court case in Washington State ruled that hospitals must pay nurses overtime when they do not get breaks during their shifts as a way "to protect health-care workers and promote patient safety and quality health care." See Washington State Department of Labor and Industries, "Nurses' Overtime," available at: http://www.lni.wa.gov/WorkplaceRights/Wages/Overtime/Nurse/default.asp (accessed April 26, 2014).
9. U.S. Department of Health and Human Services (2010).
10. Despite the existence of a set of rules and policies to minimize the use of overtime, schedulers in both the nursing homes and the hospitals we studied reported that upper management did not carefully monitor how much overtime they created. Senior managers simply expected them to pay attention to both staffing needs and the bottom line. Although we were somewhat surprised by this freedom offered to frontline scheduling supervisors, a number of factors were likely at work. First, they became supervisors because they were trusted by management, and management knew that these frontline supervisors worked extremely hard to pull together the schedules. Administrators told us, again and again, that scheduling is a difficult job. We observed schedulers at a number of sites making constant schedule adjustments, talking to sometimes crying workers about their need to go home, cajoling workers to stay, and "dialing for dollars," as one described it when she had to call

one person after another to fill a staffing hole. We saw this hard work, and so did management. Second, as management knew, schedulers often serve as the frontline supervisors who know workers best. As a result, as other researchers have suggested (Kelly et al. 2008), not only do workers approach these frontline supervisors to get help adjusting their schedules, but the schedulers sometimes use these adjustments to reward workers who help them run the schedule more smoothly. Management offers frontline supervisors some leeway in making decisions; workers use that leeway to gain some leverage over the unpredictability of their lives.

11. Gordon (2006a).
12. Golden and Wiens-Tuers (2005).
13. For the national surveys, see Golden and Gebreselassie (2007).
14. U.S. Department of Health and Human Services (2010).
15. Bae and Brewer (2010).
16. We did a content analysis of 105 contracts (dated between 2004 and 2010) from 21 EMT unions, 37 certified nursing assistant unions, and 47 registered nurse unions to examine how much contract space was devoted to various aspects of overtime (that is, the percentage of the entire text of the contract dedicated to this issue). Because doctors are far less likely to be hourly employees receiving overtime (Budrys 1997; Wine and O'Hair 2004), we do not include the 27 physician contracts in this analysis. For a detailed discussion of the methods and data as well as the findings, see Crocker and Clawson (2012), Lashway and Stein (2012), and Stein (2012).
17. See Gerstel and Clawson (2001) for the argument that unions are far from monolithic and, in particular, vary depending on the gender composition of their staff and membership. In that paper, we suggest that unions whose members are primarily women are far more likely to negotiate for "family-friendly policies" and temporal policies that support women's family responsibilities.
18. Crocker and Clawson (2012), 471.
19. The workers did not immediately strike; instead, a complicated alternative arrangement was devised where neither management nor union gave ground and workers maintained the ability to mount a campaign going forward.
20. For discussion of different compensation models, see New England Journal of Medicine Career Center (2004).
21. Note the language: the time "after five"—that is, after seeing patients—does not seem to count as working.
22. Nurses also see staying at work late as a sign of their dedication and commitment to patients, but they talk more often about what they did not have time to do during the day, and they stay to do the paperwork that must still be completed (often for billing purposes). Doctors tend to emphasize the patient who urgently needs to be seen, the need to authorize a prescription refill, or

the patient who needs to be called about troubling lab results. Doctors put far more stress on responding to patients as the reason for the extra hours.

23. Hipple (2010).

24. Going back to school did not generate any immediate income, but it was in many ways very similar to holding down a second job—something that was done in the hope of bringing in extra money (in the long term) and that required many hours beyond the basic job schedule. It was common across three of our occupations (physicians being the exception) and was often encouraged by management. Although second jobs were not a major factor in nurses' accounts of their work schedules, schooling featured more prominently. In nursing homes, about one in five nursing assistants we interviewed were attending school with the aim of becoming a licensed practical nurse; both of the nursing homes we observed had a program to pay the cost of schooling in exchange for a commitment to work for the nursing home after graduation. Although fewer EMTs were in school, many had been at one time, and a substantial number were currently enrolled, typically preparing to become paramedics or nurses. These three occupations exemplified an important characteristic of twenty-first-century society, and a major change from nineteenth- or early-twentieth-century practice: even the best on-the-job performance is not enough to move from one occupation to the next; that can only be done by returning to school.

25. Note that these rates are significantly higher than the national rates reported in the Current Population Survey (CPS), according to which firefighters and EMTs are the two groups most likely to hold a second job, but only 28 percent of firefighters and 20 percent of EMTs and paramedics do so.

26. Schor (1998).

27. The current debates over resident and intern hours came up often in our interviews with established doctors. Many, especially the older ones, insisted that the changes in the interns' hours were not such a good thing—that they were not being socialized to the patterns that would ensure a commitment to medicine and the patients they served. Note that this was another example of a generational divide we saw among doctors.

CHAPTER 7

1. Waugh (1992); see also Roediger and Foner (1989) and Rybczynski (1991).

2. Rybczynski (1991), 132.

3. The median is six days of paid sick leave, whether a worker has one, five, ten, or twenty years of service. See U.S. Bureau of Labor Statistics (2009), tables 31 (holidays), 33 (sick leave), and 34 (vacations). "According to the Bureau of Labor Statistics," Steven Greenhouse reports, "39 percent of private-sector workers do not receive paid sick leave." Steven Greenhouse, "Bill Would

Guarantee Up to Seven Paid Sick Days per Year," *New York Times*, May 15, 2009. Available at: http://www.nytimes.com/2009/05/16/health/policy/16 sick.html (accessed May 15, 2014).

4. Greenhouse, "Bill Would Guarantee. . . ."

5. Connecticut's law, which took effect January 1, 2012, mandates five sick days a year for qualifying service workers who receive an hourly wage; it does not apply to manufacturing workers, workers at nonprofit organizations, or independent contractors; see Peter Applebome, "In Connecticut, Paid Sick Leave for Service Workers Is Approved," *New York Times*, June 4, 2011. Available at: http://www.nytimes.com/2011/06/05/nyregion/connecticut-service -workers-to-get-paid-sick-leave.html (accessed May 15, 2014). Cities with legally guaranteed sick leave include San Francisco, Seattle, Washington, D.C., and New York.

6. Milkman and Appelbaum (2013).

7. Proposed federal legislation, the Healthy Families Act, would require employers with fifteen or more employees to provide seven paid sick days per year to full-time workers; these sick days could be taken for the worker or the worker's child, spouse, parent, or another close friend or family member.

8. For a workplace to qualify, it must have fifty or more employees within a seventy-five-mile radius. For a worker to qualify, he or she must have worked 1,250 or more hours for that employer in the preceding twelve months.

9. Armenia, Gerstel, and Wing (forthcoming).

10. Mishel, Bernstein, and Shierholz (2009), 367; see also Ray and Schmitt (2008).

11. See U.S. Bureau of Labor Statistics (2009), tables 31, 33, and 34.

12. Cited in *Daily Hampshire Gazette*, September 3, 2012.

13. From the confidential survey results sent to us by the survey company.

14. When people self-regulate and are responsible to each other, they make every effort to do the work if they possibly can. This is a result of the structure of work, not simply a male privilege (although the two are related). Although it applies above all to doctors, one other group—a set of six salaried nurse-midwives who together staffed a hospital's maternity operation—had a similar situation. Like doctors, they developed the schedule together and, filling in for one another, changed it around as needed. Like doctors, they never called out sick because of their sense of autonomy and responsibility to their coworkers: "We never call in sick, because if you call in sick one of your partners has to do your work. It's not like the patients don't keep coming. So it's very rare that any of us calls in sick. . . . I worked with a broken toe, we work when we feel like crap, because you know that the work doesn't go away and it just lands on the shoulders of the people you work with. So we don't call in sick."

15. The term "mental health day" deserves more investigation. According to the *Merriam-Webster* online dictionary, it was first used in 1971. In our own study,

it was used moderately often by nurses and EMTs, but almost not at all by doctors or nursing assistants. (Doctors probably did not use the term because they did not believe in taking sick days, and CNAs probably never used it because they had enough difficulty getting time off even for physical illness.) A scan of online hits for the term shows others using the term in ways that roughly correspond to how our respondents used it—ranging from "Screw you, I'm taking off to enjoy myself and there's nothing you can do about it" (an often overlooked form of resistance), to "I'm feeling stressed and think it's legitimate to stay home to refresh myself," to "I'm just as ill as if I had a physical ailment." Although workers used the term among themselves, it is highly unlikely that they would use the term in reporting to their employer why they needed the day off (however much some mental health advocacy groups might wish it could be otherwise).

16. Deutsch (2007).
17. David Johnson, Chief, Social, Economic, and Housing Statistics Division, U.S. Census Bureau, personal communication with the author, January 2012. These figures (for all occupations) need to be treated with caution because the BLS sample size for any given occupation is small.
18. As discussed later in this chapter, at the Berkman nursing home, if a nursing assistant called out within ninety days of her most recent call-out, she would receive a written disciplinary warning. Here, if a firefighter did *not* call out, he received a bonus day.
19. EMTs' casual attitude toward vacations might also have been influenced by the fact that work itself had a lot of downtime, so they may have felt less of a need to get a break from it.
20. Lopez (2006). On Walmart, see Brown (2013).
21. The penalty is for each call-out, not for each day of missed work. Thus, if a nursing assistant calls to say that she has pneumonia and will miss a week of work, that is only one call-out. However, if she tries to come back after four days and then becomes ill again, that is two call-outs.
22. Compare this thinking to Thompson's (1967) discussion of natural necessity (getting in the harvest, taking advantage of the tide) versus clock time.
23. At a negotiation session attended by about two hundred workers at a union-ized small chain of nursing homes, we observed a similar policy almost lead-ing to a strike.
24. All the examples of such "abuse" language we heard came from black im-migrant workers—Africans or West Indians. Considering that only a few of them made such comments, however, this may have been chance.
25. This worker had been employed at the nursing home less than two years.
26. Society for Human Resource Management (2012).
27. Note that workers at Berkman, to avoid being charged with a call-out, had to

call out two days ahead and have their absence approved by the director of nursing.

28. Workers were required to leave a minimum of forty hours in their vacation bank so that if they needed time off a reserve would be available. At least one nursing assistant complained about this, wanting the right to cash in all of her time.

29. Williams (2011).

CHAPTER 8

1. Jacobs and Gerson (2004).
2. On spouses' work hours and shifts, see Cha (2010) and Presser (2003); on the division of domestic labor, see Bianchi, Robinson, and Milkie (2006); on stress levels in marriage, see Larson, Richards, and Perry-Jenkins (1994); and on connections to kin networks, see Hansen (2004) and Sarkisian and Gerstel (2012).
3. On families' influence on hours and schedules with respect to wives and mothers, see Bianchi et al. (2006), Blair-Loy (2003), Mason, Wolfinger, and Gouldner (2013), and Stone (2007); for the literature focusing on husbands and fathers, see, for example, Cooper (2000), Deutsch (1999), Townsend (2002), and Williams (2011).
4. On the polarization of good and bad jobs, see Kalleberg (2011).
5. For marital data, see website table 8.1.
6. For one such study of lower-level supervisors, see Dodson and Zincavage (2007).
7. See Pugh (2009) for a discussion of parents buying goods for their children so they will not feel different from their peers and will have a sense of belonging. For many of the nursing assistants in our study, their inability to provide these goods was particularly difficult for them precisely because they knew and even shared this model of parenthood.
8. Murray (2012).
9. Dodson (2009).
10. Dodson and Dickert (2004).
11. Dodson and Dickert (2004); see also East, Weisner, and Reyes (2006).
12. Our data correspond to national data. In 2008, 6 percent of registered nurses were single mothers (U.S. Department of Health and Human Services 2010, A-55, appendix table 54). Among married nurses and those in domestic partnerships, 51.7 percent had children in the home, compared to 25.3 percent of unmarried nurses. In addition, 15.2 percent of married nurses and those in domestic partnerships and 18.1 percent of unmarried nurses had dependent adults in the home; combined, "approximately 55 percent of RNs working in

nursing reported having household dependents, either adult or children" (ibid., table 7-11).

13. Acker (1990).

14. An older literature suggested that "women's jobs" (whether nursing or teaching) are organized around women's shifting life-course responsibilities—asserting, for example, that women can withdraw from such jobs and reenter with little penalty to their career for there are no career ladders in these jobs. For an updated version of this argument and its flaws in the contemporary setting, see Moen and Roehling (2005). Here we argue that such responsiveness to domestic responsibilities is not encouraged or allowed in all jobs where women predominate, but rather characterizes only professional (or what used to be called "semiprofessional") women's jobs, not low-wage women's jobs.

15. Hochschild (1989). This division of labor was likely to have been shaped by their husband's occupation: our research suggests, for example, that a nurse married to a doctor would be more gender-conventional than one married to an EMT; the power dynamics are very different (see Perry-Jenkins and Folk 1994). But we do not have the data to do a systematic analysis of this pattern.

16. Emphasis added.

17. On economic penalties, see Budig and England (2001), Correll, Benard, and Paik (2007), Goldin and Katz (2011), and Mason et al. (2013).

18. Macdonald (2009).

CHAPTER 9

1. Ridgeway (2011), 95.

2. In this respect, EMTs differ from nursing assistants, whose second jobs usually involve fixed and invariant hours.

3. Williams (2000, 2010).

4. Even though female nurses and male EMTs, in saying that they were deeply involved in doing the work of family, may only have been saying what people, regardless of gender, like to claim these days. But it is noteworthy that we did not hear this from doctors. Of course, if we had interviewed their spouses, perhaps they would have told us something different.

5. This EMT was willing to be docked a day's pay (which he would make up through sick leave pay). It did not even occur to him that he might face a penalty beyond that. Nursing assistants were not only docked a day's pay but reprimanded and, if they left too often, fired.

6. Presser (2003).

7. Perlow (1999).

8. Williams (2000).

9. This was about double the national rate for the population as a whole (U.S. Census Bureau 2012).
10. Cha (2010).
11. Shows and Gerstel (2009).
12. As mentioned in the previous chapter, this is precisely what the nurse married to a doctor suggested. It would have been interesting and useful to get data from the spouses/partners on these issues, but limited resources (of both time and money) made it difficult to do so.
13. Stone (2007).
14. Note that even though we discuss women physicians here, we have discussed female EMTs much less and do not discuss male nurses or CNAs at all. That is in part a result of our methodological decisions: there were very few male nurses or nursing assistants to be found. And as we suggested, at least in our study, among EMTs women and men look quite similar in work hours, second jobs, and family work. In contrast, women physicians differ significantly from their male counterparts, and perhaps because doctors have more choice than those in any of the other occupations (as we suggest later), it is important to discuss those differences.
15. For a discussion of women physicians and their families, see Boulis and Jacobs (2008).
16. Cha (2010), 315.
17. Emphasis added.
18. Stone (2007).
19. See Pyke (1996) and Deutsch (1999).
20. Connell (1995). On the relationship of masculinity to paid work and domestic life, see Coltrane and Adams (2008), Cooper (2000), and Townsend (2002).
21. Connell (1995), 735.
22. To be sure, as chapter 11 explores in some depth, the CNAs occasionally speak of the benefits of escaping their homes to go to their jobs.

CHAPTER 10

1. On critiques of organizational rules and policies, see Jasper (2011), Taylor (1903/1947), and Weir (1973); on employees protecting each other in the face of punitive policies, see Sloan (2012).
2. See, for example, Burawoy (1979), Clawson (1980), Graham (1995), Hodson (2001, 2008), Roethlisberger and Dickson (1939), Roy (1952, 1954), and Taylor (1903/1947).
3. Stone (2007), 99; see also Blair-Loy (2003), 101.
4. Ryan and Kossek (2008), 306.
5. Lambert and Henly (2012), 156.

6. Jillian Crocker (2013) used data from our study to examine the breaks that workers take.

7. Weir (1973) and Jasper (2011).

8. For discussions of firefighters and hegemonic masculinity, see Crocker and Clawson (2012) and Shows and Gerstel (2009).

9. Kanter (1977) and Hertz (1996). The head of the union in one fire department where this issue arose insisted that "it is not tolerated among the bargaining unit. We will not have that here. This is not a bargaining unit that promotes hostile work environment anywhere. And I won't have that on my watch." In urban areas, race is often a bitter dividing line, especially around promotions to officer, but in our study area there were few black or Latino firefighters, and they appeared to be respected and valued by their white coworkers.

10. For many of these factors, the lines are not necessarily clear-cut. Nursing assistants and doctors often have long-term relations with patients, who might not be happy about a switch, and even within a long-range project there may be discrete tasks that can be assigned to a worker on a switch. Similarly, there is room for maneuver on what constitutes appropriate skills: can a sociologist of work cover a course on family or culture?

11. Workers sometimes argued that a swap did not in fact change the total overtime the employer would be paying, but simply changed which worker got the overtime. Therefore, workers thought such a swap should be permitted, but management was usually unwilling to do so.

12. And at least to the administrator, it went without saying that permitting a nurse to take a two-week vacation is not a unit need.

13. Mauss (1925/1967), Clawson, Neustadtl, and Scott (1992).

14. On generalized reciprocity, see Yamagishi and Cook (1993).

15. On the "norm of reciprocity," see Gouldner (1960).

16. Meaning, if the nursing home management will not authorize overtime pay.

17. This complicates the entire idea of "vacation" and muddies any attempts at quantitative analysis of the use of vacations in these situations. This is one of the reasons why, in our analyses of churning at the Berkman nursing home, we counted all days not worked according to schedule as churning.

18. Burawoy (1979).

19. Marxists like to talk about the self-organization of the working class and argue that the new world is developing within the shell of the old and that conditions are being created for an alternative way of organizing society.

CHAPTER 11

1. Mike Duke, "Walmart's Enduring Values," Walmart shareholders' meeting, Bentonville, AR, June 2012.

2. Malcolm (2013).

3. Adam Lashinsky Sr., "Larry Page: Google Should Be Like a Family," CNN Money, January 19, 2012, available at: http://tech.fortune.cnn.com/2012/01/19/best-companies-google-larry-page/ (accessed April 30, 2014).

4. Lakoff (1992), 5; Kovecses (2010), 68.

5. Note that the term "nursing *home*" is a familial term for a facility where *dependent* residents receive considerable care from CNAs. In contrast, the term "assisted living" is used for a facility where residents are more *independent* and receive less care.

6. Lasch (1977).

7. Hochschild (1997).

8. Ibid., 104, 34.

9. See Becker and Moen (1999), Clarkberg and Moen (2001), Cooper (2000), Jacobs and Gerson (1998), Maume and Bellas (2001), Meiksins and Whalley (2002), and Reynolds (2005).

10. Pager and Quillian (2005).

11. Larson, Richards, and Perry-Jenkins (1994).

12. Ibid., 1034.

13. Rubin (1976), 159, 169.

14. See also Dodson and Zincavage (2007).

15. See Centers for Disease Control and Prevention (CDC), "National Nursing Home Survey: National Nursing Assistant Survey," table 6 (August 2008), available at: http://www.cdc.gov/nchs/nnas.htm (accessed March 15, 2012).

16. A practice that Dodson and Zincavage (2007) also report.

17. Leif and Fox (1963).

18. Folbre (2012) and Pfefferle and Weinberg (2008).

19. Lisa Dodson and Rebekah Zincavage suggest that to some extent nursing homes exploit the CNAs' relations with residents by using emotional or interpersonal rewards in place of material rewards (Dodson and Zincavage 2007). See also Gabriel Winant's (2013) argument that worker connection and commitment to residents reduces the labor union's ability to build power.

20. At one nursing home where we observed, nursing assistants with some seniority regularly worked with the same residents and might have done so for years; newer CNAs, especially those who worked reduced hours, worked with the same set of residents less often. Systematic data on such policies and their consequences could usefully be the subject of future research.

21. In a personal communication (2013), Lisa Dodson said that she too found that nursing homes told CNAs to keep their distance from residents and discouraged them from grieving too much when a patient of theirs died. But simultaneously, she said, when it was useful to the nursing homes, they encouraged CNAs to think of residents like family. For example, in the field she would hear management repeatedly saying, "Take care of them the way you

do your grandmother." In this way, intrinsic rewards could substitute for extrinsic rewards.

22. See also Pfefferle and Weinberg (2008).
23. McPherson, Smith-Lovin, and Cook (2001).
24. Moen and Roehling (2005).
25. Centers for Disease Control and Prevention (2014).
26. Almost none of the male nurses brought this up, and the one who did explicitly disagreed with the idea of being drawn to work as an escape from home.
27. Garson (1975), 219.
28. Cowan and Cowan (2000).
29. See Gerstel (2011), Sarkisian and Gerstel (2012), and Gerstel and Clawson (2014).
30. Lamont (2000).
31. Note, however, that despite the close relationships nursing assistants reported having with these (often affluent) nursing home residents, almost no one spoke of what the residents had done for the nursing assistants. Today obituaries do sometimes contain expressions of gratitude to nursing homes, sometimes listing the specific people who gave care to the deceased, but one hundred years ago an affluent elderly person might leave a bequest to the caregiver (Hartog 2012). Today nursing homes often do not allow that.
32. Coontz (2005), Stone (1977), and Cherlin (2009).
33. Lakoff and Johnson (1980), 458.
34. Sherman (2006).
35. Ibid., 261.
36. Lareau (2003), Edin and Kefalas (2005), and Furstenberg (2009).
37. One of the nursing homes we studied had a very low nursing assistant turnover rate—about one-fifth the national average (Donoghue 2010). We have only systematic turnover data on one of the organizations, a nursing home. It would be useful for future research to look at the relationship between turnover and the kind of patterns we focus on here.
38. Milkman and Appelbaum (2013).
39. Besides Hochschild, also expounding on this theme are Viviana Zelizer (2005), Juliet Schor (2004), Daniel Cook (2004), Marion Fourcade and Kieran Healy (2007), and Allison Pugh (2009), to name but a few.

CONCLUSION

1. The most important exception is the pioneering work by Susan Lambert and Julia Henly, who have not only developed good original data but also made insightful analyses. Others, such as Jennifer Swanberg and Liz Watson, as well as Karen Lyness, Janet Gornick, Pamela Stone, and Angela Grotto, have also written useful and important analyses of these issues.

2. Granovetter (1985).

3. See Kalev (2009), Smith-Doerr (2004), and Stainback and Tomaskovic-Devey (2010).

4. Goldin and Katz (2011).

5. Ridgeway (2011), 30.

6. Bianchi et al. (2012).

7. See, for example, Etzioni (1969) and Oppenheimer (1973).

8. Sandberg (2013).

9. On "undoing gender," see Deutsch (2007).

10. Bernard (1972).

11. Mills (1959), 8.

12. Friedan (1963).

13. See, for example, the public policy agenda of Take Back Your Time, an initiative to address "time poverty relief" in the United States by guaranteeing paid leaves for all parents, a week of paid sick leave for all workers, three weeks of paid vacation, and limits on compulsory overtime and making it easier for Americans to choose part-time work. For information, see the group's website at: http://www.timeday.org/time_to_care.asp (accessed April 30, 2014).

14. Some nursing unions have been demanding two weeks of vacation in the summer.

15. Stephanie Luce (2004) argues that workers can be sure of receiving the mandated living wage only if there is both a specific government body charged with enforcement *and* an external movement monitoring enforcement.

16. See, for example, Christensen and Schneider (2010), Gornick and Meyers (2003), Heymann (2007), Jacobs and Gerson (2004), Kelly, Moen, and Tranby (2011), Kelly and Moen (2007), Lambert (2009a, 2009b), Milkman and Appelbaum (2013), Perry-Jenkins and MacDermid-Wadsworth (2013), and Williams (2006). A number of useful websites discuss these issues; see, for example, the Institute for Women's Policy Research (http://www.iwpr.org [accessed April 30, 2014]), the Mobility Agenda (http://www.mobility agenda.org/home [accessed April 30, 2014]), the Center for Work Life Law (http://worklifelaw.org/pubs/ImprovingWork-LifeFit.pdf [accessed April 30, 2014]), and the Center for American Progress (http://www.american progress.org [accessed April 30, 2014]).

17. For discussion of inequalities in policies, see, for example, Williams and Boushey (2010) and Heymann (2007).

References

Accreditation Council for Graduate Medical Education. 2014. "ACGME Duty Hours." Available at: http://www.acgme.org/acgmeweb/tabid/271/Graduate MedicalEducation/DutyHours.aspx (accessed March 30, 2014).

Acker, Joan. 1990. "Hierarchies, Jobs, and Bodies: A Theory of Gendered Organizations." *Gender & Society* 42(2): 139–58.

———. 2006. "Inequality Regimes: Gender, Class, and Race in Organizations." *Gender & Society* 20(4): 441–64.

Aiken, Linda H., Ying D. Xue, Sean P. Clarke, and Douglas M. Sloane. 2007. "Supplemental Nurse Staffing in Hospitals and Quality of Care." *Journal of Nursing Administration* 37(7-8): 335–42.

Americans for Effective Law Enforcement (AELE). 2010. "Minimum Staffing: Firefighters and EMS." *AELE Monthly Law Journal* (September). Available at: http://www.aele.org/law/2010all09/2010-09MLJ201.pdf (accessed May 15, 2014).

American Hospital Association (AHA). 2001. "The Hospital Workforce Shortage: Immediate and Future." *AHA Trend Watch* 3(2): 1–8.

———. 2008. *AHA Guide 2009: United States Hospitals, Health Care Systems, Networks, Alliances, Health Organizations, Agencies, Providers.* Washington, D.C.: AHA.

Appelbaum, Eileen, Peter Berg, Ann Frost, and Gil Preuss. 2003. "The Effects of Work Restructuring on Low-Wage, Low-Skilled Workers in U.S. Hospitals." In *Low-Wage America: How Employers Are Reshaping Opportunity in the Workplace,* ed. Eileen Appelbaum, Annette Bernhardt, and Richard J. Murnane. New York: Russell Sage Foundation.

Armenia, Amy, Naomi Gerstel, and Coady Wing. Forthcoming. *Work and Occupations.* "Workplace Compliance with the Law: The Case of the Family and Medical Act."

Bae, Sung-Heui, and Carol Brewer. 2010. "Mandatory Overtime Regulations and Nurse Overtime." *Policy, Politics, Nursing Practice* 11(2): 99–107. doi:10.1177/0730888413502657.

Barker, James. 1999. *The Discipline of Teamwork: Participation and Concertive Control.* Thousand Oaks, Calif.: Sage Publications.

Baum-Snow, Nathaniel, and Derek Neal. 2009. "Mismeasurement of Usual Hours Worked in the Census and ACS." *Economics Letters* 102(1): 39–41.

Becker, Penny, and Phyllis Moen. 1999. "Scaling Back: Dual-Earner Couples' Work-Family Strategies." *Journal of Marriage and Family* 61(4): 995–1007.

Bernard, Jessie. 1972. *The Future of Marriage.* New York: World Publishers.

Berney, Barbara, Jack Needleman, and Christine Kovner. 2005. "Factors Influencing the Use of Registered Nurse Overtime in Hospitals, 1995–2000." *Journal of Nursing Scholarship* 37(2): 165–72.

Bernhardt, Annette, Laura Dresser, and Erin Hatton. 2003. "The Coffee Pot Wars: Unions and Firm Restructuring in the Hotel Industry." In *Low-Wage America: How Employers Are Reshaping Opportunity in the Workplace,* ed. Eileen Appelbaum, Annette Bernhardt, and Richard J. Murnane. New York: Russell Sage Foundation.

Bianchi, Suzanne M., John P. Robinson, and Melissa A. Milkie. 2006. *Changing Rhythms of American Family Life.* New York: Russell Sage Foundation.

Bianchi, Suzanne M., Liana C. Sayer, Melissa A. Milkie, and John P. Robinson. 2012. "Housework: Who Did, Does, or Will Do It, and How Much Does It Matter?" *Social Forces* 91: 55–63.

Blair-Loy, Mary. 2003. *Competing Devotions: Career and Family Among Women Executives.* Cambridge, Mass.: Harvard University Press.

Boulis, Ann K., and Jerry A. Jacobs. 2008. *The Changing Face of Medicine: Women Doctors and the Evolution of Health Care in America.* Ithaca, N.Y.: Cornell University Press.

Bourdieu, Pierre. 1984. *Distinction: A Social Critique of the Judgment of Taste.* New York: Routledge, Kegan and Paul.

Braga, Anthony A., Andrew V. Papachristos, and David M. Hureau. 2010. "The Concentration and Stability of Gun Violence at Micro Places in Boston, 1980–2008." *Journal of Quantitative Criminology* 26(1): 33–53.

Brotman, Daniel J., and John R. Nelson. 2011. "Hospitalists, PCPs, Specialists, and Non-physicians: Too Many Cooks in the Kitchen?" *Journal of Hospital Medicine* 6(8): 433–34.

Brown, Jenny. 2013. "Paid Sick Leave, at Last?" *Labor Notes* (May 13). Available at: http://www.labornotes.org/2013/05/paid-sick-leave-last (accessed May 13, 2013).

Brown, William E., Drew E. Dawson, and Roger Levine. 2003. "Compensation, Benefits, and Satisfaction: The Longitudinal Emergency Medical Technical Demographic (LEADS) Project." *Prehospital Emergency Care* 7(3): 357–62.

Budig, Michelle, and Paula England. 2001. "The Wage Penalty for Motherhood." *American Sociological Review* 66(2): 204–25.

Budrys, Grace. 1997. *When Doctors Join Unions.* Ithaca, N.Y.: ILR Press/Cornell University Press.

Burawoy, Michael. 1979. *Manufacturing Consent: Changes in the Labor Process Under Monopoly Capitalism.* Chicago: University of Chicago Press.

Burgoon, Brian M., and Fabian Dekker. 2010. "Flexible Employment, Economic Insecurity, and Social Policy Preferences in Europe." *Journal of European Social Policy* 20(2): 126–41.

Castle, Nicholas G., John Engberg, and Aiju Men. 2008. "Nurse Aid Agency Staffing and Quality of Care in Nursing Homes." *Medical Care Research and Review* 65(2): 232–52.

Centers for Disease Control and Prevention (CDC). 2014. "Faststats: Hospital Utilization (in Non-Federal Short-Stay Hospitals)." Available at: http://www.cdc.gov/nchs/fastats/hospital.htm (accessed January 26, 2014).

Centers for Medicare & Medicaid Services. 2012. Available at: http://www.cms.gov/Research-Statistics-Data-and-Systems/Statistics-Trends-and-reports/NationalHealthExpendData/NationalHealthAccountsHistorical.html (accessed April 30, 2014).

Cha, Youngjoo. 2010. "Reinforcing Separate Spheres: The Effect of Spousal Overwork on Men's and Women's Employment in Dual-Earner Households." *American Sociological Review* 75(2): 303–29.

Chang, Lin Chiat, and Jon A. Krosnick. 2003. "Measuring the Frequency of Regular Behaviors: Comparing the 'Typical Week' to the 'Past Week.'" *Sociological Methodology* 33: 55–80.

Charles, Maria, and David B. Grusky. 2004. *Occupational Ghettos: The Worldwide Segregation of Women and Men.* Stanford, Calif.: Stanford University Press.

Chase, D., and Geoffrey Godbey. 1983. "The Accuracy of Self-reported Participation Rates: A Research Note." *Leisure Studies* 2(2): 231–33.

Cherlin, Andrew. 2009. *Marriage Go Round.* New York: Alfred A. Knopf.

Chetkovich, Carol A. 1997. *Real Heat: Gender and Race in the Urban Fire Service.* New Brunswick, N.J.: Rutgers University Press.

Christensen, Kathleen, and Barbara Schneider. 2010. *Workplace Flexibility: Realigning Twentieth-Century Jobs to a Twenty-First-Century Workforce,* ed. Kathleen Christensen and Barbara Schneider. Ithaca, N.Y.: Cornell University Press.

Clarkberg, Marin, and Phyllis Moen. 2001. "Understanding the Time-Squeeze: Married Couples' Preferred and Actual Work-Hour Strategies." *American Behavioral Scientist* 44(7): 1115–36.

Clawson, Dan. 1980. *Bureaucracy and the Labor Process: The Transformation of U.S. Industry, 1860–1920.* New York: Monthly Review Press.

———. 2003. *The Next Upsurge: Labor and the New Social Movements.* Ithaca, N.Y.: Cornell University Press.

Clawson, Dan, Alan Neustadtl, and Denise Scott. 1992. *Money Talks: Corporate PCAs and Political Action.* New York: Basic Books.

Coltrane, Scott, and Michele Adams. 2008. *Gender and Families.* 2nd ed. Lanham, Md.: Rowman & Littlefield.

Connell, R. W. 1995. *Masculinities.* Berkeley: University of California Press.

Cook, Daniel T. 2004. *The Commodification of Childhood.* Durham, N.C.: Duke University Press.

Coontz, Stephanie. 2005. *Marriage, a History: How Love Conquered Marriage.* New York: Penguin.

Cooper, Marianne. 2000. "Being the 'Go-To Guy': Fatherhood, Masculinity, and the Organization of Work in Silicon Valley." *Qualitative Sociology* 23(4): 379–405.

Correll, Shelley J., Stephen Benard, and In Paik. 2007. "Getting a Job: Is There a Motherhood Penalty?" *American Journal of Sociology* 112(5): 1297–1339.

Cowan, Carolyn, and Phillip Cowan. 2000. *When Partners Become Parents: The Big Life Change for Couples.* Hillsdale, N.J.: Lawrence Erlbaum Associates.

Crocker, Jillian. 2013. "'We Will Handle It Ourselves': Rules, Norms, and the Micropolitics of Resistance Among Nursing Assistants." Paper presented to the meeting of the Labor and Working Class History Association Conference. New York (June 7).

Crocker, Jillian, and Dan Clawson. 2012. "Buying Time: Gendered Patterns in Union Contracts." *Social Problems* 59(4): 459–80.

Cummings, Kristin, and Kathleen Kreiss. 2008. "Contingent Workers and Contingent Health: Risks of a Modern Economy." *Journal of the American Medical Association* 299(4): 448–50.

Cunningham, Peter. 2011. "Non-urgent Use of Hospital Emergency Departments." Statement before the Senate Health, Education, Labor, and Pensions Committee, Subcommittee on Primary Health and Aging, hearing on "Diverting Nonurgent Emergency Room Use." May 11.

Deutsch, Francine. 1999. *Halving It All: How Equally Shared Parenting Works.* Cambridge, Mass.: Harvard University Press.

———. 2007. "Undoing Gender." *Gender & Society* 21(1): 106–27.

DeVault, Marjorie. 1999. *Liberating Method: Feminism and Social Research.* Philadelphia: Temple University Press.

Devoe, Sanford, Bryon Lee, and Jeffrey Pffeffer. 2010. "Hourly Versus Salaried Payment and Decisions About Trading Time and Money over Time." *Industrial and Labor Relations Review* 63(4): 627–39.

Diamond, Timothy. 1992. *Making Gray Gold: Narratives of Nursing Home Care.* Chicago: University of Chicago Press.

Dodson, Lisa. 2009. *Moral Underground: How Ordinary Americans Subvert an Unfair Economy.* New York: New Press.

Dodson, Lisa, and Jillian Dickert. 2004. "Girls' Family Labor in Low-Income Households: A Decade of Qualitative Research." *Journal of Marriage and Family* 66(2): 318–32.

Dodson, Lisa, and Rebekah Zincavage. 2007. "'It's Like a Family': Caring Labor, Exploitation, and Race in Nursing Homes." *Gender & Society* 21(6): 905–28.

Donoghue, Christopher. 2010. "Nursing Home Staff Turnover and Retention: An Analysis of National-Level Data." *Journal of Applied Gerontology* 29(1): 89–106.

East, Patricia, Thomas Weisner, and Barbara Reyes. 2006. "Youths' Caretaking of Their Adolescent Sisters' Children: Its Costs and Benefits for Youth Development." *Applied Developmental Science* 10(2): 86–95.

Edin, Kathryn, and Maria Kefalas. 2005. *Promises I Can Keep*. Berkeley: University of California Press.

England, Paula. 2010. "The Gender Revolution: Uneven and Stalled." *Gender & Society* 24(2): 149–66.

———. 2013. "How Is Inequality in the U.S. Changing?" Paper presented to the annual meeting of the American Sociological Association. New York (August 10–13).

Epstein, Cynthia Fuchs. 1993. *Women in Law*. Champaign: University of Illinois Press.

Etzioni, Amitai. 1969. *The Semi-professions and Their Organizations*. New York: Free Press.

Fields, Barbara Jeanne. 1990. "Slavery, Race, and Ideology in the United States of America." *New Left Review* 181(May-June): 95–119.

Folbre, Nancy. 2012. *For Love and Money*. New York: Russell Sage Foundation.

Fourcade, Marion, and Kieran Healy. 2007. "Moral Views of Market Society." *Annual Review of Sociology* 33: 14.1–14.27.

Friedan, Betty. 1963. *The Feminine Mystique*. New York: W. W. Norton.

Fuchs, Victor. 2012. "Major Trends in the U.S. Health Economy Since 1950." *New England Journal of Medicine* 366(11): 973–77.

Furstenberg, Frank. 2009. "Diverging Development: The Not-So-Invisible Hand of Social Class in America." In *Families as They Really Are*, ed. Barbara Risman. New York: W. W. Norton.

Garey, Anita Ilta. 1999. *Weaving Work and Motherhood*. Philadelphia: Temple University Press.

Garson, Barbara. 1975. *All the Livelong Day: The Meaning and Demeaning of Routine Work*. Garden City, N.Y.: Doubleday.

Gawande, Atul. 2009. "The Cost Conundrum: What a Texas Town Can Teach Us About Health Care." *The New Yorker*, June 1. Available at: http://www.new yorker.com/reporting/2009/06/01/090601fa_fact_gawande (accessed May 15, 2014).

Gerstel, Naomi. 2011. "Rethinking Families and Community: The Color, Class, and Centrality of Extended Kin." *Sociological Forum* 26(1): 1–20.

Gerstel, Naomi, and Dan Clawson. 2001. "Unions' Responses to Family Concerns." *Social Problems* 48(2): 277–98.

———. 2014. "Low-Wage Care Workers: Extended Family as a Strategy for Survival." In *Caring on the Clock*, ed. Mignon Duffy, Amy Armenia, and Clare Stacey. New Brunswick, N.J.: Rutgers University Press.

Giddens, Anthony. 1973. *The Class Structure of the Advanced Societies*. London: Hutchinson.

Gilder, George. 1981. *Wealth and Poverty*. New York: Basic Books.

Golden, Lonnie. 1996. "The Expansion of Temporary Help Employment in the U.S., 1982–1992: A Test of Alternative Economic Explanations." *Applied Economics* 28(9): 1127–41.

———. 2001. "Flexible Work Schedules: Which Workers Get Them?" *American Behavioral Scientist* 44(7): 1157–78.

Golden, Lonnie, and Eileen Appelbaum. 1992. "What Was Driving the 1982–88 Boom in Temporary Employment?" *American Journal of Economics and Sociology* 51(4): 473–93.

Golden, Lonnie, and Tesfayi Gebreselassie. 2007. "Overemployment Mismatches: The Preference for Fewer Work Hours." *Monthly Labor Review* 130(4): 18–37.

Golden, Lonnie, and Barbara Wiens-Tuers. 2005. "Mandatory Overtime Work in the United States: Who, Where, and What?" *Labor Studies Journal* (1): 1–25.

Goldin, Claudia, and Lawrence Katz. 2011. "The Cost of Workplace Flexibility for High-Powered Professionals." *Annals of the American Academy of Political and Social Science* 638(1): 45–67.

Gordon, Suzanne. 2006a. "Suzanne Gordon: A Nurses' Week That Really Honors Nurses." *The Progressive,* May 4. Available at: http://progressive.org/media_mpgordon050406 (accessed April 30, 2014).

———. 2006b. *Nursing Against the Odds: How Health Care Cost Cutting, Media Stereotypes, and Medical Hubris Undermine Nurses*. Ithaca, N.Y.: Cornell University Press.

Gordon, Suzanne, John Buchanan, and Tanya Bretherton. 2008. *Safety in Numbers: Nurse-to-Patient Ratios and the Future of Health Care*. Ithaca, N.Y.: ILR/Cornell University Press.

Gornick, Janet C., and Marcia K. Meyers. 2003. *Families That Work: Policies for Reconciling Parenthood and Employment*. New York: Russell Sage Foundation.

Gornick, Janet C., Harriet Presser, and Caroline Batzdorf. 2009. "Outside the 9-to-5." *The American Prospect* (June 9): 1–3.

Gouldner, Alvin W. 1960. "The Norm of Reciprocity: A Preliminary Statement." *American Sociological Review* 25(2): 161–78.

Graham, Laurie. 1995. *On the Line at Subaru-Isuzu: The Japanese Model and the American Worker*. Ithaca, N.Y.: ILR Press.

Granovetter, Mark. 1985. "Economic Action and Social Structure: The Problem of Embeddedness." *American Journal of Sociology* 91(3): 481–510.

Hansen, Karen V. 2004. *Not-So-Nuclear Families: Class, Gender, and Networks of Care*. New Brunswick, N.J.: Rutgers University Press.

Harlow, David. 2009. "No Ambulance Diversion Rule Takes Effect in Massachusetts." HealthBlawg: David Harlow's Health Care Law Blog, January 1. Available at: http://healthblawg.typepad.com/healthblawg/2009/01/no-ambu

lance-diversion-rule-takes-effect-in-massachusetts.html (accessed January 21, 2010).

Hartog, Hendrik. 2012. "A Lost World of Care? Reflecting on Inheritance and Old Age, 1850–1950." Paper presented to the meeting of the Eastern Sociological Society. New York (February 24).

Hegewisch, Ariane, Hannah Liepmann, Jeffrey Hayes, and Heidi Hartmann. 2010. "Separate and Not Equal? Gender Segregation in the Labor Market and the Gender Wage Gap." Briefing Paper. Washington, D.C.: Institute for Women's Policy Research (September).

Henly, Julia R., H. Luke Shaefer, and Elaine Waxman. 2006. "Nonstandard Work Schedules: Employer- and Employee-Driven Flexibility in Retail Jobs." *Social Service Review* 80(4): 609–34.

Hertz, Rosanna. 1996. "Guarding Against Women? Responses of Military Men and Their Wives to Gender Integration." *Journal of Contemporary Ethnography* 25(2): 251–84.

Heymann, Jody. 2007. *Forgotten Families: Ending the Growing Crisis Confronting Children and Working Parents in the Global Economy.* New York: Oxford University Press.

Hipple, Steven. 2010. "Multiple Job-Holding During the 2000s." *Monthly Labor Review* 133(7): 21–32.

Hochschild, Arlie. 1989. *The Second Shift.* New York: Penguin.

———. 1997. *The Time Bind: When Work Becomes Home and Home Becomes Work.* New York: Metropolitan.

Hodson, Randy. 2001. *Dignity at Work.* New York: Cambridge University Press.

———. 2008. "The Ethnographic Contribution to Understanding Coworker Relations." *British Journal of Industrial Relations* 46(1): 169–92.

Hoff, Timothy. 2010. *Practice Under Pressure: Primary Care Physicians and Their Medicine in the Twenty-First Century.* New Brunswick, N.J.: Rutgers University Press.

Hout, Michael. 2008. "How Class Works: Objective and Subjective Aspects of Class Since the 1970s." In *Social Class: How Does It Work?*, ed. Annette Lareau and Dalton Conley. New York: Russell Sage Foundation.

Institute of Medicine. 2007. *Emergency Medical Services: At the Crossroads.* Washington, D.C.: National Academies Press.

Jacobs, Jerry. 1998. "Measuring Time at Work: Are Self-Reports Accurate?" *Monthly Labor Review* 121(42): 42–53.

Jacobs, Jerry A., and Kathleen Gerson. 1998. "Who Are the Overworked Americans?" *Review of Social Economy* 56(4): 443–60.

———. 2004. *The Time Divide: Work, Family, and Gender Inequality.* Cambridge, Mass.: Harvard University Press.

Jasper, James M. 2011. "Emotions and Social Movements: Twenty Years of Theory and Research." *Annual Review of Sociology* 37: 14.1–14.19. Available at: http://www.jamesmjasper.org/files/ARS_2011.pdf (accessed May 30, 2013).

Joyce, Kelly A. 2008. *Magnetic Appeal: MRI and the Myth of Transparency.* Ithaca, N.Y.: Cornell University Press.

Juster, F. Thomas, Hiromi Ono, and Frank P. Stafford. 2003. "An Assessment of Alternative Measures of Time Use." *Sociological Methodology* 33(1): 19–54.

Kalev, Alexandra. 2009. "Cracking the Glass Cages? Restructuring and Ascriptive Inequality at Work." *American Journal of Sociology* 114(6): 1591–1643.

Kalleberg, Arne. 2009. "Precarious Work, Insecure Workers: Employment Relations in Transition." *American Sociological Review* 74(1): 1–22.

———. 2011. *Good Jobs, Bad Jobs: The Rise of Polarized and Precarious Employment Systems in the United States, 1970s to 2000s.* New York: Russell Sage Foundation.

Kanter, Rosabeth Moss. 1977. *Men and Women of the Corporation.* New York: Basic Books.

Kelly, Erin, Ellen Kossek, Leslie Hamer, Mary Durham, Jeremy Bray, Kelly Chermack, Lauren Murphy, and Dan Kaskubar. 2008. "Getting There from Here: Research on the Effects of Work-Family Initiatives on Work-Family Conflict and Business Outcomes." *Academy of Management Annals* 2(1): 305–49.

Kelly, Erin, and Phyllis Moen. 2007. "Rethinking the Clockwork of Work: Why Schedule Control May Pay Off at Work and at Home." *Advances in Developing Human Resources* 8(4): 487–506.

Kelly, Erin, Phyllis Moen, and Eric Tranby. 2011. "Changing Workplaces to Reduce Work-Family Conflict: Schedule Control in a White-Collar Organization." *American Sociological Review* 76(2): 265–90.

Kletke, Phillip R., David W. Emmon, and Kurt D. Gillis. 1996. "Current Trends in Physicians' Practice Arrangements: From Owners to Employees." *Journal of the American Medical Association* 276(7): 555–60.

Kocher, Robert, and Nikhil R. Sahni. 2011. "Hospitals' Race to Employ Physicians—The Logic Behind a Money-Losing Proposition." *New England Journal of Medicine* 364(19): 1790–93.

Kovecses, Zoltan. 2010. *Metaphor: A Practical Introduction.* New York: Oxford University Press.

Lakoff, George. 1992. "The Contemporary Theory of Metaphor." In *Metaphor and Thought,* 2nd ed. Cambridge: Cambridge University Press.

Lakoff, George, and Mark Johnson. 1980. *Metaphors We Live By.* Chicago: University of Chicago Press.

Lambert, Susan J. 2008. "Passing the Buck: Labor Flexibility Practices That Transfer Risk onto Hourly Workers." *Human Relations* 61(9): 1203–27.

———. 2009a. "Lessons from the Policy World: How the Economy, Work Supports, and Education Matter for Low-Income Workers." *Work and Occupations* 36(1): 56–65.

———. 2009b. "Makin' a Difference for Hourly Employees." In *Work-Life Policies*

That Make a Real Difference for Individuals, Families, and Organizations, ed. Ann C. Crouter and Alan Booth. Washington, D.C.: Urban Institute Press.

———. 2012. "'Opting In' to Full Labor Force Participation in Hourly Jobs." In *Women Who Opt Out: The Debate over Working Mothers and Work-Family Balance,* ed. Bernie D. Jones. New York: New York University Press.

———. 2014. "The Limits of Voluntary Employer Action for Improving Low-Level Jobs." In *Working and Living in the Shadow of Economic Fragility,* ed. Marion Crain and Michael Sheradden. New York: Oxford University Press.

Lambert, Susan J., Anna Haley-Lock, and Julia R. Henly. 2012. "Schedule Flexibility in Hourly Jobs: Unanticipated Consequences and Promising Directions." *Community, Work, and Family* 15(3): 293–315.

Lambert, Susan, and Julia Henly. 2012. "Frontline Managers Matter: Labor Flexibility Practices and Sustained Employment in Hourly Retail Jobs in the U.S." In *Are Bad Jobs Inevitable? Trends, Determinants, and Responses to Job Quality in the Twenty-First Century,* ed. Chris Warhurst, Françoise Carré, Patricia Findlay, and Chris Tilly. London: Palgrave Macmillan.

Lambert, Susan J., and Elaine Waxman. 2005. "Organizational Stratification: Distributing Opportunities for Work-Life Balance." In *Work and Life Integration: Organizational, Cultural, and Individual Perspectives,* ed. Ellen Ernst Kossek and Susan J. Lambert. Mahwah, N.J.: Lawrence Erlbaum Associates.

Lamont, Michele. 2000. *The Dignity of Working Men: Morality and the Boundaries of Race, Class, and Immigration.* New York and Cambridge, Mass.: Russell Sage Foundation and Harvard University Press.

Lareau, Annette. 2003. *Unequal Childhoods: Class, Race, and Family Life.* Berkeley: University of California Press.

Larson, Reed, Maryse Richards, and Maureen Perry-Jenkins. 1994. "Divergent Worlds: The Daily Emotional Experience of Mothers and Fathers in the Domestic and Public Spheres." *Journal of Personality and Social Psychology* 67(6): 1034–48.

Lasch, Christopher. 1977. *Haven in a Heartless World: The Family Besieged.* New York: Basic Books.

Lashway, Mary, and Jackie Stein. 2012. "Class and Gender Inequality in Overtime." Paper presented to the meeting of the Eastern Sociological Society. New York (February 24).

Leif, Harold I., and Renée C. Fox. 1963. "Training for 'Detached Concern' in Medical Students." In *The Psychological Basis of Medical Practice,* ed. Harold I. Leif. New York: Harper & Row.

Lipsey, Mark W., and David B. Wilson. 1998. "Effective Intervention for Serious Juvenile Offenders." In *Serious and Violent Juvenile Offenders: Risk Factors and Successful Interventions,* ed. Ralph Loeber and David P. Farrington. Thousand Oaks, Calif.: Sage Publications.

Lopez, Steven Henry. 2006. "Culture Change Management in Long-Term Care: A Shop-Floor View." *Politics and Society* 34(1): 55–80.

Lorber, Judith. 2005. *Breaking the Bowls: Degendering and Feminist Change.* New York: W. W. Norton & Co.

Luce, Stephanie. 2004. *Fighting for a Living Wage.* Ithaca, N.Y.: ILR/Cornell University Press.

Lyness, Karen, Janet C. Gornick, Pamela Stone, and Angela R. Grotto. 2012. "It's All About Control: Workers' Control over Schedule and Hours in Cross-National Context." *American Sociological Review* 77(6): 1023–49.

Macdonald, Cameron. 2009. "What's Culture Got to Do with It? Mothering Ideologies as Barriers to Gender Equity." In *Gender Equality,* ed. Janet Gornick and Marcia Meyers. New York: Verso.

Maguire, Phyllis. 2009."What's the Ideal Number of Patients to See?" *Today's Hospitalist* (July). Available at: http://www.todayshospitalist.com/index.php?b=articles_read&cnt=824 (accessed August 15, 2009).

Malcolm, Janet. 2013. "Nobody's Looking at You: Eileen Fisher and the Art of Understatement." *The New Yorker,* September 23.

Manias, Elizabeth, Robyn Aitken, Anita Peerson, Judith Parker, and Kitty Wong. 2003. "Agency Nursing Work in Acute Care Settings: Perceptions of Hospital Nursing Managers and Agency Nurse Providers." *Journal of Clinical Nursing* 12(4): 457–66.

Marmot, Michael. 2005. *The Status Syndrome: How Social Standing Affects Our Health and Longevity.* New York: Macmillan.

Marx, Karl. 1867. *Capital: A Critique of Political Economy,* vol. 1. Moscow: Progress Publishers.

Mason, Mary Ann, Nicholas H. Wolfinger, and Marc Gouldner. 2013. *Do Babies Matter? Gender and the Family in the Ivory Tower.* New Brunswick, N.J.: Rutgers University Press.

Maume, David, and Marcia L. Bellas. 2001. "The Overworked American or the Time Bind? Assessing Competing Explanations for Time Spent in Paid Labor." *American Behavioral Scientist* 44(7): 1137–56.

Mauss, Marcel. 1967. *The Gift: Forms and Functions of Exchange in Archaic Societies.* New York: W. W. Norton. (Originally published in 1925.)

McKinlay, John B., and Lisa D. Marceau. 2002. "The End of the Golden Age of Doctoring." *International Journal of Health Services* 32(2): 379–416.

McPherson, Miller, Lynn Smith-Lovin, and James Cook. 2001. "Birds of a Feather: Homophily in Social Networks." *Annual Review of Sociology* 27: 415–44.

Mechanic, David. 2006. *The Truth About Health Care: Why Reform Is Not Working in America.* New Brunswick, N.J.: Rutgers University Press.

Meiksins, Peter, and Peter Whalley. 2002. *Putting Work in Its Place: A Quiet Revolution.* Ithaca, N.Y.: Cornell University Press.

Milkman, Ruth. 2009. "Flexibility for Whom?" In *Work Life Policies*, ed. Ann Crouter and Alan Booth. Washington, D.C.: Urban Institute.

Milkman, Ruth, and Eileen Appelbaum. 2013. *Unfinished Business: Paid Family Leave in California and the Future of U.S. Work-Family Policy.* Ithaca, N.Y.: Cornell University Press.

Milkman, Ruth, Ana L. Gonzalez, and Victor Narro. 2010. *Wage Theft and Workplace Violations in Los Angeles: The Failure of Employment and Labor Law for Low-Wage Workers.* Los Angeles: University of California, Institute for Research on Labor and Employment.

Mills, C. Wright. 1959. *The Sociological Imagination.* New York: Oxford University Press.

Mishel, Lawrence. 2013. "Vast Majority of Wage Earners Are Working Harder, and for Not Much More: Trends in U.S. Work Hours and Wages over 1979–2007." Issue Brief 348. Washington, D.C.: Economic Policy Institute.

Mishel, Lawrence, Jared Bernstein, and Heidi Shierholz. 2009. *The State of Working America 2008–2009.* Ithaca, N.Y.: Economic Policy Institute/ILR Press/Cornell University Press.

Moccio, Francine. 2009. *Live Wire: Women and Brotherhood in the Electrical Industry.* Philadelphia: Temple University Press.

Moen, Phyllis, and Patricia Roehling. 2005. *The Career Mystique: Cracks in the American Dream.* Lanham, Md.: Rowman & Littlefield.

Murray, Charles. 1984. *Losing Ground: American Social Policy, 1950–1980.* New York: Basic Books.

———. 2012. *Coming Apart: The State of White America, 1960–2010.* New York: Crown.

New England Journal of Medicine Career Center. 2004. "Physician Compensation Models: The Basics, the Pros, and the Cons." September. Available at: http://www.nejmcareercenter.org/article/2184/physician-compensation-models-the-basics-the-pros-and-the-cons (accessed April 30, 2014).

Oppenheimer, Martin. 1973. "The Proletarianization of the Professional." *Sociological Review Monograph* 20(2): 213–17.

Organisation for Economic Cooperation and Development. 2012. "Average Weekly Hours Worked on the Main Job." Available at stats.oecd.org (accessed April 29, 2014).

Pager, Devah, and Lincoln Quillian. 2005. "Walking the Talk? What Employers Say Versus What They Do." *American Sociological Review* 70(3): 355–80.

Peppe, Elizabeth, Jim W. Mays, Holen C. Chang, Eric Becker, and Bianca DiJulio. 2007. "Characteristics of Frequent Emergency Department Users." Issue Brief. Menlo Park, Calif.: Henry Kaiser Family Foundation (October).

Perlow, Leslie. 1999. "The Time Famine: Towards a Sociology of Work Time" (meeting abstract). *Academy of Management Proceedings* (August): 244–48.

———. 2012. *Sleeping with Your Smartphone*. Cambridge, Mass.: Harvard Business Review Press.

Perry-Jenkins, Maureen. 2005. "Work in the Working Class: Challenges Facing Workers and Their Families." In *Work, Family, Health, and Well-Being*, ed. Suzanne Bianchi, Lynn Casper, Kathleen Christensen, and R. B. King. Mahwah, N.J.: Lawrence Erlbaum Associates.

Perry-Jenkins, Maureen, and Karen Folk. 1994. "Class, Couples, and Conflict: Effects of the Division of Labor on Assessments of Marriage in Dual-Earner Families." *Journal of Marriage and Family* 56(1): 165–80.

Perry-Jenkins, Maureen, and Shelley MacDermid-Wadsworth. 2013. "Work and Family Through Space and Time." In *Handbook of Marriage and the Family*, edited by Gary W. Peterson and Keven Bush, 549–73. New York: Springer.

Pfefferle, Susan G., and Dana Beth Weinberg. 2008. "Certified Nurse Assistants Making Meaning of Direct Care." *Qualitative Health Research* 18(suppl. 1): 952–61.

Phibbs, Ciaran S., Ann Bartel, Bruno Giovannetti, Susan K. Schmitt, and Patricia W. Stone. 2009. "The Impact of Nurse Staffing and Contract Nurses on Patient Outcomes: New Evidence from Longitudinal Data." Working paper. New York: Columbia Business School.

Pierce, Jennifer. 1995. *Gender Trials: Emotional Lives in Contemporary Law Firms*. Berkeley: University of California Press.

Piore, Michael J. 1986. "Perspectives on Labor Market Flexibility." *Industrial Relations* 25(2): 146–66.

Pope, James Gray. 2012. "Letter to the Editor." *New Labor Forum* 21(3, Fall): 124–25.

Presser, Harriet. 1999. "Toward a Twenty-Four-Hour Economy." *Science* 284(5421): 1778–79.

———. 2003. *Working in a 24/7 Economy*. New York: Russell Sage Foundation.

Pugh, Allison. 2009. *Longing and Belonging: Parents, Children, and Consumer Culture*. Berkeley: University of California Press.

Pyke, Karen. 1996. "Class-Based Masculinities: The Interdependence of Gender, Class, and Interpersonal Power." *Gender & Society* 10(5): 527–49.

Ray, Rebecca, and John Schmitt. 2008. "The Right to Vacation: An International Perspective." *International Journal of Health Services: Planning, Administration, Evaluation* 38(1): 21–45.

Reis, Ricardo A. M. R. 2012. "Social Transfer Programs." Talk delivered at Visiting Scholars Seminar, March 14. New York: Russell Sage Foundation.

Relman, Arnold. 2007. *A Second Opinion: Rescuing America's Health Care*. New York: Public Affairs (Century Foundation).

Reynolds, Jeremy. 2005. "In the Face of Conflict: Work-Life Conflict and Desired Work Hour Adjustments." *Journal of Marriage and Family* 67(5): 1313–31.

Ridgeway, Cecilia. 2011. *Framed by Gender: How Gender Inequality Persists in the Modern World*. New York: Oxford University Press.

Roediger, David R., and Philip S. Foner. 1989. *Our Own Time: A History of American Labor and the Working Day.* New York: Verso.

Roethlisberger, Fritz J., and William Dickson. 1939. *Management and the Worker.* Cambridge, Mass.: Harvard University Press.

Roy, Donald. 1952. "Quota Restrictions and Goldbricking in a Machine Shop." *American Journal of Sociology* 57(5): 427–42.

———. 1954. "Efficiency and 'the Fix': Informal Intergroup Relations in a Piecework Machine Shop." *American Journal of Sociology* 60(3): 255–66.

Rubin, Lillian. 1976. *Worlds of Pain: Life in the Working-Class Family.* New York: Basic Books.

Ryan, Ann Marie, and Ellen Ernst Kossek. 2008. "Work-Life Policy Implementation: Breaking Down or Creating Barriers to Inclusiveness?" *Human Resource Management* 47(2): 295–310.

Rybczynski, Witold. 1991. *Waiting for the Weekend.* New York: Penguin Books.

Sandberg, Sheryl. 2013. *Lean In: Women, Work, and the Will to Lead.* New York: Alfred A. Knopf.

Sarkisian, Natalia, and Naomi Gerstel. 2012. *Nuclear Family Values, Extended Family Lives: The Power of Race, Class, and Gender.* New York: Routledge Press.

Schor, Juliet B. 1992. *The Overworked American: The Unexpected Decline of Leisure.* New York: Basic Books.

———. 1998. *The Overspent American: Upscaling, Downshifting, and the New Consumer.* New York: Basic Books.

———. 2004. *Born to Buy: The Commercialized Child and the New Consumer Culture.* New York: Simon & Schuster.

Scott, James C. 1985. *Weapons of the Weak: Everyday Forms of Peasant Resistance.* New Haven, Conn.: Yale University Press.

Sherman, Rachel. 2006. *Class Acts: Service and Inequality in Luxury Hotels.* Berkeley: University of California Press.

Shows, Carla, and Naomi Gerstel. 2009. "Fathering, Class, and Gender: A Comparison of Physicians and Emergency Medical Technicians." *Gender & Society* 23(2): 161–87.

Sloan, Melissa. 2012. "Unfair Treatment in the Workplace and Worker Well-Being: The Role of Coworker Support in a Service Work Environment." *Work and Occupations* 39(1): 3–34.

Smith, Vicki, and Esther B. Neuwirth. 2008. *The Good Temp.* Ithaca, N.Y.: ILR Press / Cornell University Press.

Smith, Tom W., Peter Marsden, Michael Hout, and Jibum Kim. 2013. *General Social Surveys, 1972–2012.* Machine-readable data file. Chicago and Storrs, Conn.: National Opinion Research Center and University of Connecticut, Roper Center for Public Opinion Research.

Smith-Doerr, Laurel. 2004. *Women's Work: Gender Equality vs. Hierarchy in the Life Sciences.* Boulder, Colo.: Lynne Rienner.

Society for Human Resource Management (SHRM). 2012. "2012 Employee Benefits Research Report: The Employee Benefits Landscape in a Recovering Economy." Alexandria, Va.: SHRM (June 22). Available at: http://www.shrm.org/research/surveyfindings/articles/pages/2012employeebenefitsresearchreport.aspx (accessed October 30, 2012).

Stainback, Kevin, and Donald Tomaskovic-Devey. 2010. "Organizational Approaches to Inequality: Inertia, Relative Power, and Environments." *Annual Review of Sociology* 36: 227–47.

———. 2012. *Documenting Desegregation: Racial and Gender Segregation in Private-Sector Employment Since the Civil Rights Act.* New York: Russell Sage Foundation.

Standing, Guy. 2011. *The Precariat: The New Dangerous Class.* New York: Bloomsbury.

Steele, Shelby. 1991. *The Content of Our Character: A New Vision of Race in America.* New York: Harper Perennial.

Stein, Jackie. 2012. "Inequality in Overtime: An Examination of Class and Gender Differences in Collective Bargaining Agreements for Nurses, Emergency Medical Technicians, and Nursing Assistants." Paper presented to the meeting of the Eastern Sociological Society. New York (February 24).

Stone, Lawrence. 1977. *The Family, Sex, and Marriage in England, 1500–1800.* New York: Harper & Row.

Stone, Pamela. 2007. *Opting Out? Why Women Really Quit Careers and Head Home.* Berkeley: University of California Press.

Taylor, Frederick W. 1947. "Shop Management." In Frederick Winslow Taylor, *Scientific Management.* New York: Harper & Brothers.

Thompson, Edward P. 1964. *The Making of the English Working Class.* New York: Pantheon.

———. 1967. "Time, Work Discipline, and Industrial Capitalism." *Past and Present* 38: 56–97.

Tilly, Charles. 1998. *Durable Inequality.* Berkeley: University of California Press.

Tilly, Jane, Kirsten Black, Barbara Ormond, and Jennie Harvel. 2003. *State Experiences with Minimum Nursing Staff Ratios for Nursing Facilities: Findings from Case Studies of Eight States.* Washington: U.S. Department of Health and Human Services.

Todd, S. Rob, Bridget N. Fahy, Judy L. Paukert, Dottie Mersinger, Melanie L. Johnson, and Barbara L. Bass. 2009. "How Accurate Are Self-Reported Resident Work Hours?" *Journal of Surgical Education* 66(2): 69.

Townsend, Nicholas. 2002. *Package Deal: Marriage, Work, and Fatherhood in Men's Lives.* Philadelphia: Temple University Press.

U.S. Bureau of Labor Statistics. 2009. *National Compensation Survey: Employee Benefits in the United States, March 2009.* Bulletin 2731 (September). Available at:

http://www.bls.gov/ncs/ebs/benefits/2009/ebb10044.pdf (accessed January 22, 2010).

———. 2010. *National Occupational Employment and Wage Estimates.* Available at: http://www.bls.gov/oes/2010/may/oes_nat.htm (accessed April 30, 2014).

U.S. Census Bureau. 1980. *Statistical Abstract of the United States 1980.* Washington: U.S. Government Printing Office.

———. 1983. *Statistical Abstract of the United States 1983.* Washington: U.S. Government Printing Office.

———. 2010. *Statistical Abstract of the United States 2010.* Washington: U.S. Government Printing Office.

———. 2012. *Statistical Abstract of the United States 2012.* Washington: U.S. Government Printing Office.

U.S. Department of Health and Human Services. Health Resources and Services Administration. 2010. "The Registered Nurse Population: Findings from the 2008 National Sample Survey of Registered Nurses." September. Available at: http://bhpr.hrsa.gov/healthworkforce/rnsurveys/rnsurveyfinal.pdf (accessed March 16, 2012).

Wachter, Robert, and Derek Bell. 2012. "Renaissance of Hospital Generalists." *British Medical Journal* 344: e652.

Wachter, Robert, and Lee Goldman. 1996. "The Emerging Role of 'Hospitalists' in the American Health Care System." *New England Journal of Medicine* 335(7): 514–17.

Watson, Liz, and Jennifer E. Swanberg. 2011. "Flexible Workplace Solutions for Low-Wage Hourly Workers: A Framework for a National Conversation." *Georgetown Law, Workplace Flexibility 2010* (May). Available at: http://www.workplaceflexibility2010.org (accessed April 30, 2014).

Waugh, Douglas. 1992. "TGIF." *Canadian Medical Association Journal* 147(11): 1687.

Webster, Eddie, Rob Lambert, and Andries Bezuidenhout. 2008. *Grounding Globalization: Labour in the Age of Insecurity.* Malden, Mass.: Blackwell.

Weir, Stan. 1973. "The Informal Work Group." In *Rank and File: Personal Histories of Working-Class Organizers,* ed. Alice Lynd and Staughton Lynd. Boston: Beacon Press.

West, Candace, and Don Zimmerman. 1987. "Doing Gender." *Gender & Society* 1(2): 125–51.

Williams, Christine. 1992. "The Glass Escalator: Hidden Advantages for Men in the 'Female' Professions." *Social Problems* 39(3): 253–67.

Williams, Joan. 2000. *Unbending Gender: Why Family and Work Conflict and What to Do About It.* New York: Oxford University Press.

———. 2006. "One Sick Child Away from Being Fired: When 'Opting Out' Is Not an Option." Report from Center for Work Life Law. San Francisco: University of California, Hastings College of Law.

———. 2010. "The Odd Disconnect: Our Family Hostile Public Policy." In *Workplace Flexibility: Realigning Twentieth-Century Jobs to a Twenty-First-Century Workforce*, ed. Kathleen Christensen and Barbara Schneider. Ithaca, N.Y.: Cornell University Press.

———. 2011. *Reshaping the Work-Family Debate: Why Men and Class Matter*. Cambridge, Mass.: Harvard University Press.

Williams, Joan, and Heather Boushey. 2010. *The Three Faces of Work-Family Conflict: The Poor, the Professionals, and the Missing Middle*. San Francisco: University of California, Hastings College of Law, Center for Work Life Law.

Winant, Gabriel. 2013. "'You Will Feel Good About Yourself and Your Job': Gender, Class Formation, and Health Care Work in and Around Pittsburgh, 1975–1985." Paper presented to the Labor and Working-Class History Association Conference. New York (June 7).

Wine, Charles J., and H. Dan O'Hair. 2004. "Factors Which Influence Physicians to Join Labor Unions." *Journal of the Oklahoma State Medical Association* 97(3): 114–17.

Wright, Erik Olin. 1979. *Class Structure and Income Determination*. New York: Academic Press.

———. 2008. "Logics of Class Analysis." In *Social Class: How Does It Work?*, ed. Annette Lareau and Dalton Conley. New York: Russell Sage Foundation.

Yamagishi, Toshio, and Karen S. Cook. 1993. "Generalized Exchange and Social Dilemmas." *Social Psychology Quarterly* 56(4): 235–48.

Zelizer, Viviana. 2005. *The Purchase of Intimacy*. Princeton, N.J.: Princeton University Press.

Zerubavel, Eviatar. 1979. *Patterns of Time in Hospital Life: A Sociological Perspective*. Chicago: University of Chicago Press.

———. 1981. *Hidden Rhythms: Schedules and Calendars in Social Life*. Chicago: University of Chicago Press.

Zussman, Robert. 1992. *Intensive Care: Medical Ethics and the Medical Profession*. Chicago: University of Chicago Press.

Zweig, Michael. 2000. *The Working Class Majority: America's Best Kept Secret*. Ithaca, N.Y.: Cornell University Press.

Index |